T0361038

ROUTLEDGE LIBRARY EDITIONS:
SOCIAL THEORY

Volume 63

THE SHAPING OF
SOCIO-ECONOMIC SYSTEMS

THE SHAPING OF SOCIO-ECONOMIC SYSTEMS

The Application of the Theory of Actor-System Dynamics to Conflict, Social Power, and Institutional Innovation in Economic Life

THOMAS BAUMGARTNER, TOM R. BURNS
AND PHILIPPE DEVILLE

With a preface by
AMITAI ETZIONI

Routledge
Taylor & Francis Group

LONDON AND NEW YORK

First published in 1986

This edition first published in 2015
by Routledge
2 Park Square, Milton Park, Abingdon, Oxon, OX14 4RN

and by Routledge
711 Third Avenue, New York, NY 10017

Routledge is an imprint of the Taylor & Francis Group, an informa business

© 1986 Gordon and Breach Science Publishers S.A.

British Library Cataloguing in Publication Data
A catalogue record for this book is available from the British Library

ISBN: 978-0-415-72731-0 (Set)
eISBN: 978-1-315-76997-4 (Set)
ISBN: 978-1-138-78399-7 (Volume 63)
eISBN: 978-1-315-76339-2 (Volume 63)

Publisher's Note
The publisher has gone to great lengths to ensure the quality of this reprint but points out that some imperfections in the original copies may be apparent.

Disclaimer
The publisher has made every effort to trace copyright holders and would welcome correspondence from those they have been unable to trace.

Printed and bound by CPI Group (UK) Ltd, Croydon, CR0 4YY

Foreword

The Shaping of Socio-Economic Systems was first published in 1986. It followed the publication of an earlier volume (Burns et al., 1985), which presented the theoretical framework of "actor-system dynamics approach" (ASD). The conceptualization developed in the 1985 book laid out the foundations for empirically oriented research. The new theoretical framework was used to analyze a variety of scientific and policy problems from a multi-disciplinary and dynamic perspective: the complex interplay between economic and socio-political institutions, conflicts and struggles over economic resources and economic institutions, problems of development and under-development, and inflation and unemployment. The result of this research was the publication of this book. The reprint of this book gives us the opportunity to reflect on its foundations and relevance after almost 30 years.

The book's major underlying themes are:

- Conflict over economic institutions and policies and over the distribution of economic resources.
- The structural bases of economic inequality and conflict—and their instability.
- The shaping and reshaping of socio-economic institutions and the contradictions and conflicts and instabilities which such developments evoke.
- The failure of orthodox economic theories, including Keynesianism, in the face of recurrent economic crises and instabilities.

All of the papers collected here deal, in some sense, either with social power, conflict, and struggle regarding economic resources and institutions or the structural and other factors which underlie powering, conflict, and struggle (Burns and Hall, 2012).

Two fundamentally different conceptions of the human being and human action as well as system behavior underlie most modelings of social behavior and social systems. In one, social actors are viewed as essential forces that structure and restructure social systems and the conditions of human activity and development. The individual, historic personality enjoys an extensive freedom to act within and upon social systems, and in this sense is to some degree independent of them. In the other view, social actors are either not found or are automata following the established rules or given roles and functions in a world which they cannot change. Social action and movements as creative–destructive forces are absent.

To a large extent, systems theories have been based on the second view under the influence of the deterministic natural science paradigm and, in a certain sense, akin to system engineering (e.g., Forrester's system dynamics (1961, 1968); Meadows et al., 1974; and many others). This approach tends to ignore or even deny freedom of decision and transformative opportunities available to human agents in much of this system modeling and analysis. System sustainability and evolution tend to be considered "natural" and taken for granted, rather than being treated as problematic and subject to social struggle and transformation, and possibly even collapse as in the approach of ASD.

This book and our related work have shown that social systems modeling and analysis are compatible with, and can readily incorporate, concepts relating to the cognitive, decision-making, and strategic capabilities of social actors as purposeful, self-reflexive, and transformative beings. Such social actors or agents refer not only to individuals but to social groups, organizations, alliances, and nations, which have the capability of making collective decisions and carrying out collective action. The processes and social logic of making decisions and acting could obviously be very different for individuals or small groups compared with large collectivities.

The 30-year period between the original publication of the book and this reprint has been marked by intense debates and new questions and challenges relating to conceptual and empirical work in our systems perspective. This reprint invites us to critically reflect on three key issues which emerged from that period: (I) the theoretical-methodological underpinnings of ASD; (II) the relevance of the theoretical and empirical work almost 30 years after; and (III) what's next: new challenges and issues.

I. The theoretical-methodological-ontological underpinnings

The book made two major contributions: (A) it expanded and applied the dynamic, actor-oriented systems theory (ASD theory) and (B) it developed coherent ways of overcoming the separation between economics and sociology in a new transdisciplinary synthesis: "socio-economics". Later on, Amitai Etzioni, who wrote the Preface to the first edition, would launch in 1989 his "Society for the Advancement of Socio-economics" in which several of us participated for a number of years.

A. Development and application of a dynamic, actor-oriented systems theory

The ASD approach addresses, in general, questions about complexity and the organization of complexity in social systems. More specifically, it deals with questions of how socio-economic and other systems function and evolve, how systems interact with one another, how they impact on one another and their environments, and how unexpected outcomes and developments emerge from system processes and interaction. In contrast to other systems approaches in the social sciences[1], our systems theory is based upon active, creative, normative (moral), transformative agents (individuals as well as collectives). With the exception of the work of Talcott Parsons (whose approach nevertheless remained in large part static), most systems approaches are largely devoid of systematic agential, cultural, and institutional conceptualization[2]. Actors in our theorizing are participants in social systems as well as part of the dynamics of transformations of these systems and in the construction of new ones. Social systems consist of institutional, cultural, and material structures. Hence, our research network early on had a substantial group of "institutionalists", developed rule system conceptions (see below) as a coherent social scientific foundation, and made extensive use of descriptions and analyses of institutions and cultural formations, as it still does.

Key conceptual innovations have been and still are the mark of ASD theory. First, social beings are creative and self-transforming agents. Human consciousness is viewed in terms of self-representation and self-reflectivity on collective and individual levels. Second, cultural and institutional formations are seen as constituting the major environment of human behavior, an environment in part internalized in social agents in the form of *shared rules and systems of rules*. Third, interaction processes and games are considered embedded in and context dependent on cultural and institutional systems that facilitate, constrain, and, in general, influence the actions and interactions of human agents (Granovetter, 1985). Fourth, social systems are conceptualized in ASD in multi-level terms, for instance, as hierarchies of games where a higher level interaction process sets the functions and parameters of lower level interactions and related processes; this multi-level property is crucial in generating endogenously the dynamics of the system, although of course external forces also produce dynamics (see below). Fifth, ASD social systems are considered to be open to, and interacting with, their environment. Through interaction with their environment and through internal processes, such systems acquire new properties, and are transformed, resulting in their evolution and development. Sixth, social systems in the ASD perspective entail complex configurations of tensions and dissonances due to the conflicting interests and power struggles among groups. The latter lead to the generation of contradictions in institutional arrangements and cultural formations. And seventh, rule systems (the bases of institutions and cultural formations) evolve as a function of (a) human agency realized through interactions and games, and (b) selective mechanisms in part constructed by social agents in forming and reforming institutions, but also in part a function of physical and ecological environments.

The ASD conception of *social rules and rule systems* is a particularly major innovation in this and related work (Burns et al., 1985; Burns and Flam, 1987; Burns and Hall, 2012). Social rule systems and rule processes are universal in human groups and organizations and are the building blocks of institutions and cultural formations; they are produced by and embodied in the practices of groups and collectivities of people: language, customs and codes of conduct, norms, laws, and the social institutions of family community, state, and economic organizations such as business enterprises and markets. Most human social activity—in all of its extraordinary variety—is organized and regulated by socially produced rules and systems of rules. Rule processes—the making, interpretation, and implementation of social rules as well as their reformulation and transformation—are often accompanied by the mobilization and exercise of power, and by conflict and struggle. Social rules and systems of rules are, therefore, *not* transcendental abstractions in the ASD perspective.

As a consequence, human actors (individuals, groups, organizations, communities, and other collectivities) interpret, adapt, implement, and transform rules, sometimes cautiously, other times radically (Burns and Dietz, 2001). Such behavior explains much cultural and institutional dynamics. Major struggles in human history revolve around the formation and reformation of core economic, administrative, and political institutions of society, the particular rule regimes defining social relationships, roles, rights and authority, and obligations and duties as well as the general "rules of the game" in these and related domains of social action.

Of particular interest in the context of our approach is the concept of meta-power, based on the capability to shape and reshape institutional arrangements, the rules of the game, and the access of actors to key resources and corridors of power. Exercise of such power is observable in the struggles to maintain or change socio-economic and other societal systems (Burns et al., 1985; Burns and Hall, 2012).

In addition to presenting a brief introduction to the ASD conceptual framework (see Chapters 1 and 2), the book provides a number of methodological and modeling innovations: multi-level models (Chapters 3, 4, 6, and 10), system models with multiple phases (Chapters 4, 6, 7, and 10), multi-game systems and hierarchies of game systems (Chapters 3, 4, and 6), and multi-agent structural models (Chapters 4, 5, 9, and 10).

B. The synthesis and integration of economics and sociology (as well as history and political economy)

The various topics of the book dealing with socio-economic issues clearly differentiate our work from that of mainstream economics. The ASD approach to human behavior does not rely on the axiomatic of rational choice theory. Perfect foresight, perfect knowledge, and perfect information about the available choice sets and their elements, the capacity to optimize on the part of individuals and collectives; in brief all the usual *homo oeconomicus* behavioral assumptions are definitely incompatible with our own. On one side, they are more encompassing, on the other they are more restrictive. As indicated above, social beings are for us active, self reflecting, creative, normative (morally conscious), transformative agents (individuals as well as collectives). But, in an almost paradoxical way, they also have imperfect information, limited knowledge, unequal powers, myopic foresight, and "irrational behaviors". In addition, they may be faced with "radical uncertainty" (Frank Knight, John Maynard Keynes) and limited capacity to compute. All of these assumptions are close to the "bounded rationality" assumption argued by Herbert Simon (1969). Such a conception makes appropriate our treatment of economic processes in behavioral, conflictive, and powering terms. It enables us to address issues such as the mobilization and exercise of power in shaping and constraining institutional development, blocked or distorted development, and socio-economic crises and their dynamics.

At the same time, it has been somewhat unusual for sociologists to consider topics such as inflation, the structuring and restructuring of markets, the shaping and reshaping of entire economic systems, the development and functioning of alternative socio-economic systems such as the former Yugo-slavia, the facilitators of and constraints on technology transfer, and the wealth and poverty of nations, among other socio-economic topics and issues. From the start, our team (economists and sociologists) jointly conducted early trans-disciplinary research on these and related topics and issues, which, as we suggest below, continue to be relevant and challenging almost 30 years later.

We recognize that the predictive capability of our models, in the usual sense, is very limited. However, aside from some very short-run predictions, traditional economic models have not scored very well either, especially when economies have been faced with brutal shocks, structural failures, and insti-tutional incoherence and degeneration. We felt, however, that our framework might prove itself fruitful in many ways, allowing for the identification of capabilities and for predicting system potentialities and limitations in a range of situations. It enables us to identify key social agents involved, their cap-abilities and potentialities, their social judgments and likely choices, their strategic behavior leading to inflationary, contracting or other economic pressures, and to constraints on such processes. Socio-economic developments are not, in the ASD perspective, the result of blind, mechanical forces but the result, to a substantial degree, of *human individual and/or collective actions— based on good as well as bad judgments*—even when it comes to institution building and reform.

In sum, ASD conceptualizations and analyses are not only contributions to the development of social systems theory and methodology but to economic theorizing and analysis, which often fails to conceptualize power and conflict processes, institutional arrangements and their dynamics and transformations, the evolution of socio-economic systems, and a great deal of non-equilibria phenomena.

II. Relevance of the theoretical and empirical work.
After almost 30 years what is the relevance?

In reviewing this work, we find ourselves surprised at what appears to us and to many of our scientific friends as substantial evidence of the continued relevance of many of the topics and issues that were addressed from almost 30 years ago to the present time.

Capitalism and its discontents continue more than ever (Burns and DeVille, 2006; Burns and Hall, 2012). Conflicts and struggles are endemic on all levels and in all sectors, not only in labor markets but commodity and money and financial markets. Power, conflict, and institutional analyses continue to be relevant to specific socio-economic systems, as we tried to show in the cases of Belgium, Mexico, the former Yugoslavia, and Latin America (Chapters 4, 5, 7, and 10).

Socio-economic development is highly uneven (with well-supported development in some cases and blocked or distorted development in others (Chapters 5, 7, 9, 10, and 11)). There is not only a wealth but a poverty of nations, regions, and sectors. This is the institutionalized logic of capitalism as we know it, producing inequality and uneven development along with its massive outputs and flows of goods and services (often at the expense of degrading societal conditions and the natural environment).

Much of the book is devoted to the analysis of inflation and its causes, an issue of great scientific and policy concern during the 1970s. Eventually, advanced economies found ways to regulate inflation, shifting from accommodation to wage, price, and taxation demands, on the one hand, to a monetarist regime which focused on regulating credit to households, enterprises, and government, on the other hand. At the same time, developing countries such as China, Korea, and Taiwan were and still are exporting relatively cheaper, although increasingly sophisticated, commodities to advanced economies, helping the latter to constrain their inflationary pressures.

As we have argued since the early 1980s, conflicts and struggles over income distribution issues generates inflationary pressures in such countries as Belgium, Iceland, Italy or Sweden, but particularly in developing countries with limited economic and political means to deal with and mitigate those tensions and conflicts. However, in some sense (see Chapter 4, p. 89) we have been wrong in our argument that monetarism could not counter inflationary pressures because it could not address distributional conflicts. During a long period of money and credit creation, inflation could in most instances be kept at relatively low levels because it contributed to mediating societal tensions and conflicts. Only after the highly destabilizing crisis of 2007, and afterwards, do we see the imposition once again of powerful constraints, especially in Europe, leading to the introduction of austerity policies reducing disposable real income, thereby intensifying competition and conflict potentials, as experienced recently by Greece, Italy, Spain, and Portugal, among others. Modern democratic governments are only able, to a limited degree, to address directly the conflicts over the distribution of income among societal groups. Their best strategies have been accommodation to demands (from private companies, government agencies, and households) by expanding government budgets, subsidies, and debts contributing to inflation as it took place from the late 1960s to the early 1980s and by allowing for the massive expansion of credit (from the 1970s onward) for households and businesses. That policy mix reached its limits by 2010 with the sovereign debt issue in Europe.

After the appearance of this book in 1986, the former Yugoslavia dissolved (early 1990s). Already, our article (Chapter 7) identified the underlying crisis, related conflicts and their inflationary consequences. The inability of the political elite to deal with these and related crises has been blatant. This was the context that led to the dissolution of Yugoslavia in the early 1990s and the wars, destruction, and mass murder that followed. Nowadays, international banks and the IMF impose "austerity measures" on several European countries, often again in the context of weakened political leadership, shrinking resource bases, and continually rising expectations and demands. And recent events in several of these countries are signs of increasing tensions and conflicts, as it is the case, for example, in France.

In Latin America, while the powerful pressures producing inflation continued (and continue), dramatic changes have taken place. Many Latin American countries have made considerable progress toward more democratic orders: Argentina (1983), Bolivia (1982–5), Brazil (1985), Chile (1989), Paraguay (1991–2), and Uruguay (1984), among others.

As emphasized in this book, the international capitalist system enables the reproduction of inequality, unequal exchange, and uneven development. But it does also allow for the advancement of some, while sustaining substantial inequality in the wealth and poverty among nations. The following are relevant historical developments.

- The New International Economic Order (NIEO) was historically a major concept pushed by developing countries (for instance, the Group 77 (1964) and the United Nations General Assembly (1974)). However, this normative idea had insufficient real power mobilization behind it at the time. Interestingly, in the meantime, the emerging BRIC nations (Brazil, Russia, India, and China) have not only ideas about a new international economic order but begin to mobilize the global power to push effectively for it. Under their influence, there are emerging strategies and pressures in that direction.
- The ASD approach has also been applied to an analysis of financial systems as complex, dynamic, and unstable systems (Burns and DeVille, 2003; DeVille and Burns, 1976). The 2007+ crisis has been analyzed as a *systemic crisis*; it is argued that a major re-design will be required if stabilization is to be achieved (Burns et al., 2013). But such a re-design is unlikely to happen in the present context, given the opposition of major world banks and financial interests and their supporting countries. Nevertheless, the need remains and will be with us for some time. We will probably have to wait for the occurrence of the next major crisis (within the next five to ten years (Burns et al., 2013)) for the global system of banking and finance to be seriously confronted and subject to substantial reform.

- With respect to the issue of ecological sustainability, DeVille and Burns (1976) had already suggested in the mid-1970s that the major factor undermining capitalism would not be class and other societal struggles, but ecological and natural constraints (class and other struggles appeared intense in the 1960s and 1970s and made up the historical context of much of what was written in this book). This prediction, based on a systemic analysis, seems to be more pertinent than ever.

III. Conclusion and what next

A major challenge remains. We and others should keep expanding and elaborating the theory of ASD, in the face of the terrible fragmentation of knowledge and the frustrating and costly inability to address many current problems with systematic knowledge and analysis. The current increasing violence both among and within countries testifies to the urgent need to have better integrated, encompassing but coherent social science to identify and limit the many dangers which are threatening the future of humanity. ASD theory seems to remain a most promising basis for such a development. Social systemic analyses pinpointing the drivers and dynamics of links and processes are on the one hand needed, and on the other hand should be expanded beyond socio-economics and political economy.

This book is addressed to social scientists concerned with socio-economic issues, institutions, and development and is based on what was then (the late 1970s and early 1980s) a new social system theory. For the future, the need for further linking up with other social sciences such as anthropology, cultural geography, and history, as well as the humanities (philosophy, linguistics, literary analysis, etc.) is clear. Moreover, there is also an urgent need for closer linkages between the social sciences and humanities, on the one hand, and the natural, life, and engineering sciences, on the other hand. The "tower of Babel" metaphor (see Chapter 1) applies today as much as then, if not more so. The task at hand for upcoming research is on the further elaboration of the theory of ASD beyond its socio-economics comfort zone into its potential as a powerful tool of systematic analysis of complex, dynamic social systems and their interaction with technological as well as ecological systems, thus linking social, natural, and engineering sciences.

Today we are faced with something described elsewhere as the "perfect storm" of social systems in disarray (unstable financial systems and ineffectual global institutions, declining welfare, failed states, warring regions), together with serious and immediate ecological disturbances and, in some cases, irreversible destruction, all feeding into cycles of social violence and further social and ecological degradation (adaptation of a remark thanks to Paul Ehrlich). It is thus imperative to understand these systems, their cycles, processes, and local–global strategic linkages in order to further develop the necessary scientific and policy capacity to respond to and operate on them on a long-term basis.

In the face of diverse, complex social systems—government, finance systems, socio-technical systems, regional systems, and the global system—which are unstable and in disarray, the conceptual and methodological toolbox which ASD offers is still useful, but at the same time requires extension of its scope. As we wrote in the early 1980s (see Chapter 3, p. 91), the major challenge today for appropriate societal transformation is that the institutional means are not available, and, moreover, there are powerful vested interests and antagonistic nation-state regimes opposing appropriate change. Cleavages and struggles at the international as well as other levels are much deeper and the basis or potentialities for shaping global consensus less feasible than earlier in the case of many advanced nation-states. In light of our arguments, we came to pessimistic conclusions: the necessary transformation of international conditions and regimes will have to await a much more profound crisis (September, 1983; repeated, November, 2013). But, we also know the dangers and the appalling human costs of such tragedy. As social scientists, it is our responsibility to develop tools and analyses to avoid or mitigate, as much as possible, such a catastrophe.

Notes

1 In particular that of Talcott Parsons (1951) and later Niklas Luhmann (1995) as well as many natural science and engineering approaches (von Bertalanffy, 1968; Forrester, 1961, 1968; Klir, 1969), and more recently the group Biomatrix approach (Dostal, 2005), among others.
2 This was to be expected of von Bertalanffy, Forrester, and Klir as well as even World System Theory (Wallerstein, 2004) and structural Marxism (Althusser and Balibar, 1970).

References

Althusser, L. and E. Balibar 1970 *Reading Capital.* London: New Left Review
von Bertalanffy, L. 1968 *General System Theory: Foundations, Development, Applications.* New York: George Braziller, revised edition 1976
Burns, T. R. and P. DeVille 2003 "The three faces of the coin: A socio-economic approach to the institution of money." *European Journal of Economic and Social Systems*, 16(2): 149–195
Burns, T. R. and P. DeVille 2006 "Dynamic approaches in social system theorizing." In: *Handbook of 21st Century Sociology*. Eds. C. D. Bryant and D. L. Peck. Thousand Oaks, CA: Sage
Burns, T. R. and T. Dietz 2001 "Revolution: An evolutionary perspective." *International Sociology*, 16(4): 531–555
Burns, T. R. and H. Flam 1987 *The Shaping of Social Organization: Social Rule System Theory with Applications.* London: Sage
Burns, T. R. and P. Hall 2012 *The Meta-power Paradigm: Impacts and Transformations of Agents, Institutions, and Social Systems – Capitalism, State, and Democracy in a Global Context.* Frankfurt/NewYork/Oxford: Peter Lang

Burns, T. R., T. Baumgartner, and P. DeVille 1985 *Man, Decisions, and Society.* London: Gordon and Breach

Burns, T. R., A. Martinelli, and P. DeVille 2013 "A socio-economic systems model of the global financial crisis of 2007+: Power, innovation, ideology, and design failure." In: *Financial Crises and the Nature of Capitalist Money.* Eds. J. Pixley and G. Harcourt. London: Palgrave/Macmillan

DeVille, P. and T. R. Burns 1976 "Institutional responses to crisis in capitalist development." *Social Praxis,* 4: 5–46

Dostal, E. (in collaboration with A. Cloete and G. Jaros) 2005 *Biomatrix: A Systems Approach to Organizational and Societal Change.* 3rd ed. Cape Town: Imaging Data Solutions

Forrester, J. 1961 *Industrial Dynamics.* Cambridge, MA: MIT Press

Forrester, J. 1968 *Principles of Systems.* Cambridge, MA: MIT Press

Granovetter, M. 1985 "Economic action and social structure: The problem of embeddedness." *American Journal of Sociology,* 50: 481–510

Klir, G. 1969 *An Approach to General Systems Theory.* New York: Van Nostrand Reinhold

Luhmann, N. 1995 *Social Systems.* Translated by John Bednarz, with Dirk Baecker. Stanford, CA: Stanford University Press

Meadows, D. H., D. L. Meadows, J. Randers, and W. Behren II 1974 *Limits to Growth.* 2nd ed. New York: Universe Books

Parsons, T. 1951 *The Social System.* Glencoe, IL: Free Press

Simon, H. A. 1969 *Sciences of the Artificial.* Cambridge, MA: MIT Press

Wallerstein, I. 2004 *World-systems Analysis.* Durham, NC: Duke University Press

The Shaping of Socio-Economic Systems

The Application of the Theory of Actor-System Dynamics to Conflict, Social Power, and Institutional Innovation in Economic Life

THOMAS BAUMGARTNER

TOM R. BURNS

PHILIPPE DEVILLE

with a preface by
AMITAI ETZIONI

GORDON AND BREACH SCIENCE PUBLISHERS
New York   London   Paris   Montreaux   Tokyo

P.O. Box 786
Cooper Station
New York, NY 10276
United States of America

P.O. Box 197
London WC2E 9PX
England

58, rue Lhomond
75005 Paris
France

14-9 Okubo 3-chome
Shinjuku-ku
Tokyo 160
Japan

Library of Congress Cataloging in Publication Data

(Studies in Cybernetics, ISSN 0275-5807; v. II)
Includes index.
1. Social sciences—mathematics models. 2. Industrial management. 3. Economic
development 4. System theory. I. Burns, Tom R. II. DeVille, Philippe. III. Title. IV. Title:
Socio-economic systems. V. Series.
H61.25.B38 1984   300'.724   84–10222
ISBN 2–88124–003–5 (France)
PBK: 2–88124–027–5

Contents

Introduction to the Series

The subject of cybernetics is quickly growing and there now exists a vast amount of information on all aspects of this broad-based set of disciplines. The phrase "set of disciplines" is intended to imply that cybernetics and all the approaches to artificial (or machine) intelligence have a near identical view-point. Furthermore, systems analysis, systems theory and operational research often have a great deal in common with (and are in fact not always discernibly different from) what is meant by cybernetics, as far as this series is concerned: inevitably, computer science is bound to be involved also.

The fields of application are virtually unlimited and applications are discovered in the investigation or modelling of any complex system. The most obvious applications have been in the construction of artificially intelligent systems, the brain and nervous system, and socio-economic systems. This can be achieved through either simulation (copying as exactly as possible) or synthesis (achieving the same or better end result by any means whatsoever).

The range of applications today has become so broad it now includes such subjects as aesthetics, history and architecture. Modelling can be carried out by computer programs, special purpose models (analog, mathematical, statistical, etc.), and automata of various kinds, including neural nets and TOTES. All that is required of the system to be studied is that it be complex, dynamic, and capable of 'learning' and also have feedback or feedforward or both.

This is an international series.

FRANK GEORGE

Preface

Once upon a time progress was believed to be in differentiation, in parcelling out, in specializing, both in institutions and matters of the mind. Out of family and community there grew segregated places of work, schooling, worship. Out of dogma, humanities and science were segregated. And then there were additional specializations — kinds of work, levels of schools, divisions of humanities. Finally, political economics, once a comprehensive study of society, was split up into ideology, politics — and modern day economics.

And then we learned that progress was no simple matter. Yes, differentiation allowed specializations, but the pieces were nearly impossible to fit together, and individually they made little sense. One reaction was to return to the womb, to recapture the lost fusion in society and the world of reflection. Back to the community, family, nature — and political economics. However, we soon learned it is impossible to return the genie into the bottle, to return to innocence. We tasted the fruits of division and are reluctant to do without them. We desire a true synthesis of the unfragmented past and the divided present. This is what the book before us is all about.

It deals with systems, as it ought. This is one way the parts are integrated but not meshed. Indeed the system idea is as pivotal to post-modern social science as the wheel to mechanics. It points to interactive effects among the parts, their inter-relationships, the wholes they make. The three authors make excellent use of the concept and in the process enrich it.

Economics for them is not a market place sealed in a vacuum, but an integral part of a societal system, a polity, a community. If readers will gain nothing out of this work but a sense of socio-economics, it will be well worth their effort of studying this book.

Last but not least, the view is dynamic. None of the never-never-land of ossified structures here. Process, conflict, democracy are key themes. If we can, using such concepts and insights, render our society responsive to our needs — our world will become more peaceful and more humane. Division will not vanish, but the piece will come together.

AMITAI ETZIONI
University Professor
The George Washington University, and
Director
Center for Policy Research

Acknowledgements

"The Shaping of Socio-Economic Crisis: Societal Change and Theoretical Failure" was part of the paper presented at the Xth World Congress of Sociology, Session on Economy and Society, Mexico City, August 16–20, 1982. A somewhat different version of the chapter appeared in the *International Journal of Comparative Sociology* in 1984.

"Inflation, Politics and Social Change: Actor-Oriented Systems Analysis" consists largely of material previously published in a paper with the same title in R.F. Geyer and J. van der Zouwen (eds.), *Uneven Development in the World System*, 1981. Permission to reprint has been given by Pergamon Press, Oxford.

"The Dynamics of Inflation and Unemployment in Belgium; Actors, Institutional Setting, and Social Structure" and "Socio-Political Cleavages: The Illegitimate State and Inflation in Latin America" are reports from "The Inflation Project", directed by Tom R. Burns and financed by the Social Science Research Council (HSFR) of Sweden. They have not been previously published.

"Conflict Resolution and Conflict Development: the Workers Take Over at the Lip Factory" is a slightly edited version of a paper with the same title that appeared in L. Kriesberg (ed.), *Research in Social Movements, Conflicts, and Change*, Vol. 1, in 1978. Permission to reprint has been given by JAI Press, Greenwich (Connecticut).

"Yugoslav Post-War Development Patterns and Dialectics: Self-Management, the Market, and Political Institutions in Conflict", appeared as "Self-Management, Market and Political Institutions in Conflict" T.R. Burns, L.E. Karlsson and V. Rus (eds.) in *Work and Power*, 1979. Permission to reprint has been given by the International Sociological Association. The paper has been slightly edited.

1

Introduction

Tom R. Burns

1. Issues and Problems

The papers collected in this book concern socio-economic issues, institutions and developments. A new theoretical framework, actor-system dynamics, is used to analyze a spectrum of scientific and practical problems from a multi-disciplinary and dynamic perspective: the complex interplay between economic and socio-political institutions, conflicts over economic resources and over the organisation of economic systems, contemporary inflation and stagnation, problems of development and underdevelopment.

The book is addressed to social scientists who are concerned about such problems, theoretically as well as practically. It should also be of interest to policy-makers and practitioners who seek new concepts and tools of analysis to tackle a world which is increasingly complex. The book's major underlying themes are:

- conflict over economic institutions and the distribution of economic resources

- the structural bases of economic inequality and conflict

- the shaping and reshaping of socio-economic institutions and the contradictions and conflicts which such developments generate

- the failure of orthodox economic theories, including Keynesianism, in the face of the current economic crisis.

All of the papers collected here deal, in a certain sense, either with social conflict and struggle over economic resources and institutions or with the structural and other factors which underlie such conflict and struggle. The conflicts concern in some instances the distribution of income, as in the papers on inflation and stagnation in Part 1. In other cases, the conflicts or potential conflicts concern the formation and development of economic institutions and organizations (Part 2 and to a large extent Part 3), as dif-

1

ferent classes and groups struggle to maintain or change socio-economic forms.

Socio-economic systems and their effects can be examined, therefore, not only as "targets of social struggle" between different social classes or groups but also as sources of contradiction and conflict. The latter, particularly structural sources, are examined in most of the papers:[1]

• systems of production and distribution generate or reproduce inequality, uneven development and socio-political cleavages.

• market, negotiation, and administrative systems determine income distributions which are unacceptable to particular groups or segments of society and this leads to social struggles over income distribution. Under some conditions, these assume violent, political forms; under others, they are manifested as inflationary developments.

• on the regional, sector and enterprise levels within countries (Yugoslavia in this case), there may be patterns of resource control, relations of dependency and uneven development, which make for rich and poor regions and produce deep social cleavages.

• on the international level, resource control, relationships of dependency, and uneven development contribute to the maintenance and development of inequalities in the world today, the wealth and poverty of nations.

Capitalist, decentralized market systems, nationally and internationally, are *inherently unstable* (contrary to the belief among the few optimists left and the many during the 1960s that effective policy and "fine-tuning" would stabilize capitalism). The instability derives from several interrelated factors: social struggles over income distribution, over economic policies and the shape of socio-economic systems, the use in these struggles of power and influence in different, including non-economic forms, and innovation and restructuring attempts which both reflect struggles and generate them. In our view, this pattern of conflict, the exercise of social power, and innovation explains in large part why *crisis is endemic in capitalist systems* (see DeVille and Burns, 1977).

A core process of capitalist market systems is the struggle, nationally and internationally, among social agents (individuals, groups, organizations, classes, and nations) over the distribution of money income in order to improve their own income shares. Indeed, in a monetary economy, this is the only way in which social actors can try to control their *real* incomes. Struggles over the distribution of money income manifest themselves in a number of different socio-economic and political processes. If the economy-and-society were a purely competitive, production-exchange one, the processes by which social agents could attempt to modify their nominal income would be relatively simple to analyze. But in a society where the state is a central institution capable of affecting many economic processes, where there are both private and public sources of money and credit creation, and where economies are open and interdependent both in terms of trade and capital flows, the ways by which social agents can attempt to modify their income shares are many, intricate and often involve complex strategies.

In terms of the perspective sketched above, "exchange" is not the primary or characteristic social process of capitalist economies. Conflict and struggle are equally, if not in many instances, more important processes. At the same time, social conflicts and struggle invariably raise questions of social power. Power relations — and different types of influence and control processes — are essential ingredients in any analysis of contemporary capitalism.

Of particular interest in the context of the work presented in this book is the concept of structuring or *meta-power*, the power to shape and reshape institutional arrangements. Exercise of such power is observable in the struggles to maintain or change socio-economic systems (see companion volume). At the same time, systems of production, exchange and distribution result in differential resource control and opportunities to maintain or to restructure socio-economic arrangements. Such dynamics are described and analyzed in our studies of Yugoslavia (Part II) and in the relationships between First and Third World countries (Part III).

The articles collected here have been published previously in whole or in large parts, with the exceptions of Chapters 3 and 4 dealing with the Belgian and Latin American economic crises, respectively, which have appeared as research reports. We have made a number of editorial changes, adding and deleting material in order to sharpen or extend the analyses found in the original articles. All of the articles were written to stand on their own. Still, we want to stress from the outset — more than we did with the individual articles — that there is a framework underlying each of them which has structured the data gathering, model-building and analyses.

In the following sections, we shall present briefly the core elements of the framework, actor-system dynamics, hereafter abbreviated as ASD. (In some of our earlier articles, it is referred to as actor-oriented systems theory). We eventually go on to suggest how ASD provides a basis for interdisciplinary collaboration and for genuine social science research. The more purely theoretical and methodological aspects of ASD theory are dealt with in the companion volume, *Man, Decisions, Society* (Gordon and Breach, 1985).

The framework offers theoretical concepts and methods, in preliminary forms, for the description and analysis of socio-economic systems:

• as dynamic and subject to restructuring

• as characterized by interlocked markets, bargaining and administrative systems for allocating economic and other resources

• as frameworks for social agents or groups of agents to not only produce and exchange but to exercise power and to conflict, as well as to innovate and to carry out socio-economic transformations.

We address several questions, which in our view economic theory has difficulty specifying and explaining adequately as well as offering a solid basis for policy:

1) it has difficulty offering intelligent explanations of the current economic crisis, with stagnation, inflationary pressures and the complicated interplay between the economy and politics (Chapters 2, 3, 4 and 5).

2) it has failed to explain satisfactorily, and to indicate useful strategies to overcome, underdevelopment and the great division in the world today between rich and poor countries (Part III).

3) it has been unable thus far to identify systematically, and to suggest policies and strategies to overcome, the barriers to technology transfer and, in general, the structural constraints on the use in the Third World of modern technology, and capital generally (Chapters 11 and 13).

4) it does not specify and analyze systematically the concrete processes of institutional innovation and reform, technological developments, as well as socio-political struggles which make economic practices and institutions potentially unstable (rather than tending toward equilibrium) (Parts I and II).

5) it is unable to specify and analyze conflict and power processes relating, for instance, to social struggles over income distribution and to struggles to maintain or change socio-economic arrangements (Parts 1, 2 and 3).

We do not claim that the framework and applications presented in this book manage to solve major problems where economic theory has failed. Rather, in some instances, they revise and fill in gaps in economic theory, and in a certain sense, complement the theory; in others, they address important problems and areas of socio-economic research which economic theory has neglected or failed to deal with adequately, above all questions concerning socio-economic power, conflict, and institutional change.

What is offered here is largely incomplete. It is more the first steps, a promising beginning as we see it. It should be read with this understanding. Very substantial problems and challenges remain, and we hope that others will be inspired to take up some of these. The tragic waste, and anxiety about the future, in connection with the current crisis call for the use of our imaginations and a collective openness to new approaches.

2. Toward a New Framework

Two fundamentally different conceptions of man and human action underlie most modeling of social behaviour and social systems. In one, social actors are viewed as essential forces that structure and restructure social systems and the conditions of human activity. The individual, the historic personality, as exemplified by Schumpeter's entrepreneur, enjoys an extensive freedom to act within and upon social systems, and in this sense is independent of them. In the other view, social actors are either not found or are faceless automata following iron rules or given roles and functions in a world which they cannot basically change. Incompatible goals, divided loyalties, and conflicts are excluded. Social action as a creative-destructive force is absent.

To a large extent social systems theories have been based on the second view, reflecting the influence of the deterministic natural science paradigm and, in a certain sense, an affinity to systems engineering (e.g., Forrester's system dynamics (1961, 1968), Meadows et al., 1974).[2] This type of approach tends to deny free decision and restructuring opportunities to human agents.

System maintenance and reproduction, rather than being treated as problematical and subject to social struggle, are considered 'natural' and taken for granted in system modeling and analysis.[3] Purposeful action to assure system reproduction is seen as unnecessary; struggles to reshape and transform social systems are given minimal attention, if they are recognized at all.

We intend to show that social systems modeling and analysis is compatible with and can incorporate concepts relating to the decision-making and strategic capabilities of social actors as purposeful, self-reflexive beings. Social actor or agent refers not only to individuals but to social groups, organizations, networks and alliances, as well as nations which have the capability of making collective decisions and carrying out collective action (albeit the processes and logic of making decisions and acting are obviously very different for individuals or small groups and large collectivities).

Actor-system dynamics has drawn on the rational choice approach, particularly game theory, in its development. Game theory is grounded in concepts of actors, their interests, conflicts of interests, decision-making, and strategic actions between and among actors. However, the games are conceptualized and analyzed as *closed systems*. This neglects an important feature of real-life 'games' and interaction situations governed by social rules and institutions, namely that actors often transform unsatisfactory 'game structures' (see Burns and Meeker, 1978, Chapter 4 in this volume, and the companion volume).

In this context we want to emphasize that social decision-making, and negotiations and conflicts in particular, are not "games". The occasional use of game theory terminology here and in other chapters simply reflects an open acknowledgement of debt to the valuable research and conceptual development found in the game theory tradition.

Actor-system dynamics, while trying to incorporate into a more global framework the valuable analytical approach provided by game theory, treats games as open, multi-level systems of social action. They change and develop. Game structuring and restructuring are identified as meta-level processes that maintain or change interaction situations or game components. Our investigation of such *game transformation* has three major concerns:

- to specify and analyze the material, social structural and cultural contexts of games or interaction settings and their role in structuring and regulating the concrete production, exchange, conflict, power, and other interaction processes which take place in societal games
- to show in what ways such social activity, partially determined by such contexts, constitute a fluid and dynamic force maintaining or changing games and their contexts
- to ground game analysis in a theory of social action, which stresses, above all, the transformational potentialities and tendencies of such action, in particular the capacity to structure and transform games.

In the first instance, attention is given to the ways in which specific aspects of the game context structure and restructure games: in particular, actors' definition of the social situation, their goals and preferences, available options, interaction outcomes, and above all the 'rules of the game'.

In the second instance, one not only investigates the extent to which actors with different social relationships and cultural understandings respond and interact differently *in the context*, for example, of 'zero-sum', 'prisoners dilemma', or other objective game conditions. But one also examines the extent to which social agents act *on the context*, structuring and transforming games. In this way, they may generate various development paths of games and game systems (see companion volume, Chapter 4).

3. Some Key Features of the Theory of Actor-System Dynamics

ASD theory takes as a point of departure a general principle as being basic to any attempt at social theory and social explanation. Human agents, individuals, groups, organizations and nations, are subject to material, social structural and cultural constraints on their actions. At the same time, they are creative, active forces; they shape and reshape social structures and institutions as well as their material circumstances. They thereby change — intentionally and unintentionally (often enough through mistakes and failures) — the conditions for their own activities and transactions. To paraphrase Marx, men make their history within certain constraints, constraints which are themselves largely the products of human action.

ASD's minimal set of concepts essential for description and model-building in social analysis is indicated below with very brief notes. The concepts and their role in description and modeling are discussed more completely and applied in the chapters of this and the companion volume.

A *social system* consists of the set of relevant actors, their interrelationships, the endogenous constraints, social activity and processes, outcomes and effects, and the structuring processes which shape and reshape actors, cultural frames, social rule systems and institutions.

Actors and Social Interaction

1) *actors or social agents.* Actors process data, evaluate, make decisions and act purposefully in and on the world around them.[4]

2) *social action and interaction.* Social agents *interact* with unequal resources and unequal opportunities to realize their purposes and interests. They engage in the concrete social activities of producing, cooperating, exchanging, exercising power, struggling, and maintaining and changing social systems. The activities affect and regulate conditions in social agents' material, social and cultural worlds.

Constraints

3) the concrete, definable *contexts or settings* which directly or indirectly structure and regulate social processes.

4) *institutions, cultural elements and social structure generally.* These structure and regulate social action and interaction. They cannot be reduced to the thoughts and acts of individuals, since they structure social relationships and organization. Such collective properties arise from the set of institutionalized relationships, not merely from the agents or elements.

5) *material and technological constraints.* Physical conditions, climate, distribution of natural resources, and technologies (which are human creations) constrain as well as provide opportunities for certain actions and interactions.

Outcomes and Developments

6) *the concrete outcomes and effects of purposeful action.* These may be intended as well as unintended. They are the immediate gains and losses as well as the material and cultural effects relating to the maintenance and transformation of social systems.

7) *structuring activity and the exercise of meta-power.* Social activity and its effects may be directed toward maintaining or changing rule systems, institutions, and cultural elements regulating key societal processes such as exchange, conflict, power and production processes. Such activity entails *relational or structural control* and is based on 'meta-power' (see companion volume).

8) *unintended and exogenous structuring of social systems.* Structuring is the result not only of purposeful activities of social agents, but also the unintended effects of human action or the effects of exogenous material and social factors which impinge on social systems.[5]

ASD theory recognizes three levels of a social system: (1) actors, (2) social action and interaction settings and processes ('games' very broadly defined), and (3) endogenous constraints, material, social structural, and cultural. Figure 1.1 represents these elements and levels and indicates their interrelationships.

Truly exogenous factors, according to ASD theory, are those which structure and influence actors, social action, and system development, but which are not influenced by them, at least not in the short-run. In the long run, agents in the social system may gain control over them, thereby making them endogenous to the social system.

Fundamentally, social systems are dynamic because exogenous factors change, causing internal restructuring, and also because of the creative properties of social action and interaction. The structuring effects of social action are represented in Figure 1.1, relating to the maintenance or change of

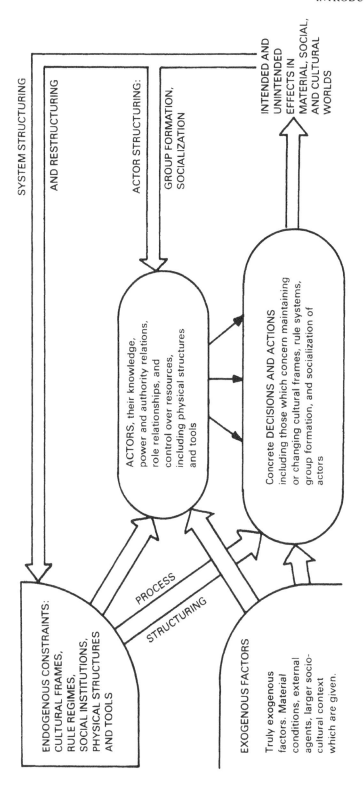

FIGURE 1.1 General model of actor-system dynamics.

endogenous constraints as well as of the actors themselves. The feedback loops make a social system not only highly dynamic, but even intrinsically unstable. Stability is not assumed unless social institutions and controls regulate and stabilize social action and system development.

Cultural frames, institutions, and physical structures and tools shape and regulate 'process-level' activities and conditions, among others, those of production, exchange, the exercise of power and conflict.

In particular, they structure such conditions of social activity as the definition of relevant issues and problems, membership or participation in the activities, permissable or acceptable activities, relationships of actors or categories of actors to one another and to forms of property or resources, the possible outcomes of activities and the distribution of benefits and costs for different actors or categories of actors involved.

The endogenous constraints which structure and stabilize to some extent social action and systems developments may appear more or less rigid. In any given instance or in the short run, some consist of structures and processes which social agents to some extent take as given, for instance the macro-social structures that impinge on, structure and regulate particular social activities of spheres or action. They may lack knowledge about their possibilities to manipulate them, or lack the will or means to do so. Above all, powerful agents and vested interests may maintain these constraints against the will of others. In this sense, key structures and processes of the social system are often experienced or defined as "exogenous", although such factors can be distinguished, at least analytically, from truly exogenous ones.

If, at a given moment, social agents manage to restructure one or more of the factors or factor-complex, then a 'break-point' or turning point takes place. Indeed, in the medium to long-run, actors learn, redefine problems, change their models of reality, develop new strategies, and create new technologies. This implies also the emergence of new actors or coalitions of actors, and the restructuring of action settings and of societal frameworks within which social action and interaction are played out.

The institutional order of a social system may be viewed then as the macroscopic resultant of multiple, often contradictory structuring processes, including purposeful social action. These produce particular social formations, for instance the systems of power, conflict, production and exchange examined in several of the Chapters (see Chapters 4, 5, 7, 9, and Chapters 3 to 8 in the companion volume). The contradictory structuring processes are also basic factors with which to explain the reproduction and transformation of social systems (see companion volume).

4.   Beyond the Babel of Two Hundred Voices[6]

There was a time when "social science" questioning and thinking were carried on within the realm of philosophy (the tower of Babel). This assured that the relatively little that was known about psychology could be readily linked in a natural way to the limited systematic knowledge available about political systems, economics, or socio-cultural development (as pointed up by the breadth of Adam Smith's work or that of Marx).

The break-away of the various social sciences from philosophy has profited them, above all in the development of more concrete empirical knowledge and a spectrum of powerful methodological tools. The price, however, has been high: systematic knowledge about man and society is highly fragmented and the social science professions are deeply alienated from one another.

The difficulties of communication and joint work among social scientists are well-known to anyone who has attempted inter-disciplinary research. Joint projects more often than not fail to function jointly and result typically in separate reports which are bound or stapled together. This would be no more than an academic problem, if there were not a demand for greater knowledge about how the economy interacts with politics, or about how social institutions such as the family and local community are affected by technological and economic developments. Our collective ability to understand and to regulate effectively modern, democratic societies is declining as they become more complex and new or more important types of interdependencies arise which are outside the domain of knowledge or competence of any single social science discipline.

Our research — and the development of ASD theory in particular — represents an effort to create a common language to facilitate communication and collaboration among the various social science disciplines.[7] Greater interdisciplinary cooperation should lead to more rapid development of analytical tools, theoretical principles and methods (see companion volume). Equally as important, it can enable social science to shed some light (of course, from different angles) on several of the key problems and issues confronting modern societies: stagflation, the current socio-economic crisis, the crisis of the welfare state, problems of development and underdevelopment, and technological change and its socio-cultural and political implications.

Key concepts introduced in Section 3 can be applied fruitfully, we suggest, to the segments of society which are defined as "economic", "political", and "social": actors and social agents which make decisions and carry out social action; rule systems and institutions structuring and regulating social action and transactions; material constraints; the structuring of action opportunities and constraints; outcomes and consequences of human activity, both intended and unintended effects; the structuring and restructuring of social systems.

Economists show an interest in certain general *categories of actors or social roles* such as buyers and sellers, owners of capital, trade unions, financial intermediaries and central banks, and increasingly politicians. They focus on particular social *decision settings* in society (production sectors and industries, markets, banking systems) which are considered "economic".

Political scientists and political sociologists tend to focus their interest on other types of actors (or in some instances the same actors play different or more diversified roles) — politicians, bureaucrats, pressure groups, the general public, political parties, public agencies and interest organizations. The decision settings of interest in these cases (political arenas, political organs and public authorities, policy-making and planning settings) are characterized by significantly different norms, rules and procedures than the economic or "market" spheres. That is, there is a different rationality or logic than that found in purely economic spheres investigated by economists.

Sociologists may study class structures and their transformation, social organization and social movements, often involving highly complex, formally organized social agents. They also study local communities, schools, hospitals, neighborhood networks and families where the actors may be individuals or small groups and where social norms and institutional regulation are substantially different from those found in more macro-level settings.

Of course, there are increasing linkages and cross-overs between the different spheres. Economists more and more deal with public choice and public regulation while political scientists and sociologists develop economic sociology and political economy. Such developments reflect in part the fact that the distinctions between political and economic sectors, and macro-society and local-society have become more diffuse in modern society, with increased and elaborate interactions and infiltration between these systems.

The ASD framework enables the systematic study of the dynamics of socio-economic systems. For instance, one finds new and emergent actors, public actors, citizen groups and workers have become involved to an increasing extent in decisions in the economic system, such as the strategic and investment decisions of enterprises, from which earlier they were totally excluded. At the same time, new types of decision settings and games have emerged. Some of these, such as tripartite negotiations and decision-making about income policies and wage and price setting rules, have changed in part the character of economic and political sectors. This is another way of saying that the "mixed economy" or "welfare capitalism" is a different species than "capitalism" as Marx or liberal economists understood it.

ASD theory suggests how one may go about identifying and relating in a systematic way a variety of different social decision settings or spheres in a modern society, each setting with certain actors, 'rules of the game', and issues. The linkages among settings entail information flows, influence and regulative relations, money and debt connections, flows of goods and services. While some of these can in large part be understood as "economic", they also have obvious political and socio-cultural characteristics in that non-economic actors and institutions may be involved. Other areas such as public administration, community politics, and government policy-making have been nearest to political science and to a lesser extent sociology's domains. Once again, contemporary research suggests that economic actors, such as a major employer and source of income, or a lobbyist, are often intimately involved in these "political arenas".

In sum, we want to suggest that out of the work carried out thus far there is emerging slowly — and in a yet incomplete way — a framework for the social sciences which can contribute in the long run to the development of a more unified language and methodology fo the study of man and his societies.

5.   Issues and Applications

The Chapters are divided into three distinct groups, although the issues and analyses in the three parts overlap partially.

Part I, Modeling Socio-economic Systems and Problems, deals with some aspects of the current socio-economic crisis, in particular in Chapter 2, with problems of inflation, stagnation and unemployment with a stress on the first in developed countries. One of our case studies, that of Belgium, is presented in Chapter 4. Our thesis is quite simple: institutional arrangements in advanced welfare capitalist societies make them prone to inflation and/or stagnation. The ability — and the commitment — of the state to deal with the current crisis is strictly limited, as we argue in Chapters 2 and 3. Chapter 5 deals briefly, from the same perspective developed in earlier chapters, with problems of stagflation, economic and political crisis in Latin America.

Part I also presents and applies a methodology developed within ASD theory, with which to build structural models of socio-economic systems. These models permit the knowledge of different social science professions to be combined in systematic ways.

We show how a socio-economic system with its various institutional spheres and sectors can be modeled as a set of social decision and activity nodes. Particular social agents are involved at each node, governed by specific rule regimes (see Burns *et al.*, 1985). Actors cooperate, conflict, negotiate, make decisions, and in general transact at these nodes. They do this in response to certain data and information inputs. The decisions made determine such variables and conditions, for example, as wages, price levels, investment levels, credit creation and allocation, money supply, and so forth. Models of decision nodes, the actors involved and the rules governing their decision-making and activities are qualitative in character, even if information inputs may be quantitative (as well as qualitative). The decisions made affect quantitative variables and relationships such as general price level, unemployment, investment rates, inflation and employment relationships, the relationship of consumption to income. Decisions, for example in the form of legislation or government policies, may also determine particular rules and rule systems such as those governing collective bargaining and wage developments. These quantitative and qualitative factors, in turn, may feedback to affect actors' perceptions, strategies, negotiations and transactions. Changes in rule regimes and the institutional framework may also be brought about.

Some of the decision nodes are linked to one another directly, others only indirectly. The nodes are also linked to real processes and developments in the social economy, such as levels of investment and government expenditures, balance of payment developments, and rates of economic growth. The structuring of such systems, the meta-processes and social struggles which maintain or change them, the role of different social agents and coalitions of agents in the shaping and reshaping of such systems are all important questions which, in our view, can be systematically investigated. The knowledge gained can be integrated with the existing knowledge and insights of economic science. Ways in which this can be done are suggested in Chapters 2, 3, 4 and 5.

Chapter 9 also takes up modeling problems, in this case dealing with the concept of dependent development. This is defined in terms of the structuring and constraining of causal structures within a political economy. A methodology for such structural analysis is outlined.

Part II of the book deals with attempts to shape and develop innovations in socio-economic institutions and organizations. Such innovations are viewed in a historically given, economic and political context. This sets the stage for major conflicts and even confrontations between those committed to existing economic arrangements and those determined to bring about restructuring.

The specific focus of Part II are studies of institutional innovation to realize in practice the concept of "worker control". In one case, discussed in Chapter 6, workers at the Lip watch factory in Besançon, France took over the running of the factory after a period of confrontation with management. This action was not their initial intention. However, the dynamics of the labor-management conflict led them to the notion of "workers' control" and ultimately to the social action to realize it.

The other two chapters in Part II deal with Yugoslavia, the first major attempt on a societal level to institutionalize a form of "workers' control" or *self-management*. This endeavor was not the result of an utopian vision of a new, alternative socio-economic system and society. Rather, the political elite in Yugoslavia invented the system out of necessity. Faced with growing tension and confrontation with the Soviet Union, it chose to break away, rather than remain within the "Soviet sphere". The leadership believed themselves to have the military capability and sufficient internal (and international) support to carry out this maneuver. At the same time, it was not prepared to return to some form of private capitalism. For dedicated communists, this was simply out of the question. But how to call themselves socialists, and at the same time distinguish themselves from Soviet state socialism? Self-management was the social invention which resolved this dilemma. It ultimately combined "workers' control" with market institutions and a variety of semi-public institutions designed to serve as alternatives to "statism", the all encompassing and powerful state. The "self-management principle" and ideology allowed a communist regime to differentiate itself from a powerful rival and, at the same time, legitimize itself as a socialist society.

The Yugoslav self-management system is interesting on the level of praxis as well as of social science theory. Practically, it represents a "third way" between capitalism and private ownership of the means of production and a planned society with an all powerful state, "state socialism". Scientifically, the Yugoslav development has entailed a variety of institutional innovations, institutional conflicts, learning and restructuring. Its history is a formidable challenge to institutional analysis. It is also a case that points up the limits of traditional economic approaches.

The Yugoslav experiment, as we argue in Chapter 7, has not been without serious problems. Many of these problems have become much more serious since Tito's death. Unfortunately, perhaps, the highly innovative ideas, and the great energy which has gone into the realization of the self-management concept has not found the most suitable milieu in Yugoslavia, with its historically deep social cleavages and its low level of initial economic development.

Social institutions and organizations are human constructions to deal with certain problems or to realize certain values or goals, including the maintenance or transformation of social power structures. This idea is a major consideration in Part II as well as in other parts, and is consistent with the challenge of William F. Whyte (1982) to investigate systematically "social inventions for solving human problems."

Social agents may feel it necessary to change institutional arrangements, to invent entirely new systems, or to introduce new strategic possibilities and new interpretations and models of the situation in order to be able to effectively realize their values, goals, or interests.

Innovation and social restructuring is attempted under conditions such as the following:

1) Economic or socio-political elites initiate changes in socio-economic institutions which fail to serve their interests adequately or which seem to block effective problem-solving in areas they consider important. This may concern either economic or political issues or both, as illustrated in the numerous reforms and innovations carried out in the course of Yugoslav post-world war II development (Chapter 7).

2) A shift in power favors actors with a different image or principle of appropriate institutional arrangements. They may be critical of existing socio-economic institutions, because they fail to deal with issues or problems which they consider essential to solve. Or they may judge the arrangements to be unjust or incompatible with important social values and norms. We see this in the various proposals and struggles related to a new international economic order (NIEO) (Chapters 9 and 11).

3) Social agents in conflict try individually or collectively to restructure "rules of the game" or other features of the socio-ecnomic order because they cannot find mutually acceptable settlements or resolutions *within* the existing institutional arrangement (Chapter 6). In this sense, "unmanageable conflicts" become forces for institutional innovation and development.

Innovations in socio-economic institutions may themselves be sources of tension and struggle. In some instances, they are too radical for their social environment, or at least for powerful groups or elites in that context. The "threat to the social order" may be apparent almost from the beginning, as in the case of the worker take-over of the Lip factory (Chapter 6), or it may be "revealed" in the course of working out the implications of major institutional reforms as in Yugoslavia (Chapter 7). Elites mobilize to correct "deviations", to try to re-establish more acceptable conditions and arrangements. Often, this 'counter-revolution' itself entails innovations. This should be stressed, since it is often assumed that there is simply a return to what obtained earlier. Usually, this is not the case. To a certain extent, some of the elements or features of the institutional innovations which provoke counter-measures are incorporated into the arrangements established through the 'counter-reformation'.

More generally, we are interested in the relationship between institutions, as social constructions and rule systems organizing and regulating socio-economic behavior, the ways in which different institutions interact, limit or reinforce one another. The multiple institutions which typically apply to a sphere of socio-economic activity may be more or less contradictory or incompatible. This sets the stage for social confrontation and struggle among social groups adhering to or anchored in the different institutional set-ups. Additional questions are: what implications do institutional reforms or inventions have for the performance of the established arrangements. Chapters 8 and 11 analyze some of the ways in which institutions such as product and financial markets allocating resources and stimulating competition and improved economic performance, on the one hand, contradict, on the other, principles of organizing self-managed enterprises or self-reliant economies. Or, on the contrary, stress on self-management or self-reliance may interfere with or limit economic performance.

Part III of the book deals with problems of development and underdevelopment. We suggest in Chapter 9 that the international division of labor, and the wealth and poverty of nations, are coupled in a way analogous to the linkage inside societies between unequal resource control and uneven development (for instance, in the case of Yugoslavia). We try to specify and analyze some of the major factors which produce and maintain inequalities in wealth and power between "developed" and "less developed" countries. The main thesis is that the organized system of inequality between developed countries and underdeveloped countries and their respective economic agents tends to maintain and reproduce itself. Participation in such a framework leads to or reinforces inequalities in wealth, power and capabilities for further socio-economic development, for instance, unequal possibilities to take advantage of new opportunities for profit and economic growth, or to avoid losses and negative effects of economic downturn or crisis. In short, the development tendencies and conditions of the world economic system result not only in the production of greater wealth but also the production of relative poverty and a system of uneven development and dependence among nations of the world.

Chapter 10 takes up the problem of dependent development, where dependency is defined in terms of external factors and conditions structuring and constraining causal structures within a political economy. The analysis is applied to the case of Mexico's recent development, to explore the possibilities of Mexico reducing its level of dependence. The prognosis at the time (1980) the paper was written was pessimistic, and developments in Mexico since then have only confirmed this assessment.

Chapter 11 takes up the issue of technology and under-development. It questions the thesis that technology transfer, the massive input of industrial technology into under-developed countries (UDCs) will bring about socio-economic development, and improvement in general welfare. The analysis considers the relationship between developed countries (DCs) and UDCs and the contraints on and selectivity of technology transfer. It also examines the internal conditions of UDCs which limit the possibility to absorb and make effective use of DC technology. We suggest an approach, *compatibility analysis*, with which to analyze the likelihood that a new technology or technological development will fit into and prove productive in the societies in which the development or introduction takes place.

6.   Conclusion: Structuralist and Rational Choice Approaches to Socio-economic Analysis

The stress on innovation in socio-economic processes, the concrete activities of structuring and restructuring socio-economic systems, and conflict and struggle among groups about institutional innovation and change clearly distinguish our approach to the study of socio-economic systems, and society in general, from that of ahistorical structuralism (Althusserian Marxism, Parsonianism, among others) as well as rational choice and related actor-oriented approaches. In the ASD framework, the dichotomy between freedom and determinism — and that between intentional and causal methodologies — are replaced by the concept of deciding and acting *within* systems and acting *on* systems. The dichotomy between equilibrium and disequilibrium is replaced by the concepts of structuring and restructuring of systems, with the question of system stability and change a matter for empirical and theoretical investigation.

ASD theory differs at a fundamental level from both rational choice and structuralist approaches. This can be summed up in terms of three major theoretical concepts in ASD theory: human creativity, social structuring and relational and collective properties. In each case, the concepts link human agents with the structures and systems *in* which and *on* which they act.

Human creativity   A basic premise of ASD theory is that human action can entail or lead to innovations and creative developments, in particular the invention or transformation of particular social systems. On the one hand, structuralists largely ignore action and actors and, therefore, there is no real place within their frame for creative human action or creative actors and entrepreneurs. On the other, the rational choice approach takes for granted or ignores the structuring of decision systems and games and, therefore, lacks the notion of "choice about choice" and relational control. There is simply no major concept or sustained theoretical development within the rational choice tradition concerning the capability of actors to creatively transform their preferences, the set of options, and the outcomes, or the entire decision and game systems, or to be creative in any other way.[8]

Social structuring   The concept of structuring has two components, the *structural and the actional.* Structural determinists stress the first and rational choice theorists the second. Structuralists ignore human action as a component in the structuring and restructuring of social systems. However, the rational choice approach largely takes for granted or ignores the structural component of social structuring — social institutions, rule regimes, cultural forms and other social constraints — which shape and reshape preferences, options and outcomes. The latter are quite simply given or the point of departure for rational choice models.

Relational and collective properties   Concepts such as institutions, cultural forms, legitimacy, ideology and principles of justice are relational and structural in character. They cannot be reduced to individuals. They apply to groups, organizations, networks, nations and other collectivities. Individual as well as collective actors are constrained by such structures at the same time that they shape and change them, at times in very innovative ways.

   Through structuring activity, humans create, maintain and change *collective or organized agents*, groups, movements, organizations, the state (in each case made up of course of individuals). Within these collectivities certain rule regimes and cultural forms govern the relationships among actors and their social action and interactions. The members of the collectivity also share some minimum *common identity* and cultural symbols and forms. The collective or organized agents are capable of making decisions and acting, and of exercising power with respect to other actors and agents, as well as particular individuals and groups within the collectivity. They can carry out collective action and exercise power on a structural or systematic level, for example to shape and reshape macro-structures, or to produce public goods. The state, for example, as a collective actor or more precisely a complex of collective actors with a monopoly of legitimate coercion, can determine many of the basic rules of the game, property rights and other institutions, which determine the action opportunities and outcomes of particular decision processes and games in society (North makes this point in his critical review of Mancur Olson's recent book, *The Rise and Decline of Nations* (1982).

Collective and relational properties, organized actors, collective action, and the dynamic interplay between actors and systems cannot be adequately described and analyzed in terms of individuals acting and inter-acting as purely independent units, each privately making optimal decisions. In part, human agents find themselves embedded in complex systems where their options are strictly limited.

Moreover, in many instances, the effects of joining or not joining a collective action are too complex or uncertain to allow for a rational choice in the strict meaning. Besides, many social organizations and movements are ideologically motivated (Etzioni, 1975), or are grounded in principles of justice or other legitimizing principles which have meaning only in a relational or collective sense. Quite simply, rational choice theory lacks the language and tools of analysis with which to deal with collective and rela-tional properties of socio-economic systems.

On the other hand, structural determinists lack a language and an analytical framework with which to describe and analyze human action, including collective choice, as well as the dynamic structuring processes through which collective agents and movements build up and maintain as well as transform socio-economic structures. It is not possible within such intellectual traditions to specify and analyze systematically the dialectical interplay between social actors and macro-structures, including large scale organized agents.

Figure 1.2 sums up in a very rough manner our preliminary attempt to characterize ASD theory and to place it in the "space of social science theories", distinguished on two strategic dimensions: subjectivism/objectivism, static-ahistorical as opposed to dynamic-historical approaches.[9]

A common criticism of the social systems approaches which Boulding, Buckley, Deutsch, Easton, and Etzioni, among others have tried to develop is that such approaches allow the formulation of certain general models and hypotheses, but these are too abstract or general to be applied directly to concrete analysis or data. The work collected together in this and the companion volume suggests that this is not the case. Although the empiri-cal and policy studies included here are far from finished studies, they point up that an empirically and policy-oriented ASD research program is capable of developing and applying new analytical tools and can be used to investigate a wide range of socio-economic problems. On-going projects entail further development and application of ASD theory and methodology.[10]

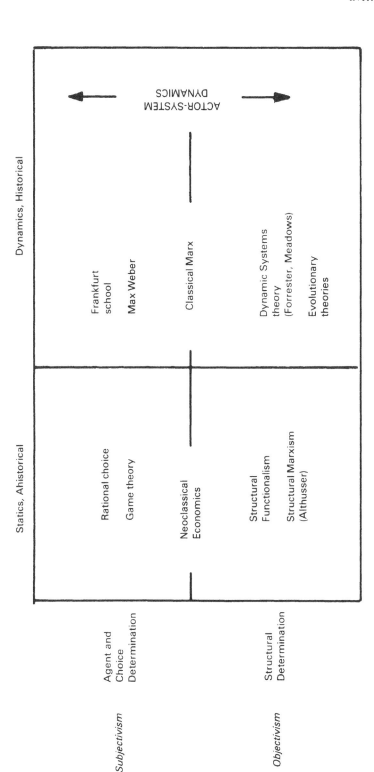

FIGURE 1.2   Social science approaches distinguished in terms of the subjectivity/objectivity and statics/dynamics dimensions.

Note: Such a scheme fails, of course, to capture the extent to which different approaches in the social science are multi-dimensional undertakings. Marx, in particular, is particularly difficult to place, in part because he addressed himself to problems of subjectivism and objectivism. However, Marx failed to develop a systematic framework and methodology for combining actor and system levels, subjectivity and objectivity. This is reflected today in the various "Marxist schools".

The framework introduced and applied in the papers collected together here and in the companion volume appear to us to be a promising beginning for investigating and analyzing socio-economic phenomena. It also implies new ways of viewing social life. Through its role in, and effects on, policy analysis and institutional reform, it may contribute to reshaping circumstances. Existing socio-economic arrangements, which in large part structure our conditions and opportunities, generate uneven development, inequality and conflict. These institutions can be reformed or transformed. The possibilities of creativity, innovation and experimentation in the development of socio-economic institutions have only been explored superficially. In part, this reflects the power of vested interests in existing arrangements. In part, however, it reflects the failure of social and economic theory to help us learn and to discover better ways to organize and to conduct our lives.

NOTES

1. In general, there is substantial incompatibility between the aims and ambitions of economic welfare (and possibly greater equality) and development, on the one hand, and, on the other, the existing institutional frameworks for production, exchange and distribution, which frustrate these aims.
2. Important exceptions to the general pattern are found in the works of Alker (1979), Buckley (1967), Deutsch (1968), Etzioni (1968), and Geyer (1974,1976).
3. This type of approach tends to treat as purely hierarchical the relationship between environment and system processes. The environment is simply given and determines processes and their outputs. The latter are rarely seen to affect or to transform the environment and its structure through multi-level feedback linkages (see Burns et al, 1985). This is the case with most economic growth models whose mathematical structure remains unaffected by model output. Similarly, macro-economic models have to be frequently re-estimated, particularly during periods of actual structural transformations, so that new data 'bends' coefficients, at least to some degree, in the right directions.
4. Following Simon and others who have stressed imperfect information in human decision-making and action, we assume in our models that knowledge is incomplete for two reasons:

    (1) No complete, finite description is possible of what has happened in the past, what is happening at present, and what could happen in the future. Rationality is therefore always strictly limited in the sense that actors can never have complete knowledge, and invariably also make miscalculations and mistakes.

    (2) Also, the 'game character' of many social relationships and interactions motivate actors to manipulate information, to deceive, lie, and so forth.

    The result is invariably unintended and unanticipated consequences of purposeful action.
5. Agents may or may not be aware that they cause a shift or transformation, for instance when peasants clear forests and trees from their lands and set in motion erosion and climatic changes which reduce the agricultural productivity of the land and their ability to sustain themselves and their institutions.
6. J. Conrad's phrase, 'in the babel of two hundred voices, he would forget himself.'

7. The language of ASD theory, through its close but independent ties to general systems science, allows social scientists to carry on intelligent dialogue and to collaborate with engineers and natural scientists, for instance in studies presently being prepared on the societal impact of new technologies and technological developments.

8. Classical game theorists (von Neumann, Nash, Harsanyi, and Howard, among others) transformed decision structures and games in order to solve problems or anomalies. However, they did not allow their 'players' to enjoy such initiative. In this sense, the models are static ones, and they neglect completely the creative and truly dynamic aspects of human choice and rationality (Burns and Meeker, 1978).

9. The format of Figure 1.2 has been inspired by the somewhat different scheme which Burrell and Morgan (1979:29) present in their survey of organizational theory paradigms.

10. Among others, a comparative international study of inflation and stagnation, a comparative international study of collective bargaining and wage patterns, energy policy-making and implementation in Scandinavia, strategic decision-making and labor union influence in Swedish enterprises, a national survey.

REFERENCES

Alker, Jr., H.R., J. Bennett and D. Mefford, (1979) Generalized precedent logics for resolving insecurity dilemmas. Project Working Paper, MIT Center for International Studies, Cambridge.

Buckley, W., (1967) *Sociology and Modern Systems Theory*. Englewood Cliffs: Prentice-Hall.

Burns, T.R., T. Baumgartner and P. DeVille, (1985) *Man, Decisions, Society*. London: Gordon and Breach.

Burns, T.R. and D. Meeker, (1978) Conflict and structure in multi-level, multiple objective decision-making systems. In C.A. Hooker (ed.), *Foundations and Applications of Decision Theory*. Dordrecht, Holland: Reidel.

Burrell, G. and G. Morgan, (1979) *Sociological Paradigms and Organizational Analysis*. London: Heinemann.

Deutsch, K., (1968) *The Analysis of International Relations*. Englewood Cliffs: Prentice-Hall.

DeVille, P. and T.R. Burns, (1977) Institutional response to crisis in capitalist development. *Social Praxis* 4: 5-46.

Etzioni, A., (1968) *The Active Society: A Theory of Societal and Political Processes*. New York: Free Press.

Etzioni, A., (1975) *A Comparative Analysis of Complex Organizations*. New York: Free Press.

Forrester, J., (1961) *Industrial Dynamics*. Cambridge: MIT Press.

Forrester, J., (1968) *Principles of Systems*. Cambridge: MIT Press.

Geyer, R.F., (1974) Alienation and general systems theory. *Sociologia Neerlandica* X: 18-40.

Geyer, R.F., (1976) Individual alienation and information processing: A systems theoretical conceptualization. In R.F. Geyer and D. Schweitzer (ed.), *Theories of Alienation — Critical Perspectives in Philosophy and the Social Sciences*. The Hague: Martinus Nijhof.

Meadows, D. *et al.*, (1974) *Limits to Growth*. 2nd ed. New York: Universe Books.

North, D.C., (1982) A theory of economic exchange: Review of Mancur Olson *The Rise and Decline of Nations*, *Science* 219: 163-164.

Whyte, W.F., (1982) Social inventions for solving human problems. *American Sociological Review*, 47: 1-13.

Modeling Socio-Economic Systems and Contemporary Problems

2

The Shaping of Socio-Economic Crisis: Societal Change and Theoretical Failure[1]

Thomas Baumgartner   Tom R. Burns
Philippe DeVille

Part 1 of this chapter singles out several of the more important socio-economic and political developments which have made inflation endemic in modern capitalist societies and which also limit the ability of the welfare state to regulate inflation and at the same time prevent economic stagnation. Part 2 goes on to suggest some of the reasons that contemporary economic theory and policy are unable to deal adequately with the current crisis. We go on to indicate several of the requirements for a new framework.

The analyses in this chapter as well as in Chapters 3 and 4 represent the preliminary findings from a long term, comparative and multi-disciplinary project to investigate inflation as well as stagnation processes in several industrialized countries (with detailed case studies of Belgium, Great Britain, Iceland, Sweden and Switzerland) as well as a number of Latin American countries (Chapter 5). The research makes use of the considerable data and analytical material available in published and unpublished economic and other social science reports.[2] Such material has been complemented with interviews of knowledgeable researchers as well as persons in key positions in major socio-economic institutions (central bank authorities, industrial leaders, government policy-makers and authorities, labor leaders, among others) in the countries under investigation.

Our research points to the development of what we refer to as *inflationary societies*, that is a strong tendency toward inflation. The degree to which modern Western societies are inflationary varies (see Table 2.1). But all have experienced historically high and rising rates during the early 1970s and also declining real economic growth. The future will tell if the falling rates of the early 1980s signal a turning point. We are sceptical. Our reasoning is quite direct: A complex of institutional conditions and processes have emerged over the past 35 years which have contributed to making inflation endemic in capitalist welfare societies. The welfare state also has been unable to control inflation without producing serious economic stagnation and unemployment.

Part I The Emergence of the Inflation Society

Six developments contributing substantially to the emergence of inflationary society are:

• Distributional conflicts are more and more difficult to settle or manage, particularly under conditions of economic stagnation.

• The economy is regulated increasingly by multiple negotiations in different segments and sectors of society. These are interdependent. At the same time there is no effective coordination and regulation of the diverse negotiations.

Claims advanced in market and negotiation settings are formulated in nominal terms (prices, wages, entitlements, government budgets). However, the real outcomes are determined only through the aggregate or macro effects of all major market and negotiated claims.

• Social structures have changed, reflected in increasing economic concentration, innovation in and restructuring of the strategic financial and banking sectors, the institutionalization of non-economic values, and the development of the "mixed" market/politically administered economy.

• Struggles over resources and inflationary pressures in the international system have substantially increased.

• The role of the state in the national economy has changed dramatically, and its ability to make policy and to stabilize the economy have become at the same time increasingly problematic because of changes in internal social structure, economic internationalization, and the development, both at the national and international levels, of complex financial institutions which are relatively autonomous from central government and central bank control.

• The conceptionalization and measurement of inflation as well as other socio-economic indicators has not kept pace with societal shifts and transformations.

We discuss these interrelated points in the following six sections.

TABLE 2.1
Economic Performance of Selected OECD Countries, 1961-1970 and 1970-1979

	Increase in real GDP (in %)		Increase in consumer price indices (in %)		Average rate of unemployment (in %)		Increase in civilian employment (in %)
	1961-70	1970-79	1961-70	1970-79	1961-70	1970-79	1970-79
Austria	51	41	35	70	2.72	1.95	2.6
Belgium	48	38	27	71	3.7	7.5	—
France	62	40	39	115	—	—	3.9
Germany (FRG)	50	29	27	56	0.97	2.85	− 4.3
Italy	61	30	42	225	5.14	6.37	5.5
Sweden	48	19	42	120	1.70	2.05	8.4
Switzerland	46	07	41	60	—	—	− 5.1
United Kingdom	27	21	43.45	196	2.0	4.1	1.7
United States	42	33	27.13	76	5.27	6.20	23.3
TOTAL	55	36	36	106	—	—	10.1

Sources: OECD, National Accounts of OECD countries 1950-1970, vol. 1, Paris 1981, OECD, Main Economic Indicators, Historical Studies 1960-1970, Paris 1980. Adapted from Scharpf (1981).

1. Distributional Conflicts and Inflationary Societies

Societal groups have increasingly organized and developed strategies to articulate claims on economic resources, goods and services, both private and public. Political parties, business organizations, labor unions, and a variety of other organized interests perform their roles and justify their existence to their members by advancing new claims or by protecting established ones. The aggregate of these claims tends to exceed available real goods and services, particularly under conditions of economic stagnation. This sets the stage for *distributional conflict*, in many instances for an intensification of such conflicts. In modern welfare societies, these tend to be "settled" or regulated through bilateral negotiations and decisions increasing *nominal* monetary claims: wages, prices, entitlements, budget allocations. Various government policies and measures enable the expansion of total money expenditures to take place. Inflation is the ultimate result.

More specific observations in this context are:

• Government agencies, large oligopolistic enterprises, crisis industries, trade unions, and a variety of organized pressure groups struggle to maintain or increase their real income, even though these demands in the aggregate may exceed available real output.

Even pensioners, the handicapped and other resource weak groups — or professionals acting in their name — are able to pressure many governments to maintain services for them and their standards of living in the face of economic downturn.[3]

• Rising expectations and a growth culture emphasizing material growth are firmly rooted in our value structure, our high standards of living notwithstanding. Everybody feels entitled to the maintenance of her or his standard of living and even its future improvement. This presupposes continued economic growth whatever its consequences for resource base, environment and social health.

• All who experience, or are threatened with, income set-backs struggle in market, negotiation, administrative, or political settings to regain or to prevent losses. The aggregate claims on income have more and more tended to exceed the resources available for distribution.

• It has become increasingly difficult in most Western societies to maintain growth of productivity and of real output, especially since the early 1970s. This is due to changing patterns of work life, constraints on business expansion, declining investment in production facilities, and shifts to services and other types of "less productive" activity.

- The distributional conflicts are "settled" in part by allowing the claimants to realize their nominal, monetary claims. That is, negotiated wages, prices, entitlements, taxes, and budget allocations are paid even if it requires the borrowing or printing of money. Total monetary expenditures in society tend therefore to exceed real output which is available for the satisfaction of claims.

- Government policies to a greater or lesser extent *enable* such an expansion of total monetary expenditures through appropriated budget, taxation, monetary, and credit policies.

The state feels obliged to insure a sufficient level of demand to ensure purchase of the available output at prices covering production costs. Otherwise, workers will be laid off eventually, plants will be closed, enterprises go bankrupt. Selling prices tend to be raised if costs are subject to pressures from income demands by workers, by suppliers, including the international suppliers of commodities such as oil, and even by the state through higher taxation. (During the post-war period of growth, productivity gains covered a significant part of expanding income claims.)

The state may in this situation expand credit and money supply to finance the resultant growth in government expenditures and to satisfy the growing credit demand of industry and households. The Thatcher and Reagan governments have tried to break this pattern. There is little evidence that this will help them to achieve long-term control over inflation. In fact, our research suggests the contrary, as pointed out later.

- The welfare state and political leaders find it difficult to settle conflicts either by political persuasion or by force. Persuasion would entail convincing most groups to reduce or to hold back their expanded claims in favor of other groups. Real income might have to be taken away from some groups, or at least real increases denied them for the benefit of others or for the entire social economy.

In some countries, such as the U.S. and Great Britain, high rates of unemployment, promises of improvements, and even various forms of coercion operate to restrain claims and therefore inflationary pressures.

Repression is a particularly prominent strategy of the weak nation states with low political legitimacy found in Latin America. Such strategies are unacceptable in many European countries, e.g., Scandinavia, Austria, Germany, and the Netherlands.

The concept of distributional conflict — and that of the negotiation economy discussed below — might well suggest direct confrontation among societal groups, as in bargaining between representatives of capital and labor. While such confrontation is obviously an important part or aspect of distributional conflict, they are by no means the only or the major ones.

There are a large number of *indirect* distributional conflicts where the actors are not engaged in any direct negotiations or direct conflicts over income distribution. They are acting inconsistent with each other by simply pushing their claims for scarce resources, especially if they try to maintain or expand real income in face of economic contraction.

Claims are advanced — sometimes openly, at other times not — in a variety of institutional settings. Class conflict is not the only competitive conflict axis in modern welfare societies. Different occupational and labor groups "compete" with one another in negotiating for wages and fringe benefits: white collar workers oppose blue collar ones; public sector workers insist on comparability with private sector workers; skilled workers fight to maintain or enlarge their differentials to unskilled workers; workers in the old smoke-stack industries try to maintain their position at the top of the wage hierarchy despite the collapse of their industries; and so on.

Old urban centers demand transfer payments and subsidies from the surrounding subsurbs or from the central government. Peripheral and mountain regions want equality with services in central and highly industrialized ones. Central and local governments struggle about who can tax what and at what rates; each tries to gain transfers from the other while attempting to shift responsibilities and tasks. Government agencies struggle to have their programs expanded while others should could back theirs.

The private sector would like reductions of its tax burdens while insisting the government pay for infrastructure development and maintenance, and letting it also pay for the negative social effects of business activities, such as pollution, congestion, occupational disease, and the unemployment, retraining and early retirement of people with outdated skills. And so it goes. Each group, sector, and segment pursues its own more or less legitimate interests.

2.   The Negotiated Economy

The economy of a modern welfare society can be to a great extent characterized as a negotiated one (Johansen, 1979). Markets and capitalist institutions in their strictest meaning have come to play less and less of a role in shaping and regulating wages and prices. Instead, organized groups meet in institutionalized bargaining settings and negotiate their claims and counterclaims. "Tripartite bargaining" about wage and price development guidelines, now increasingly coupled to taxation policies, is an obvious example of bargaining replacing or strongly interfering with capitalist institutions. This does not imply in our view that market mechanisms are no longer important in general. We believe simply that their role in terms of determining the distribution of income is becoming less important. Political and administrative negotiations play an increasingly central role in those societies, particularly in Western Europe, where the welfare state has come to exercise influence over a larger and larger share of the national product.

The numerous negotiations concerning wages, prices, entitlements, public services and expenditures, government budgets, central bank policies, etc. take place in different institutional settings. Many of the decisions or their outcomes will affect one another, that is they are inter-dependent. Thus, the decisions reached between employers and labor unions about a wage package or between price leaders about a concerted price push in an industry may led to rising unemployment. This in turn pushes up government social security expenditures as well as other budgets related to income maintenance programs. Government attempts to reduce budget deficits through taxation can in turn affect wage negotiations and price decisions of enterprises; or financing the deficit through borrowing can push up interest rates and squeeze business.

The numerous and diverse negotiations and decisions relating to the distribution of the national product are clearly *interdependent*. But their *co-ordination* is very weak or even non-existent. There are strong pressures — and in some instances concerted efforts — toward coordinating and linking negotiations. Wage settlements contain price indexation clauses, and moderate wage settlements are sometimes pushed through with the help of taxation concessions. Efforts to link questions of public expenditures, the level and coverage of public services, standards for pensioners, and even credit policies with wage negotiations are likely in the future. But it is still unclear how these linked negotiations — and the resulting "packages" or "social contracts" — will be accepted or legitimized.[4]

The results of poor coordination are apparent. The aggregate of claims in a society — or on the international level — tends to substantially exceed available resources. Inflationary pressures result. Societal actors, including policy-makers, experience a social reality they did not intend to create and over which they cannot exercise suitable control. As one economic policy-maker put it to us: "We know something must be done. In some instances we know what has to be done. But we do not know how to change the rules of the game. Politically it is not possible."

3. Inflation and Changing Social Structures

The development of inflationary societies in the West is in part linked to changing social structures and power relationships in and between societies. Constitutional and government reforms, the emergence of new interests, powerful organizations and movements, new coalitions, the shift in values and definitions of social reality tend to alter power relations and this affects negotiation systems.

Such changes affect in particular the relative bargaining power among actors involved in concrete decisions settings relating to the distribution of resources. They also affect linkages among negotiation settings and among actors in different settings, and, indeed, the entire structure of and the dominant forces in the negotiated economy. Political weight may thus be added to the demands of previously neglected groups; or the relative weightings of the demands among powerful vested interests — for instance private industry versus the state — may be shifted. Such alterations in negotiation sytems and processes affect the extent to which claims of different actors, groups, organizations, and coalitions can be advanced and gain substantial influence in the struggle over income distribution.

We discuss below eight major structural shifts.

Increases in Economic Concentration

Strengthened oligopolies and monopolies have transformed market pricing into administered pricing. Cost consciousness is reduced, especially when the (growing) public sector is the major customer. Market power and the ability to administer prices is used to increase prices even during economic downturns in order to cover large fixed costs and ensure satisfactory profit levels.

Organized Wage Bargaining

In many Western countries, particularly in Europe, wages are to a large extent determined through collective bargaining. In many countries (such as the Scandinavian countries, Belgium, Austria and Germany) these cover whole industries if not the entire manufacturing sector, the public sector, and important parts of the private service sector as well. Sector-wise or even more centralized wage bargaining tends to reduce the risks connected with wage increases. Individual managements are more willing to go along with wage increases knowing that their domestic competitors face more or less the same wage costs.

Expansionary Government Policies Shape "Sellers' Markets"

Keynesian demand management through government policies and

programs maintains if not increases total money expenditures in society. Most economic agents were, at least until very recently, convinced that government was committed to acting consistently on this basis, even at the cost of inflationary pressures. Managements, able to pass on increased labor and input costs, were therefore more willing to grant increased labor and input costs. At the same time, labor and other sellers learned to expect management readiness to give in to demands.

Institutionalized Power of Previously Resource-weak Groups

Power of labor as well as other resource-weak groups has been institutionalized to a greater or lesser extent in advanced welfare societies. This has led to an increased ability to realize ever increasing demands for higher real incomes, better income maintenance, substantial improvements in fringe benefits (vacation time, pension plans), and increased provision and quality of public services.

The Emergence and Institutionalization of Non-economic Values

The consequences of rapid economic growth have threatened non-economic values at the same time that increasing standards of living have strengthened commitment to them. Groups have organized and succeeded to some extent to realize environmental protection, increased work and product safety, and improved quality of work life. These gains add in most cases to costs of production or constrain the growth in productivity, thus limiting economic growth and the quantity of goods available for distribution. (But see Section 6 for a counter-argument.)

The Development of Banking and Financing Institutions

Since World War II, the financial service sector, including banking, has grown substantially in response to, e.g., economic growth, higher standards of living, and the development of new customer and consumer needs. Profitable marketing opportunities and intense competition have changed the behavior of financial institutions, above all banks. They have shed their traditional conservatism, becoming much more *marketing* oriented. Banks and other financial institutions vie with each other for fast growth and greater size.

This transformation has gone farthest in the U.S., but all industrialized countries have experienced the change. Specialization among different types of business and financial institutions — e.g., commercial, savings and investment banks; stock and commodity brokers; investment funds, insurance companies — has tended to break down. New types of financial organizations have emerged: credit agencies, leasing companies, investment funds, quasi- or fringe banks, etc. Attempts are being made to create all-purpose financial conglomerates, in some instances even under the control of non-financial companies. The reorientation has led to the development of new products: combined checking and saving accounts, credit cards, electronic fund transfer; investment certificates, money market certificates, certificates of deposit; share options, future certificates, etc.

Organizational and product development have made regulation and control of the financial sector and of credit and money creation much more difficult. This is not surprising. These innovations were not only designed to exploit new opportunities, they were often explicitly created to overcome regulatory barriers and break through regulatory constraints on growth.

Theoretical and statistical developments lag seriously behind these market developments so that regulatory bodies have to do with only partial (and often low quality) knowledge of credit and money developments. Nor has the concept and the statistical definition of money kept pace with the emergence of all these quasi-monies and financial claims.

The Internationalization of Banks and Financial Market

Rapid world growth, the emergence of multinational corporations, international travel, and the increasing speed and falling costs of international communications have led to and facilitated the increasing international integration of national financial markets and the development of international banks. The number of foreign branches and total assets in foreign branches of national banks has grown substantially. International borrowing and lending has become extremely important for many domestic banks. Off-shore money and capital markets have greatly expanded in part because financial institutions, multinational corporations and other agents wanted to avoid national taxation and regulation of capital flows, in part because national money and capital markets failed to develop and grow in response to the needs of ever larger and more international enterprises. Profit opportunities through international arbitrage have expanded just at a time when international organizations (such as banks and MNCs) have become able and willing to seek profits through the global management of their idle funds.

The volume of internationally mobilizable credit and money flows is by now so large that central banks and government regulators have lost the ability to manage interest and exchange rates for domestic purposes without losing control over capital inflows and outflows and the money supply. The flows are large enough to affect interest and exchange rates of even the largest countries, thereby providing powerful incentives for the mobilization of large volumes of capital in search of quick, speculative gains.

Yet, banking and financial market regulation remains national. This leaves increasingly important parts of the activities of international banks free from national control at a time when the potential for spectacular banking crashes force central banks to support shaky banks and nervous financial markets through the generous provision of central bank credit.

The transformation and internationalization of banking have made regulation of and control over banks and other financial institutions increasingly problematic. This is, in particular, the case with money supply (just at a time when "monetarist theory" successfully established itself as an analytic and policy approach to problems of inflation). This assures that both on national and international levels long-term stability of prices and other variables are quite unlikely.

The Welfare State as a Major Actor Complex in the Economy

The state has grown absolutely and also relatively to the private sector over the past thirty years. Yet, the state is not a single actor but a complex of actors with often competing and even conflicting interests. The state plays multiple and diverse roles in the negotiated economy, and does so in almost all the sectors and at different levels of society. The state engages in policy-making, shaping constraints and opportunities for many of the major negotiations and decisions in the economy. But the state is also engaged in many of them as an active participant. The state regulates the relationship between capital and labor through labor market regulations and interventions in wage negotiations, yet it is itself a major employer, often with the claim or the obligation to be a particularly progressive one. The state similarly regulates the banking system and the financial markets, yet the state is a major debtor.

The structural transformations of modern capitalist systems have severely limited the state's ability to solve stagflation problems. We will take up this problem in more detail below in Section 5.

4.   International Economic Struggle and Inflation

Conflict over the distribution of income and resources is international. This is pointed up by OPEC's struggle with OECD countries, the more general struggle between "North" and "South", between Poland and other Eastern European countries and their Western creditors, as well as the competition among Japan, US, and EEC countries.

An obvious instance of international struggle over income with inflationary consequences was OPEC's greater claims on world resources through dramatically increasing oil prices during the 1970's.

During the Vietnam War, the US could lay claim on international resources by creating and exporting dollars — to pay for both "guns and butter".[5] In this way, it was able to some extent to reduce national distributional conflicts arising from having to choose between "guns and butter". At the same time, its strategy created considerable international liquidity with world inflationary effects, given increasing oil and other commodity prices, which many countries paid for by making use of available "Euro-dollar" credits.

5.   The Ambivalent and Increasingly Problematic Role of the State in Socio-economic Policy-making

The links between institutional and sectoral price, wage, and budget setting processes, on the one hand, and inflationary developments, on the other, are established through the *processes of money and credit creation*. Such creation is realized through government fiscal policy, monetary policy, and the regulation of credit, financial markets, and exchange rates. It is these which determine in which ways, and to what degree, incompatible income claims are related to the production capacity of the economy:

  • through a growing money stock, credit expansion, and inflation;

  • through deflationary policies trying to impose price and wage moderation by means of recession and unemployment;

  • or through direct or indirect intervention into price determination processes (through income policies, industrial restructuring policies, market regulation, etc.)

Governments may utilize various strategies and regulatory mechanisms in order to try to control inflation, that is, to keep it within acceptable limits:

  • monetary and fiscal policies;

- price and income policies;

- consensus building strategies and institutional arrangements for negotiations relating to compatible wage, price, and budget determinations;

- intervention in and regulation of wage and price contract negotiations at the national, sectoral, and even enterprise level;

- direct intervention in key enterprises and branches to assure the production of goods and services in demand.

These government policies and strategies define rules and many of the constraints and opportunities within which income distribution games are played. State agencies regulate relationships among major participants as well as create new games, actors and arenas. Government agencies are participants in many of the games and negotiations which their policies are ostensibly formulated to regulate. These policies, and in particular monetary and fiscal policies, are clearly not exogenous to society and the negotiated economy. Policies are themselves the result of complex games and negotiations whose outcomes can determine the distribution of income and resources.

Policies are made and remade by people, politicians, and administrators. Politicians and administrators depend for reelection and for effective decision-making on the goodwill of voters and interest group representatives. Politicians are of course often interest group representatives. Both politicians and administrators are subject to heavy lobbying. Assar Lindbeck (1976) refers to the "endogenous politician" and the literature on regulatory organizations demonstrates that the adminstrator does not stand above the fray but is part of it. This structural situation makes highly ambiguous the state's role in money creation, credit expansion, and other processes with inflationary potentials.

The ambiguity also arises because the state plays a policy-making role with respect, e.g., to money and credit creation while it is at the same time a substantial net debtor, benefiting itself from inflationary developments. Also, policies to stabilize prices may interfere with or undermine other political or economic goals of governments, e.g., the political necessity of preventing excessive unemployment or assuring the viability of economically and politically important production sectors. *It is therefore not surprising that governments rarely apply their monetary and price stabilization policies in a consistent manner.*

The overall impact of the modern state on the social economy is substantial. Yet the state is severely constrained in its action possibilities in relation to problems such as stagflation:

1) In a democratic society, the state gains legitimacy by being ready to

respond favorably to what is presented as justified claims.

2) The state's own engagement as multiple participant in many of the negotiations and decisions — which it is supposed to regulate — compromises the exercise of its discretionary powers in fiscal, monetary, and other policies of economic management.

3) The state's established programs and institutions have acquired vested interests. They cannot simply be eliminated or cut back. Elimination or cutback is subject to negotiation and struggles within the state as well as between state agencies, political leaders, and external interest groups. The number of authorities, commissions, quasi-independent agencies, etc., has grown rapidly over the last decades. They are part private, part public and often have overlapping areas of responsibility and conflicting authority. Yet they are also channels through which vested interests can find access to the state.

4) Government debts are often so large today — in contrast to the 1930s — that the state cannot disregard them when making a choice of policy. There exist today serious risks that a failure of expansionary policies to stimulate the economy will simply further increase state debt, stimulate inflation, without however getting the economy going again. Stagflation is the result, even in Western economies which have considerable unused production capacity. It is of course difficult to judge whether this unused capacity could be utilized for the production of goods for which there exists a profitable demand. The constraints on capital, labor and management mobility in steel, shipbuilding and car production are so substantial that the likelihood of rapid conversion of this capacity is small.

5) A number of major economic forces and sources of problems lie outside the sphere of influence or effective regulation of the nation state. This is certainly true for most internationally traded commodities including oil; for the international banking system; for many transnational corporations and their development plans and strategic moves. This does not mean that some states or groups of states lack more opportunities to exercise influence and control than others. OECD countries could together solve major problems in the international banking system. OPEC could have managed the adjustment to higher oil prices in a more controlled way. It is increasingly apparent, however, that the nation-state's limited scope for action and influence in an internationally dependent domestic economy is a major source of uncertainty and therefore a key factor in the reluctance of governments and enterprises to "invest in the future".

Governments cannot be certain that their domestic pump-priming efforts will get the economy going — and eventually pay for the resultant budget and balance-of-payments deficits. The risk is very great that they will simply unleash inflationary forces. This is also in part the explanation why none of the major countries in the West (the U.S., Japan, Germany) or no group of smaller OECD countries is willing to start the pump-priming effort on a global level. Fears of being left alone in this endeavour are based on the open hostility to the pump-priming strategy among several of the OECD countries. The initiating country or group of countries risks growing balance-of-payments and budget deficits at the same time. Balance-of-payments problems may force a devaluation and unleash renewed inflationary pressures. Budget deficits often require a credit and money expansion and lead in this way to inflation.

No Western government has found an effective strategy to deal with this dilemma. It is in this sense that one may speak of an "institutional crisis".

6. Conceiving of Inflation. Possible Mismatches between What is Actually Produced and What is Measured as Produced

There are challenging problems connected with defining and measuring inflation. Currently, the rate of inflation is usually expressed through changes in a suitably defined "price index". This index is almost entirely based on statistics collected for the purposes of national income accounting. In this accounting system, important categories of goods and services, such as government production, which are not transacted through markets, are subject to arbitrary rules of definition and valuation. The values assigned may have only the most tenuous connection with the actual value of the goods and services to individuals and groups in society, or to the society as a whole.

In addition, it is commonly recognized that national income accounting measures only a limited spectrum of the outputs of economic activity. There are many and various benefits and costs relating to the social and natural environments which are not accounted for. For instance, *the accounting measures exclude all pollution-reducing results. Yet, these entail actual gains in benefits or value.* At the same time, the production of such results involves *economic costs.* Hence, the "conclusion" that investment in pollution reducing equipment is "non-productive", at least as measured by current economic statistics. It therefore contributes to cost increases, and hence generates inflationary pressures.

Denison (1981) provides evidence that in the USA net productivity declined in the period between 1965 and 1975 due to "changes in the industrial and human environments within which business must operate."

This decline can be attributed to two major factors: 78 % of it is due to increased costs of safety on the job and costs of air and water pollution control. The remaining 22 % is attributable to increased needs for surveillance of potentially dishonest employees, customers, contractors and thieves. The resources, invested in work and occupational safety and cleaner air and water, are a net gain to society, even if they tend to result in increased production costs and prices (in some instances, less business profitability).

In a certain sense one may speak of a "mismatch" or incompatibility between *measured costs*, which enter into the calculation of productivity and the determination of prices, and the *actual benefits* gained by individuals, groups as well as society as a whole. Viewed in this way, inflation is a particular — statistically structured — perception of reality. That is, inflation is in this sense *a purely statistical phenomena* which does not necessarily have any real meaning beyond what we are making of it on the basis of our wrong perception.

To put it differently, inflation may, given the present theory, statistics and accounting conventions, indicate a growing gap between measured nominal and real incomes. Yet our experience of an improving quality of life, a cleaner environment, better work environments, improved community life and social services may actually make us feel richer and more satisfied than we should be according to the published statistics. We are unfortunately living in the information age where published numbers are so powerful that they tend to shape our perception of reality more than our own life experiences.

This of course suggests that one challenging solution to the stagflation problem lies in finding systematic ways to account for and evaluate not just the traditionally measured economic costs and benefits, but also the beneficial effects of quality of life improvements even though they are not exchanged in markets and often are truly public goods.

Part II Old and New Paradigms

Contemporary economic theory and policy is incapable of dealing successfully with the current crisis of stagflation. There exists a serious, irredeemable mismatch between economic models and actual economic and socio-political developments. Such models can neither make intelligible the role of socio-political and institutional factors in contemporary inflation and stagnation, nor provide a solid basis for effective policy and strategy.

Some economists have recognized the importance of such socio-political and institutional factors. The following quotes speak for themselves:

...the long struggle over relative shares has implanted a chronic tendency to inflation in industrial countries, which no resort to monetary stringency can master.

Joan Robinson (1977)

Inflation lets this struggle proceed and blindly, impartially, and non-politically scales down all
its outcomes. There are worse methods of resolving group rivalries and social conflict.

James Tobin (1972)

I have always assumed the money supply to be sociologically determined.

Richard Cooper (quoted in Hirsch and Goldthorpe, 1978)

Inflation is the only politically feasible way that democratic governments have found for allocating increased real costs, or what is equivalent, for reducing people's standard of living, or at
least retarding improvements in them. Its silent, impersonal, unconscious workings allows
people to disavow responsibility for the result, while continuing to pursue their own personal
well-being.

R. Fuller (1980)

A pessimist or a cynic may even be tempted to say that the most severe difficulties of economic
policy are imbedded in the political rather than the economic system and that the main
obstacle for a successful stabilization policy is ... the government itself.

Assar Lindbeck (1976)

Yet no major economist has tried to initiate a radical restructuring of the
conceptual and analytical apparatus of economic theory. They remain
largely content to retouch the margins, whereas it is the core that needs
rethinking. At most they engage in policy analysis which remains completely separated from the analytical core of economic theory.

In Section 1 we suggest why contemporary economic theory and policy
is incapable of dealing with the current crisis. In Section 2 we go on to
indicate several of the questions which a new theoretical framework or
paradigm should address.

1.   The Failure of Contemporary Economic Theory and Policy

The capitalist economies up to the 1930s were shaken by recurrent depressions. The greatest crisis of them all, the world depression of the 1930s, led
to the introduction of "New Deal" programs in various Western countries
in order to alleviate or counteract tendencies towards overproduction and
stagnation, unemployment, falling investment, and bankruptcies.

The Keynesian theoretical framework provided a model and guidelines
for social policy, which to a greater or lesser extent "worked", more effectively in some countries than others.

It should be stressed from the outset that the Keynesian framework took certain societal conditions for granted. It assumed that the institutions essential for formulating and carrying out fiscal and monetary policies were or could be established, and that there existed a definite potential for shaping "legitimate" demands and for meeting them through the utilization of unused capacity. But in the absence of, for instance, appropriate fiscal and monetary institutions under the control of a general political agent there can be no Keynesian program. This was and still is the case in Switzerland, for example. Its central bank is private and lacked until recently all the rights necessary to operate a monetary policy except through interventions on foreign exchange markets. Central and local governments can increase spending and change taxes only through the most difficult and uncertain political processes. In the case of Latin American countries, external forces shock and destabilize their economies at the same time that the governments lack the institutional means, which the Keynesian strategy takes for granted, to buffer and stabilize the economies. The smaller European countries also seem to have encountered considerable difficulties during the 1970s in dealing effectively with oil price shocks and large, speculative international money flows.

The economy and society which the Keynesians took as a point of departure has undergone substantial changes in the last fifty years. The image of society underlying the Keynesian framework had very little ressemblance to the real world, especially the one of the 1930s. Keynesianism assumes a society free from conflict. In unemployment equilibrium everybody loses: workers suffer unemployment and capitalists have to write down inventories.[7] Everyone should expect to gain from the stimulation of demand and from growth.[8] Distributional aspects, above all the distribution of wealth, are not important from such a perspective and do not have to be dealt with. The state is seen as a neutral regulator, serving the general public interest.

The economy-and-society at the times Keynes formulated his theory has undergone substantial changes. Some of these changes could have been anticipated already in the 1920s and 1930s, since they entailed simply a further development of existing or emerging tendencies: increased economic concentration, administered pricing, increased labor unionization, restructuring of financial institutions, development of new forms of credit and money, and continued internationalization of domestic economies.[9] In addition, some changes have been brought about by the interventionist state, in its very engagement in and regulation of the economy, along the lines of thought initiated by Keynes and others. Systems of policy and regulation were established or activated which enabled the parallel expansion of demand, credit and money and, ultimately, growth in production and employment. This system, along with tendencies in capitalist development mentioned above, have made the fall in prices (and wages) increasingly difficult and price (and wage) increases more usual. As Heilbroner (1979) pointed out:

'It is no longer taken for granted that what goes up must come down; on the contrary, what goes up will probably continue to go up indefinitely. With such attitudes, corporations do not feel a need to furl sails rapidly the instant a recession blows up, nor do households feel a need to practice thrift, even if their incomes fall. Unions are emboldened to ask for aggressive wage settlements because they know their members have the backstop of unemployment compensation behind them. The unemployed do not feel the necessity of taking any kind of work, because the welfare system permits individuals to refuse work they do not like. And so, in one way and another, with results some people celebrate and some people deplore, government has made everyone more secure, and this generalized state of security helps breed attitudes and behavior that push up demand and jack up costs.

The old tendencies towards depression became therefore replaced by tendencies towards inflation, the development of "inflationary societies."

Given this development, discussed more fully in Part I, the socio-economic world in which Keynesian policies and programs are carried out is very different from the pre-World War II world, or even the world of the 1950s and 1960s. The Keynesian strategy made the non-economic, indeed the political value of "full employment" into a major goal. This was probably unintended but unavoidable given the period of the Great Depression in which Keynesianism was born.

The Keynesian revolution implies politicalization of the economy. After all, Keynesianism proposed a political solution to the economic crisis of the 1930s: the emphasis on state intervention, and the inevitable mixing of political and economic institutions and processes in order to expand demand and to stabilize the economy at near or full employment.

Yet, the language, concepts, principles and analytical tools of Keynesianism remain grounded in economics. It — together with neo-classical micro-economics, which Keynesianism simply adopted — does not provide a fully suitable language and analytical framework for the study and analysis of political actors and processes, and their interaction with "economic sytems". Hence the irony of history: Keynesianism contributed to making a political economy for which it became increasingly unsuitable. Therefore, it also became more and more inadequate as a solid basis for policy.[10]

The failure of Keynesianism to deal with contemporary problems of resource scarcity, declining industries, de-industrialization, stagnation and inflation has allowed or facilitated the (re)emergence of monetarism and supply-side economics for example, and of their political expressions in Thatcherism and Reagonomics. They are sold as new approaches, or as old ones in new form, with which to tackle the complexity of current problems. They all advocate a radical reduction in government intervention and participation in the economy.

These approaches will not succeed because they are even further away than Keynesianism from a relevant or adequate model — and a solid basis for effective policies — of contemporary welfare capitalism. They offer a profound lack of historical perspective, in that they have failed to demonstrate that a return to a pre-Keynesian separation of politics from the economy will not result in the cycle of ever worsening depressions which, after all, was the reason for inventing Keynesianism in the first place.

The approaches fail, above all, to recognize and to provide models with which to analyze inflation as the consequence of institutionalized struggles over the distribution of income which are settled through granting of higher nominal claims (prices, wages, profits, entitlements, government budgets) of major groups and social agents in society. Indeed, we argue later that such struggles tend to be intensified over the long run by the measures proposed by Thatcherism and Reagonomics because they result in economic stagnation if not deep recession, generating more "zero-sum" like situations.

2. The Challenge to a New Paradigm

A new paradigm is needed which will provide an adequate model of contemporary economy-and-society, above all of the relationship between economic and political processes. This entails a number of capabilities.

1) The paradigm should be capable of specifying and analyzing the causes of imbalances between income claims and available resources as well as the effects and dynamics of such imbalances. The concepts of supply, demand and competitive market equilibrium have never been adequate for this purpose, certainly not in the case of a mixed economy where so much production and distribution is administered instead of organized through markets.

This calls for determining in what ways claims come to exceed or to grow faster than available resources. Claims are certainly shaped as much through "sociological" and "political" processes as through the economic ones of production and exchange. Issues of fairness, distributive justice and income relativities play a major role in the claims groups make and in their opposition to the claims of others. The capability to make claims — and to oppose the claims of others — ultimately relates to the acquisition and exercise of power (administrative, market, and other forms of social power). Such questions as these have been much more central to political science and sociology than to economics.

2) A new paradigm should enable specification and analysis of the various ways claims are "negotiated" and decided in different institutional settings such as markets, wage bargaining situations, administrative milieus, and political and legislative settings. It is important here to identify the participating actors and groups, the "rules of the game" in force, and the linkages among the settings.

A central question concerns the ability of the state or other socio-political agents to regulate or limit income claims or to bring about consensus among groups and segments of society on suitable levels of claims. This is a particularly difficult question because the state itself and its various segments are directly involved in making claims on scarce resources.

3) The framework should make intelligible why claims agreed to in the various social decision settings tend to result in increased wages, prices, taxes and budgets. It should specify how these increases are accommodated concretely, in part through debt expansion, and how they are ultimately translated into inflation.

4) A new paradigm has to provide an adequate model of economy-and-society in its global resource and international contexts. It should shed light on related questions, such as:

• To what extent is scarcity of basic resources, with energy scarcity an obvious but not exclusive example, related to inflation? Through which institutional frames and social processes is such scarcity translated into inflationary pressures. It would seem that some actors with control over scarce strategic resources, such as oil, have been able to use this control to increase their income claims (price) and to change to some extent the global distribution of income.

• On the other hand, inflationary pressures do not appear to be simply the result of the oil and commodity price shocks as well as instability in the international monetary system of the 1970s. Inflationary pressures predate the turbulent 1970s. After all, Sweden imposed a prize freeze in 1970 and, even more noteworthy, the U.S. did so in 1971 under a conservative Republican president (Nixon).

• To what extent are ongoing socio-cultural and political changes in Western countries related to inflationary pressures: value shifts, the increased importance of non-economic values, environmental protection, quality of life, work environment and occupational health measures, and so forth? And if so, in what concrete ways do these shifts and reforms concretely influence price determination processes?

- To what extent have inflationary pressures, and struggle over income distribution, been intensified, and become more difficult to deal with, as a result of social learning and the development of interest group rationality. Individuals, groups, and organizations articulate systematically their income claims. They exhibit less "self-sacrifice" for the benefit of others or for the common good. Greed has become institutionalized. The readiness to sacrifice for the common good has lost social force and legitimacy.

- Is there a growing tendency to use income for private and public consumption, allocating less for investment purposes? To what extent, and in what ways, does any such tendency reflect socio-cultural and political changes in contemporary societies?

- Is there a growing tendency for investments to go either abroad or into speculative and non-productive ventures (real estate, gold and silver, art, prestige projects) which do not contribute to eventual real economic growth?

If there is such a tendency, to what extent and in what ways does it reflect the institutionalization of non-economic values and changes in social structure making investments less profitable or more risky and providing alternative channels of investment? Or is it simply a reaction to inflation experience?

Answering such questions requires a transdisciplinary paradigm. We are convinced that the new paradigm will not emerge from within economics, sociology, or political science, but only from the nexus between the various disciplines.

NOTES

1. The research reported in this chapter has been supported by the Social Science Research Council (HSFR) in Sweden.
2. Typically, because of the professional barriers among social science disciplines, the materials are isolated from one another. Sociological and political science research dealing with income expectations, questions of distributive justice, changing attitudes about work and occupational safety, and the declining legitimacy of political decisions may not be known or readily available to economists; similarly, the latters' research results, which often has a bearing on socio-political and socio-cultural developments, may be scarcely known to or utilized by sociologists and political scientists.
3. 'Non-monetary claims' in a monetized economy typically have a monetary side, since labor and other resources will have to be used to satisfy the claim. Even a 'free and cheap public service' requires real resources for its production and distribution, implying a charge on the budget of the public sector.

4. An important element, as suggested in Chapter 3, is the grounding of such contracts in concepts and principles of *distributive justice.* At present, however, there are no obvious institutional frames and strategies for coordinating the vast number of negotiations and decisions in modern society which relate to income distribution.

5. The US could do this because the US dollar, in contrast to the currencies of most other countries is used as an (the) international reserve currency. Most other countries must concern themselves with the impact on exchange rates and balance of payments of excessive increases in domestic money supply.

6. Keynes argued that the traditional Walrasian concept of equilibrium where supply has to be equal to demand (which implies, of course, full employment on the labor market) is not valid and relevant in a monetary economy. Not only are there institutional wage and price rigidities, but above all financial speculation on the assets and money markets causing deep instability. They allow the economy to come into an 'equilibrium' where both involuntary unemployment and excess supply on commodity markets may obtain, a possibility that was denied by previous economists. Since Keynes believed that social control and policy objectives were difficult to achieve on the cost side, he put all the emphasis on policies and strategies relating to aggregate demand management. Thus, the state's role was determined: government spending — and policies to stimulate private spending — would be the key control variables to affect the entire macro-economic environment.

7. This is true in large part for the case of short-run unemployment equilibrium. In the longer run insufficient productive capacities due to profit requirements of corporations tend to generate unemployment equilibria where 'only' workers loose, as appears to be increasingly the case now.

8. In this sense, the Keynes unemployment equilibrium is essentially a collective action problem. The solution calls for a central authority which transcends the myopic interests of each group or class.

9. The systemic conditions structured by the state through its policies allowed corporations and households as well as the state itself to accumulate debt on an unprecedented scale. In the USA for example, corporate debt between 1955 and 1975 appears to have increased from eight times of after-tax profits to more than fifteen times. Household debt increased from 65% of disposable income to 93% over the same period.

10. In general, the failings of Keynesianism (as distinct from Keynes own thinking!) is the result of:

    1) neglect of increased interdependence between national economies both in terms of trade in goods and services and capital flows.

    2) neglect of the impact of capital accumulation on the structure of the world economy (related to point 1)).

    3) insufficient analysis of the monetary and financial processes in relation to capital accumulation and its impact on socio-economic stability.

    4) a relatively superficial tratment of the state as totally coherent, relatively autonomous and quite 'enlightened', a sort of benevolent dictator.

REFERENCES

Denison, E.F., (1981) *Effects of Selected Changes in the Institution and Human Environment upon Output per Unit of Input.* Washington, D.C. Brookings General Series Reprint Nr. 335.

Fuller, R., (1980) *Inflation: The Rising Cost of Living on a Small Planet.* Washington, D.C., Worldwatch Paper Nr. 34.

Heilbroner, R., (1979) Inflation. *The New Yorker*, October 8.

Hirsch, F. and J.H. Goldthorpe (eds.) (1978) *The Political Economy of Inflation*. London: Martin Robertson.

Johansen, L., (1979) The bargaining society and the inefficiency of bargaining. *Kyklos*: **32**, 497-522.

Lindbeck, A., (1976) Stabilization policies in open economies with endogenous politician. *American Economic Review*: **66** (Proceedings): 1-19.

Robinson, Joan, (1977) What are the questions? *Journal of Economic Literature*: **15**, 1318-1339.

Scharpf, F., (1981) *The Political Economy of Inflation and Unemployment in Western Europe: An Outline*. Berlin; Wissenschaftszentrum. Discussion Paper IIM/LMP 81-82.

Tobin, J., (1972) Inflation and unemployment. *American Economic Review*: **62**, 1-18.

3

Inflation, Politics and Social Change[1]: Actor-Oriented Systems Analysis

Thomas Baumgartner   Tom R. Burns
Philippe DeVille

Inflation at a very high rate, or even at a moderate rate for a long period of time, is closely linked to socio-political crisis. This is most obvious in Third World countries. But it is also increasingly apparent in the case of industrialized countries, particularly when inflation can only be regulated at the substantial cost of high unemployment and the under-utilization of production capacity. Economic advisors and political leaders seem powerless to deal with such a situation. In any case, they have failed thus far to come up with a coherent counter-inflationary strategy which is effective as well as politically sustainable over the long-run.

Our point of departure in approaching the inflation problematic is the thesis that inflation is one of several possible outcomes of institutionalized societal struggles over the distribution of income. The state, unable to resolve these conflicts through other means, accommodates them — with the intentional or unintentional cooperation of the banking system — through an expansion of credit and of the money supply at a rate in excess of what is necessary to finance the actual increase in the production of marketable resources.

The distributional conflicts manifest themselves in a finite set of social decision settings or "games". In Section 1 we introduce the concepts of game, actors, rules of the game, and indicate their role in our conceptualization and analysis of inflationary processes. A second section presents the main elements of our approach to inflation conceived as one among several outcomes from the system of relevant games, that is those relating directly or indirectly to inflationary pressures and developments. We define a minimal set of games or social decision settings for the modelling and analysis of contemporary inflation in industrialized countries.

Section 3 suggests how specific game configurations combine to produce

51

several of the vicious circles underlying inflationary developments. In Section 4 we present 11 theses on inflation based on the preliminary results of our research. Section 5 returns to the theme introduced in Chapter 2, "the shaping of inflationary societies", and leads into our concluding Section 6, where we take up several of the normative and practical implications of the framework presented in this chapter.

1.   Inflation as the Result of a Complex Social Game

Inflation can be conceptualized and analyzed as one of the outcomes from a system of interrelated games. The concept of a game refers simply to interaction settings entailing social decision-making processes and outcomes. The inflationary game system has "collective action properties", as suggested by Keynes:

> An individual cannot by saving more protect himself from the consequences of inflation if others do not follow his example; just as he cannot protect himself from accidents by obeying the rule of the road if others disregard it. What is to the advantage of each of us regarded as a solitary individual is to the disadvantage of us regarded as members of a community. We have here the perfect opportunity for social action, where everyone can be protected by making a certain rule of behavior universal law.

The collective action aspects of inflationary situations can be formulated as follows.[2] The game set-up is characterized by conflicts of interest about the distribution of resources among multiple actors (labor, management, consumers, and government). For each actor, the eventual outcome does not depend entirely on their own choices, but on those of others over whom they have limited or no control. The collective action (or "prisoners' dilemma") property refers to a social setting where the best individual strategy (buy-in-advance, borrow, make excessive wage demands, increase prices as much as possible) is collectively the worst one. Individual sacrifice — for instance, by not making as large a wage demand, restraining price increases, limiting budget requests, etc. — will *not* reduce the rate of inflation, unless all others do the same. But no actor or group of actors can afford to withhold their claims without running the risk of loosing in real income or purchasing power over time. Yet, as each actor or coalition of actors tries this, the result is continued if not increased inflation, with many, although not all left worse off.

Of course, the situation is much more complicated than this general orientation suggests. Different social games relating to price and wage determination as well as public budget determination occurs in concrete institutional and organizational settings. In these settings multiple social agents are involved in negotiating and making decisions about wages, prices, entitlements, and budgets. Moreover, price, wage, entitlement, and budget determinations are affected by a complex matrix of pricing rules, indexation clauses, management-labor negotiation frameworks, market and adminstrative power factors. This matrix also shapes the opportunities and limitations for actors to translate income demands and cost increases into relative income adjustments (prices, wages, entitlements and budgets) and new contractual obligations (such as indexation of wages or of pensions and welfare payments).

The dynamics of inflationary processes in any historically given society is related to the changing societal conditions under which distributional games are played: changing power relations among actors, changes in their perceptions about the nature of the games or their possible outcomes, changes in the national or international environments and in the constraints (norms, rules, values) within which games are played out.

Analysis of inflation and related economic problems requires a clear identification (1) of the socio-economic processes that manifest themselves in an inflationary situation and (2) of the social actors and their strategies in the games and related processes which generate inflationary pressures. Particular stress is placed on the linkages that exist both *among actors* and *among games*, e.g. linking games in the private sector with public sector games. Such linkages provide an understanding of the "*vicious circles*" which we use to explain the existence of sustained or accelerating inflationary processes; or, on the contrary, "dampening processes" that lead to deflationary situations.

The dynamics of inflation can be viewed, therefore, as a temporal succession of *different phases*. Each phase has its own specific characteristics in terms of game structure and linkages, relationships among actors, and the stabilizing or destabilizing nature of the various outputs of the games.

Our approach to inflation makes use of traditional inflation theories but goes beyond them in readily incorporating into *social system models* political and sociological variables and relations along with economic factors. The traditional theories are often monist in the sense that they single out a particular unique causal factor — wage-push, demand-pull, money-supply — in explaining inflation. They proceed then to either ignore or at best leave implicit the social transactions and political processes that lead from the causal factor(s) (input) to the inflationary outcome (output). Such a black box approach suggests why policy failures cannot be readily explained by traditional theories which have abstracted from concrete social processes as well as break-points or substantial changes in these.

2. The Research Approach: Actor-Oriented Systems Dynamics

Our approach to the investigation and analysis of inflation in modern societies is based on actor-oriented systems theory (AOS) The theory deals explicitly with three levels of a social system:

1) The *system* consisting of societal structures and processes, i.e. the framework *within* which actors in different institutional, cultural and material settings operate.

2) *Social decision-making and transaction settings* — or societal games for short — involving multiple actors and groups of actors. These games are the institutionally and culturally defined *settings* of society in which actors struggle, negotiate, and decide on prices, performances, and claims to societal resources and wealth.

3) *Actors* (organizations, groups, individuals) as agents playing societal games and struggling with unequal resources and opportunities to realize their interests and goals. Actors act within certain systems constraints: material conditions, resource and knowledge limitations, institutional and organizational frameworks, rules of the game, limited opportunities and capabilities for learning and innovation. But at the same time, actors have some — unequally distributed — opportunities to maintain or change systems constraints.

The AOS approach to inflation entails investigating two types of social action:

1) Negotiations about and determination of prices, wages and budgets and the resultant income distributions within different institutionalized game situations.

2) The decision-making and activities oriented toward maintaining or changing institutionalized game situations, and, ultimately, the system itself. In addition, the analysis of societal action takes into account the actors' definitions of their situations, their problem-solving models and strategies. These depend on their knowledge, beliefs, norms and values oriented to the concrete game situations in which they act.

In the perspective of AOS-theory, learning and restructuring are characteristic features of society.[3] The 'game about games', i.e. politics, and the emergence of new concepts and models through the concrete struggle over the distribution of income and resource control imply that a social systems framework for dealing with societal conflicts over income distribution and systems development is not stable, but is subject to change. Hence, inflation is more than a 'price spiral'. It entails actors learning, redefining problems, changing expectations, and developing new strategies. This implies the emergence of new actors or coalitions of actors, and the restructuring of games and of societal frameworks within which the games are 'played'.

2.1. Inflation: The Perspective of Actors, Games and Systems

In approaching the study of inflation on the three system levels described above, AOS-theory stresses that:

1) Inflation can be usefully analyzed as consisting of self-amplifying 'vicious circles', generated by actors competing and conflicting with one another over the distribution of limited resources in society. Inflation as well as other socio-economic performances and developments, as system-level properties, are modeled in AOS-theory as resulting in large part from the outcomes and developments from a set of interlinked societal decision settings or games.

2) The different societal games are played in concrete settings with their particular histories, institutionalized values and social arrangements, established actors, rules of the game, and resource distribution patterns: for example, capital-labor negotiations over wages and salaries in different sectors, or the struggles between state agencies and their demands for increased public expenditures and transfer payments, on the one hand and, on the other, private interests pressing for the maintenance of, or increase in, levels of private consumption.[4] The context dependence of the games and their interlinkages over time give inflationary processes *their particular character in each society.*

3) Actors engaged in these games learn and sometimes try to restructure the rules of the game and the institutional framework, thereby changing the context for economic action. Also, actors may organize and reorganize in these struggles, leading to new structures and structural conflicts. These conflicts are manifested in legislative, administrative and judicial initiatives and struggles.

2.2. Inflation: Imbalances between Resources and Claims on Resources

Inflation is the result of persistent imbalances between the set of monetized claims on resources made by institutionalized actors and the resources available for distribution. The claims on production as well as productive activities are shaped through a complex of institutional, organizational, and socio-political arrangements. An explicit 'societal choice', e.g. by the state, among the competing claims for the resources cannot or will not be made.

The state is at the same time unwilling to tolerate open conflict where its claims to legitimacy might be called into question and where socio-political and economic instability is made more likely. Conflict regulation is achieved through negotiations which result in settlements that increase prices, wages and government budgets.[5] These increases are ultimately validated through an expansion of the credit and money supply.

Key societal processes in inflationary imbalances are (1) the creation of products and resources, (2) the shaping of expectations and demands among actors, and (3) the creation of credit and money, and of the claims to products and resources implied by them. The decisions and developments around these processes occur in different social spheres. These are linked but poorly coordinated, thus providing some of the conditions for imbalance.

Imbalances, as a result of the set of claims growing faster than the growth of available resources or of production, can occur in a variety of ways, among others:

1) the erosion of social controls, growing societal fragmentation, and escalating conflict may result in self-interested maximizing behaviour and increasingly excessive claims by different groups and classes in society.

2) the constraints on increased societal production may intensify: constraints on the factors of production, particularly due to raw material and energy shortages, non-substitutability, unwillingness on the part of those having financial resources to invest them in 'productive capital', introduction of social controls and regulations which have reoriented investments into 'non-productive improvements', such as pollution control, improved work environment, etc.

Imbalances between available resources and claims on resources are not merely the outcome of poor coordination; they also reflect special interests and the exercise of power which, intentionally and unintentionally, maintain imbalances.

2.3. *Modelling a Socio-Political Economy*

In the perspective of AOS-theory, inflation is a societal phenomenon. It can only be effectively described and analyzed through a social systems analysis.[6] Such an analysis has to be based on a model of the socio-political economy of the case to be studied. This perspective has not only implications for the modelling and analysis of a socio-political economy but also for policy-making and strategic action. Regulation of any sphere of social life requires a model of that sphere. Failure to adequately represent the

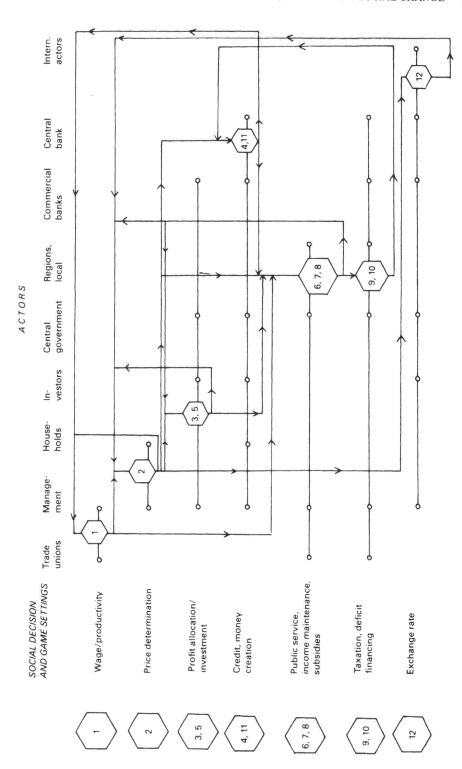

FIGURE 3.1   Societal game interaction matrix.

strategic factors and processes in and around that sphere results in serious policy and regulatory failures.

Models can be built with different levels of resolution and they can focus on one or more spheres or subsystems of a socio-political economy. Our most general model consists of four subsystems:

1) The enterprise production and market subsystem (settings 1, 2, 3 and 5 in Table 3.1.)

2) The banking subsystem (settings 4, 11 and 12)

3) The public administration and regulatory subsystem (settings 6, 7, 8, 9 and 10)

4) The socio-political and socio-cultural subsystem (settings 13 and 14).

These subsystems are mutually linked with each other (Baumgartner, 1978). Each subsystem consists of a set of social decision situations or settings. These involve multiple actors (at least two) with mutual inter-dependencies (Johansen, 1979). These settings vary considerably in their properties as to social organization and rules governing actors' behaviors. Markets, bargaining situations, planning situations, political choice situations and settings for value formation are basic examples.

The process of building up a model of the socio-political economy of a country on the basis of social decision-settings and their interrelationships involves four steps:

1) Identify specific social *decision- or game-settings* through which institutional actors make claims to resources and purchasing power in a money economy.

2) Identify *actors* who participate in the various social decisions.

3) Identify *linkages* between and among games on the basis of theoretical and empirical information. Linkages can be of different forms: real flows (goods and services), money flows, liability and asset flows, information flows, and so forth.

4) Identify and analyze feedback *loops*, in particular loops relating to wage, price, and government budget developments. (Section 3 deals at length with this aspect.)

The description of decision-settings and of the actors involved in them (steps 1 and 2) includes a number of elements. The most important are:

- the main actors involved;
- the actors' domains of possible action and of resources available;
- the organization of the actors and their relation to one another;

• the rules and institutions which regulate and coordinate the actors in relation to one another. It is important here to identify the rules and institutional arrangements which are specific to each country;

• the problem situation(s) in which actors find themselves, their interests and the relationships among their interests, the models they use to interpret the problem situation(s) and to arrive at analyses and strategies for action;

• the actions considered by the actors and the constraining factors associated with each of them. It is important here to identify the action possibilities which actors exclude from detailed consideration or which they feel unable to consider in the first place;

• the actors' assessment of alternatives and their outcomes, and the eventual decisions taken, or not taken, and how these feed into the flows of the system.

Table 3.1. lists 14 decision-settings which we have used so far in our analysis of inflation processes. Of course, decision-settings may be specified in less detail, or they may be differentiated much further. Country characteristics and the needs of the analysis determine the degree of differentiation. A comparison of the settings listed in Table 3.1. with those used in Figure 3.1. and in the models of 'vicious circles' presented and discussed in Section 3 provides examples for both of these procedures. For example, one may find it necessary to distinguish within setting 1 (wages and productivity) between a decision process with respect to wage determination and one with respect to productivity determination — these may be coupled to varying degrees. Likewise, setting 7 (income maintenance) may be differentiated into processes (and specific settings) deciding unemployment compensation, health insurance and old age pensions.

Another type of distinction, between different economic sectors and branches, is employed later in Section 3 in relation to setting 1 (wages and productivity) and setting 2 (prices and consumption). For example, we differentiate between farm and non-farm sectors, and between export-oriented and import-competing sectors, and the protected production sectors. Obviously the analysis of inflation in Third World countries would in most instances require a different type of differentiation reflecting those activities which are in the money economy and those which are outside of it, or those which are based on older technologies and modes of operation (see Chapter 5 in this volume).[7]

TABLE 3.1

Social decision settings and their actors

---

1   *Wages and Productivity*

Wages, labor effort and output are determined here. Trade unions and employers/ managers are the principal actors. Government, as a major employer, is also involved. In addition the government may participate as a third party, mediating the negotiations as well as setting income guidelines.

2   *Prices and Consumption Patterns*

Product prices and consumption patterns are determined here. Pricing rules range from 'administered prices' to 'market determined prices'. Management and consumers are the major actors. Their respective influence over prices varies with their relative power in different markets. The government may also participate as buyer, and as controller of prices.

Consumers, including consumers of producer goods, make decisions about the 'packages of goods and services' they intend to buy. The allocation of income between spending and saving (or borrowing) is also decided here.

3   *Earnings Distribution*

Decisions concerning the distribution of earnings between retained profits, dividends, etc. are made here. Participants are managers, owners, investors and the state. Tax policies may affect the distribution decisions.

4   *Credit Creation and Distribution*

Banks and investors on one side, and households and enterprises and governments on the other decide here about the volume of credit created and the credit distribution. The central government and the central bank are involved through their monetary and credit policies.

5   *Investment*

Enterprise decisions about investments involve managers together with investors, banks and, in some cases, the government. The latter intervenes with tax and subsidy policies.

6   *Public Services and Investments*

Decisions concerning the public infrastructure (roads, airports, schools, hospitals) and public services (education, health care, transportation, police, information) are made here. The government and its agencies are involved in the decision-making together with trade unions, managers, and public interest groups as well as local governments.

7   *Income Maintenance*

Transfer payments concerning unemployment, sickness and old age are made here. Major actors involved are the government, trade unions, managers and households.

8   *Government Subsidies*

Government aid to enterprises for investment and employment purposes, and subsidies for sectoral and regional development are decided here. Actors are the government, trade unions, managers, investors as well as regional and other growth-oriented interests.

9   *Taxation*

Here decisions are made about raising revenues through direct (enterprise profit, household income, wealth) and indirect (sales and value-added) taxes. Tariffs are also decided here. The government, trade unions, management and various interest groups are participating in this setting.

10   *Budget Deficit Resolution*

Decisions about covering the deficit through borrowing or the creation of new money are made here by the government together with the central bank, commercial banks and other investors, and public pressure groups.

TABLE 3.1 continued

---

11   *Money Creation*
      Central actors here are the central bank and the commercial banks together with the government. Decisions are closely intertwined with those from setting 4 (Credit creation and distribution). Managers, home buyers and creditors, etc. may directly or indirectly intervene here.
12   *Exchange Rate Determination*
      The government and the central bank have the final say here. But enterprises (especially those involved in exports and imports), the commercial banks and trade unions are also involved. Of course, foreign actors of various types are intimately participating in the decisions about exchange rates.
13   *Political Decisions*
      Here the leading ideas, guidelines and pressures are generated which enter as inputs into public administration. Decisions here affect government behavior. The participating actors may be any of those mentioned so far as well as many ad hoc or organized groups such as political parties, social movements, the military and the police. Participation depends on the configuration of, and social relations among groups and interests in the society. Foreign actors often participate here.
14   *Social Value and Interest Formation*
      These are central decision processes providing inputs into all the decision settings from 1 to 13. The processes here are closely intertwined with the political decisions because they have to do with learning and socialization. They occur in family, school, work and political settings.

Figure 3.1. presents one way of combining information about the actors participating in particular decision-settings and the linkages among these settings. *Decision-settings, actors and linkages are likely to be country-specific.* For example, the central bank in the case of England would have to be considered, to some extent, a part of the actor 'government'. In the case of Switzerland the central bank should be conceived as an independent actor, while it could be merged with the actor 'banks' in the case of Belgium.

The framework suggested above for modelling a socio-political economy seems to imply a rather isolated social system. However, the international context can be introduced readily in the form of additional games (e.g. about international trading), new actors (International Monetary Fund, multinational corporations, and foreign governments); or, as we do in Section 3 and as we have suggested here, through differentiating within the settings defined in Table 3.1.

3.   Vicious Circles and Inflation

Decision settings are interlinked. The outcomes and developments from some settings feed directly into others. Also, some of the outcomes and developments from the latter may feedback directly or indirectly to the former. Some of the feedback loops are the self-amplifying ones, vicious circles, which underlie the persistent increases in price-levels, i.e. inflation.[8]

Below, we present several of the self-amplifying loops[9] which our research has identified as underlying inflationary developments in some countries. Several are rather well known, whereas in other cases, as a result of using our approach, we have identified and analyzed new loops.

In Figure 3.1., we show the input and output linkages among several of the social decision-settings defined in Table 3.1. The output of a setting is a function of inputs into it and of its state, including the states of the actors participating in it.

The Wage-Price Spiral

The vicious circle involving games 1 (wages) and 2 (prices) may be initiated by exogenous factors, e.g. an oil price shock, and/or endogenous factors such as a devaluation, a value and norm shift, or a new phase of struggle among social groups over the distribution of income. The vicious circle would be dampened if, for instance, wage payment increases were only partly translated into higher prices. This link depends on pricing rules (e.g.

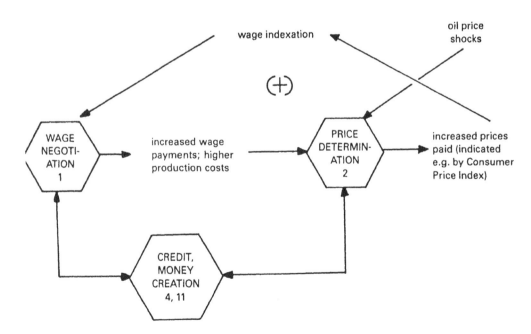

FIGURE 3.2   The wage-price spiral.

mark-up rules), market structure, and productivity developments.[10] Similarly, increases in the price level may only partly feed back into wage increases (see Figure 3.2).

However, this wage-price linkage is only part of the vicious circle. Increased payments for wages and for goods and services require increased purchasing power. An enabling flow of increasing credit and money (games 4, 11) to both games 1 (wages) and 2 (prices) complements the vicious circle. A weakening of this enabling flow will contribute to dampen the vicious circle under conditions where actors' expectations about wage and price developments are affected by such a development.

The Devaluation-Price Spiral

This vicious circle entails an elaboration of the previous one. It represents a particularly powerful mechanism for inflationary developments in societies with considerable import/export linkages. The latter condition is of course typical for many Third World countries. Games 2A and 2B represent the disaggregated price-setting game where sectors A and B represent domestic (protected) and export sectors respectively, (see Figure 3.3).

In Iceland, for example, devaluation serves to maintain the profitability of the fish export sector which is squeezed between rising domestic costs and fixed international prices. Yet, devaluation sets off import price increases which contribute directly to consumer and production cost increases and which affect indirectly consumer prices through the generation of domestic cost-push pressures. The monetary enabling flow is linked to the financing needs of the fish sector, which are of course increasing as domestic costs and export prices (in domestic currency) go up as a consequence of devaluation.

The Government Demand-Pull Circle

This system incorporates the loop described in Section 3.1. But it involves in addition the government's expanding public services and investments (game 6), which, through demand-pull, can lead back to increased costs for the government and thus to an inflationary spiral. The government must obtain increased purchasing power to finance this expansion. If funds cannot be raised through taxation, e.g. because of the political costs involved, then the increased purchasing power is likely to be created through monetary expansion, (see Figure 3.4).

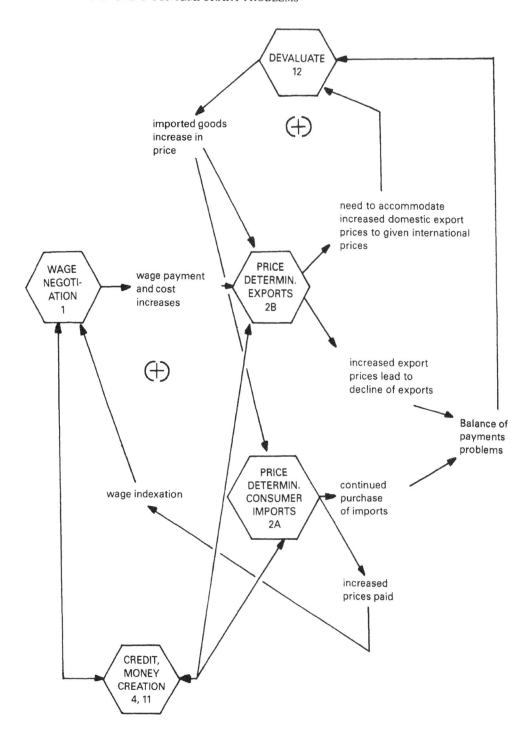

FIGURE 3.3   The devaluation-price spiral.

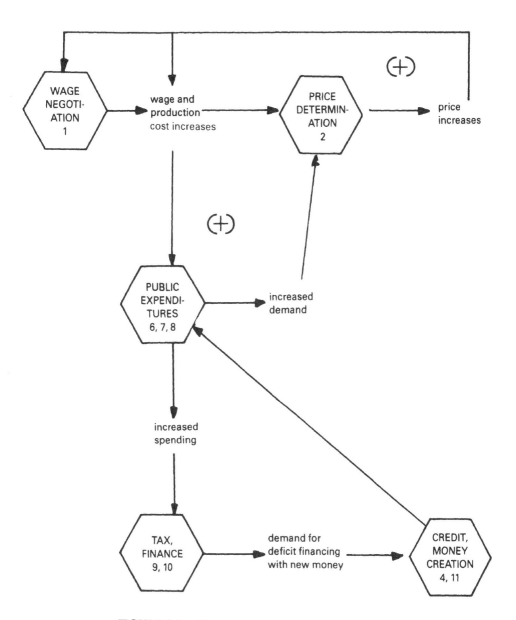

FIGURE 3.4   The government demand-pull price loop.

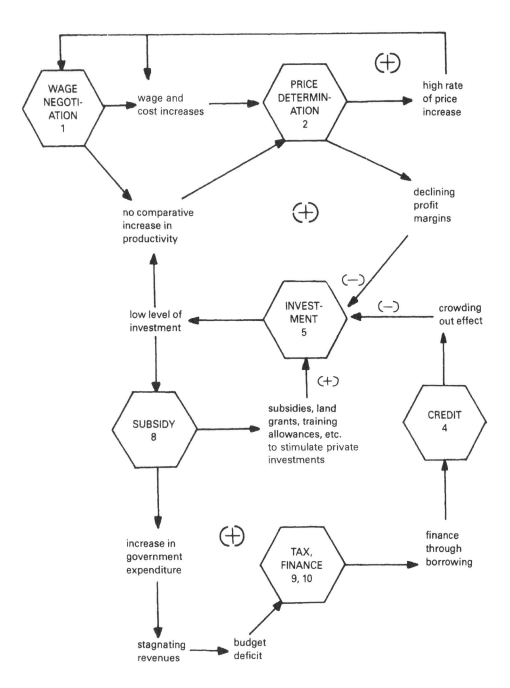

FIGURE 3.5   Stagflation-government expenditure loop.

The Stagflation-Government Expenditure Loop

In the model of Figure 3.5 economic stagflation leads the government to try to increase private investment by providing incentives as inputs to decision-settings 4 (credit) and 5 (investments). This increase in government expenditures under conditions of economic stagflation often leads to a budget deficit (game 10), which is then financed through increased borrowing on capital markets (decision-setting 4). The increased government competition in the credit distribution game 'crowds out' private investment, thereby closing the loop. Alternatively, the budget deficit may be financed through the creation of new purchasing power (game 4/11), thus avoiding the 'crowding out effect'. However, this contributes to increased demand and price and wage pressures, which in turn may affect profits and profit distribution negatively, depressing private investments.

The Farm Price-Industrial Price Interaction

Figure 3.6 represents an inflationary mechanism which is common to the European Economic Community (EEC), but elements of which are also found in the Scandinavian countries and Switzerland. Farm prices are negotiated between the political leadership and representatives of the farmers. A characteristic feature of these negotiations is the close linkage of farmers' incomes to those of workers in the manufacturing sector.

In particular, decision-making about food prices is tied to wage negotiations and to the pricing of manufactured goods.

Rising fuel costs act as an exogenous driving impulse to the mechanism. In the diagram, A and B represent non-farm and farm sectors respectively. 1A and 1B represent the settings where income demands are presented and negotiated. The outputs of 1A feed into the price determination decisions, as represented earlier. In the case of the farm sector, B, there is a close coupling and direct feedback loop between negotiations about farm prices (2B) and negotiations about the income of farmers (1B).

The process described above may be dampened through the state subsidizing farmers in order to hold down price increases (see Figure 3.7). However, the subsidies themselves may contribute to inflationary developments. This occurs whenever the state must resort to inflationary financing to cover the expenditures, as is especially likely to happen under conditions of stable or declining government revenues (a stagnant or 'zero-sum' economy). On the other hand, attempts to reduce the budget deficit by lowering subsidies on food prices may unleash inflationary pressures through the food-price and wage-push loop (see Figure 3.2).

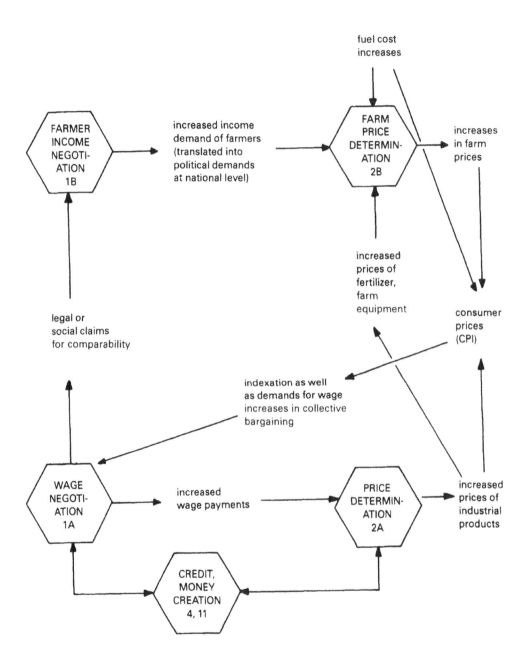

FIGURE 3.6   The farm price-industrial price interactions.

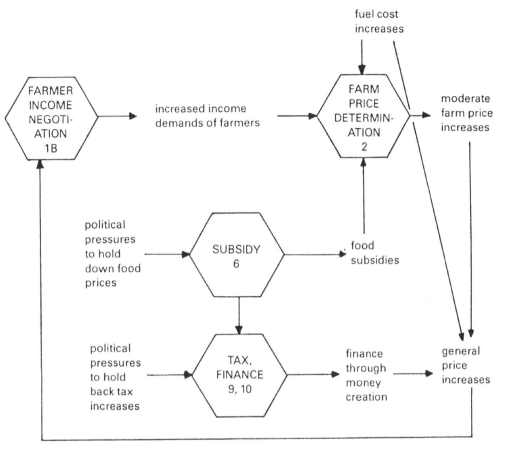

FIGURE 3.7   Food price subsidies as a dampening factor.

4.   Theses About Inflation

Several of the preliminary conclusions and theses of the project are suggested below. These propositions are still tentative although they are based on considerable empirical and analytical work. They are formulated as strongly as possible in order to provoke thought and further analysis.

Thesis 1: Inflation arises whenever monetized claims to resources exceed the available resources.   Inflation will be generated whenever the rate of increase of monetized claims on resources exceeds the rate of increase in the available resources.[11] Such imbalances can arise through pressures and developments on the 'claim' or on the 'supply' side:

1) International or domestic developments can lead to a cutback in resources available to satisfy a historically given level of expectations.[12] Expectations cannot be quickly enough adjusted downwards to match the reduced capacity of the economy to provide goods and services. In Third World countries, such a resource contraction is often induced through a shift in the terms of trade following developments in the industrialized countries.

2) The monetized claims grow more rapidly than the expansion of the resource base and the economic capacity to provide goods and services. Here, the ability of the government to control the money creation process is crucial. The ability of banks to expand credit and invent new forms of 'monies' in pursuit of profits and in satisfying demanding clients is also important.

Thesis 2: Inflation in contemporary societies reflects competition and struggle among actors over resources. Groups of actors push their claims and struggle with one another within institutionalized social decision settings. The system as a whole is characterized by conflicts of interest about the distribution of income and resources among multiple actors in society, such as owners of capital, labor, consumer groups, pensioners, government agencies, etc.

For instance, employers' associations act to assure that the profits of enterprises are maintained or increased. Labor unions as well as other interest groups work to provide their members with increasing standards of living (above all defined in monetary terms). Interest organizations contribute to raising expectations and demands in the course of their activities, strategy developments and negotiations. Refraining from raising demands for the overall good would be a futile gesture, given the collective action situations in which interest organizations operate. A singular sacrifice would have little or no impact on the overall escalation of demands and claims. Interest organizations making sacrifices in the name of the general interest could even be accused by their members — and above all by competitors for leadership in the organization — of damaging the membership's interests. Political parties and the leadership of government are also oriented towards encouraging rising expectations and demands, rather than toward trying to deliver results.

Thesis 3: Inflation is a political problem. Inflation is not a purely economic problem. It is a political problem. It involves the regulation of distributional conflicts either directly through income, price and property rights policies, or indirectly through the shaping of market and public allocation systems.

The expansion of the state and the increased flood of laws and regulations reflect the shift to the political regulation of economic interaction. This is one aspect of the political nature of inflation. The other aspect is that politicians, and increasingly government administrators as well, have to be seen as an integral part of the system of distributional conflicts and their settlement. Measures taken to deal with inflation entail a distribution of costs and benefits. Some actors inevitably will suffer reduced benefits and income claims.[13] Politicians are really endogenous to the economic system and its inflationary situation (Lindbeck, 1976). The monetarist argument that price inflation is 'caused' mainly by governments which irrationally or irresponsibly allow the amount of money in the system to increase too fast is a crude oversimplification of a complex social reality. This is an especially serious oversimplification when politicians and policy-makers accept monetarist arguments as a basis for action as is the case with 'Thatcherism'. The supply of money is of course an important factor in inflationary developments and in counter-inflationary policies. However, there is not simply an actor, e.g. the central bank, standing outside of society, merely creating money 'for the hell of it'.

Thesis 4: Actors in modern society pursue contradictory social goals.   Actors in complex, highly differentiated societies make what often are irreconcilable demands on the economy. These demands underlie several of the major social conflicts and struggles chacteristic of modern Western society:

• between labor and capital over the relative shares of wages and profits as well as over work conditions and productivity;[14]

• between those striving for an improved quality of working life and those demanding a rapid expansion in material standards of living;

• between those wanting higher private consumption and those stressing the expansion of public consumption (including the maintenance of national security);

• between the environmental protection movement and those commited to economic expansion.

Sometimes different actors or groups of actors push for different developments. Sometimes it is one and the same actor striving in an inconsistent manner for contradictory goals; he may not be fully aware that 'one can't have one's cake and eat it too'. Or he may hope that a resolution of the contradiction will be found at the cost of another actor or group of actors.

Thesis 5: Governments find it increasingly difficult to resolve distributional conflicts.   A major function of government consists in balancing conflicting demands and social goals. But contemporary democratic governments find it difficult or impossible to resolve these conflicts in part because they themselves reflect many of the societal divisions and contradictions. In many societies there is a lack of established, agreed-upon models and consensus-building processes which could help resolve the conflicts mentioned under Thesis 4. Particularly critical problems are:

- the fragmentation of knowledge about the system;

- the fragmentation of societal institutions which are specialized in different spheres and domains of social life.

Such fragmentation manifests itself in a variety of instances:

1) There is a general tendency to look to the state to solve a range of different problems such as unemployment, regional economic and industrial decline, help to resource-weak groups, etc. At the same time, there is a growing unwillingness to pay higher taxes and an insistence that the government keeps its budget balanced.

2) Demands for public services, claims and entitlements realized through the state are largely separated from the responsibility for financing them, although, of course, the 'government' as an abstraction stands for the balance.

3) Decision-making is disjointed so that actors in one decision setting pass on to others problems which they cannot or will not solve by themselves. Thus labor unions and employers' associations may make decisions concerning substantial increases in wages under difficult economic conditions which result in increased rates of unemployment. The consequences from unemployment are then handled by the government through unemployment compensation, retraining programs, and subsidized employment schemes. The government, in turn, passes on the financing problem to taxpayers and society as a whole, through increased taxation and inflationary deficit financing.

4) There are increasing demands for resources, goods and services at the same time that there are growing constraints and limitations on the possibilities of increasing production. In some instances, the new demands and the growing constraints have been pushed as a result of the same shift in

values, for instance the shift relating to the demand for improvements in the work environment.

Thesis 6: The monetary financing of contradictory claims provides a short-term settlement. Capitalist and socialist systems and their governments derive their legitimacy from satisfying group interests and increasing claims to resources. The legitimacy of a pluralist system also depends on the 'appeasement of grievances' short of a group's actual walk-out or undertaking of disruptive action.

One method to readily appease demands and 'satisfy' incompatible expectations and demands when available resources are limited is to increase the supply of credit and money. This allows price, wage and budget increases above those consistent with available resources.[15] Tobin (1972: 13) concludes:

Inflation lets this struggle proceed and blindly, impartially, and non-politically scales down all its outcomes. There are worse methods of resolving group rivalries and social conflict.

Thesis 7: Inflation is international. The struggle over the distribution of income and resources is not only a national phenomenon, but also an international one as pointed up by OPEC's struggle with the OECD countries, and the more general struggle between the 'North' and the 'South' over a New International Economic Order (NIEO). Struggles are also occurring within the 'South' between oil-exporting and resource-poor countries, and within the 'North' between Japan and the other OECD countries and between Europe and the U.S.

Obvious manifestations of this struggle have been the U.S. dollar glut following the monetary financing of the 'Guns *and* Butter' strategy during the Vietnam war. The dramatic increases in oil prices determined by OPEC during the 1970's also reflect OPEC's greater claims on world resources. The OECD countries, and the U.S. in particular, were unable to prevent this, although there were threats, even of military action, on the part of the U.S.

These claims came into conflict with those of OECD countries and their domestic interests and actors, wishing to maintain and even increase their standards of living and wealth. National governments of OECD countries could not or would not try to resolve these conflicting claims. They are unwilling and unable, given the present institutional set-up and the expectations of their populations, to permit a substantial loss of income to occur. The governments of OECD countries responded to the OPEC challenge with expansionist fiscal-monetary policies in order to 'reexport' the inflationary pressures to the OPEC countries and other raw-material-exporting Third World countries.

Thus, while the OPEC nations succeeded initially to a large extent with their claims on world resources, they did not have sufficient military or institutional power to impose a noninflationary redistribution of world resources, or to establish a New International Economic Order. Developing this line of reasoning, Whitehead (1979: 577) points out:

'Inflation' is the logical outcome where all political actors share a common interest in the preservation of the existing system of decision making but are unable (or unwilling) to accept an authoritative mechanism for making and upholding specific distributional decisions.

Thesis 8: Inflation is one among several conflict resolution mechanisms. Struggles over income distribution may be dealt with or resolved through several different mechanisms, which are typically and not mutually exclusive:

1) *Work and growth mechanism.* Productivity and output are increased. Economic growth provides increased resources with which to satisfy growing claims. This has been, at least until the turbulent 1970s, the "positive sum" strategy of post-world war II Western countries.

2) *Inflationary mechanism.* Nominal income claims exceeding available resources are acceded to by raising prices and wages, increasing entitlements, and increasing government budgets, accommodating the increased income claims through the expansion of credit and money supplies (without corresponding increases in capacity or utilization of unused capacity).

3) *Borrow-now abroad, pay-later mechanism*[16] Economic agents or the state may borrow abroad to enable (temporary) satisfaction of the excessive claims of groups and agents in the society. (Of course, under proper conditions, the loans may be used to increase productive capacity and to make the economy grow.) This mechanism has been increasingly common in the 1970s both in developed as well as underdeveloped countries.

4) *Process of consensus building and normative persuasion.* This entails persuading societal groups to lower their income expectations and income claims, to reduce their efforts to advance their claims, or to accept redistribution schemes.

5) *Repressive mechanism.* Police and military force as well as more subtle coercive forms (such as high unemployment rates) are used to force working class and other groups to reduce their income claims or hold back their efforts to advance their claims. This is a particularly common strategy in Latin America, often combined also with the inflationary mechanism.

The relative role of these mechanisms in controlling or resolving income struggles varies from country to country and also from period to period in any one country. A particular constellation of mechanisms will reflect the institutional or cultural framework, the relative power and interests of social agents, policy-makers and powerful coalitions, as well as the available resources and pressures on resource distribution.

What is increasingly apparent is that the growth and international borrowing mechanisms have for most countries been substantially exhausted by the early 1980s as *reliable* means of resolving domestic conflicts over income distribution. Some countries (such as Austria, Belgium, France and Sweden) are undergoing a very slow, difficult process of normative persuasion and consensus building relating to income distribution issues. The strategy entails shaping consensus around implicit or explicit income policies where groups accept substantial real income reductions and restrain their efforts to push claims for compensation.

Massive use of force is a common strategy in Latin America. Labor union activity is repressed, and wages set by administrative fiat. Public resources are reallocated, with minimum concern about the needs or preferences of any but a narrow cluster of interests at the top of the power structure (Foxley and Whitehead, 1980). Such repression may be temporarily successful, as for example, the "achievements" of the post-populist regimes in Chile and Uruguay in the 1970s. However, economic stagnation and deep-felt issues of justice and income distribution set the stage for renewed struggle and intensified inflationary pressures, sooner or later. The prognosis for future civil peace and economic stability is indeed bleak. The socio-economic history of Latin American countries, with persistently high inflation rates, is precisely all about deep societal cleavages and intense struggles over income distribution (see Chapter 5).

Inflationary pressures in relatively democratic countries such as the USA and Britain have been temporarily contained through substantial deflation and extremely high unemployment rates (which border on being repressive). In view of the economic stagnation — and the zero-sum struggle which this implies — one may anticipate sooner or later renewed inflationary pressures, in the absence of societal consensus about income distribution.

What is particularly noteworthy in the cases of the USA and Britain is the extent to which the Reagan and Thatcher governments have been prepared to sacrifice the post World War II consensus that the state should prevent high unemployment, intervene to prevent recession, and maintain general welfare. This was a basis or legitimation of the socio-economic system and Keynesian theory (in part the 'historic compromise' between capital and labor manifested in 'welfare state capitalism'). The relinquishment or erosion of the consensus sets the stage for intensified income struggles — and even greater inflationary pressures — in the future, but also reduces legitimacy and capability of the state to resolve these through non-repressive means. Latin American countries are informative in this respect: given a lack of general consensus and legitimacy, policy choice is reduced to two strategies with which to resolve income struggles: inflation or repression.

Thesis 9: There is no single cause and no simple solution to inflation. Inflation is a system phenomenon. There is no single factor generating inflation. Any of the following may be important: increasing competition among actors in relation to income distribution games, wage or cost-push pressures, money creation processes, excessive demand, or even value and norm shifts. However, each factor or set of factors must be seen in the larger economic and social context, i.e. in relation to other processes, factors and conditions which together shape inflationary situations or an 'inflation sytem'.

Thesis 10: Inflationary situations are unique. It is possible to identify sets of factors which underlie inflationary developments in general (see Section 3). In practice, however, each society has a more or less unique set of factors. Moreover, money creation processes, budgetary processes, or wage and price negotiations and determinations take on specific forms and are influenced by the conditions and mechanisms specific to each country.

Thus, each society, even if its inflationary profile is similar in many ways to that of other countries, faces a unique situation. For each country has its economic structure; its institutions shaping price and wage determinations; its specific class and group relations; its identifications with certain ideologies and theoretical models of the economy and of appropriate economic and political behavior; and its various historical experiences which have shaped socio-cultural, political and economic patterns of behavior.

In particular, each country has its production profile and structure, its resource base and specific areas of knowledge and capability specializations. Iceland is dependent on fish production and exports, Belgium and Switzerland are manufacturers of high value-added products. Britain and Sweden have some natural resources. Britain and Belgium have long industrial traditions. Because of the more or less unique profile of each country, it experiences a given type of international or domestic economic shock in a particular manner.

Moreover, each country is constrained differently in its possible responses to shocks. Iceland has had to assure the well-being of its fish sector. Belgium has had to absorb falling terms of trade with falling real wages in order to avoid inflationary wage-cost pressures which would have resulted in a substantial loss of export markets. Switzerland could export its foreign workers, thereby finding a 'costless' and domestically non-contradictory solution to the anti-inflationary recession after the first oil-price shock.

In sum, the institutional response to an inflation problem assumes specific or unique features in each national setting. Money creation, control processes, budget decisions, wage and price negotiations and policies have to be fitted into what already exists and have to be made compatible with existing institutions, social relationships, ideologies and values. An incomes policy in Britain assumes a completely different meaning than it does in Iceland, even in the case where the formal content of the two policies is the 'same'. Moreover, an incomes policy which is conceivable in some countries, such as Iceland or Norway, would be totally unthinkable in the decentralized Swiss system with its fragmented price and wage negotiation patterns and complex, hence extremely slow, economic and social policy consultation mechanisms.

The arguments above point up that the concrete anti-inflationary strategies which are pursued will tend to be — *and should be* — different in different countries. Moreover, they will be supported by different elite coalitions. And finally, they are likely to differ in their effectiveness and their structural consequences for the society.

Thesis 11: Factors underlying inflation change over time.   The world does not stand still. The conditions and processes whereby a country comes into inflationary vicious circles, and the conditions and processes whereby these are maintained and develop, differ substantially over time. Inflationary pressures may be initiated by external shocks. Responses of economic agents, policy-makers, and interest groups may result in expectations, strategies and institutional changes which in themselves become inflationary.

5.   The Shaping of Inflationary Society

It will have become clear by now that inflationary processes and developments relate to basic societal processes such as:

1) the shaping of actors' expectations and demands,
2) the production of goods and services,

3) the bargaining over and the settlement on prices, incomes, budgets and property rights in general,

4) the allocation of public goods and services and of tax and governmental financing burdens,

5) the creation and allocation of credit and money, and

6) the integration and differentiation of society.

Several central aspects of the relationship between these societal processes and inflationary processes and developments in contemporary societies are briefly discussed below.

Processes (1) and (2) relate to inflation in terms of the creation of resource-expectation gaps. Such gaps set the stage for distributional conflicts. These assume a particular structure and characteristic features depending on negotiation and allocation processes (3) and (4). The creation of credit and money (5) as an expanding basis for claims on societal resources is of crucial importance here, as are the processes which generate societal integration and differentiation (6).

5.1. The Shaping of Expectations and Demands

Actors and groups of actors develop expectations about and seek to make or maintain corresponding claims on goods and services they expect they should have access to. They also aspire to certain positions within the distribution of income and wealth. Government agencies and specialized organizations speak in the name of weak or poorly organized groups, claiming for them certain benefits and improvements. There appears to have been an increase in the number of claimants and in the intensity of their pressure since the late 1960's, symbolized of course by 'May 1968':

• increasing pressure for groups to be able to participate and, among other things, to influence the distribution of income in society;

• increasingly competitive pressures from different social groups for greater shares in the distribution of national product and changes in the structure of income;

• implicit social understandings, where groups 'knew their place' and relative positions, have given way to higher levels of questioning, assertion of new claims, competition and instability.

5.2. The Production of Goods and Services

Production processes are constrained and facilitated by a number of factors. The shaping of new constraints on economic expansion and on growth in productivity has increased in intensity since the 1960's:

Demographic constraints.   The lack of a growing labor supply, for instance labor freed from the countryside or high rates of reproduction, has been overcome to some extent in countries such as Switzerland, Germany and Sweden by a high import of foreign labor. This led to social and political problems which generated pressures for restriction on labor importation, especially in some countries.

Constraints on business activity and production.   These pressures have been carried forward on a wave of growing suspicion towards business and industrial activity shared by substantial parts of the population, worried about environmental degradation, increasingly obvious health hazards, and stressful work conditions.

Emergence of resource scarcity.   The move towards more costly energy resources has led to a politically motivated scarcity, above all of oil. Increased uncertainty and political instability have also led to scarcities in other raw materials. Substitution and adjustments require long-term efforts.

Low R & D.   Growing pessimism and uncertainty about future enterprise liquidity, profits, and financing charges have led to a reduction of R & D and of investments in productivity-increasing activities (including training and education). Part of this is the result of the constraints described under point (b) above. Part of it is a consequence of inflation which favors 'investment' in speculative activities based on real estate, gold, and art works.

5.3 The Setting of Wages, Prices and Profits

Through the setting of wages, prices and profits, expectations are translated into demands and ultimately into some form of exchange and, possibly, into contractual obligations over a considerable length of time. These contracts can involve the provision of labor and capital services, and the supply of resources, goods and services. In these settings, enterprises and administrative units decide on price changes; these decisions are influenced by multiple social actors and many factors. Pricing rules, indexation clauses, management-labor negotiation frameworks, and market and administrative power factors form a complex pattern for price determination. This pattern shapes opportunities for and restrictions on price increases. It defines the possibilities of different actors to translate income demands and cost increases into relative price adjustments and new contractual obligations, such as indexation of wages, farm prices, pensions and welfare payments. Government fiscal, credit and monetary policies have weakened to some extent price and wage discipline. Market actors learned about the erosion of discipline and exploited it increasingly.

For instance, labor expected that it could press for wage increases without risking unemployment, and managers tended to give in to such demands, because they expected to be able to raise prices sufficiently to cover their increased costs. In some industries, it appears that management set prices high enough to maintain or establish old levels of profitability with the expectation that expansionary fiscal and monetary policies would generate the necessary demand.

Until matters started to get out of hand in the 1970's, the general rule seemed to be that the government would guarantee full employment and an expansionary economy regardless of wage and price developments.

5.4. The Setting of Claims to Public Goods and Services

Value shifts supporting, and commitments to, increased participation in important societal decision-making have legitimized the efforts of groups to seek redress for reduced life-chances and for wrongs suffered. At the same time, groups have learned to organize and to use the mass media to generate public support for their demands and to put pressure on the government to respond favorably to their requests. Governments themselves have taken initiatives to assume responsibility for correcting and regulating market failures, partly because of the need to maintain legitimacy, partly in response to pressures from organized groups and social movements, and partly in response to the interests of professionals in government service.

The assumption of such responsibilities — largely open-ended with regard to additional future responsibilities — has led to increased government expenditures, in the form of transfer payments, tax rebates, subsidy programs as well as wage payments and payments for public investment and the production of public services. Particular interests and the 'institutionalization of values' develop around the government's production of services and its transfer of resources to particular groups. They contribute toward making these activities and expenditures almost *irreversible.* Resistance to the open financing of these excess expenditures has been growing at the same time that some of the measures taken, e.g. concerning work environment and control over industrial pollutants, have resulted in substantial constraints on productivity and productivity gains.

5.5. *The Monetary Resolution of Distributional Conflicts*

Contemporary democratic governments find it increasingly difficult to resolve the conflicting interests and demands. Some of the critical conditions are:

• There are substantial constraints on increasing the supply of goods and services, and resources for distribution generally, as well as on the resources the government can claim for itself.

• On the demand side, governments find it difficult or impossible to limit or reduce expectations and demands of actors in society. This may be, in part, because the "government" is not perceived as "above the games", but one of the parts and also closer to some of the parts than others.

Governments are tempted to follow a line of least resistance, particularly if subject to frequent electoral and voting tests. They may have the opportunity to do so by increasing the available credit and money supply. To follow a harsher line, as in Britain today, generates hostility and opposition. There may be other reasons which make the expansion of credit and money a compelling line of least resistance, e.g. governments may lack organizational capabilities to collect taxes effectively.

The gap between expected and realizable income and wealth patterns is partially resolved through *nominal* satisfaction of expectations and demands, at least for some actors and groups of actors. Conflict games are transformed into nominal positive-sum games.[17] This is achieved through the monetary *financing* of government budget deficits and the expansion of credit to governments, enterprises and households in order to enable them to complement their revenues, which fall short of their expectations and demands for purchasing goods and services.

The monetary resolution of conflicting demands can only provide an apparent, and therefore temporary, resolution of distributional conflicts. Some if not most income and revenue recipients sooner or later come to realize that the nominal claims and entitlements they are receiving provide them with less access to resources, goods and services than they had expected and counted on.

Expectations frustrated in this way lead to raising of expectations and claims in order to compensate for past losses. These are pushed through with greater aggressivity in order to protect one's interests. Inflationary losses are even calculated in advance and then become the basis for compensatory demands.

This general loss of money and price standards leads to intensified efforts to protect one's historical position in the distribution of income and wealth.[18] This of course serves to rigidify relative prices and production structures, just at a time when some of the shocks (e.g. the oil crisis of 1973-1974), which plunged economies into inflationary developments, require changes in relative prices, quantities, and qualities.

5.6. Inflationary and Counter-Inflationary Social Processes

The present inflation is not an economic problem which has popped up recently. It is the result of a longer-term societal development since the end of World War II. Common features underlying this development have been:

1) Changing social power relationships, both nationally and internationally.

2) Rising expectations and demands for incomes, both nationally and internationally.

3) Increasing difficulties in appeasing and satisfying the claims to income.

4) A tendency to settle conflicts with short-term solutions entailing credit and money expansion.

The changes in power relationships which occurred have enabled previously weak or unorganized groups, both internationally and nationally, to increase their claims and to influence the distribution of income. At the same time, however, previously dominant groups have not lost their ability to influence income distribution processes, and struggle, sometimes successfully, to maintain the status quo. These remarks apply not only to the relative power of labor groups to claim and realize increasing real incomes. They also apply to the relative power of different sectors and regions of society in making claims on public investment, state subsidies, income maintenance programs, etc. At the same time, there have been increasing constraints on the growth of productivity and economic expansion, due to social movements and government regulators pushing to bring about improvements in work environments and occupational safety and in the natural environment.

The policies and programs of pluralist, democratic states have contributed, in many instances unintentionally, to the shaping of 'inflationary societies'. The maintenance of full employment and high rates of growth became dominant economic policy goals after World War II. The successful economic performance during the 1950's and 1960's made these goals seem fully realizable and even encouraged actors to expect them almost as "natural rights".

This has provided a context for shaping vicious circles relating to growing claims and stagnating production. A major factor in facilitating or inhibiting the development of an inflationary society is the extent to which key groups of actors in society share a model of acceptable income, wealth and resource distribution. Such a model both guides, and is verified by, the "meta-level" exchanges among the key groups in society.

There may be a clear ideological and cultural basis for the presence or absence of such a shared model. But real interests and payoff structures also play a significant role, as suggested below.

5.6.1. The virtuous circle. Under conditions where major groups of actors believe that they would gain from *cooperative exchange* — for instance between management and labor, or between the government and the business world — these beliefs become validated under a range of conditions. The process works as follows:

• Labor exercises wage restraint and shows a willingness to accept changes in work organization, technology, occupational identity, productivity and rationalization measures.

• The public sector exercises restraint by means of limiting tax increases and by not financing government deficits in ways which are either inflationary or crowd out private investments.

• The profitability of enterprises is facilitated.

• Profits go into, and reinforce, the level of investments.

• Investments contribute to the growth of the economy and of employment.

• Labor and government tend to experience real income gains.

As a result of such a process, the beliefs and intentions underlying the cooperative exchanges tend to be *validated,* at least when certain enabling conditions obtain (see below). Labor and government will then be inclined to hold such beliefs and pursue the cooperative strategy, and the virtuous circle is more likely to be maintained.

However, the virtuous circle may be destabilized due to a breakdown of the conditions supporting it, which made cooperative agreements between governments, labor, and capital mutually fruitful. Thus, labor and governments may cooperate with management and capital, but profit margins and/or investments may decline:

• Markets decline or collapse, so that even with labor and government restraint profits decline.

• There may develop a weak connection between profitability and investment due to general pessimism or belief that future profitability will not be as good as it has been, and moreover that profitability elsewhere, abroad or in real estate, is better.

• Constraints on growth develop.

• Competition from the Third World is increasing.

The result may be a break-down of restraint on claims from labor and government, thereby bringing about the vicious circle.

5.6.2. The vicious circle. Labor and/or the government may refuse to engage in cooperative agreements with management and capital concerning long-term developments. This may be because they believe that wage or tax income given over to profits will not or does not benefit labor or the government, respectively. Or labor-actors and the government may be under pressure, for example due to inflation, to push for short-term gains. If labor, through collective bargaining, and the government, through taxation, are strong enough to cut into enterprise profits, the result may be a vicious circle of declining investments, poor enterprise competitiveness, declining economy and employment, still greater pressure on the part of labor and the government to increase their income (see Figure 3.9).

Crouch (1980) points out some of the circumstances which shape such a vicious circle:

• There is no shared model and there are no government initiatives to convince workers (1) that they would gain substantially in eventual income if they exhibited wage restraint and (2) that adequate alternative employment would be available if they cooperated in the improvement of labor productivity.

• At the same time, labor is strong enough to resist rationalization and reduction in manning levels and work practices made possible by advanced

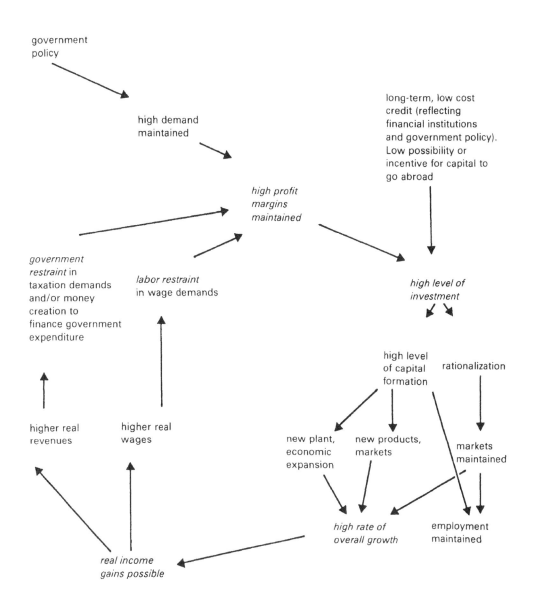

FIGURE 3.8   Virtuous circle of economic expansion and cooperation concerning income distribution.

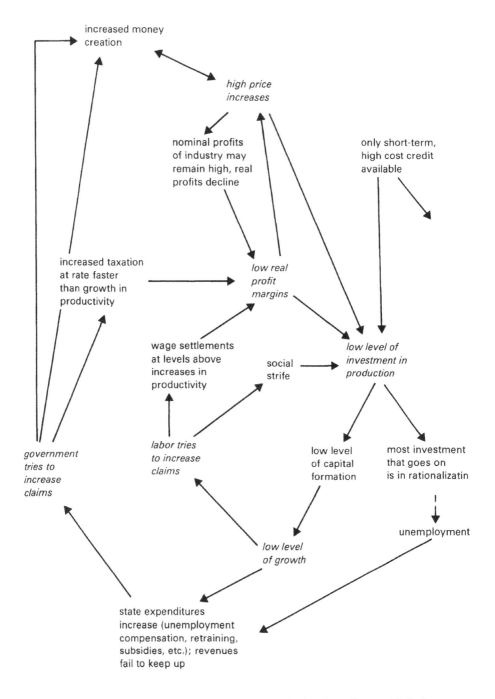

FIGURE 3.9   Vicious circle of stagnation, distributional conflicts, and inflation.

technology — indeed to resist the technology itself, at the same time that money wages can be maintained.

● Capital goes along with this pattern because 'money illusion' makes managers and investors believe that profits are reasonable. Anyway, owners of capital have the possibility to channel resources for investment abroad. This exit opportunity enables them to escape the profit consequences which their acquiescence is producing in the first place.

● Credits are available, but only for short terms. They are therefore costly. Financial institutions which could channel financial resources into long-term investments in industry for productive purposes do not exist.

6.   The Modelling of Inflationary Society

Models should enable us to explore the ramifications of policies and measures taken to deal with inflationary developments, particularly the unintended consequences of action in a complex system. That is, government measures to reduce inflation often produce other, unintended effects, which are inflationary. Monetary control, particularly the simplistic versions of it formulated by some monetarists, can be shown to have multiple effects, some of which are under most circumstances clearly deflationary. For instance, policy measures lead to increased unemployment, thereby dampening the wage demands of labor unions, at least in the short run. Yet, other effects are likely to be inflationary, particularly in a modern, complex economy. For instance, high interest rates contribute to cost-push pressures for enterprises with high debt-equity ratios. High unemployment, arising from deflationary monetary policies, is likely to contribute to increased government expenditures, at the same time that tax revenues tend to decline. The resulting budget deficit has to be financed through money creation, contributing to inflationary pressures. Even attempts to reduce government deficits and the need for inflationary deficit financing may, under some condition, contribute to *other* inflationary mechanisms. For example, the government raises the charges for public services. Through indexation this leads to increases in wages and pensions, and thereby to inflationary pressures.

In such ways, the model developed and used here can be used to specify and analyze the multiple processes which make up a complex economy, and to point out the unintended consequences of proposals to deal with complex problems, such as inflation, in a modern society.

The framework may also be used to develop strategies and policies for structural and institutional changes to dampen or to break inflationary vicious circles: above all, by restructuring societal games and the linkages among games, input-output linkages, rules of the game, participation of different societal actors in strategic games, etc.

The games societal actors play, and the ways in which they play these games reflect the constraints and loop-holes, the reward and penalty structures into which the social system locks them. The complex, modern system of institutionalized income distribution games — at the sector, national, and international levels — tends to produce inflation and unstable development. At the same time, it limits the capacity of most societal actors (1) to understand the nature of the social system and the games they are locked into playing and (2) to develop means or strategies to intelligently restructure the social system and the 'rules of the game' whereby social decisions and transactions are carried out. The ultimate aim of the present project is an emancipatory one: to assist actors in developing such capacities.

Several of the more specific normative questions which the research has addressed are as follows:

1) If inflation represents a particular mode of resolving distributional conflicts — and if its costs in terms of sustaining an effective economy are excessive — then alternative strategies and institutions for resolving distributional conflicts should be considered:

• research should identify the key axes of competition and conflict relating to distributional questions.

• efforts should be made to explore ways to discuss distributional conflicts more openly and possible measures to deal with the conflicts in a manner consistent with greater price stability.

• in consideration of policy and institutional responses to inflation problems, stress should be placed on *long-term* developments as much as on short-term stabilization: industrial restructuring and re-orientation, enhancement of consensus building and conflict resolution processes and institutions.

• It follows that short-term measures to achieve price stability, which at the same time undermine long-term socio-political capabilities to resolve or to regulate conflict must be avoided. All too often, as we see in the present case of the UK, short-term measures are pursued to stabilize price developments. However, they tend to intensify conflict potential and the likelihood that struggle over the distribution of income will be pursued again, with renewed vigor, once the government will allow or set in motion a "go period" (which within a relatively short time it must do with a view to the next election).

• Monetarism — and monetary policy as an instrument of social control — cannot be an effective counter-inflationary means, given that *distributional conflicts* underlie inflationary pressures. Quite simply, such means tend to depress the economy, reducing real income available for distribution, *thereby intensifying competition and conflict potential.* In the medium- and long-run, according to our analyses, strict monetarist policies are likely to amplify inflationary potential.

Even if monetary solutions could be shown to be optimal on grounds of economic theory, such solutions are unsuitable in most instances on social and political grounds, and, therefore, ultimately, on economic grounds.

Fiscal policy is also inadequate in these terms, since it is not designed to or capable of addressing directly the conflicts over the distribution of income among societal groups. Indeed, such policies tend to be caught up in or are an integral part of the conflict processes, encouraging the continual expansion of government budgets and growth in credit and money supply, in part in order to finance the expansion.

Special institutions, such as indexation, are simply ways of trying to protect groups against some of the negative effects of inflation. They do not resolve the underlying conflicts and demands that give rise to inflation in the first place.

2) The above arguments suggest that institutions for building consensus about income distribution and for coordinating and limiting claims on the national product should be established or developed.

3) This will require in our view: (1) some concept or framework about *distributive justice*; (2) a forum or forums to carry on *open dialogue about the distribution of available real income*; (3) greater stress on socio-political and socialization processes which would contribute to consensus formation about income distribution and to the restructuring of income expectations and claims of societal groups as well as individuals.[19]

These are subjects which sociology and political science are fully capable of shedding light on and contributing ideas toward institutional innovation. Even such recent innovations as "social contracts" and "tripartite negotiations and agreements" have as much sociological and political science relevance as economic. Obvious major questions here concern the political and socio-cultural conditions under which such institutions are likely to be accepted or found legitimate. What social and political consequences are

their use likely to have? In raising and researching such questions, sociologists and political scientists have much to contribute to discussions and
strategies relating to price stablization in modern society.

Epilogue

Only time will tell if the drop in current inflation rates in OECD countries
represents a permanent solution to the inflation crisis, or a temporary
respite. In our view, the national and international struggles over income
distribution will continue, and inflation will remain a serious problem. In
non-OECD countries, in particular Latin America, we see that inflationary
pressures are far from under control.

In the USA, income distribution questions appear to have been partially
resolved in favour of the middle classes and the employed through tax
reduction. On the other hand, substantial budget deficits, high interest rates
as well as tragic unemployment levels (particularly among youngsters) are
part and parcel of income distribution struggles, nationally as well as internationally.

At the national level, the government budget deficits and high interest
rates impede credit-needy and interest-sensitive sectors, contributing to
high rates of unemployment and bankruptcy in some sectors. On the other
hand, the conditions provide opportunities for less-interest-rate sensitive
sectors such as services, non-durable goods and defense products. The
interest rates (as prices or claims on resources) have brought, and continue
to bring, massive profits to banks, particularly international banks.

Internationally, the high US interest rates force many other industrialized countries to maintain higher interest rates than they would otherwise
do, given policy objectives to encourage investment and economic growth.
These other countries must defend themselves against USA policies and
strategies, in the absence of an international authority or rule regime controlling strictly such competitive games.

The high international interest rates, in large part driven by the USA,
have an even more disastrous effect on under-developed countries. The
recession in OECD countries prevents them from earning the hard currencies with which to service their increasingly expensive debts. High interest
charges impose an extra claim (capital outflow). Possibilities to borrow for
further investment and economic expansion are effectively eliminated.
Internal income struggles are intensified.

But the international income distribution game is far from played out.
The possibility of Third World countries collectively declaring bankruptcy

cannot be ruled out, as one among a number of strategic responses. This would set the stage for an even more serious crisis in the entire international economy

We are faced today with a global crisis: stagnation and unemployment in developed countries, inflationary pressures, stagnation and widespread hunger and poverty in underdeveloped countries. The Great Depression — and Keynes theory — prepared us for increased government intervention, the activist state. Today, that state is incapable of dealing effectively with crisis on the international level, the level at which major problems and conflicts originate and develop, for example between the USA and other OECD countries, or between them and their financial and other economic agents, on the one hand, and, on the other, underdeveloped countries.

The situation clearly calls for the introduction of a world authority in some form. Its responsibility would be to regulate the international financial system and control world monetary expansion and credit availability (for the moment these are under the control of a very few OECD countries). The authority would also engage in international fiscal policy, redistributing income from rich countries to the poor regions and classes of the Third World. This would imply in one form or another a progressive income tax at the international level, probably coupled with negative income taxes for those living at subsistence or lower levels.

In the face of the Great Depression, many countries had the institutional means, or were able to shape the necessary institutional means to deal with the crisis. The major problem today is that either the institutional means are not available or powerful vested interests, in the form of nation-states and particularly powerful nations, oppose any major restructuring of international regimes. Cleavages and struggles at the international level are much deeper and the basis or potentialities for shaping international consensus much less feasible than in the case of most nations. In light of this argument, one must conclude pessimistically. The necessary transformation of international conditions and regimes will have to await a much more profound crisis. (September, 1983).

NOTES

1. The research reported in this chapter has been supported by the Social Science Research Council (HSFR) in Sweden.
2. This approach to collective action problems is found in Burns et al., (1985), and Burns and Meeker (1978). Maital (1979) has recently pointed in a similar direction for inflation analysis.

3. In contrast to the assumptions of classical or neo-classical economic theory, there is no tendency toward equilibrium, except to the extent that actors with social power mobilize to realise a 'social equilibrium', i.e. the maintenance of the status quo.

4. We want to stress that societal competition and struggles over income are not 'games' in the sense of playing and gambling. The use of game theory terminology and a social game framework reflects a desire to draw on a valuable research tradition. Yet, we differ from this tradition in that we view games as potentially open, dynamic systems. Emphasis is placed on the relationship between conflict and social change, in particular the relation of conflict activity to structure maintaining and structure changing processes in societal development.

5. See Chapter 6 for a discussion of the difference between conflict resolution — which is temporary — and conflict settlement which is more permanent.

6. From this perspective 'wage-cost-push', 'profit-cost-push', 'demand pull' and 'overexpansion of the money supply' are not necessarily inconsistent explanations. They may simply represent important but partial components of complex, dynamic social economies. Thus, the problem of inflation is not, in our view, so much a question of Keynesianism versus monetarism, *but both and much more.*

7. In Figure 3.1. we have collapsed a few games into one another compared to the settings listed in Table 3.1.:

   — Game 4 (credit availability and distribution) and game 11 (money creation).

   — Games 6 (public services and investments), 7 (income maintenance) and 8 (government subsidies).

   — Games 9 (taxation) and 10 (budget deficit).

   In each case, the different games are closely linked to each other. The reduction in the number of settings listed facilitates the exposition without detracting from the major idea of the figure.

8. Inflation can be understood in a limited sense as a persistent increase in the price level, measured by the consumer price index (CPI) or GNP deflator. Of course, not all prices increase at the same rate: some remain constant, some may even drop.

9. Mainstream economists sometimes recognize the self-amplifying nature of inflation, but complex feedback systems are not a central part of their paradigm and approach to modelling and analyzing inflation.

10. 'Virtuous circles' may also obtain where, for instance, decision setting 1 results in substantial productivity increases but moderate wage increases. This results, other things being equal, in price constraint, good profit margins and high levels of investment which, in turn, stimulates productivity.

11. The monetization of claims is essential to money inflation. But claims greater than available resources can be created in other ways. for example, individuals or groups may claim *rights* to the use of a good such as health care, which one does not buy on a market, but waits in line for. 'Inflation' resulting from increased scarcity, would then be manifested in *increased* waiting times for the service, which of course involves a 'price' or 'cost'.

12. Cutbacks may result from natural catastrophes, shifts in values which lead to constraints on exploitation of the natural environment or on production, for instance in the name of improving the quality of life, and power shifts which enable a foreign actor (an oil cartel for example) to substantially increase its claims on the resources of a country or group of countries.

13. This involves not only the 'politics of distribution', but also the socio-cultural and ideological aspects of distribution. *Inevitably, the question arises of how the costs or*

burdens of reducing inflation will be legitimized, what values and arguments will serve to convince most actors, or the most important actors, that specific sacrifices have to be made, and why they should be willing to make them.

14. Other more abstract contradictions concern movements to promote economic equality or economic democracy, often in forms which are detrimental to economic growth, at least in the short run.

15. There are a variety of conditions which make the inflationary settlement of conflicts the solution of least resistance:
    — frequent voting and electoral tests;
    — threat of political instability and 'pronunciamentos';
    — compensation for the lack of government ability to levy and collect taxes.

16. In the age of colonialism and direct exploitation, it was possible to extract resources from colonies and defenseless groups and to use them at home to resolve income struggles. The contemporary form for such exploitation is indirect. Developed countries or their social agents can sell their goods and services at inflated prices to underdeveloped countries.

17. That is, through nominal increases in payoffs, conflicts over resources may be resolved temporarily. Indeed, individual actors or groups of actors find that the most advantageous strategy for each, in potentially inflationary situations where the demands of actors exceed the available resources, is to seek to increase wage demands, increase prices, increase government budgets, borrow, buy-in-advance. *Collectively*, of course, this is the worst strategy, since it intensifies scarcity and inflationary pressures.

    Note also that individual sacrifice through restraining one's demands for income — for instance, by not making as large a wage demand as originally intended, by holding back price increases, limiting budget requests, etc. — will not reduce the rate of inflation, unless all or most other actors do the same. But no actor or group of actors can afford to withhold its claims without running the risk of loosing in real income or purchasing power over time. Above all, this occurs with respect to others who have shown no restraint. Yet, as each actor increases his demands in the different institutionalized settings for income distribution decisions, this results in inflationary pressures and developments, with many, although not all, worse off.

18. In Switzerland during some periods, one has had substantial increases in the money supply, but actors were still willing to hold Swiss money since they had the expectation that the value of the money would be stable, and *the belief contributed to making this true.*

19. Institutional means — political and socio-cultural — must be developed to limit growth in claims, to maintain claims and demand in balance with capacity and resource availability and to govern the distribution of available income among claims with consideration not only about distributive justice but about balancing consumption and investment.

REFERENCES

Baumgartner, T., (1978) An actor-oriented systems model for the analysis of industrial democracy measures. In R.F. Geyer and J. van der Zouwen (eds.), *Sociocybernetics*: **1**. Martinus Nijhoff, Leiden, pp. 55-77.

Burns, T.R. and L.D. Meeker, (1978) Conflict and structure in multi-level multiple objective decision-making. In Hooker, Leach and McClennen (eds.), *Foundations and Applications of Decision Theory*: **1** Dordrecht, D. Reidel, pp. 67-114.

Burns, T.R., T. Baumgartner and P. DeVille, (1985) *Man, Decisions, Society.* New York: Gordon and Breach.

Crouch, C., (1980) Varieties of trade union weakness: Organised labour and capital formation in Britain, Federal Germany, and Sweden. *Western European Politics:* **3**, 87-106.

Foxley, A. and L. Whitehead, (1980) Economic stabilization in Latin America: Political dimensions — Editor's Introduction. *World Development:* **8**, 823-832.

Johansen, L., (1979) The bargaining society and the inefficiency of bargaining. *Kyklos*, **32**, 497-522.

Maital, S., (1979) Inflation as a prisoners' dilemma. *Challenge*, **22**, 52-54.

Whitehead, L., (1979) The political consequences of inflation. *Political Studies:* **27**, 564-577.

4

The Dynamics of Inflation and Unemployment in Belgium:[1] Actors, Institutional Settings, and Social Structure

Philippe DeVille

1. The Approach

The objective of this chapter is to provide a systematic analytic framework that would be useful to understand the dynamics of both inflationary and deflationary processes in Belgium since 1970.

Traditional macroeconomic theory has developed for the past thirty years a theory of inflation of its own. No one ever talks about a corresponding theory of deflation!

Thus from the start a typical asymmetry between the study of inflation and the study of deflation must be pointed out.

This curious state of affairs undoubtedly comes from the fact that the last twenty years have not experienced periods of decrease in the general price level. As an example, for the country under review in this study, Belgium, the last sensible absolute decrease in the consumption price index dates back from 1955 and lasted only three quarters (see Figure 4.2). In this respect the contrast with the pre-World War II period is striking. But to justify a theory of inflation in itself one needs more than simple empirical justification. It requires the theoretical proposition that inflation is a qualitatively different phenomenon than deflation, requiring an explanation of its own. And this is exactly what traditional macroeconomic theories try to do.

Indeed the current state of inflation theory is based upon two basic propositions:

1) the effective rate of inflation can be decomposed into two components: one is the underlying persistent trend in the general price level of

what could be called in the traditional neo-classical approach the "equilibrium" component of the inflation rate. Let us call it $\dot{p}^x$. The other is its temporary component; cyclical variations in the inflation rate which are due to shock-induced disequilibrium: $\dot{p}'$.

Thus $\dot{p} = \dot{p}^x + \dot{p}'$

2) inflation theory is really concerned with the explanation of $\dot{p}^x$ and not of $\dot{p}'$ which is the concern of short-run macroeconomic theory. It is in the identification of the causal determinants of $\dot{p}^x$ that two lines of reasoning seem to depart from each other: the monetarist "demand-pull" explanation of inflation and the neo-keynesian cost-push (especially increases in unit labor costs) inflation theory.[2]

$\dot{p}^x = M\,(\dot{m})$ the monetarist approach
$\dot{p}^x = K\,(\dot{w})$ the neo-keynesian approach

They appear to be conflicting alternative theories. But to appreciate the difference, we should identify their underlying hypothesis. The monetarist approach presupposes an inherently stable private market economy where real wages like any other relative prices is determined by market equilibrium: they are thus endogenous. But the rate of growth of the nominal money supply $\dot{m}$ is exogenous. Since money is not considered per se as an asset, its rate of growth necessarily determines directly aggregate demand and thus governs the rate of change of the general price level. On the other hand, the cost-push approach disconnects some of the nominal cost elements (i.e. especially wage costs) from market determination processes: they are exogenous and, in this sense, a market economy is not inherently stable at full employment. Neo-Keynesians have to introduce monetary accommodation processes for the cost-push induced increase in prices to be sustained: the money supply is endogenous. Quite obviously, behind the mere choice of deciding what is exogenous and what is endogenous in the model, are hidden more fundamental assumptions about the way in which our socio-economic systems are structured and functioning.

In both cases anyway, the ultimate explanation of inflation relies upon changes in exogeneous variables on one hand, and specific assumptions about the transmission mechanism between these changes and the general price level. There are two consequences of this: first, the inflationary processes appear very much as the outcome of a black-box system where the role payed by the actual social actors involved and their degree of control both on these "exogenous" variables and on the "transmission mechanism" is simplistic and mechanical, if not totally unidentified. As a result most policy recommendations made along these lines are rather crude: control the money supply (and reduce inflationary expectations) or reduce money wages. But the ability of social actors to adjust themselves and to circumvent such regulating measures is never taken into account.

Finally, we can question also the validity of separating "permanent" and "transitory" components of the inflation rate. Such a procedure is justified only if it can be asserted that the trend of the inflation rate is totally independent from these temporary disturbances. Quite clearly, this decomposition is again based upon the fundamental hypothesis of the inherent stability of a private market economy.

The starting point of our approach is different although not contradictory in itself to the economic theories of inflation. It just takes up the argument at a more fundamental level: inflation (or deflation for this matter) is viewed as *one* of the possible outcomes of a conflict over the existing distribution of income and wealth. To state it like this is not arbitrary. It puts emphasis from the start on what is the core process of a capitalist decentralised market society: the struggle among social actors (individuals, groups, classes, etc.) over the distribution of *money* income in order to improve their own income shares. Indeed in a monetary economy, this is the only way by which social actors can try to control their *real* incomes.[3]

However this conflict over the distribution of money income manifests itself in a number of different processes. If we had a purely competitive production-cum-exchange society, the processes by which a given social actor can attempt to modify its nominal income are relatively simple to analyze. But in a society where the state is a central institution capable of affecting many economic processes, where there are both private and public sources of money and credit creation, where economies are open and interdependent both in terms of trade and capital flows, the ways by which social actors can attempt to modify their income shares are many, intricate and involving complex strategies. In such a society where the illusory transparence of the social relations postulated in the purely competitive exchange economy has been put aside, power relations are an essential ingredient of the analysis of macroeconomic processes like inflation.

The departure of our approach from traditional economic theories of inflation can now be clarified. Once the importance of complex social, political and institutional processes is recognized both as instruments and constraints for social actors to improve their income shares, the distinction made by economists between endogenous and exogenous variables in their approach to inflation seems no longer acceptable. At a systemic level, it is absurd to consider the money supply as well as nominal wages exogenous. Propositions like "excess money growth above the trend of real income growth is a necessary *and* sufficient condition of inflation" are unwarranted as generally and universally meaningful propositions about systemic conditions. But they might nevertheless be true. On the other hand, in our view conflicts over the distribution of money income are a necessary *but not* a sufficient condition of inflation. The aim of our systemic analysis is precisely to find these sufficiency conditions.[4]

In other words, we believe that the inflationary processes should be analyzed in terms of being a possible outcome of a series of different "games". The concept of game used here refers simply to any social interactive scheme which involves a "collective" decision making process and outcome.

The dynamics of inflationary processes is then basically related to the changing societal conditions under which these distributional "games" are played: changing power relations among actors, changes in their perceptions about the nature of the game or its possible outcomes, changes in the international environment and in the constraints (norms, rules, values) within which these games are played. Such analysis thus requires at the same time a clear identification of the economic processes that manifest themselves in an inflationary situation and of the social actors and their strategies which underly and structure the various games that lead to such processes. Particular emphasis should be placed on the linkages that exist both among actors and among games. Such linkages provide an understanding of either "vicious circles" that explain the existence of sustained or accelerating inflationary processes or on the contrary "dampening processes" that lead to deflationary situations. Inflationary processes are thus going to be associated with a particular linkage network. More precisely, they will be associated with a particular hierarchy among games. Such a hierarchy will depend on the ability of the different actors to intervene in the various games involved and their respective power in imposing a particular game as the important one.

The dynamics of inflation can then be viewed as a temporal succession of different phases, each of them having its own specific characteristics in terms of game structure and linkages and in terms of the stabilizing or destabilizing nature of the various outputs of these games.

2. Inflation and the Dynamics of Societal Games

In the following section, we will introduce the essential elements of game description and analysis and summarize the main conclusions of our study.

Inflationary processes appear to be characterized by a precise periodization (1970-1974, 1975-1977, 1977-1980, 1981 ...), that can be explained in terms of specific game structures and consequently of policy orientations.

2.1. Structural Background

Belgium led the industrialization on the continent: today's economic structure is that of a highly industrialized, small, open economy. Belgium is today rather resource-poor; its exports, as most of its production, are import-intensive, turning Belgium essentially into a net exporter of value-added. Being considered as the main driving force of the Belgian economy, the open sector has to be differentiated from the domestic or "protected" sector concentrated mainly in the services.

Precise criteria for classifyng a particular branch in the open or the protected sector are not easy to establish. The "law of a single market price" for defining the open sector never applies purely: not only pure price competition never excludes completely some price differentiation among producers but also non-price competition is an important factor to take into account. One has thus to rely on more qualified criteria like the intensity of *external* competition on both the domestic *and* the external market to define the open sector. But of course one should then also consider for example the importance of subsidies given to domestic producers (implicit protectionism) or of public orders that might discriminate against foreign competitors. Unfortunately the available data base does not allow for such a detailed analysis. For the data base used in this report, the open sector is mainly defined as the agricultural sector and almost the entire manufacturing industry. The protected sector comprises energy, most of transport and communications, construction and all private marketed services.

The importance of the "open sector" is considerable. Table 4.1 indicates its share in G.D.P.[5] Of course, exports as a percentage of GNP is a much higher figure: it was 47 % in 1970, 68 % in 1981. As said before, imports content of exports is quite high in Belgium. The country being thus a net exporter of value-added, good management-labor relations have always been a key factor for the performance and stability of the Belgian economy. Social consensus is usually achieved through a very extensive set of collective bargaining institutions. As a result Belgium has enjoyed so far a rather high standard of living and strong labor unions have succeeded in institutionalizing an extensive welfare system, including a rather complete wage indexation scheme. It is only during the last three or four years that the substantial and continuous slowing down of real growth has created increased tensions over the maintenance of such social legislation which in a context of stagnation has implied an increased transfer of income from enterprises to households.

TABLE 4.1
Gross Value Added, by Sector. Belgium 1960-1980*

	Protected Sector	Open Sector	Public Sector	G.D.P.**
1960	490.6 (.41)	386.9 (.32)	140.7 (.12)	1210.7
1973	917.7 (.41)	732.1 (.32)	285.7 (.13)	2253.8
1975	945.2 (.41)	705.5 (.30)	306.4 (.13)	2313.1
1980	1110.3 (.41)	792.8 (.29)	361.8 (.14)	2680.0
Δ 1973-1960	+427.1 (+87.1%)	+345.2 (+89.2%)	+145.0 (+103.1%)	+1043.1 (+86%)
Δ 1980-1973	+165.1 (+17.5%)	+62.7 (+8.6%)	+76.1 (+26.7%)	+426.2 (+18.9%)

Source: estimates from data of the Planning Bureau
* in billions of Belgian Francs, in 1975 prices.
** Sum of the three sectors does not equal G.D.P. since the latter includes Households' value-added.

TABLE 4.2
Total Employment, by Sector. Belgium 1960-1980*

	Protected Sector	Open Sector	Public Sector**	Total
1960	1488.2 (.43)	1605.8 (.46)	395.6 (.11)	3489.6 (1.0)
1973	1810.2 (.48)	1445.7 (.38)	527.3 (.14)	3783.2 (1.0)
1975	1866.0 (.49)	1371.9 (.36)	545.8 (.14)	3783.6 (1.0)
1980	1987.8 (.53)	1164.6 (.31)	645.5 (.17)	3797.9 (1.0)
Δ 1973-1960	+322 (+21.6%)	-160.1 (-10%)	+131.7 (+33.3%)	+293.6 (+8.4%)
Δ 1980-1973	+177.6 (+ 9.8%)	-281.1 (-19.4%)	+118.2 (+22.4%)	+14.7 (+0.4%)

Source: estimates from data of the Planning Bureau
* in thousands
** includes unemployed enrolled in temporary public employment programs.

Since World War II, the state has increasingly become a crucial element in the maintenance of the social consensus. It has always guaranteed and enhanced the good functioning of the bargaining institutions at the highest level ("concertation sociale"). But its importance as a social regulating mechanism is no longer confined to the class dimension (labor-management relations). The emergence of regional differences and conflicts has led to substantial political battles among political parties — entirely organized on a regional basis — about the control of the central state.

The state has thus become totally involved in regional issues on public programs: public infrastructure, subsidies to enterprises, cultural and educational questions. Such involvement has become even more important once the world-wide recession has started to uncover structural imbalances among regions between old declining industries and more modern advanced sectors. Increased awareness of regional differentiation and the consequent claims for increased regional autonomy have culminated in the 1980 state reforms which give the regional institutions legislative competences and executive powers on many social and economic matters although with extremely limited financial means. Two years later, it appears however quite clear already that the decentralization process is still very much unstable and that new heated debates on the limits of regional autonomy are again taking place.

A final but very important characteristic of the Belgian economy has been the existence of a strong banking and financial sector. Financial holdings became very early in the economic history of Belgium powerful actors. They do control now large segments of strategic branches like steel, chemical, metals, etc ... But at the same time, they have gotten involved more and more in international operations: direct foreign investments or portfolio activities. In this sense, one could say that they have never been, and are still not, nationalistically oriented, although in this respect also regional differences among banks have been important.

2.2. Actors and Games

From the previous description of the Belgian socio-economic factors, we will now identify what are the key actors involved in the inflationary processes in Belgium. *Primary-level actors* are social groups identifying themselves around common objectives and strategies, institutionally organized to some degree and being parties in social decision-making processes. They do take part in such processes explicitly whenever institutional arrangements allow them to do so and their own strategies imply acceptance of bargaining and concerted action. If these conditions are not met, they still can take part in the process as outside "pressure groups". These primary-level actors are production management, trade-unions, banks and other financial intermediaries, consumer and ecology groups. These actors are not necessarily internally homogenous. This is of particular importance in Belgium where regional differentiation can be important within each group. Production management from both regions agree on most of the short-run stabilization policies. They do disagree however on more long-run considerations like industrial restructuring and the corresponding industrial policies. On the other hand, and irrespective of their regional origins, production management from the open sector might disagree with their counterpart of the protected sector on some stabilization policy issues. Similar remarks can be made about regional and sectoral differentiation within trade-unions. *Meta-level actors* are mainly political entities. One could argue that they are not actors by themselves to the extent that they are representatives of primary-level actors. Such argument has to be rejected because it neglects two important considerations. First it confuses the political parties and government and public administration. The former in a certain sense can not indeed be considered as actors. On the issues that we are dealing with in this report, they do express, although most often in a composite way, the essentials of the objectives of the primary-level actors. Of course, the same thing could be said about the government which, in our parliamentary system, is closely linked to political parties. However government strategies cannot be reduced to the strategies of the political parties supporting it since in Belgium there are only coalition governments. Coalition governments in Belgium impose on the political parties that are part of it either cooperative strategies and compromise solutions or "exit" strategies. But these compromises very often transcend political parties' strategies: in many instances in the past, governments had to impose on their coalition members solutions that they would not accept by themselves. This justifies in our view the inclusion of central and regional governments in our list of meta-level actors. Identical arguments could be developed along similar lines for the central bank.

To summarize, one has the following list of actors:

Primary-level Actors

- management $\left.\vphantom{\begin{matrix}a\\a\end{matrix}}\right\}$ with due account for regional and sectoral
- trade-unions $\left.\vphantom{\begin{matrix}a\\a\end{matrix}}\right\}$ differenciations
- banks and other non-bank financial intermediaries
- consumers and ecology movements

Meta-level actors:

- national government
- regional governments
- central bank

In the analysis of the inflation history of Belgium provided in this report, it is argued that the actors are involved in a series of strategic "games":

1) the "wage-price-productivity-employment" game between management and trade-unions;

2) the "credit availability" game where financial intermediaries, enterprises and the central bank are mainly involved;

3) the "public investment and public services" game, which consists mainly of the expenditure side, net of transfer payments, of the government balance sheet. Aside from the government itself, trade-unions, regions, and management are involved;

4) the "income maintenance and social security" game which involve mainly the government, trade-unions and management;

5) the "subsidy" game, where the issues are all the transfer payments or subsidies made to enterprises by the government. Regions, management, unions and the government are the main actors;

6) the "taxation" game; the receipts side of the government balance sheet, involving trade-unions, management and the government;

7) the "budget deficit financing" game where collective decision making involves the government, the financial intermediaries and the central bank;

8) the "money creation" game, involving the central bank, financial intermediaries and the government. This game covers also the obviously related issue of exchange rate policy.

Figure 4.1. summarizes the actors and games structure of our analysis of inflation in Belgium. This analysis will consist of identifying the inflationary nature of the outputs of these games and the cumulative or dampening effects of these inflationary impulses which may depend on the specific nature of the linkages existing between these games.

2.3 The Inflation Story: Descriptive Facts

Belgium, as any other industrialized country, has experienced historically

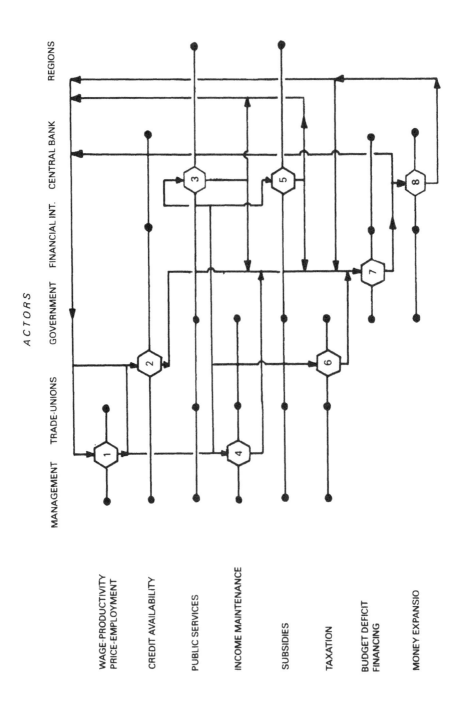

FIGURE 4.1 General game interaction matrix for Belgium.

high rates of inflation during the years 1974-1976 (see Figure 4.2.) Yet, the decade of the 70's started out with annual rates of inflation of around 4 %. Belgium achieved again rates of around 5 % at the beginning of the 80's.[6] This inflation rate has slowly increased again from 1981 up to now.

In some sense Belgium is a low inflation country. Its CPI-rate has generally been lower than the average rate for the OECD and the EEC countries (see Table 4.3). Here the years 1974-1975 are a slight exception: the Belgium inflation rate was just average. The effort at reducing the level of inflation has therefore born some fruit, at a substantial price however as we will mainly show later. The indicator of such a price is Belgium's performance in terms of unemployment. Table 4.4 clearly indicates that Belgium has experienced higher than average unemployment rates since 1974. Yet, similar to other countries, the last few years seem to have resulted in an underlying inflationary base which is above those of earlier periods from

TABLE 4.3
Belgian Inflation Rate: International Comparisons

Country	Change over the Period of 12 Months ending in								
	1972 Dec.	1974 Dec.	1976 Dec.	1978 Dec.	1979 Dec. in%	1980 Dec.	1981 Dec.	1982 Dec.	1983 March
*USA	3.4	12.2	4.8	9.0	13.3	12.4	8.9	3.9	3.6
*Japan	5.3	21.9	10.4	3.6	5.7	7.5	4.3	1.8	2.3
*Germany	6.4	5.8	3.7	2.4	5.4	5.5	6.3	4.6	3.5
*Netherlands	7.9	10.8	8.5	4.0	4.8	6.7	7.2	4.3	2.7
*Belgium	6.4	15.7	7.6	3.9	5.1	7.5	8.1	8.1	8.9
Switerland	6.9	7.6	1.3	0.7	5.2	4.4	6.6	5.5	4.8
*United Kingdom	7.6	19.2	15.1	8.4	17.2	15.1	12.0	5.4	4.6
*Italy	7.3	25.3	21.8	11.9	19.8	21.1	17.9	16.3	16.4
*Sweden	6.1	11.5	9.5	7.3	9.8	14.1	9.2	9.6	8.4
*France	6.9	15.2	9.9	9.7	11.8	13.6	14.0	9.7	8.9
*Canada	5.1	12.3	5.9	8.4	9.8	11.2	12.1	9.3	7.2
Austria	7.6	9.7	7.2	3.7	4.7	6.7	6.4	4.7	3.5
Denmark	7.0	15.6	13.0	7.1	11.8	10.9	12.2	9.0	7.5
Spain	7.3	17.9	19.8	16.6	15.5	15.2	14.4	13.9	12.8
Finland	7.1	16.9	12.4	6.4	8.6	13.8	9.9	9.0	7.5
Greece	6.6	13.4	11.7	11.5	24.8	26.2	22.5	19.1	23.1
Ireland	8.2	20.0	20.6	8.0	15.9	18.2	23.3	12.3	12.5
Norway	7.8	10.4	7.9	8.1	4.7	13.7	11.9	11.7	9.2
Weighted Average of the 'Group of Ten'[1]	5.1	14.5	7.8	7.3	11.2	11.6	9.0	5.6	4.8

*Member of 'Group of Ten'
[1]Weighted with Gross National Products of 1981
Source: B.I.S., Annual Report, 1983.

TABLE 4.4

Belgian Unemployment Rate: International Comparisons

Country	1974	1976	1978	1979	1980	1981	1982	1982 Dec.	1983 March
	Annual Averages, in % of the Active Population								
USA	5.6	7.7	6.1	5.9	7.2	7.6	9.7	10.8	10.3
Canada	5.3	7.1	8.4	7.5	7.5	7.6	10.8	12.8	2.6
Japan	1.4	2.0	2.2	2.1	2.0	2.2	2.4	2.4	2.6
Germany	2.7	4.6	4.4	3.8	3.9	5.6	7.7	8.5	9.3
France	2.3	4.3	5.3	6.0	6.4	7.8	8.8	8.9	8.8
United Kingdom	2.6	5.2	5.5	5.1	6.5	10.2	12.0	12.7	13.0
Italy	5.4	6.7	7.2	7.7	7.6	8.4	9.1	$9.8^{1,2}$	n.a.
Netherlands	3.3	5.5	5.1	5.9	9.0	12.3	14.1	16.5^{3}	
Sweden	2.0	1.6	2.2	2.1	2.0	2.5	3.1	3.4	3.6
Belgium	2.6	5.7	7.0	7.2	7.9	9.4	11.0	11.6^{2}	12.2^{2}
Switzerland	0.0	0.7	0.3	0.3	0.2	0.2	0.4	0.7	0.8
Group of Ten	3.7	5.5	5.1	5.0	5.7	6.6	8.1	8.8	8.8

[1]1st week of Jan. 1983 [2]Not seasonally corrected [3]New Series as of Jan. 1983
Source: B.I.S., Annual Report, 1983.

1950 to the early sixties. In this, an underlying trend towards higher rates of inflation, despite all the efforts to combat it, becomes visible.

If we now focus on the most recent years, from 1970 to 1982, it appears, as it can be seen from Figure 4.2, that the inflation in Belgium seems to have gone through four different phases:

• from 1970 to 1974, a slowly, but subsequently at the end of the period a rapidly, accelerating rate of inflation;

• from 1975 to the end of 1977, early 1978, a continuing slowing down of the inflation rate;

• from 1978 to 1980, a stable or slowly accelerating inflation rate;

• from 1981 up to now, a more noticeable increase in the inflation rate.

Taking these four phases as working hypotheses, we analyze each of them on the basis of the existing quantitative and qualitative data available and we attempt to elucidate the underlying game structure and linkages. The way the outputs of these games feed on each other to produce either vicious circles or dampening processes is one of the key factors in explaining the dynamics of the inflationary process.

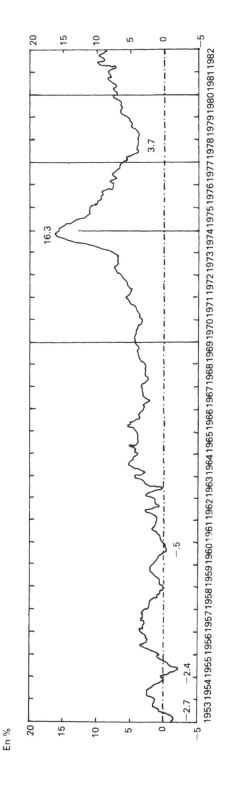

FIGURE 4.2

Graph: Annual Change (in each month)
Numbers: Extreme Monthly Values

© Res. Louvain-la-Neuve

3. The Dynamics of Inflation in Belgium

Phase 1: 1970-1974 Inflation-Expansion   After a little downturn in 1970-1971, the Belgian economy operated in a favorable international environment. Exports increase continuously from the end of 1971 up to the Fall of 1974 resulting in a balance of current account surplus. The favorable impact of external demand conditions on the level of economic activity was strengthened even further by increases in domestic demand especially for capital formation. In such a favorable situation, the distributional issue was essential: the wage-price productivity game became the central game. There was a general consensus among key actors (especially management and trade-unions) on evaluation of the state of the economy and on positive expectations about the future. Unions were able to obtain high increases in real wages: good performance and expectations in terms of productivity increases (especially in 1972 and 1973) did not lead management into strong resistance. Unit labor costs did not rise dramatically and profit margins were still improving up to 1973 for the protected sector but were already slowly decreasing for the export sector.

All the other games followed the same logic: the public expenditures game, where regional conflicts had already became serious, was relatively easy to handle because of the reasonable size of the budget deficits and the government's easy access to borrowing. There were no serious liquidity constraints thus far although long term interest rates started rising in 1972. Similarly, the income-maintenance game did not lead to serious collective decision-making problems: extensions of the social security system were granted to self-employed persons.

As far as monetary policy is concerned, it should be mentioned that the Belgian monetary authorities let the Belgian franc actually devaluate by 3 % respective to the Dutch guilder and the German mark when these two currencies were reevaluated in 1973. As usual, devaluation had both cost-push and demand-pull inflationary effects, the former being the most important in the short-run. Such a policy decision thus created additional inflationary pressures. On the other hand, to fight against the accelerating inflation, the Central Bank introduced already in 1972, but more strongly in 1973, quantity measures (reserve requirements) to control the expansion of liquidity. These measures were ended during the next phase in mid 1975. Thus the money expansion game and the credit availability game became important; on this issue conflicts between banks, financial intermediaries and the Central Bank had to be and were solved. But the government was involved also since the reserves had to be invested in treasury certificates!

The combined effects of these various cost-push and demand-pull pressures explain some of the increase in the inflation rate in 1973 but two external shocks affected dramatically the situation: the oil crisis and the resulting import prices increase in 1973 and the world economy downturn in 1974.

The key argument related to the sudden and important increase in the inflation rate in 1974 (12.6 %) is that the external developments did not affect key actors' basic perceptions, and assumptions about specific institutional features (i.e., the extensive indexation system for wage and transfer payments) did not allow for a major restructuring of the situation.

The collective decisions related to the wage-price-productivity game and the other games mentioned above were still based on the same perceptions and strategies that were prevalent among the actors up to 1973. Real wages increased by almost 8 % in 1974. Capital formation increased at a rate substantially higher (9.5 %) than its average in the past. But the high rate of increase in import prices (25.9 %) led, partly directly, partly indirectly through the indexation system, to a rate of increase in the CPI of 12.8 % and in the index of the domestic goods prices of 20.1 %. The balance of payments surplus provided the accommodating monetary expansion. The price-wage inflationary spiral was thus in full gear.

Figure 4.3 attempts to illustrate the logic of the inflationary process during Phase 1. It suggests that the two dominant games in that period were the wage-price-productivity game and the money-creation game, although the former constrains the latter.

The Figure shows also that the inflationary vicious circle started by the favorable external conditions and the overall optimistic expectations dominated the entire period despite the attempt made by the Central Bank to increase its control over liquidity creation.

The impact of these restrictive monetary measures came too late. Credit to the private sector and the overall liquidity (taking M_2 as its proxy measures) were still above their trend values in 1973 and 1974 despite the substantial decrease in their annual rate of change. In other words, monetary and credit creation mechanisms were able to validate the accelerated inflation rate induced by direct cost-push pressures (wage cost increase), imported inflation (import price increase) and indirect cost-push pressures (through the indexation scheme which translated into additional wage costs the increase in these import prices and domestic prices; the latter coming especially from services where productivity growth was lower).

This vicious circle was also sustained by the fact that expectations among the main actors about future economic performance were optimistic and convergent. Indeed in this period there was general consensus among the key actors about what went on in the economy, what were the major prob-

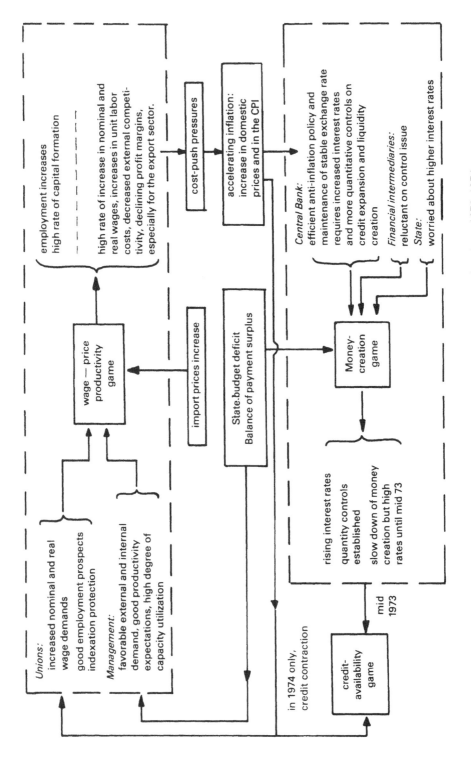

FIGURE 4.3   Game structure phase 1: Inflation-Expansion from 1970-1974.

lems, in which ways the problems were to be dealt with, and what the future was likely to bring. This consensus cut across all games, and concerned the following points or propositions:

- Business is doing well, and will do better.
- The growth of wealth is satisfactory.
- There is a set of institutionalized games to decide who gets what (income), and these are functioning satisfactorily.
- The central game is the wage-productivity game between management and labor. Business agrees that productivity is growing and wages could be increasing.
- Public expenditures are growing but no great deficits. No serious social welfare problems.
- Self-employed and professionals should be provided social security, which is bound to be costly, but the overall growth of the economy allows it.
- Regional conflicts are serious but relatively easy to handle because of resources available for distribution. Politically difficult problems, e.g. the Louvain University crisis in 1968 (split between French and Flemish speaking) led to the decision in 1969 to build a new university, which was started in 1972 and eventually entailed for the government heavy financial burdens.

Changes in perceptions and initiatives to restructure the hierarchy of games eventually came from those actors that were structurally dominant and immediately affected by the two external shocks, the oil crisis and import price increases in 1973. In Belgium, the open sector management represented through the Federation of Belgium Firms (FEB) is a key actor here. On one hand, it has always been recognized that the open sector was the main driving force of the Belgian economy. This group also strongly connected itself with the financial intermediaries and the Central Bank: its protests were always heard. On the other hand, the open sector in 1974 was most immediately hit by the two shocks: squeezed between cost-push pressures because of import prices and labor cost increases and having to compete mainly as "price-takers" on world markets, their profit margins started declining rapidly in 1973 and even further, after a pause, in late 1974 because of the contraction of world demand.

Phase 2: 1975-1977, Inflation-Recession   The downturn of the world economy struck rapidly the Belgian economy: the 1975 growth rate of

GDP in real terms was substantially negative (-1.8%) and this for the first time since 1958. But in this respect, Belgium did not differ significantly from its other main European partners.

At that time, none of the main social actors would have argued that this was the beginning of a major change in the medium-run growth prospects. Consequently the vicious circle started in the earlier period, which was centered around the wage-price-productivity game, kept going but this time in a drastically changed environment. Wage cost pressures and import price increases fed into the Consumer Price Index and led through the indexation scheme to inflationary increases of domestic prices. These processes were validated through credit and money creation. Wage and price pressures were amplified by the secondary games where various social groups (regions, segments of income earners) attempted to improve or to maintain their relative socio-economic positions. The brutal contraction of external demand affected this overall structure because of its differentiated impact on the open sector versus the protected sector. Although wage cost pressures and import prices increased and the usual cyclical downturn drop in productivity affected both sectors, lack of external demand and the levelling of the world prices explain the much more rapid decrease in profit margins in the open sector compared to the protected sector where costs increases may be shifted more easily to price increases.

The consensus built up earlier around the wage-price-productivity game finally broke down at the end of 1975 because of the change in attitudes and strategies of the dominant open sector. Leading voices of that sector raised the issue of wage moderation and indexation through the channels of the Employers' Association (FEB) and to some extent through the central government's analyses. To protect the indexation scheme, trade-unions reluctantly accepted real wage moderation under the tacit agreement that the employment situation would not deteriorate further than expected, as we said before, from what was appearing as a severe but *only cyclical* downturn (with a doubling of the unemployment rate from 1974 to 1976). Substantial real wage moderation was obtained in late 1975 and continued thereafter up to 1979. To that extent, the key issues were no longer related to the wage-price-productivity game but to the credit-availability game, the budget-deficit game and the money creation-exchange rate policy game.

The maintenance of a stable exchange rate of the Belgian franc became the main objective of the Central Bank, with which the government and at least part of the open sector agreed. In 1975 the inflation rate peaks and the rate of growth of the money stock remained high: this can only partly be explained by the balance of payments' monetary impacts, its surpluses both on current accounts and capital having become very small. There was, in addition, throughout 1975 a noticeable increase in credit expansion by banks and other financial intermediaries to the non-financial sector of the economy.

But part of the increase was also due to the monetary financing of the government budget deficit, which ultimately increased the monetary base and after a lag, the overall liquidity position of the financial intermediaries. The money-creation game became strongly linked to the budget-deficit game.

Indeed, substantial increases in transfer payments to households (especially unemployment compensations) and to enterprises (subsidies to overcome financial difficulties, a problem greatly exacerbated by its regional implications), led to increased budget deficits: their percentage with respect to GDP increased continuously after 1974.

The Central Bank tried maintaining a stable exchange rate, against losses of exchange reserves due to speculations on the franc and progressively larger trade balance deficits. At the same time it was forced to provide the monetary financing required by the government deficits. The Central Bank was thus placed in a central position of arbitrage between two possible strategies: either to maintain the overall liquidity of the system, which could imply a devaluation, or to accept some liquidity squeeze and possibly rising interest rates to keep a stable exchange rate. The Central Bank chose the strategy of a restrictive monetary policy, justifying its choice by the argument that a devaluation would have a limited positive impact on the performances of the open sector. A devaluation, it was argued, would entail import price increases and increased inflationary pressures. The actual restraint of the policy is hard to measure: the annual rate of growth of the money stock decreased in 1976 and stabilized in 1977 in a context of a continuously decreasing inflation rate. Long-term nominal interest rates remained fairly stable throughout the period, this implying increased real rates. Changes in discount and short-term rates deal with the destabilizing effects on capital flows of speculation against the franc.

Credit availability, money creation and exchange rate policy became the dominant games in this period. Their linkages and the strategies of the actors involved (especially of the more powerful ones in this situation, i.e. the open sector and the Central Bank, led to a mildly deflationary policy. The policy, especially the relative decrease in import prices due to the effective reevaluation of a Belgian franc closely linked to the German mark, combined with wage moderation led to a substantial decrease of the inflation rate. But the impact of such a policy entailed a restructuring of the game situation. (See Figure 4.4.)

The shift from the previous period in the hierarchy of games can be explained by a shift from a preoccupation with wage costs to credit availability. Labor costs pressures were dealt with at least temporarily. The

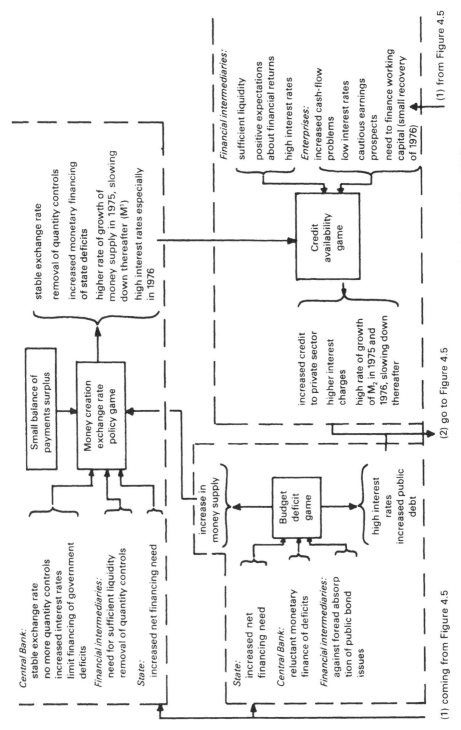

FIGURE 4.4   Game structure phase 2: Inflation-Recession from 1975 to 1977.

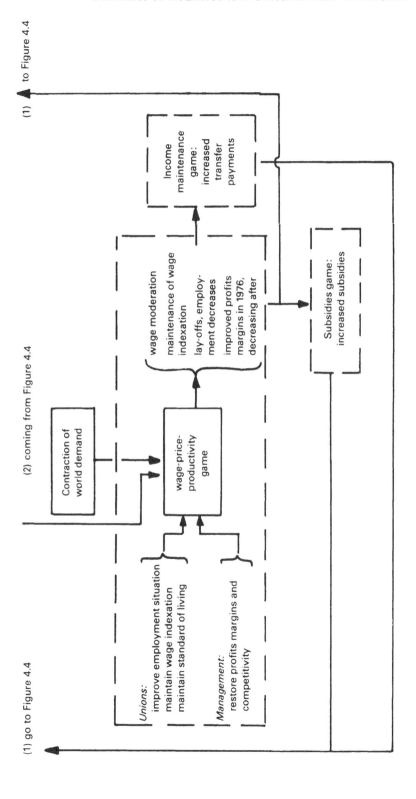

FIGURE 4.5   Game structure phase 2: Inflation-Recession from 1975 to 1977.

crucial problem for many enterprises was how to manage a difficult financial situation where both short-term and long-run endebtment might be essential for their survival.

At this time, the various conflicts of interest and the resulting contradictory requirements imposed on monetary policy began to appear clearly and were well reflected in the Central Bank analysis of the situation. On one hand, an anti-inflation policy must be maintained: Inflation, despite its reduction and the overall economic downturn, was still latent. This required a stable exchange rate and a restrictive monetary policy. On the other hand, credit demand from enterprises was rising and so was the net financing need of the government due to increased transfer expenditures (unemployment compensation) and lack of additional fiscal revenues. The only solution to this contradiction for the Bank was to progressively remove quantity controls on liquidity creation that were established in 1973, limit as much as possible the monetary financing of the government deficits and let the interest rates adjust upward. This last element would be a positive factor for the balance of payments. In other words, the Central Bank wanted to switch from a quantity rationing scheme to a price rationing mechanism; its argument was that interest charges are a negligible part of total production costs and that their increase will have a limited impact on price formation.

Such a policy proposal was not met with unanimous approval. Financial intermediaries were favorable especially because of the removal of quantity controls. But government officials were worried about its impact on interest rates and about the removal of the "monetary reserve" quantity control on liquidity creation. The latter was a convenient institutional rule guaranteeing easier access to bank financing of the public debt.

As illustrated in Figure 4.4, the result of the money creation game was a compromise situation where each actor got more or less what he wanted. Interest rates did not decrease substantially and actually went up in 1976. This situation created problems later on for management, especially for the small- and middle-size export-oriented industries which were very sensitive to credit market conditions. Also, the money supply increased at a substantial rate in 1975 and 1976, decreasing thereafter. The Central Bank complained about the situation, arguing that the financing of the budget deficit prevented the implementation of an adequate restrictive monetary policy. This prefigured its future requests for a strengthening of such restrictive monetary policy.

In summary, one could argue that the period 1975-1977 was a transition period. Expectations and strategies which had led to the inflationary vicious circles, characteristic of the first period, disappeared progressively. The fundamental distributional issue raised by the choice of adjustment processes to the two external shocks — import prices increases and contraction of world demand — concerned the question of which groups were going to bear most of the burden of the adjustments. Since the structural nature of the crisis was not clearly perceived, most actors adopted essentially short-run, defensive strategies focusing on short-run immediate interests. Contradictory processes, as manifested for instance in the money creation games, reflected the uneasy arbitrage between conflicting interests.

The progressive perception of structural problems and the dissatisfaction of some actors with the partly contradictory nature of the policies adopted and their outcomes entailed a new restructuring of the situation.

Phase 3: 1978-1980, Deflation-Stagnation   There was a slight upturn in 1976 (mainly due to a temporary improvement of external demand and reconstitution of domestic inventories but not to an overall improvement in productive capital formation). Nevertheless, the preceding phase ended up with a very low growth rate of GDP (1 %), low degree of capacity utilization (around 72 %) and still rising unemployment. The partial improvement of 1979 did not really improve the overall picture. The rising unemployment rate could be explained in part by a growing labor force (increased labor force participation of women and demographic factors). It could also be explained in part by the negative impact on employment of rationalizing investment made in some important segments of the open sector where the rates of growth of productivity exceeded those of output. Despite temporary public employment programs (Plan Spitaels) the employment issue became a crucial one, because trade-unions felt that they had been cheated: the continuing wage moderation in the private sector had *not* been offset by improved employment conditions. Also, expectations about the future on the part of trade-unions as well as large segments of businessmen and public decision makers became in this period much more pessimistic about the medium run. The crisis was no longer viewed as a cyclical problem but rather as one involving structural inadaptation to a rapidly changing international division of labor. Increasingly, there were strong indications of the inadequacies of the Belgian economy in a changing world economy, particularly for the steel, textile, ship-building, and glass industries. The long-run problems were compounded by the low rate of capital formation in Belgium (although with important sector differences). Such a lack of dynamism in terms of investment plans, product differentiation and development of new technologies, was itself aggravated by short-run considerations, especially the increasing liquidity squeeze caused by a growing deficit of both the balance of payments and of the government budget, only partly financed through direct or indirect money creation. In addition, the second oil shock of 1979 puts additional pressures on the profitability of the open sector.

The wage-price-productivity game became important again but under a different form. The questions raised by the unions (although with some hesitations and internal divisions) did not address themselves so much directly to the wage moderation strategy as to the reduction of work time through work sharing job creating schemes. The obvious issue linked to the work time reduction notion is the degree of wage compensation. In 1979 the dominant position among trade-unions called for full compensation, implying increases in hourly wage costs and thus of unit labor costs. Management fought this issue and won, the arguments being that it decreased flexibility of the labor market and increased costs, thereby even further threatening competitivity. Only marginal reductions of work time were implemented without apparent employment compensation.

Restructuring of the game hierarchy from Phase 2 occurred above all because of the changes in actors' perceptions and consequently of their strategies. More than two years of wage moderation did not lead to employment improvements. Unions felt that the "structural" longer-run nature of unemployment was a central concern. As a result, they decided to concentrate their defensive strategy on another front: the maintenance of the social security system and especially the unemployment compensation regulations. The income maintenance game became crucial.

Belgium has a rather "generous" unemployment compensation scheme. Management and public officials began to raise the question of the state's ability to sustain such a liberal scheme. The central argument was not so much to increase the unemployed's incentives to work as to decrease transfer expenditures and consequently reduce the budget deficits that had grown to an alarming size (9.0 % of GNP including public capital formation: almost highest among OECD countries aside from Italy). Not only was the unemployment scheme at stake; the overall social security expenditures were now debated. The social security deficit was an important part of the overall deficit. The only alternative to cutting expenditure would be to increase socal security contributions, which would affect either enterprises' cost structure or households' overall fiscal burden (see Figure 4.6).

Structural problems were a concern not only for trade-unions but for management as well. The near financial collapse of the steel industry in Wallonie, the deteriorating situation of important sectors like textile, glass, ship-building also made the subsidies games more complex. The financial aide required to help these sectors to restructure and modernize put the state under strong pressure. Since the required financial commitments were beyond its capabilities, the state negotiated medium-run plans with management, unions and banks, entailing a mixture of subsidies and bank loans. Thus far private financial intermediaries have shown a reluctance to

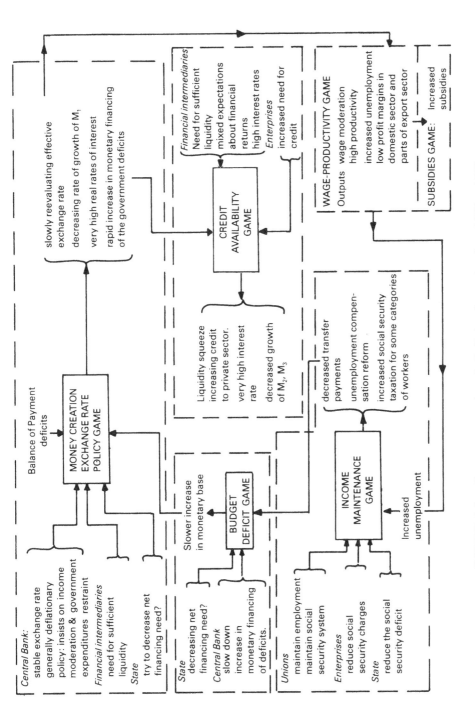

FIGURE 4.6   Game structure phase 3: Deflation-Stagnation from 1978 to 1980.

enter such negotiations or to comply with the terms of the agreements.

The accumulation of claims upon the state implied that budget deficits became less and less controllable. The monetary financing it required was increasingly incompatible with the restrictive monetary policy which the Central Bank wanted to follow. For this reason the Bank insisted on the absolute necessity to improve the government budgetary situation in order to restore balance of payments equilibrium and preserve the stability of the Belgian franc exchange rate. To achieve such objectives, the Central Bank proposed a reform of the social security system, in particular decreasing the net transfers paid to households, but also a stop in the earlier practice of subsidizing marginally inefficient enterprises. Despite the increased monetary financing of deficits, the government deficits put financial markets under pressure. The slow decrease of the households' savings rate, especially their financial saving rate, and the increased credit demand from the private enterprises also contributed to these pressures. Finally, increasingly large balance of payments deficits, both on current and capital accounts, had a negative impact on the monetary base. All these factors contributed to a liquidity squeeze which was further exacerbated by the limited cyclical upturn in 1979.

The increased need for financing the state deficits, which was met only partly by domestic borrowing, partly by money creation (either directly or through foreign borrowing), meant that the money-creation exchange-rate-policy game and the credit-availability game were, as in the preceding phase, still crucial.

But now the issue was no longer simply a question of the relaxation of liquidity constraints. These constraints had indeed put excessive pressures on small and middle-size enterprises faced with short-run, recurrent cash-flow problems and long-run indebtment. Voices coming from both the open sector and the domestic one complained about excessive (increases in) interest rates. Indeed nominal interest rates increased dramatically for two years. Given the low rates of inflation, real interest rates in Belgium were the highest among OECD countries.

Such high real rates were supposedly to help the capital account of the balance of payments. The increase in real rates was caused by the overall increase in foreign interest rates, especially those in the U.S. But the interest rate *differential* between foreign and domestic rates was amplified by the need to offset capital outflows. There was a lack of confidence, in what appeared to many to be an obviously, overvalued exchange rate in view of the deterioration of the current account and of the size of the government financing needs. The established rate seemed too difficult to be maintained. These pessimistic expectations put additional pressures on domestic interest rates.

Thus the question became now "what medium-run monetary policy to follow"? Was a deflationary strategy still appropriate when Belgium had almost the highest unemployment rate among EEC countries, a low level of capital formation, an increased number of bankruptcies? The money-creation game and the credit-availability game are complex because they involve the difficult reconciliation between short-run objectives and medium-run considerations. How is one to deal in an appropriate and efficient manner with structural problems and issues like the necessary adaptation of the open sector in terms of developing new product lines rather than continuously increasing through rationalization the efficiency and competitiveness of old ones? This was still an open question (but it should be noted that the record on these points of such deflationary policy was not obvious). On one hand, wage moderation and the control over the "imported inflation" had led to improvements in the open-sector competitivity (measured by the change in unit labor costs in Belgian francs). But on the other hand such improvement had been substantially offset by the implicit and continuous reevaluation of the currency (effective exchange rate). In addition as mentioned above, the liquidity squeeze created serious problems, especially for small and medium-sized enterprises. The Central Bank and some of the leading figures from business organizations had already made clear in 1979 their answer: push the deflationary policy further but now in terms of both income moderation and wage moderation.

This amounted to slowing down even more the already low rate of increase of household disposable income by decreasing simultaneously wage income and net transfer payments from the state. Cuts should be made also in the provision of some public services. These measures aimed to progressively stop the deterioration of the government budget, to improve the balance of current accounts and finally to maintain a stable exchange rate. They would also improve still further the cost structure of the open sector by wage moderation and productivity increases. Once profitability of the open sector improved, increased cash-flows would relax the liquidity constraints. All these factors should have ultimately helped the productive sector to undertake the necessary structural adaptations. This is what could be called the longer view.

The restructuring taking place in phase 3 indicates all the games strongly linked together; this translates the effort made by the central actors, Central Bank, the state, management, to overcome the previous contradictions that characterized the earlier phase by a *general* deflationary policy that would affect systematically all the games.

Was Belgium entering a vicious circle of deflationary processes that Keynes in his time denounced so vigorously and that Belgium experienced between 1930 and 1935 when, the economy being close to near collapse,

Phase 1: 1970-1974

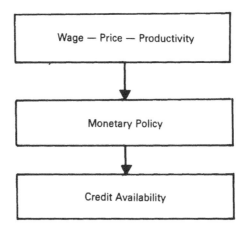

Phase 2: 1975-1977

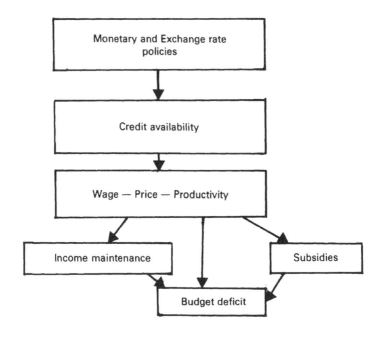

FIGURE 4.7A   Game hierarchy, phase 1 and phase 2.

Phase 3: 1978-1980

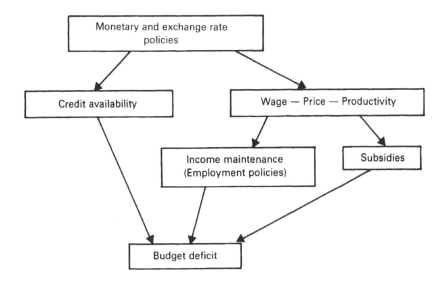

Phase 4: 1981 . . .

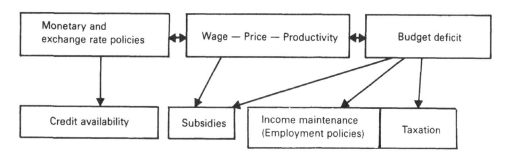

FIGURE 4.7B   Game hierarchy, phase 3 and phase 4.

the Belgian franc was devaluated?

The defensive stand taken by unions in the wage-productivity game, the pressure put on the government by the financial intermediaries and the Central Bank to balance its budget improved the balance of payments situation. The stability of the exchange rate was kept under control and inflation was maintained at a reasonable level but it was far from obvious to what extent, aside from an unlikely rapid increase of world demand, such policy would lead back to an accelerated rate of capital formation, a decrease in unemployment and a higher rate of growth of GNP. Alternative scenarios were indeed possible: the improvement in the export sector and of the balance of payments, allowing the maintenance or possible continuing reevaluation of the Belgian franc. This might have to be paid for by the overall contraction in internal demand, decrease in the household disposable income, decrease in the net public spending, accelerated substitution of domestic products by imported products, deterioration of the profitability of domestic industries, increased unemployment which, because of its impact on the government deficits, require even more deflation, etc ...

Phase 4: 1981-1983: Recession, Rising Inflation and Redistribution   At the end of 1980, the policy followed thus far in Belgium led clearly to a dead end. Indeed, the kind of stalemate among social actors that was prevalent blocked *any* dynamic adjustment of the system. The lack of adaptation led to a further deepening of the internal contradictions of the socio-economic system, particularly around the wage-price-productivity, budget deficit and income maintenance, and economic policy games.

These contradictions were structured in the following way:

1) The contradiction around the *wage-price-productivity game*. The latter created a complex pattern of segmentation both within management and within the labor force.

a) within management: the contradiction between the open and the protected sector becomes more and more apparent, but is still unresolved. The former tried to resist the external competitive pressures and the unfavorable demand conditions by planned or forced rationalizations. This process led to capacity losses and job destructions. To that extent, the open sector was preoccupied with wage moderation. The protected sector, on the other hand, was increasingly hit by contraction of domestic demand. Passing on at least part of its costs (i.e. wage increases) in prices, it added some cost pressure on to the open sector.

b) within the labor force: an implicit "segmentation" arose more and more between three groups of workers. First, there were those who were employed in the open sector, increasingly threatened by job insecurity, and pressured to accept further wage moderation. Secondly, those who were employed either in the protected sector or in the public sector were increasingly split into two subcategories; one which began to resemble the category of the open sector; the other able to count on substantial job security and fairly good wage conditions. The public sector employees were more or less in the same condition since the state had not so far dared to solve its budget deficit problem by laying off public employees or decreasing their wages. And finally, there were increasing numbers of unemployed, still predominantly old and young workers, female workers, immigrants, with very low qualifications, but also more and more prime age male workers. They lived on unemployment allowances which of course involved for them a substantial cut in *real disposable income* in contrast to the employed still protected by the indexation scheme and still enjoying *real* wage increases although at very low rates.

2) The contradictions around the *budget deficit* and the *income maintenance game.* The cumulative impact of the recession and the accumulated deficit dramatically increased the net financing need of the government. Interest charges on the public debt multiplied by five between 1974 and 1982. Even taking into account the inflation effect, the real burden of the debt has been estimated to have increased roughly by three between 74 and 82. But the domestic and external borrowing capacity has limits even for the government. Hence, the necessity of reducing such deficits. But any attempt to do so aggravates further the contraction of the domestic demand. In addition these were very difficult decisions to be made by a government where the socialists held important ministeries.

3) The emergent contradiction between the central government and the regions on economic and industrial policy issues. The new law voted in August 1980 on regional executives, assemblies and their respective authority provided for some degree of regional intervention into economic and industrial policy matters, although severely limited by the small size of the regional budgets. But only the central government had authority to deal with five strategic sectors (coal, ship-building, glass, steel and textile). The impact of the crisis on these sectors had been regionally differentiated, especially for the steel industry. This exacerbated regional tensions. Flanders argued that the central government gave more subsidies to the south part of the country. On the contrary, argued Wallonie, if the large public investment projects in infrastructure were to be taken into account (e.g. the Zeebruggen port and gas terminal), the balance might shift the other way around.

These contradictions manifested themselves in the very adverse economic conditions of 1981. A major shift in policies was called for, at least in short run stabilization policies. This shift took place in two different steps although the logic underlying each one of them was the same. Such logic is quite simple: in macroeconomic terms it amounts to inducing income transfers from households to enterprises as well as to the state in order to simultaneously increase industry competitivity and reduce state budget deficits. This helps either directly or indirectly to resorb the current account deficit of the balance of payments.

The first step which took place in 1981 can be called "moderate wage restraints and implicit devaluation".

The second step can be characterized by "strong wage restraints and explicit devaluation".

In early 1981, the government hoped for a national agreement between trade-unions and management on "wage development". The negotiations were very difficult but the government pressured both parties. The final agreement limited real wages increases for 1981 to 1 per cent maximum. Later that year, a special "solidarity tax" was imposed on the wages of public employees. The funds collected were used to finance part of the deficit of the unemployment compensation scheme of workers of the private sector. The main policy decision in this period was the so-called "operation MARIBEL".

It was a decision to *decrease* by 30 billion francs the employers' social security contributions for *blue collar* workers and, in order to make it neutral for the government budget, to increase the basic value-added tax rates by 1% which would bring in additional tax revenues by approximately the same amount. It should be noted that such a tax rate increase would have had effects on wages through the indexation scheme. It was decided to neutralize these effects on the indexation scheme. Other things being equal, the measure implied *a decrease in real wages and disposable incomes.*

We call this an "implicit devaluation scheme" since the measure concerned only blue-collar workers concentrated in the manufacturing industry and thus in the open sector. Such a measure affected differentially the open sector compared to the protected one. On the other hand, since exports (but not imports) are by definition exempted from the value-added tax, the measure had a symmetric impact on the taxation side. It should be noted also that at that time, thanks to the revaluation of the US dollar, the British pound and to some extent the Japanese yen, the effective exchange rate of the Belgian franc fell for the first time since 1976.

Such a strategy, although the first step towards a broader redistributive scheme, was still a "compromise". The amounts involved were limited; the impact on households' disposable incomes was not very restrictive. At the end of 1981, it was indeed quite obvious that this was not enough. Extremely bad results for the economy called both directly and indirectly (through their impact on actors' strategies) for more drastic measures.

The widespread destruction of jobs put the trade-unions on an even more defensive stand. Poor export performance and lack of profitability reinforced managements' point of view calling for much stronger wage moderation. The government budget deficits were totally out of control, putting the government in a very difficult political situation. All of this culminated at the end of the year in extremely severe balance of payments problems and strong speculations against the franc.

Since no "progressive" alternative policy could be clearly defined, a new "right-wing" political coalition was put together. General elections were called for in late fall. A new coalition government emerged, formed by the social christians and the liberals (right-wing parties), the socialists being now excluded from power. But within this government, christian-democrats (the left-wing of the social-christians) held some important key ministeries (budget, social affairs). This was an important political asset for the government since it allowed to divide (et impera), at least on the Flemish side, the trade-union movement between the christians and their socialist partners.

At the end of 1981, very strong speculative pressures against the Belgian franc on most exchange markets forced the Central Bank to massively intervene. The discrepancy between the regulated exchange market (where the Central Bank intervened) and the free exchange market became intolerably high. In February 1982, the Belgian franc was officially devalued by 10 %. At the same time, the government, through an emergency procedure in the parliament, introduced temporary price and wage controls and at the same time decided to suspend the indexation mechanism for all incomes exceeding the guaranteed minimum income.

The games structure was thus completely transformed again: the wage-price-productivity game and the money-exchange rate policy game became dominant. The central issues concerned the substantial redistribution of income from households to enterprises to improve the relative performance of the open sector compared to the protected one. It was also hoped that the expansionary effects of the devaluation would allow a restrictive budgetary policy: the negative income effects of the latter being compensated by the positive income effects of the former.

4.   Concluding Remarks

The preceding analysis of the various phases of the inflationary processes in Belgium suggests that the societal logic upon which each of these phases is based can usefully be approached in terms of differences in the hierarchical structure of these societal games. This raises two questions: what do we mean by "hierarchical structure"? What determines such a structure?

We can define a hierarchical structure of games in the following way: a game is said to be "hierarchically dominant" if the outcomes (output) of this game act as constraints upon the other games.

A hierarchical structure of games is the recursive structure that links the various games among themselves.

But what determines such a structure? There are three elements that have to be taken into consideration. First, there are objective processes that link the outputs of the various games *independently* of the specific strategies adopted by the different actors: in a certain sense these are the processes that are described by the various equations that one finds in the usual macroeconomic models. These models have their own recursive structure, their own 'hierarchy''. However such hierarchy is given once and for all: the models are so-called structurally stable. Our approach is different: the structure is changing over time. It changes because actors might change their objectives and strategies and also because power relations among actors might also change.

Let us give a simple example. Obviously the income maintenance game, the taxation game and the subsidy game are interrelated. Macroeconomic models handle this in a straightforward fashion. Income maintenance, taxation and subsidies are dealt with by means of their own specific equations (or they are postulated exogenously) and they feed into an accounting identity which computes the difference between expenditures and receipts, thus the budget deficit. According to our previous definition, these games hierarchically dominate the budget deficit game. What this means implicitly is that these social decision making processes (taxation, transfers, etc.) and the social agents behind them *do not take into account the size of the budget deficit as a constraint.* But the financial requirements of such a deficit could imply that the size of the deficit might be an important variable which feeds into other parts of the system affecting the same and/or other actors in a positive or negative way. Consequently, they will adopt new strategies. This means that in a different context with changing attitudes, strategies and power relations, the budget deficit could become hierarchically dominant with respect to these other games.

The different game structures of the various phases discussed in this chapter are summarized in the following comparative charts (see Figure 4.7). The hierarchy of the games indicated in these diagrams are thus suggestive of *what are considered to be the main issues by the various actors.* In phase 1, the main issue was the functional distribution of income between workers and the other actors in the productive sector. All the other issues are considered to be of secondary importance. Phase 2 and 3 indicate how real adjustments that were supposedly necessary given the exogenous shocks were induced by capital and the state.

Power relations between the trade-unions and the other actors allowed the unions to successfully "displace" the problem at least partly. The wage-price-productivity game was no longer in forefront: monetary policy became the main issue as the essential instrument to combat inflation and restore competitivity. The former was more or less successfully achieved, the second was not. Indeed, although wage and productivity developments allowed a substantial improvement in unit labor costs in Belgian currency, the overvalued exchange rate offset such developments. Consequently there emerged a competitivity gap when measured in common currency. External balance was still worsening and the rise in unemployment implied further increases in transfer payments aggravating budget deficits and the resulting interest charges on the public debt.

Phase 4 indicates a drastic change in policy orientations. This had to take place because of the disastrous results of 1981. It was made possible by the change in power relations that came about after the general election of the Fall of 1981. The new government, much more conservative in spirit and thus more willing to confront the unions on policy issues, brought up to the forefront monetary policy and the exchange rate, wage-price productivity, and budget deficit games.

The objective was to restore competitivity by using simultaneously the instruments of devaluation, and of substantial nominal and real wage restraints both directly and indirectly through the suppression, at least temporarily, of much of the indexation scheme. Other measures would be taken also in terms of income maintenance and subsidies in order to slow down the increase in transfer payments: the primary objective was no longer to sustain domestic demand through budgetary policies but on the contrary to impose a stabilization and slow decrease of the budget deficit itself as the primary constraint.

Epilogue: Late 1983

Recent developments in late 1983 indicate that the dynamics of the societal game structure presented in the analysis of phase 4 is continuing with the

TABLE 4.5
Phase Analysis of the Evolution of Some Key Variables

Variables†	Phase 1: 1970-1974	Phase 2: 1975-1977	Phase 3: 1978-1980	Phase 4: 1981-
Consumer prices	slowly accelerating up to 1973, rapidly rising in 1974	peak in first quarter 1975, constant deceleration thereafter	low in 1978, slowly rising thereafter	rising slowly in 1981, more rapidly in 1982
Wage costs	slowly rising up to 1973, rapidly in 1974	peak in 1975, brutal deceleration until mid 1976, slowly decreasing or stable in 1977	decreasing slowly in 1978, almost stable in 1979	decrease in 1981, stable or very limited increase in 1982
Productivity	rapid increase in 1971, 72, decrease in 1973, up again until third quarter of 1974	substantial drop in 1975, recovery in 1976, down again in 1977 but around average level	recovery in 1978, but slowing down in 1979	increase in 1981, slowly declining thereafter
Unit labor costs	increase in 1970, relative slow down in 1971, 72, increase 1973, rapid increase in 1974	peak in 1975, rapid decline in 1976, small increase in 1977	drop in 1978, small increase in 1979	substantial decrease in 1981, very slight increase in 1982 and 1983
Competitivity (index: inverse of unit labor costs in dollars)	decreasing with fluctuations due to productivity changes (see above)	decline in 1975, recovery in early 1976, but increased discrepancy with the index without exchange rate effect	slow improvement with fluctuations in 1978, in 1979 even larger discrepancy	very rapid movement in 1981 and 1982. Much smaller discrepancy with the index in domestic currency
Industrial productivity (deviation from trend)	higher than trend value, except for end 1971, early 1972	drop in 1975, recovery late 1975 — early 1976, although below trend, declining thereafter	stabilizing at the lowest deviations from trend for the entire period	slight increase in 1981, stable on the average but with short-run cycles in 1982
Capacity Utilization (in per cent)	follows the same pattern as industrial productivity	idem	bottom early 1978, increasing thereafter, still below the average 1970-1974	
Wage employment (private sector)	increasing at an average rate of 1.9% except in 1972 (−0.7%)	important decrease in 1975 (−2.7%), decreasing thereafter around 1.2%	decrease by 1.5% in 1978	
Profit margins: domestic sector (%)	on the increase but with cyclical variations in	falling more slowly up to end of 1975, recovery	more or less stable in 1978, rapidly declining in 1979	slow increase in 1981 and 1982

Profit margins: export sector (%)	1971, 72, falling rapidly in 1973, early 1974 continuously declining over the entire period	early 1976, slowly declining thereafter falling rapidly late 1974, early 1975, cyclical variation around a very low average percent	on the increase continuously until mid 1979 where they stabilize	−4% in 1981, estimate approx −2% in 1982
Gross capital formation, including inventory changes	declining from 1969 to 71: absolute decrease in 1971, high rate of increase in 1973, 74	absolute decrease in 1975 (−13%), recovery in 1976 (inventories), stable in 1977	very low rate of change (1%) in 1978-879.	no data available
Import Prices	declining in 1971, stable in 1972, high rate of increase in 1973 and 1974 (+25%)	absolute decline in 1975 and 1977, up in 1976	absolute decline in 1978, up by 13% in 1979	substantial drop in 1981 −15, 7%, estimates of +5% in 1982 and −10% in 1983.
Balance of payments (annual change) on a yearly basis	surplus in current accounts, deficit, but smaller in capital, slowly deteriorating current account and improving capital accounts after mid 1973	still deteriorating current rent accounts, wide fluctuations in capital accounts: net surplus, except for 1975	substantial deterioration of current accounts for entire period and capital accounts up to mid 1979, net deficit	13,5% increase in 1981 on currents accounts, stabilisation of the deficit in 1981, reduction in the improvements on capital accounts in 1981 and to mid-1982.
Money supply M$_1$ (annual change on a yearly basis)	accelerating increase from 1971 to mid 1973, deceleration 1974	acceleration in 1975, deceleration in 1976, more or less stable increase in 1977	stable increase in 1978, but substantial deceleration beginning in 1979	slight deceleration thereafter
M$_2$	idem although still increasing up to mid 1974, drop thereafter	substantial increases in 1975 and 1976, decreasing thereafter	idem	increase in 1981, slowing down in 1981, slight acceleration beginning in 1983
Interest rates	slowly decreasing until 1972, rising thereafter up to 1974	decreasing in 1975, rising in 1976, decreasing in 1977	very slow increase in 1978, rapid thereafter	rapid increase up to 1981, slowing down in 1982 but acceleration in 1983
Public debt	slowly increasing up to end 1972, almost stable in 1973 and 1974	rapid increase throughout the period, slight slow down in 1977	continuously increasing at same rate as in 1977	increasing in 1981 up to mid-1982, slowly decreasing thereafter very large increase in 1981 and 1982, slight slowing down of the rate of increase in 1983

†Indications refer to annual rates of change except when noted.

same force as in the two previous years. The three games, monetary policy, wage-price-productivity and budget deficit, are still simultaneously dominant. In the former, real interest rates are maintained at a fairly high level to preserve external balance. On the other hand, wage developments in the private sector are still tightly controlled: indexation as of September 1983 has been partially reestablished but its effect on nominal wages is not allowed to exceed the projected increase in nominal wages in the countries of our main competitors. In the event Belgium nominal wage developments exceed those in competing countries, indexation will be suspended again, with a corresponding fall in real wages, other things being equal. Finally, the budget deficit game is crucial again: the 1984 budget proposals are the object of heated debates. It touches two very sensitive questions: wage and pension restraint in the public sector and tax cuts (real or imaginary) for holders of capital incomes (especially financial assets holders). The measures proposed for wages and pensions are justified by the government in terms of budget constraint: the absolute necessity to decrease the deficit by at least 1% of GNP. On the other hand, tax cuts for capital incomes are supposedly aimed at attracting back to Belgium private capital that has escaped from fiscal supervision and is held in foreign countries. In the context of the general policy of income moderation implemented since 1981, it is not surprising that the equity issue has been particular prominent. The general strike of public services (September, 1983) which lasted two weeks shows on the one hand the depth of resistance against further redistribution of income but also the extent of divisions in the labor movement concerning the appropriate strategy to follow: contrary to some hopes, workers in the private sector did not join the public sector in the strike.

In the introduction to the chapter we contrasted the two traditional theoretical approaches to inflation. Neither of them, taken in isolation, seems to offer fully convincing explanations of inflationary and deflationary patterns in Belgium. On the contrary such patterns seem to be the outcome of highly complex interactive schemes involving not only traditional economic processes but also multiple "strategic" interactions among agents using all their experience, learning capacities and power resources to alter in their own interests the outcomes of economic, social and political processes.

This proposition implies epistemologically an important shift in the aim of scientific explanation itself: the aim is not to provide simply for a purely causal *explanation* of inflationary processes based on a stable structure of causal linkages at the economic level and consequently providing a framework for prediction. On the contrary, our approach aims at providing a more global *understanding* of the systemic structure which might allow, under specific conditions, the emergence and continuation of inflationary processes. The predictive capability, in the usual sense, of our framework is limited. However, aside from some very short-run predictions, traditional economic models have not scored very well either. We feel, however, that the framework used in this study might prove itself in the sense of *identifying capabilities* and predicting potentialities in a situation. That is, it enables us to identify the crucial social decision making processes, and the key social agents involved, where their strategic behavior *might* lead to inflationary pressures, or to reduction in the pressures. In terms of such a view, inflation is no longer the result of blind, mechanical forces but of *human collective action.*

NOTES

1. The research reported here has been supported by a grant to Tom R. Burns from the Social Science Research Council (HSFR) in Sweden.
2. Recent developments in the theory of inflation emphasize the importance of inflationary expectations but this simply adds more refinements to the basic approaches and does not constitute by themselves an alternative to them.
3. From this, it should be quite clear that in our point of view, the classical approach where the theory of value determines the relative prices and the distribution of real incomes prior to the determination of money prices and money incomes is not relevant for the study of a capitalist market economy.
4. To find out that such sufficiency conditions would simply be the existence of monetary accomodation would still not render valid the monetarist proposition stated before. To do so would imply that income distribution conflict would *necessarily* involve monetary accomodation if it has to be inflationary.
5. Table 4.2 indicates the relative importance of each in terms of employment.
6. The CPI has undergone several changes during the 1970's. In March 1972 the weight of services was increased from 21.4% to 30%, and that of food reduced from 41.6% to 30%. The underweighting of services might have underrecorded pre-1972 inflation rates by about .3% (OECD, 1974:16).
   The index coverage until 1974 was rather narrow with 32 items for food, 29 for non-food products and 16 for services. Index calculations took simply the arithmetic means for the prices in each of the three categories.
   The new index, valid as of 1976, is based on consumer expenditure patterns of working (blue and white-collar) and non-working households for 1973/74. It includes 358 goods and services (as against 149) and weights are as follows: 25.15% for food, 42.79% for non-food, 27.06% for services and 5% for rent (the last item had not been included in the previous index). The sample is now taken in sales outlets reflecting purchasing habits. Fresh food and vegetable prices were taken out of the index in the months of July and August as of the Summer of 1976.

REFERENCE

OECD Economic Survey, (1974) Belgium/Luxembourg. Paris: OECD.

5

Socio-Political Cleavages: The Illegitimate State and Inflation in Latin America

Tom R. Burns   and   Anders Rudqvist
in collaboration with Tom Baumgartner

Introduction

In this chapter we identify and discuss several major factor complexes which help explain the persistence of high rates of inflation in Latin America. The discussion does not address the various schools of thought — monetarist, structuralist, as well as socio-political approaches — which have been applied to the analysis of Latin American economic performance and inflation. Our more unified framework of analysis specifies important socio-political and cultural factors and their interaction with economic ones. It serves therefore as a point of departure to transcend traditional approaches (at the same time, it is consistent with the type of economic framework outlined recently by Vicente Galbis (1981)).

Among the factor complexes which in our view are closely linked to Latin American inflation are the following:

1) Social struggle over income distribution.

2) Radically uneven socio-economic development which reinforces social cleavages and tensions.

3) The state's inability, due to political and administrative weaknesses, to resolve conflicts and to carry through in a consistent manner stabilization policies.

4) External dependencies, particularly those relating to fluctuating markets, strategic production technologies, and capital.

5) The use of inappropriate stabilization policies and measures, including the resort to the use of force and terror.

134

Inflationary developments are often set off by a decline in the resources available for distribution in a country or region. Also, changes in social power and structures may enable previously weaker elites or even resource poor groups to push for redistribution of income. These two developments can of course be interrelated. Resource decline may sharpen already existing cleavages, increasing the likelihood or intensity of major societal struggles and even types of civil war. Such struggles destroy resources and lower production, or at least reduce its potential rate of growth.

Shifts in power relationships are generally domestic in origin, although in some instances, particularly in Latin America, they may be brought about through foreign intervention (principally the USA). Resource scarcity arises sometimes from domestic causes such as natural catastrophes or, as mentioned above, serious civil struggles. In the case of Latin American countries, resource declines are usually the domestic consequences of external causes: international markets for key exports (agricultural and extractive products) collapse or undergo substantial price swings;[1] strategic imports are blocked or undergo large price increases. Also, increases in the dollar exchange rate effect a Latin American country's balance of payments, causing a decline in available resources through an unfavorable change in the terms of exchange: in addition, the external debt which a country must repay with its available domestic resources is expanded automatically with a devaluation.

The role of internal and external factors in Latin American inflation will be discussed in more detail after a brief outline of the major inflation patterns in Latin America. Our discussion is largely focused on Argentina, Brazil, Chile, Colombia and Mexico, although occasional reference is made to other Latin American countries as well.

2.   Latin American Inflation Patterns

Latin America has exhibited historically high rates of inflation, so much so that Maier (1978) has referred to the phenomenon of 'Latin American inflation' as a category distinct from hyper-inflation (Weimar Germany; Hungary, 1945-49, among others) and 'creeping inflation' (of the OECD variety).

Inflation in Latin America has been high, over 20 % for historically long periods. In Argentina, Brazil and Chile the inflation rate has varied between 20 % and 100 % for the past 30 years with recent peaks approaching 500 % (Argentina in 1976, Chile in 1974). The average inflation rate for 25 Latin American and Carribean countries (excluding Venezuela and Cuba) has for the last 20 years remained consistently much higher than the rate for 88 "less developed" countries as a whole. These in turn have experienced much higher inflation rates than the 24 OECD countries.

Foxley and Whitehead (1980) point out that, since the mid-1960s, the Latin American countries' average inflation rate has accelerated quite markedly: prices slightly more than doubled in the period 1965-70, but more than quadrupled in 1975-79. Even Latin American countries such as Mexico and the Central American countries, which have tended to have relatively stable price patterns earlier, have had high rates of inflation in the 1970s.

Nevertheless, there is considerable variation in Latin American inflation rates (see Appendix). More importantly, different countries appear to have diverse forces initiating or driving inflation (Galbis, 1981; see Chapter 2 for a more theoretical argument).

Domestic and external factors In traditionally inflationary countries, e.g. Brazil, Argentina, and Chile, inflation appears to have its origins to a large extent in domestic factors. This is not to overlook that the international economic environment in the 1970s was more adverse to maintaining stable development policies and prices (see below). Also, in other Latin American countries with traditionally low or moderate inflation rates, e.g. Mexico and Colombia (also Bolivia and Peru), the inflationary burst of the mid- and late 1970s was largely of domestic origin. In the particular case of Mexico it was enabled largely by developments in the world oil market, in reaction to which Mexico became within 10 years one of the world's largest oil exporter.

TABLE 5.1
Aggregate consumer price indices (1975 = 100)

	24 'developed' countries	88 'less developed' countries	Of which 25 in Latin America and the Caribbean	'World' (112)
1960	47.7	14.8	4.2	40.2
1965	54.2	27.2	13.5	48.9
1970	66.5	43.6	29.2	62.3
1975	100.0	100.0	100.0	100.0
1979(I)	135.3	218.4	419.4	146.7

Sourve: IMF Survey (12 November 1979), p. 351; Foxley and Whitehead (1980)
Notes: 'Latin America' excludes Cuba and Venezuela. 'World' excludes the centrally planned economies. National consumer price indices were averaged using geometric means. The weights are based on GDP.

TABLE 5.2
Inflation rates in industrial and developing countries: 1967-77

Group	1967-72 (annual average)	Changes in Consumer Price Index				
		1973	1974	1975	1976	1977
Industrial Countries	4.5	7.5	12.6	10.7	7.7	7.8
Oil-Exporting Countries	8.0	11.3	17.0	19.0	16.2	15.0
Non-Oil Exporting						
Developing Countries	10.1	22.1	33.0	32.9	32.3	31.5
Africa	4.8	9.3	18.6	16.4	18.8	25.0
Asia	5.4	14.9	27.8	11.5	1.5	8.8
Latin America	15.9	30.8	40.9	54.6	62.7	51.6
			(25.0)	(22.0)	(28.0)	(34.0)
Middle East	4.3	12.7	21.8	20.3	17.4	24.2

Sources: International Monetary Fund, Annual Report 1978: International Financial Statistics, Vol. 30 (May 1977) and Vol 31 (April, 1978); Cline (1981).
Note: The figures in parentheses in the Latin American Row exclude Argentina, Chile and Uruguay.

By contrast, a number of typically non-inflationary countries of Central America and the Caribbean, with relatively small, open economies, e.g. Costa Rica, as well as some others such as Venezuela, suffered significant imported inflation in the mid-1970s.

Public sector deficits   In most countries, in particular Argentina, Brazil, Chile and Mexico as well as Bolivia and Costa Rica, public sector deficits have been a major factor in either initiating or transmitting domestic inflationary pressures (Galbis, 1981). The processes generating the deficits vary somewhat from country to country: for example, subsidies in Argentina to non-financial public enterprises and autonomous government agencies; government decisions to invest in and develop the economy or to increase the public sector share of the economy as in the case of Chile under Allende or in Mexico in the 1970s with respect to the oil sector; increase welfare services and/or wages and salaries in the public sector, in each instance with the state unable to raise sufficient taxes or income through other sources to cover the increased expenditures. This last factor should be stressed since public sector expenditures consist largely of salaries and wages. Consequently, if they are indexed, expenditures tend to grow in line with inflation whereas revenues tend to lag behind (Galbis, 1981).

Credit expansion   Credit expansion is often extremely large. It may arise in response to public sector deficits, private sector problems or demands, or even difficulties in the financial sector itself. Large public sector deficits are typically financed through substantial money and credit expansion. On the other hand, in Colombia where public sector deficits have been relatively small in relation to GDP, inflation has sprung mainly from the substantial expansion of credit to the private sector. This was the result of generous, selective credit policies implemented through special central bank funds and state-owned banks, partly under the influence of the government.

In some countries, the credit expansion is linked to rescuing parts of the financial sector. In the case of Colombia, another important factor in its inflationary development in the 1970s was the necessary central bank rescue operation in 1972 of the banking system after the creation of savings and loan associations with indexed deposits (whereas bank deposits remained subject to interest rate ceilings) (Galbis, 1981). Galbis suggests also that a similar problem arose in Chile in 1974-75 when the Central Bank had to support the savings and loan association system, which had collapsed in the early stages of the financial sector reform due to unfavorable legal treatment given to it in relation to the banks and *financieras*.

Substantial expansion of credit in Latin America, either to cover public deficits or to satisfy partially unlimited private demand tends to lead either to further increases in prices or larger current account deficits in balance of payments, or both. Typically, there are one or more vicious circles operating (see Chapter 3):

1) price and wage increases lead to public deficits and also accelerating demand for credit expansion in the private sector (this is particularly the case once inflation is established and social agents adopt "debt strategies", especially with very negative real interest rates, and speculate against further inflation and devaluation). Satisfying the public and private demand for credit and money expansion tends to feed inflation, thus closing the loop.

2) if the share of trade in GDP is large — and the economy relatively open — the substantial expansion of credit and money supply is likely to spill abroad to a greater or lesser extent through deficits in the current account of balance of payments. Growth of imports accelerate in response to the pressures of domestic demand; this can dampen or retard domestic price developments in the short run, as Galbis (1981) suggests and as our own research on European countries indicates.

However, balance of payments will tend to deteriorate because of the growth of imports without necessarily any increase in exports. Indeed, if domestic inflation is greater than the country's major competitors, then export price increases will tend to retard exports and amplify balance of payment deficits. After external debt possibilities have been exhausted, possibly with a balance of payment crisis, central authorities will be forced to devaluate the national currency, activating the devaluation-inflationary spiral.

Of course, import restrictions (e.g. tariffs, quotas, restrictive import licensing regulations) or barriers to capital outflow may be imposed to prevent balance of payment problems. In this case, the substantial credit expansion, including that motivated by large budget deficits, is likely to translate more immediately into increases in domestic prices, through demand-pull. Sustained inflation will sooner or later lead to devaluation.

Wage developments   Wage pressures and struggles are exacerbated by inflation, and the inflationary pressures so characteristic of Latin American countries. At the same time, of course, they contribute to the pressures. In the public sector, growing demands of public sector workers or indexation of public sector wages tend to push up government expenditures and the public deficit. In the more highly inflationary countries, e.g. Argentina and Chile, the public deficits of the early 1970s were at least partly the result of large wage increases affecting simultaneously the public and private sectors (these increases reflected shifts in political power more favorable to the working classes). "Leap-frogging" of wage rates between the public and private sectors, and within the private sector, generate price pressures as well as demand for private domestic debt.

Management approval of, rather than resistance to, increased wage demands is an acceptable strategy under inflationary circumstances, where competitors are also expected to make such accommodations and buyers of goods and services are less price sensitive and, indeed, expect increases. Management can accommodate wage demands by increasing prices, without fear of loss in sales or market shares.

Devaluations Institutionalized exchange rate depreciations have long been part of the economic context of countries such as Argentina, Brazil and Chile with traditionally high rates of inflation. In some cases, fixed exchange rates may be maintained despite moderate to relatively high levels of inflation. This leads to the gradual worsening of the balance-of-trade deficit, the need to borrow increasingly more in international markets, and ultimately the build-up of a balance-of-payments crisis. Anticipation of this sets off a large wage of speculation against the local currency, as in the case of Mexico in 1975-76 and again in 1981-82. (The closeness to and the openness of the border to the USA have certainly contributed here as well as the gradual "dollarization" of parts of the Mexican economy).

The crisis typically ends in a large devaluation, often with attempts to over-correct in order to provide a much needed reversal in trading patterns. This, of course, generates both imported price increases as well as strong pressures for price increases in the domestic sector (in part to divert resources into export activities), at the same time that the crisis and devaluation limit the expansion of production in the import-dependent manufacturing sectors.

Foreign price developments The 1973-75 surge in the inflation rates of all Latin American countries was to a large extent due initially to their simultaneous experience of foreign price developments (Galbis, 1981; Cline, 1981; Cline and Weintraub, 1981).

The prices of imported goods increased by more than the average increases in export prices of their major industrialized trading partners (USA, Japan, and Germany). In all three of these countries there was a noticeable acceleration in the rate of increase of export prices in 1973 and especially in 1974 followed by a relatively high increase (but decelerating) in 1975 (Galbis, 1981; Cline, 1981; Cline and Weintraub, 1981). The large import price increases do not appear to be the direct consequence of oil price increases since the oil import bills of a number of Latin American countries were relatively small in relation to their total import bills. Rather, the key factor appears to have been the large increase of industrial prices. Of course, these increases were caused to some extent by oil price increases and inflationary developments in developed countries.

In those countries such as Argentina, Brazil, Chile, and Mexico suffering very high rates of inflation — several times world rates in the 1970s — domestic factors appear to have had an even greater importance than external factors in generating inflation. In view of complex multiplier and feedback effects, one cannot separate out clearly and precisely the direct effects of import price increases on the level of domestic prices from the price consequences of inflation-generating policy and strategic responses to the initial imported price increases.

In all countries there are complex interlinkages where inflation seems to feed back upon itself through multiple channels — including the enlargement of public sector deficits and deficit financing, the continuation of wage demand pressures, and devaluation. Galbis (1981) points out:

In many developing countries there is a strong feedback from inflation to public sector deficits because public sector expenditures, often consisting largely of salaries and wages, tend to grow in line with inflation, whereas revenues normally tend to lag behind. Inflation also tends to exacerbate the socioeconomic pressures that operate to maintain the income shares of various population groups. Moreover, inflationary expectations may continue to fuel those pressures long after the original underlying inflationary factors have been brought under control. All of these factors will tend to propel the continued excessive expansion of domestic credit and monetary aggregates and to perpetuate inflation.

3. The Roots of Latin American Inflation: A Preliminary Model

The following general model is our point of departure for identifying and analyzing factor complexes which appear to play an important role in inflationary pressures and developments in Latin America (Galbis, 1981; see Chapters 2 and 3). The key inter-related factors are (see Figure 5.1):

1) Social conflicts and struggles over the distribution of income

2) Radically uneven development, in particular the persistent side-by-side of modern and pre-modern sectors, and the social tensions and struggles generated by such development.

3) The political and organizational weaknesses of most Latin American governments. This is in part reflected in very weak legitimacy and the inability of the state to mediate or resolve major societal conflicts. This is in part reflected in budgetary crises which are funded through money and credit expansion. The weaknesses are further reflected in the systematic use

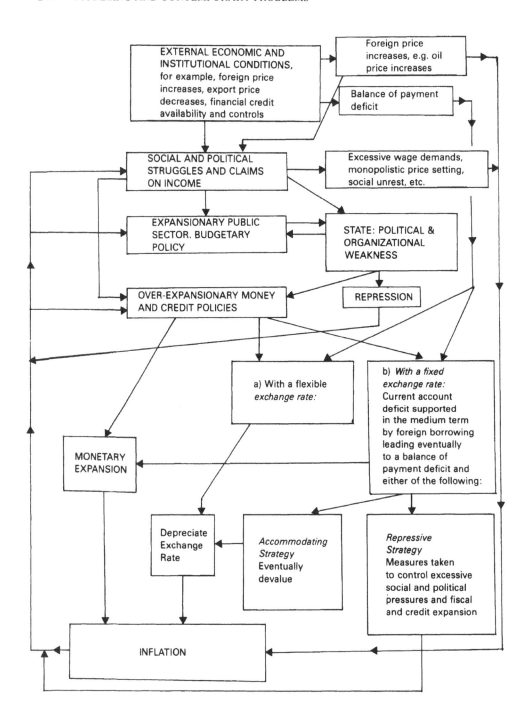

FIGURE 5.1   Socio-political and external factors in monetary expansion and inflation (based in part on Galbis, 1981).

of repression and the inability to carry through consistently stablization policies over an extended period of time. These problems are endemic and both contribute to and result from social struggle and political instability, in particular, the failure of governments having minimal legitimacy and authority to regulate and limit excessive and contradictory claims on national income.

4) The international context and constraints (trade relations and imbalances, socio-political and financial dependencies) which interact with domestic economic and socio-political processes so as to reinforce internal social conflict and inflationary pressures. For instance, external developments are linked to internal cleavages and struggles through the coupling of balance of payment crises and devaluation and internal struggles among groups to gain compensation against the losses which devaluation imposes.[2]

5) Economic policies and stabilization efforts — including frequent, systematic repression of labor movements — as part of the societal struggle; the role of international agents, in particular the IMF and international banks, in domestic economic policies and "stablization measures".

These factor complexes — and their relationships to inflationary pressures and developments — are discussed briefly in the following sections.

Social Conflict and Struggle Over Income Distribution

It is common knowledge that socio-political tensions and struggle are endemic to Latin American countries. That there are connections and interactions between such conflicts and inflation is a major thesis advanced in earlier chapters.

Attempts to realize price, wage, profit and government budget claims beyond the given value of the national product are driving forces in back of most inflation — and are in large part expressions of distribution conflicts among major groups and interests in contemporary societies.

Such conflicts take on particularly extreme forms in Latin American societies. There are deep socio-economic and political cleavages and a lack of national consensus among major societal groups (different capital and business groups, labor groups, landowners, farmers, peasants, government workers, military, etc.) about control over wealth and income distribution as well as about social and economic policies.[3] The cleavages and tensions tend to run horizontally between classes, rather than sectorally with unions and managements in one sector or segment united against those in others.[4]

In the more developed countries of Latin America (Argentina, Brazil, Uruguay as well as Chile), the political power of organized labor (the so-called populist segment composed of the new labor force at work in consumer-good industries and other new urban working groups) has been at times substantial. Labor and its allies made claims for increased income, these pressures culminating in "populist governments": in the 1940s and 50s, the Peron government in Argentina, that of Vargas in Brazil and Jiminez in Venezuela; and in the 1960s and 70s, the Goulart government in Brazil (1962-64) and that of Peron-Campora (1973-76) in Argentina. In a certain sense, the Allende government (1970-73) in Chile might be included here. However, its greater ideological precision and commitment to socio-economic transformation clearly distinguish it from traditional Latin American "populist" governments and parties. At the same time, its income distribution policies and the eventual internal crisis had inflationary consequences (see Appendix).

The labor-friendly governments resulted in serious inflationary problems and in strong political reactions and ultimately repression by rightist groups collaborating with the military. Measures to reduce inflation rates and to stabilize polity and economy entailed the imposition of wage controls and redistribution of income away from working classes. Wages were set by administrative fiat. Labor union activity was largely repressed. Systematic efforts were made to exclude labor from any political influence. Public resources were reallocated with minimum concern about the preferences or needs of any but a narrow cluster of interests at the top of the power structure (Foxley and Whitehead, 1981). Public services important to working class and marginal groups were drastically reduced.

Such repression may be *temporarily* successful in price stabilization as, for example, the post-populist regimes in Chile and Uruguay in the 1970s. However, over the period since such repressive regimes came to power, very little net investment has occurred (with the important exception of Brazil) so that there has been minimal improvement in the underlying productive capacity and growth potential of the economy. For instance, "Chilean growth" under Pinochet has been largely regaining earlier levels of production, after a period of substantial depression and unemployment. Aggregate domestic resources available for saving and productive investment have not risen to a level sufficient for self-sustaining growth.

At the same time, severe monetary constraint sharply reduces aggregate domestic demand and employment. High unemployment contributes further to weak domestic demand and crisis in domestic industries (of course, high interest rates also enter in here, see later discussion). In general, a recessionary vicious spiral is generated and sustained in case after case. Tensions and conflicts relating to income distribution are, therefore, aggravated. Without repression there would be open civil struggle and confrontation (or much more than there has been).

Uneven Domestic Development

The persistence side-by-side of modern and pre-modern segments and the social tensions and struggles generated by such development are characteristic features of most Latin American societies. To the extent that such developments undermine or block social consensus and generate societal tensions and struggle, they will in our view be contributing factors to inflationary pressures.

One important factor here is the introduction of advanced technology (capital intensive, non-labor absorbing) from industralized countries and the rapid development of the modern segment which accelerates internal cleavages and the unequal distribution of income and wealth. The modern production segment in many ways makes gains comparable to standards in developed countries, and leave behind the vast non-commercial segments as well as agricultural and manufacturing sectors characterized by more traditional production technologies.

In the advanced, modern segments, upper and middle class groups (including public employees and organized labor groups) make up what Prebisch (1982) refers to as the "privileged consumer society (*sociedad previlegiada del consumo*), who manage to a greater or lesser extent to maintain income and consumption levels even in periods of economic downturn.

The pre-modern and backward segments are weak economically. They lack resource availability, human capital, organization, and infrastructure. Therefore, they cannot provide or develop quickly a pool of unused capacity to get into the money economy when demand rises (indeed, these segments tend to be suspicious of the economic and political elites and the modern, industrial complex).

Therefore, any growth impetus runs quickly up against resource barriers and cultural and political constraints, because large, marginalized segments are unable to provide the resources required for *sustained* industrial growth. Growth periods, as a result, activate inflationary pressures due to resource shortages.

On the other hand, the relationship between uneven development and inflation is a complex one. The pre-modern and backward segments of many Latin American societies fairly readily absorb people and burdens and are forced to accept real income declines which are advantageous to other groups. To the extent that this occurs, the uneven development serves to some degree, at least in the short run, to dampen inflationary pressures.

At the same time, inflation itself, through its distributional effects, contributes to uneven development. In particular, it reinforces the uneveneness between pre-modern and modern sectors, since the latter typically have institutional and socio-political means to protect to some extent their real monetary income levels, whereas the subsistance and marginal segments lack these means.

The Political and Organizational Weaknesses of the State

There are several specific weaknesses of the Latin American state which are of particular relevance to the study:

- its difficulties or inability to regulate or deal with societal cleavages and tensions except through repression or through accommodating pressures on available real income with monetary credit expansion
- its difficulties or inability to finance its programs and activities.

The Latin American state typically lacks the capability to shape and maintain institutions which would assure consensus   In particular, it is unable to achieve relatively high consensus about the distribution of income between capital and labor, public and private sectors, civilian and military expenditures, distribution among different regions and labor groups, etc. Consensus about the use of profits for investment and development of the country is crucial in this context. "Nationalism" has been an important factor in many if not most economic take-offs and developments and is the basis of a mandate or authority of the state to act in the "general interest". The struggles for power and privilege, which are found in every society, are kept within certain 'rules of the game'. Groups and classes do not try to bring down or undermine the nation-state in order to advance their class or other interests. All major groups value the preservation of national unity above their own self-interest.[5]

In the absence of such commitments and a mandate for governing, the state finds it very difficult to regulate conflicting income claims, and also to organize or facilitate accumulation and social organization for "growth and development processes" (see Chapter 8). The 'political leadership' has essentially two options, which may also be combined in various mixes, for dealing with excessive claims on the social product:

- accommodating the excessive claims with credit and money supply expansion, i.e. resolving conflicts through inflation.[6]
- "disciplining" certain groups, particularly the working classes and other resource weak groups in order to force them to temper or limit their demands.

Both options undermine the authority of the state. Repression does this for obvious reasons. Inflation does this because it tends to reinforce or to contribute to the lack of effective government. "It dissolves the very sense that an effective public authority exists to enforce the same rules on haves and have-nots together. The loss of commonwealth is, I would argue, one of the severest tolls of inflation, but a cost that the usual welfare functions of economists cannot accommodate" (Maier, 1978:41).

The Latin American state experiences frequent financial crisis, that is large public sector deficits, which it tends to resolve through expanding credit and money supply   In countries without basic consensus and norms about the distribution of income, claims tend to exceed the social product and to grow faster than it grows. The claims originate in the various government agencies and the military, service classes, powerful agricultural and manufacturing interests (seeking subsidies; infrastructure investments; access to easy credit, etc.) and powerful organized labor groups.[7] Also, because of high rates of population growth and urbanization, there are exceptionally strong (and ever-mounting) pressures to expand employment and provide urban infrastructure and services. During periods of "political liberalization" or "populist governments", the tendency to accede to these pressures and claims is particularly high. For example, during Allende's "popular government", incomes policies led to increased wage bills in the public sector. At the same time social expenditures for goods and services were expanded. A number of key enterprises were nationalized, with compensation. Many nationalized enterprises operated at a loss. Prices and utility tariffs of public service enterprises were fixed at very low levels. It was impossible, under these circumstances, with a stagnating or declining economy, to make expenditures and revenues to match. The result was substantial deficits, which were financed through money and credit expansion, and which ultimately led to extemely high inflation rates.

On the revenue or income side, there are also serious constraints. The taxation systems tend to be weak and ineffective. Exceptions are made for various groups. Corruption is often rampant. Moreover, the governments often lack the organizational and information resources necessary to control the tax statements and returns of households and enterprises. Enterprises generally have double accounting: one for themselves, another for the state. When faced with the choice between raising its income through "taxation" or through "money creation and inflation", many if not most Latin American governments lean toward the second option.[7] In other words, *the political and organizational difficulties* of raising resources through taxes or through increasing the prices of public services are considerably greater than those involved in expanding money and credit.

Money supply and credit expansion, particularly relating to public sector debt, is an important factor in Latin American inflation. However, it should not be seen as "the cause of inflation", but rather a "proximate source". The decisions and politics around budget deficits and financing of such deficits are much more nearly "causes". *Controlling inflation — and excessive credit and money supply expansion — would require controlling the political, social and economic factors which gave rise to the expansion in the first place.*

In any case, governments have quite limited control over money supply and credit expansion. Galbis (1981) points out that when domestic credit is restricted by central bank policies, domestic borrowers find foreign finance in many instances. Even if policy makers had greater control, the question arises: Would they prevent credit and the money supply from expanding so fast so as to prevent unwanted inflation and balance of payments difficulties?

The answer to this question is suggested by our earlier comments (see also Chapters 2 and 3). Effective measures to halt monetary expansion are often more unpopular and politically destabilizing than inflation and foreign exchange shortages, particularly in countries or in periods within a given country where there is economic stagnation and low capacity to legitimately regulate income claims and conflicts. Cutting back on government spending, reducing subsidies to domestic manufacturing and large-scale agriculture, imposing credit restictions, and so forth, are all measures likely to worsen unemployment or to provoke strong opposition and tensions in societies already characterized by tensions and unemployment. Inflation may cause less social disharmony (and socio-political instability) — at least in the short-run — than its austere alternative, which helps to explain why governments are so reluctant to pursue anti-inflation policies vigorously for more than temporary interludes.

The International Context

The international context and constraints — entailing trade relations and imbalances, socio-political and financial dependencies — are important factors in the performance of Latin American economies and in particular inflationary developments (although there is considerable debate about the degree inflation depends primarily on internal or external factors or their interaction). Of particular interest are the following linkages:

Exports Both volume and prices are highly vulnerable to shocks. Most Latin American countries have exports which consist primarily of minerals or commodities subject to great price oscillation and loss of revenue: cattle and wheat for Argentina; tin, copper for Chile; coffee for Colombia, in part for Brazil; services (tourism) and now oil for Mexico. Shocks based on price or volume fluctuations as well as other external shocks (including oil price shocks) substantially alter income levels. Adjustments to these shocks are not made by reducing proportionately income demands or expectations. Rather, groups struggle intensively to maintain the levels (wages, prices, profits, entitlements, government budgets) which they are accustomed to, but which, in the face of real decline, cannot be maintained in real terms.

During the upward phase of a cycle, there are substantial income increases which often generate or contribute to generating inflationary demand pressures (and consumption of imported goods). These pressures run quickly up against production constraints which are in part due to the marginalization and underdevelopment of large parts of society. In periods of downturn the volume and/or prices of major exports decline. The loss of income spreads through indirect linkages and multiplier effects to other sectors, including the public sector. As pointed out above, actors who would be subject to 'these declines resist accepting them (wage, price, profit, entitlement, and budgetary level drops). The established real claims and entitlements cannot be sustained.

Latin American countries Those which have set out to systematically industrialize have become dependent on advanced technology (among other things, computer, electronic, and nuclear technologies) imported from and serviced by developed countries (see Chapter 11). The technology is very costly and has tended to reinforce both technological and economic dependence on industrialized countries.

Latin American inflation A typical pattern is the vicious circle or spiral linking devaluation to inflation back to devaluation (see Chapter 3). Maier (1978) points out that devaluation triggers new bouts of inflation led by higher import prices. Hence, susceptible economies have oscillated between phases of high employment and growth leading to balance of payments deficits and shortages of foreign capital, and ultimately efforts at stabilization, including currency devaluations which simply renew inflationary pressures.

Latin American dependence A particular aspect is the imposition of monetarist or anti-inflation "solutions" on the countries facing serious debt or balance of payment problems. International banks, and above all the IMF, insist on these measures. It is common knowledge now that Brazil, Argentina, Chile and Mexico have been unable to pay their large external debts — debts accumulated in large part in anticipation of sufficient growth to repay them, sustained growth which never materialized in the late 1970s. As a result, these countries have been forced to accept economic and socio-political measures imposed on them externally, e.g. reduction of public expenditures and wage restraint or reductions. This is possibly one way that the development model based largely on external dependency can be preserved.[8]

In the absence of societal consensus, a political mandate and institutionalized arrangements for effectively resolving conflicts over income distribution — and over the distribution of current burdens and future gains — the state must resort to authoritarian and repressive measures to keep order. This may "work" in the short run, but as suggested earlier, in the long run, opposition and tensions will manifest themselves in political and eventually economic destabilization.

For example, devaluation is often a measure imposed by the IMF in order to achieve "stabilization." Such stabilization is designed to redress balance of payment problems and to secure foreign capital. But devaluation leads typically not only to higher import prices but to efforts of social groups to maintain their income levels and life styles in the face of price increases. They do this by trying to increase, as appropriate in each case, wages, prices, profits, and budgets. Thus, a devaluation tends to generate secondary inflationary pressures which contribute to new balance of payment problems and further devaluations. Given the weak authority of the Latin American state, this spiral can be broken (temporarily) only by denying, *through repression*, certain groups or classes their claims (see Figure 5.1)

Stabilization Policies and Measures

The political and administrative weaknesses of Latin American governments — as suggested above, particularly as these relate to the tasks of regulating conflicting claims on economic resources and to deal with pressures for increased public expenditures and budget deficits — are likely to be reflected in, and also to explain, *the failure of stabilization policy-making and implementation.* Indeed, policy appears in many instances to oscillate between a repressive strategy and the credit expansion-and-inflationary resolution of distributional conflicts. This is not to say that these modes are not combined to varying degrees. They are. For instance, repression is used against certain groups, usually in the labor movement, forcing them to hold back their claims. Other groups, including the military and parts of the state, may be left free to continue to push their claims which are accommodated with excessive credit and monetary expansion.[9]

The vulnerability of Latin American economies to external shocks and their ramifications in their social economies makes policy-making and implementation especially difficult and uncertain in its effects. Above all, stabilization policies and measures, e.g. introduced in conjunction with a repressive regime and/or external demands (from international banking), have not only short-term economic effects, that is the degree to which they reduce inflation or solve related problems such as large budget deficits and negative balance of payments. *They have socio-political and cultural effects, intensifying or settling major societal conflicts, further eroding or building up the state's authority and ability to bring about societal consensus and to stabilize economy and polity.*

In our view, stabilization policies — in particular anti-inflation policies and measures — should also be assessed in terms of their socio-political and longer term consequences for *political stabilization* and the establishment or reinforcement of an *effective system of socio-economic accumulation and distribution.* Obviously, from such a perspective there can arise conflicts between short-term and long-term policy goals.

However, as Thorpe and Whitehead point out (1979:18-19):

Orthodox or monetarist stabilization is a term for the policy approach common to most conservative regimes in Latin America, and strongly backed, if not imposed by the IMF.

... Its underlying philosophy leads it to advocate reductions in state expenditures (rather than increased taxation), while implicit in its policy prescriptions is a belief in the power of the price system, once this has been restored to health ...

... short-term measures predominate in the 'typical package' ... Credit must be restricted, government spending cut, and tax revenue raised, so that the increase in the money supply can be kept within the limits considered to be non-inflationary. Wage and salary restraint is stressed.

Orthodox stabilization policies are not purely a question of technical economic management,or even purely a question of the distribution of material output ... in Latin America they tend to involve the forceful imposition of an entire political and social system, one which has certainly neither been spontaneously chosen nor gradually evolved by the people of the country themselves. *On the contrary* recent experiences have been of orthodox stabilisation policies being imposed by increasingly severe repression against a workforce whose collective forms of self-expression are seen as the principal obstacle to 'sound' economic policies. Further, such policies often also tend to have far-reaching social and political consequences, aggravating the social tensions and deepening the political contradictions which have been at the root of previous upsurges of inflation.

... the long-term effects of the recent wave of orthodox stabilisation policies will have been to sharpen underlying social conflicts, and to render popularly negotiable variants of the existing economic system less viable than ever.

4.   Conclusion

We have tried to suggest that there are a number of identifiable sources of inflationary pressures in open, developing economies, such as those in Latin America. Structural and socio-political conditions a well as domestic and foreign policies impinge to influence the relative importance of these various sources in the different countries and in different time periods. Given that the origins of transmission mechanisms may be diverse in the various countries, the measures and strategies to deal with inflation and socio-economic instability must be formulated accordingly (see related discussion in Chapter 3).

The problem of inflation and stagnation in Latin America is as much, if not more, a political and cultural problem as an economic one. Governments in most cases lack wide support and legitimacy. Groups try to use the state — or when in opposition, to weaken or bring it down — for their own group or class interests. Governments are unable to resolve or mediate issues of income and wealth redistribution through establishing or drawing upon a broad social consensus. There is no widely shared national framework — at least to which major societal groups adhere — with principles of distributive justice, equality, and democracy. Therefore, no state can initiate and implement effectively policies or redistribution, or effectively regulate conflicts over and excessive claims on scarce economic resources. Such weak governments are predisposed to resolve income struggles through inflation and/or repression. These strategies are institutionalized to a large extent in most Latin American countries in patterns of social policy and social action.

One conclusion must be stressed: radical deflation and high unemployment — along with repressive measures to deal with income struggles and political instability — tend to contribute in the long run to socio-economic instability and inflationary pressures. These measures are usually taken without widespread consensus and a generally accepted or normatively based scheme to distribute costs or burdens. As a result, they tend to aggravate conflicts and to reinforce societal dissension. At the same time, lack of general support or legitimacy for their policies compells those governments set on maintaining control to employ repressive measures. However, this undermines any social basis whatsoever for legitimacy and consensus-building.

The economic argument is often made that "populism" is wasteful and inflationary. On the other hand, repression is also "costly". First, resources are aborbed by the repression of politics and of opposition. Secondly, repression tends to lose its effectiveness as a means of social control over the long run, leaving only a legacy of bitterness and "readiness to take action" that adds to instability (Foxley and Whitehead, 1980). Opportunities for mobilization of societal resources and more effective investment in development are lost.

As Pothier (1982) points out about the "miracle of Argentina underdevelopment" and chronically high inflation:

> The unresolved conflict, and the resulting lack of social consensus is a key factor in Argentina economic performance. No simple economic explanation can account for either the economic stagnation ... or the chronic inflation — politics instead deserves much of the blame for arrested growth and surging price increases. At the broadest level, the political conflicts have made it difficult for Argentina to plan its development, apportion economic gain and losses and shape economic changes. At the more concrete level, the conflict is responsible for three features — populism, a rigid interest group structure, and political instability — which are crucial elements in the political economy of Argentina inflation.

Our very preliminary analysis indicates certain policy ideas and future strategies:

1) Resolution of the Latin American social struggle/inflation syndrome requires real socio-economic growth. Such growth will depend in part on opportunities to export and to gain a greater share of the world wealth (however, see discussion in Part Three of the book). This will depend partly on the stimulation and development of internal markets, which can be realized to some extent through more egalitarian income distribution and the development of production capacity to satisfy the expansion of demand.

2) Above all, growth will depend on a minimum level of economic stability. Economic stability depends not only on domestic political stability, but on stabilizing or buffering the economies from external shocks and dependencies such as those discussed on pages 140-141 and 148-150.

3) Domestic political stability requires developing political consensus and more effective government adminstration. The latter would assure better economic conditions for expansion and accumulation through policies and institutions to buffer national or regional economies from external and internal shocks. It would also assure more secure sources of government revenue as an alternative to printing money. Above all, it would provide a basis for carrying out the process of establishing greater consensus and effectively regulating or mediating income distribution conflicts. Ultimately, there will have to be "historic compromises" with relatively clear principles or ground rules and a broad commitment to overall development of society and the general welfare

4) Our analysis strongly suggest that genuine political stabilization (as

opposed to stabilization achieved temporarily through repression and police state methods) should be the first order of business. Until then, there will continue to be socio-economic instability, low or unsustainable socio-economic development, and high inflation rates.

NOTES

1. Increasingly such export products as steel and textiles, for example from Brazil; are subject to quotas or other barriers in developed countries.
2. In some instances, for example when a country manages to obtain major new loans or enjoys an upsurge of income due to commodity price increases, social tensions and inflationary pressures may be dampened.
3. Given a democratic ideology prevailing in much of Latin America, it is not possible for traditionally dominant groups simply to insist on their powers and privileges.
4. However, it seems in many cases that the urban sector (unionized labor, middle class including government employees and governing elites) is generally unanimous in keeping domestic food prices low, thereby turning domestic terms of trade against the agricultural, rural and marginal sectors.
5. Bendix (1978), in referring to Prussia and Germany before World War I, and the Weimar Republic after, notes that 'few people had internalized the 'rules of the game' of democratic politics and without that internalization, a mandate of the people cannot function'.
6. Tobin (1972) notes that inflation lets this struggle proceed and blindly, impartially, impersonally, and above all non-politically scales down all its outcomes. He suggests that there are worse methods of resolving (temporarily) group rivalries and social conflict.
7. (Also, conservative and middle class groups have the power and influence, in general, to block increased direct taxation.)

    Latin American states often tax export trade, precisely because it is easier to collect. Of course, smuggling increases. At the same time, it tends to hurt exports by removing part of the surplus, undermining or removing incentives for export activity, since producers are typically price takers for their goods.

    Also, during periods of falling export prices (e.g. copper for Chile, oil for Mexico), government revenues decline. If expenditures cannot be substantially reduced, which typically they cannot, the budget deficit must expand greatly.
8. Given the cleavages and lack of strong national identity, elite actors are usually available who find these measures acceptable or in their interest. That is, there is no general 'national defiance' to the outside. Rather, relationships 'to the outside' tend to be cooperative or dependence ties combined with opposition and struggle (from leftest national groups) against 'external agents'.

    Unified or clear-cut nationalism or national defiance would allow for greater domestic consensus on distribution of income, including agreement on unequal distribution.
9. Hirschman (1978) argues that much Latin American inflation has 'the function of denying part of what the state, in its weakness and excessive friendliness, has granted ... such a state is far from immune to pressures emanating from its own sub-divisions; with powerful and power-hungry generals heading the spending ministries the allocation of public funds can be less subject to central control than under civilian governments.' This last assertion can be questioned in light of our argument that even civilian governments may lack a broadly based authority and the 'mandate to govern'.

REFERENCES

Cline, W.R., (1981) *World Inflation and the Developing Countries.* Washington, D.C.: The Brookings Institution.

Cline, W.R. and S. Weintraub (eds.) (1981) *Economic Stabilizaton in Developing Countries.* Washington, D.C.: The Brookings Institutions.

Foxley, A. & L. Whitehead (1980) *Economic Stabilization in Latin America: Political Dimensions.* Special Issue. *World Development,* **8:** 823-832.

Galbis, V. (1981) "Effects which Alternative Monetary Policies have had on Inflation and Growth in Latin American Countries." Paper presented at the Fourth Development Banking Round Table, Interamerican Development Bank, March 2-4.

Hirschman, A.O. (1978) "The Social and Political Matrix of Inflation: Elaboration of the Latin American Experience." Washington, D.C.: Brookings Institution Paper.

Maier, C.S. (1978) "The Politics of Inflation in the Twentieth Century." In F. Hirsch & J.H. Goldthorpe (eds), *The Political Economy of Inflation,* Harvard University Press, Cambridge.

Pothier, J.T. (1982) "The Political Causes and Effects of Argentina Inflation." In R. Medley (ed), *The Politics of Inflation: A Comparative Analysis.* New York, Pergamon.

Prebisch, R. (1982) "A Historical Turning Point for the Latin American Periphery." *CEPAL Review* No. 18, December, Santiago, Chile.

Thorpe, R. & L. Whitehead (eds.) (1979) *Inflation and Stabilization in Latin America.* London: Macmillan.

Tobin, J. (1972) "Inflation and Unemployment." *American Economic Review,* **62**: 1-18.

Tumlir, J. (1982). "The Theory of Democratic Development." *Theory and Society,* **11:** 143-164.

Appendix: Growth, Inflation, Credit and Monetary Expansion and Deficits, 1970-1980

ARGENTINA	1970	1971	1972	1973	1974	1975	1976	1977	1978	1979	1980
1. Rate of change of real GDP	2.6	3.7	4.5	6.0	6.8	−2.1	−3.2	5.0	−3.7	12.0	0.6
2. Rate of change of CPI	13.5	34.8	58.4	61.5	23.5	182.8	443.0	176.0	175.0	160.0	101.0
3. Rate of population growth	1.4	1.3	1.3	1.4	1.3	1.3	1.5	1.5	1.3	1.3	1.2
4. a. Rate of unemployment	4.8	5.7	7.4	6.1	4.2	2.4	4.8	3.4	3.9	2.1	
b. Wages (manuf., ΔW)		37.6	45.8	75.8	28.7	171.4	206.5	115.0			
5. Public sector deficit (−) or surplus (+) as percentage of GDP (cent. gov't)	−1.3	−2.9	−3.0	−6.4	−6.9	−12.0	−7.3	−3.2	−2.5	−1.6	
6. Change in domestic credit (% change)	20	40	57.1	90.9	66.6	184	262	211	174	195	110
— to private sector	17.9	45.0	55.1	64.4	59.5	153	305	258	181	229	108
— to public sector	12.5	33.3	58	132	66	218	205	228	174	124	108
7. Rate of change of M_2	21.7	33.2	57.8	108.1	64.8	136.0	360.7	239.2	163.4	186.9	91.6
8. Real interest rates	−4.8	−17.1	−25.8	−27.4	−7.0	−58.2	−64.8	−23.3	−15.4	−15.4	
9. Public sector foreign indebtedness as % of GDP				4.4	5.5	5.2	5.7	6.5	8.9		
10. Foreign debt service as % of export of goods and services				19.3	16.9	26.5	23.0	14.9	13.3		
11. Specific BOP aspects: ratio of meat and grain exports to total (%)	46.8	46.5	50.0	43.4	35.6	37.2	33.4	29.7	24.1	30.1	28.2
12. Balance of payments, current account, deficit (−), surplus (+) as % GDP	−0.6	−1.4	−0.7	2.1	0.3	−3.0	1.5	2.6	4.1		
13. Exchange rate depreciation (+) or appreciation (−) in % with respect to US dollar	14.3	25.0	—	—	—	1118	350.7	117.7	67.9	61.3	39.5

BRAZIL	1970	1971	1972	1973	1974	1975	1976	1977	1978	1979	1980
1. Rate of change of real GDP	9.5	11.3	10.4	11.4	9.6	4.2	9.6	5.5	4.8	6.7	7.9
2. Rate of change of CPI	18.7	21.3	16.1	15.6	35.4	29.3	42	44	39	53	83
3. Rate of population growth	2.7	2.9	2.8	2.8	2.8	2.8	2.8	2.8	2.8	2.8	(3.7)
4. a. Rate of unemployment b. Wages (manuf., ΔW)											
5. Public sector deficit (−) or surplus (+) as percentage of GDP (cent. gov't)	−0.35	−0.24	−0.14	0.06	0.52	0.008	0.025	0.04	0.13	0.04	0.02
6. Change in domestic credit (% change)	n.a.	n.a.	52.3	51.1	51.2	58.1	64.4	55.7	50.5	75.6	75.0
— to private sector	n.a.	n.a.	48.2	48.3	60.0	60.3	61.2	52.4	46.1	68.6	74.0
— to public sector	n.a.	n.a.	111.4	78.3	−17.0	23.3	128.5	99.5	15.4	290	74.1
7. Rate of change of M_2 (money and quasi-money)	28.0	19.4	43.0	46.2	33.6	40.3	37.0	43.5	49.5	70.0	62.8
8. Real interest rates	1.3	−1.3	3.9	2.4	−17.4	−11.3	−14.0	−14.0	−6.0	−18.0	−45.0
9. Public sector foreign indebtedness as % of GDP											
10. Foreign debt service as % of export of goods and services											
11. Specific BOP aspects: ratio of coffee, soybeans, total (%)	44.5	38.5	38.0	41.2	29.3	35.5	48.8	44.1	35.5	31.9	31.4
12. Balance of payments, current account, deficit (−), surplus (+) as % GDP	−1.8	−3.1	−2.0	2.2	−7.0	−5.8	−3.9	−3.2	−3.3	−4.0	−5.4
13. Exchange rate depreciation (+) or appreciation (−) in % with respect to US dollar	12.7	15.1	12.2	3.2	10.8	19.7	31.3	32.5	27.8	49.1	95.6

CHILE	1970	1971	1972	1973	1974	1975	1976	1977	1978	1979	1980
1. Rate of change of real GDP	8.7	7.5	—	-3.7	6.0	-11.2	3.5	9.9	8.2	8.3	6.5
2. Rate of change of CPI	33.3	19.0	77.3	354.5	504.5	374.7	212	92	40	33	35
3. Rate of population growth	1.8	1.8	1.9	1.7	1.9	1.7	2.0	1.9	1.9	1.8	1.6
4. a. Rate of unemployment	7.1	5.4	3.8	4.6	9.6	16.3	16.7	13.2			
b. Wages (1975=100)	.4	.6	1.0	2.9	21.5	100	353.8	909.1	1,452	2,145	3,151
5. Public sector deficit (−) or surplus (+) as percentage of GDP (cent. gov't)	-2.1	-8.5	-12.1	-9.5	-7.4	-0.9	1.2	—	-0.4	4.8	5.5
6. Change in domestic credit (% change)	n.a.	116	159	619	452	413	153	131	85.2	47.2	50.9
— to private sector	n.a.	40	91.6	287	550	427	327	279	130	75.6	88.8
— to public sector	n.a.	170	190	717	438	411	122	80.6	9.0	4.7	-44.1
7. Rate of change of M_2	54.5	100.0	147.1	472.6	338	256.6	165.8	130.1	90.8	67.6	57.2
8. Real interest rates	-22.7	-13.4	-41.9	-77.3	-64.0	-1.5	-4.5	0.9	16.4	11.3	
9. Public sector foreign indebtedness as % of GDP				27.1	30.5	31.3	27.8	24.4	28.3		
10. Foreign debt service as % of export of goods and services			12.1	12.1	12.1	29.2	33.1	33.4	37.6		
11. Specific BOP aspects: ratio of copper exports to total (%)	67.3	70.3	73.8	83.3	66.7	53.6	59.9	54.2	49.9	47.8	45.6
12. Balance of payments, current account, deficit (−), surplus (+) as % GDP	-0.8	-2.8	-4.6	-2.7	-1.6	-4.8	1.2	-2.7	-4.9	-6.4	-7.2
13. Exchange rate depreciation (+) or appreciation (−) in % with respect to US dollar	20.0	33.3	56.3	1340	419.4	354.5	104.9	60.5	21.4	17.7	4.7

COLOMBIA	1970	1971	1972	1973	1974	1975	1976	1977	1978	1979	1980
1. Rate of change of real GDP	6.7	5.8	7.8	7.1	6.0	3.8	4.6	4.9	8.9	5.1	4.2
2. Rate of change of CPI	6.8	9.0	14.3	22.8	24.4	25.7	20	33	18	25	27
3. Rate of population growth	2.8	2.7	2.8	3.3	2.8	2.5	2.3	2.2	2.3	2.8	(4.4)
4. a. Rate of unemployment (large cities, unadj.)	10.0	11.2	10.0	10.0	10.4	12.5	11.6	8.2	9.9	9.5	10.9
b. Wages (manuf., ΔW)			9.0	13.8	18.9	23.2	24.0	25.7	29.2		
5. Public sector deficit (−) or surplus (+) as percentage of GDP (cent. gov't)	−1.2	−2.2	−2.1	−1.1	−0.8	−0.2	0.9	0.8	0.7		
6. Change in domestic credit (% change)	n.a.	n.a.	n.a.	n.a.	n.a.	26.6	23.9	27.5	25.7	17.9	47.4
— to private sector	n.a.	n.a.	n.a.	n.a.	n.a.	26.0	25.6	28.9	29.1	27.7	49.2
— to public sector	n.a.	n.a.	n.a.	n.a.	n.a.	26.2	8.0	16.9	−9.0	−111	−318
7. Rate of change of M_2	16.7	13.2	29.2	34.7	25.4	23.2	34.0	33.8	26.4		
8. Real interest rates	−2.5	−4.5	−6.2	−11.4	−12.4	−10.7	−2.9	−12.0	−2.6	−8.6	
9. Public sector foreign indebtedness as % of GDP				20.1	18.9	18.6	17.4	17.1	15.5		
10. Foreign debt service as % of export of goods and services				13.8	16.6	12.6	10.8	9.3	10.5		
11. Specific BOP aspects: ratio of copper exports to total (%)	63.4	57.9	49.7	83.3	66.7	53.6	59.9	54.2	49.9	47.8	
12. Balance of payments, current account, deficit (−), surplus (+) as % GDP	−4.1	−5.8	−2.2	−0.5	−2.9	−0.5	1.4	2.7	0.7		
13. Exchange rate depreciation (+) or appreciation (−) in % with respect to US dollar	6.9	9.5	9.0	8.8	15.3	15.3	10.2	4.5	7.6	7.3	

MEXICO	1970	1971	1972	1973	1974	1975	1976	1977	1978	1979	1980
1. Rate of change of real GDP	6.9	3.4	7.3	7.6	5.9	4.2	4.2	3.4	8.3	9.2	8.3
2. Rate of change of CPI	5.2	5.4	5.0	12.0	23.7	15.0	15.8	29.1	17.3	18.2	26.4
3. Rate of population growth	3.6	3.5	3.5	3.5	3.5	3.5	3.6	3.6	3.6	3.6	3.6
4. a. Rate of unemployment b. Wages (1975=100)	72.0	73.4	80.8	89.0	95.5	100.0	102.7	106.3	116.9	128.9	139.7
5. Public sector deficit (−) or surplus (+) as percentage of GDP (cent. gov't)	−1.5	−1.1	−3.3	−4.4	−4.1	−4.3	−5.1	−3.7	3.3	−3.3	−3.1
6. Change in domestic credit (% change)	16.4	13.5	16.3	18.3	24.9	27.2	37.7	35.0	23.5	31.4	35.7
— to private sector	18.2	14.6	13.6	14.3	18.9	23.8	38.0	−23.3	39.4	35.1	41.3
— to central gov't	10.9	10.1	25.3	30.0	40.4	34.6	37.1	67.2	13.2	31.5	30.6
7. Rate of change of M_2	10.0	7.7	17.6	26.3	20.9	17.9	48.1	24.0	24.6	(36.1)	(36.7))
8. Real interest rates	−0.4	−0.6	−0.2	−6.7	−15.5	−9.1	−9.8	−19.1	−11.0	−11.4	
9. Public sector foreign indebtedness as % of GDP				12.0	15.7	19.7	24.7	28.7	30.0		
10. Foreign debt service as % of export of goods and services				26.4	19.0	26.9	30.8	43.2	73.8		
11. Specific BOP aspects: ratio of copper exports to total (%)	2.7	2.1	1.3	1.1	4.1	15.8	15.7	22.8	30.5	43.6	63.1
12. Balance of payments, current account, deficit (−), surplus (+) as % GDP	−3.3	−2.4	−2.3	−2.9	−5.3	−6.8	−5.2	−2.5	−3.3	−3.5	−5.3
13. Exchange rate depreciation (+) or appreciation (−) in % with respect to US dollar	—	—	—	—	—	—	59.6	14.0	−0.1	0.3	2.0

Sources: IMF, *International Financial Statistics*, ILO, *Year Book of Labour Statistics* Galbis (1981).

Note to Appendix

The annual inflation rates and other statistics reported for Latin American countries should be read with great reservations, and certainly do not warrant very precise comparative analyses and conclusions. For instance, inflation indices suffer from the general statistical weaknesses common to Third World countries, including most countries in Latin America. Moreover, countries such as those in Latin America — rent by economic and social cleavages — have great difficulties and probably weak incentives to maintain detailed and correct inflation indices. The technical difficulties are formidable in any case. How can a common price index by constructed that reflects the consumption pattern of, for example in Brazil, the drought-stricken, marginal peasant in the Northeast, the Hacienda owner in the Matto Grosso, the urban rich in Copacabana, the marginales in the Rio favelas, or the car workers in Sao Paulo factories. Secondly, it is known that the Brazilian government has manipulated the index in the past — an index that is based anyway largely or only on price developments in urban areas — in order to limit wage pressures under the indexation system. Thirdly, one may ask to what extent a government acting on behalf of elite interests and relying on an inept administrative apparatus is capable of, or has an interest in, establishing a price index that can be called honest, exact, and indicative of the inflation effects on the "average" member of suppressed or exploited classes.

The fact that the statistics largely come from the IMF does not significantly change the situation. The IMF neither has the resources nor the mandate to construct its own "true" price indices for its member or client nations. Nor can it question zealously the statistics presented to it by a particular government during evaluation procedures. It is known that a large part of the time of missions is spent in delicate negotiations where the IMF and the government (or different parts of the government) try to agree on a common, acceptable set of statistics. The end result is inevitable a negotiated compromise between some 'economic reality' (as seen from Washington, D.C. and the capital of the country), domestic pride, and political expediency.

PART II

Institutional Innovation and Alternative Societal Development: Studies in Economic Democracy

6

Conflict Resolution and Conflict Development: The Workers Take Over at the Lip Factory

Thomas Baumgartner   Tom R. Burns
Philippe DeVille

This chapter utilizes the theory of Actor-System Dynamics to develop a specific framework for the description and analysis of dynamic patterns of social conflict.[1] Of particular interest are the transformation processes which generate a sequence of interaction situations or "game phases".[2] Indeed, in our view, the point of departure for any general approach to social conflict should be the recognition of (1) the transformation potentialities and tendencies of social action and (2) the interdependence between, on the one hand, social interaction processes and events and, on the other, the material, social structural, and cultural context in which they occur. Three central features of the framework presented in the paper are: the notion of the transformation of social interaction situations or games; a multi-level approach with which to describe and analyze game transformation processes, in particular, patterns of conflict resolution and conflict development; and consideration of the role of social structural and cultural context in affecting the course of a conflict, especially in bringing about conflict resolution or conflict development in concrete interaction or game settings.

Interaction conditions and rules — in general, the institutional order — may be viewed as the macroscopic resultant of multiple, often contradictory "structuring" processes, including social action (Baumgartner, Buckley, Burns and Schuster, 1976; Baumgartner, Burns and DeVille, 1977).[3] Structuring processes and conditions determine the long-term incentives, opportunities, and constraints within which action and interaction take place. That is, they provide context for and structure "process-level" conditions and activities[4] including, among other things, the definition of relevant issues and problems, membership or participation in institutional activities, permissible or acceptable activities, relationships of actors or categories of actors to one another and to forms of property or resources, and the distribution of benefits and costs for different actors or categories of actors involved in process-level activities.

Part 1 outlines the multi-level theoretical framework. The emphasis here will be on actors' interactions on the structural level — the meta-level exchanges, conflicts, and negotiations — operating to settle process-level conflicts or to bring about conflict development. Conflict resolution and conflict development processes are identified as higher or meta-level operations altering or transforming one or more components of interaction or game conditions and structure. Part 2 presents a case study, the Lip factory conflict, illustrating our approach to the description and analysis of social conflict dynamics.

1. Conflict, Conflict Resolution, and Conflict Development

Individual and collective actors in society belong to different social group-ings and classes and play different social roles. As a result of different goal orientations, action opportunities (i.e., powers), and life experiences in these roles — or in preparation for them — they develop and become iden-tified with differing ideological frameworks. These are structured in the context of variations in their social positions and social activities. The dif-ferentiation in ideological frameworks and action capabilties of actors or classes of actors leads to incompatibilities or conflicts in: (1) their goals and preference structures, (2) their viewpoints on action possibilities and deci-sion strategies, and (3) their conceptions of appropriate arrangements for social action in particular institutional areas and for the identification and resolution of conflicts in these areas. Such conflicts manifest themselves in social patterns (e.g., class conflicts). These reflect the institutional speciali-zation and the different roles various actors and groups play in the organi-zation of, and decision-making processes in, society.

For the purposes of conflict analysis in this paper we define in section 1 below social conflict and two levels on which actors may come into conflict with one another. Section 2 provides a general discussion of structural pro-cesses which are involved in conflict resolution and conflict development. Specific resolution and development patterns are examined in Section 3, while Section 4 points out several factors which make one pattern more likely than the other. In Section 5 we offer a brief discussion of certain out-comes of conflict processes.

1. Process-level and Structural Conflicts

Conflict arises when actors engaged in a situation have incompatible viewpoints, beliefs, goals or preferences with respect to conditions in that situation. For instance, states of the world or options of high rank in the eyes of actor A are of low rank in the eyes of actor B and vice versa. Table 6.1 abstractly represents situations where A and B's preferences or evaluations regarding options a_i and a_j contradict one another, in that the realization of A's preferences or goals is perceived to exclude or prevent the realization of B's preferences or goals under the given interaction conditions (Baumgartner, Burns, DeVille, and Meeker, 1975).[5]

Our multi-level framework distinguishes conflict on the process-level from conflict on structural levels. *Process-level conflict* occurs when the actors have contradictory goals, preferences, or beliefs about specific conditions, outcomes, decisions, or activties within a *given social structural or institutional context.* Management-labor opposition, e.g., about wages or working conditions, taking place within a particular collective bargaining system, is an example of such an issue conflict. In the case of *structural conflicts* the actors disagree about the conditions under which or the ways in which they are to relate to one another and interact. Such opposition is manifested, for instance, in disagreements about the institutional conditions and rules on the basis of which the actors are to identify and settle process-level conflicts. In management-labor relations the opposition may pivot on issues relating to the rights to decide on employment levels, investment policies and principles governing the distribution of income; issues concerning procedures and rules of collective bargaining institutions defining or upholding particular social relationships among the actors; or generally issues about the nature of actors' social relations.

Clearly, one may have process-level conflict without disagreement concerning the structural framework in which that conflict is embedded and possibly resolved. But structural conflicts about interaction conditions often *emerge* from conflicts over specific issues on the process-level. *Such*

TABLE 6.1
Conflicting Evaluations of Options

		Evaluation of options from actor A's perspective:	Evaluation of options from actor B's perspective:
		Ranking 1	Ranking 2
Options	a_i	high (+)	low (−)
	a_j	low (−)	high (+)

conflict "escalation" is most likely to occur when the actors are unable to resolve specific issue conflicts in mutually acceptable ways within the existing institutional framework, or when, during the course of an issue conflict, the actors become aware of other differences separating them, thus increasing the frequency or dimensionality of process-level conflicts. Such developments undermine trust in and willingess to rely on the existing institutional framework to settle conflict. It may also contribute toward making the actors aware of objective structural conflict conditions which then become issues.

It is important to note in this context that the participants at different levels often vary. *Whereas a process-level issue conflict in a limited context may remain a two-actor game, a structural conflict is more likely to became a three, four, or multi-actor game, out of which emerges an institutional order reflecting the interests of the different actors involved, rather than simply the interests weighted by the relative power of the original actors.* For instance, in the case of a labor-management dispute which concerns structural issues, the state, as well as national labor leaders, managers and owners other than those directly involved, and political parties are likely to become interested and try to influence the outcome. (One of the implications is that conflict resolution methods working effectively at the process-level with a single two-actor conflict may prove ineffective or counterproductive in multi-actor structural conflict.)

In addition to the distinction between process-level and structural conflicts, one distinguishes substantive issue or content conflicts from conflicts about the form or structure of negotiation and collective decision-making arrangements. The following table distinguishes between issue conflicts on different levels and conflicts about the negotiation or game framework within which substantive issue conflicts are to be taken up and resolved.

The interrelated social conditions to which (1,2), (2,1) and (2,2) in Table 6.2 refer make up a social structural order in relation to substantive process-level issues and events. This order provides the systemic context for the maintenance and reproduction of social relationships in process-level activities and at the same time derives coherence from these social relations (see Conclusion).

In real life, conflicts at the process and structural levels are interrelated, often in non-transparent or confusing ways to the participants. Or, if transparent to some, they may try to manipulate the conflict level or to negotiate and exchange settlements between different conflict levels in order to assume long-term structural advantages, possibly at the expense of short-term gains. For instance, one actor in a conflict persuades his or her opponent to accept a gain at the substantive process-level in return for giving up structure-level claims. Thus, management in a labor dispute may succeed in

TABLE 6.2
The Focus and Level of Conflict

| | | Focus of Conflict | |
		Substantive Issues	Game Conditions and Rules
Level of Conflict	Process level	(1.1) conflict about an issue, .e.g., about wages, working conditions, etc.	(1.2) conflict about the game conditions and rules, e.g., the form of collective bargaining, to deal with (1.1) issues.
	Structure level	(2.1) conflict about the unequal powers or rights, e.g., between capitalists and workers to determine the work environment.	(2.2) conflict about game conditions, rules, and procedures to negotiate and deal with issues of the type (2.1) and (1.2), e.g., conflict about whether (2.1) type conflicts should be dealt with and resolved within the "constitution" of a capitalist society or whether a constitutional change or revolution is called for.

"pacifying" a structure-level conflict with labor by making a generous wage settlement (p. 182).

Social conflict — viewed as social action — is social interaction where each actor in a conflict relationship attempts to carry out his or her own will over the opposition or resistance of others (Weber). (Conflictive action capabilities, mutual awareness, and intentionality are characteristic features of social conflict as social action.) That is, *such conflict occurs whenever actors involved in a concrete setting try to implement or realize incompatible goals or preferences with respect to particular conditions, interaction patterns, or outcomes in the face of one another's opposition.* For instance, the actors try to mobilize resources to expand their options at the expense of one another, to interfere with or limit one another's action opportunities, cr, through negative sanctions, to change one another's preference structures.

Here we distinguish social conflict on the process-level from structural conflict. At the process-level it is defined and takes place *within a given* institutional or social structural framework. For example, managers and workers struggle with one another over wage or employment issues according to the rules and patterns of a given collective bargaining system. Social conflict at a structural level occurs where, for instance, management and labor struggle with one another: about substantive decision-making rights or power in an enterprise (e.g., over employment or investment policies); or about the general nature of the relationship between the actors (2,1); or about procedures and rules for negotiating and settling either substantive issue conflicts (1,2), or structure-level conflicts (2,2) (see Table 6.2).

2. Structuring Processes

The resolution and development of substantive issue conflicts by means of game transformations take place through structural level processes and activities. These transformations may be carried out purposefully by the actors involved. Frequently, however, they lie outside of the complete control of the actors involved in process-level interactions; they may depend on external agents or impersonal forces, or on the unintended consequences of their own actions. We shall focus in this paper *on situations where actors have opportunities and act to transform interaction conditions.*[6] The emphasis will be on actors' interactions on structural levels — the meta-level exchanges, conflicts, and negotiations — operating to settle conflicts or to bring about conflict development. Their structure-level policies and activities change one or more components making up the interaction or game conditions:

— the rules of the game, conceptions and assumptions defining the situation, the type of game the actors are to play, the relevant issues and problems.

— the aggregate action and interaction possibilities available to the actors: for instance, the rights, perquisites, and, in general, the action opportunities of different actors or categories of actor in relation to one another and to forms of property or resources; the possibilities for certain actors or categories of actors to communicate, combine and cooperate, or to segregate and complete or conflict.

— the likely payoffs associated with particular action and interaction patterns in specific situations.

— the actors' orientations toward one another, their perceptual models and evaluative bases in the situation: for instance, the presence of distrust or a particularistic self-interest ideology or of trust and a cooperative ideology in interaction settings.

The interaction conditions and rules predispose actors to interact with, and to expect from one another, a certain range of behavior. Thus, the imposition of property concepts and assumptions, e.g., in a capitalist framework, assures a certain distribution of rights and resources and, therefore, action capabilities among the actors in relation to one another (see Part 2). On the one hand, those actors given access to and control over strategic resources have greater action opportunities including those of generating or developing new options and structuring interaction conditions favorable to themselves. On the other hand, the relatively powerless actors are constrained to engage in activities and interactions and to accept payoffs and positions of dependency which they could prevent or would be likely to reject if they were in relatively more powerful positions.

Similarly, procedural rules — e.g., collective bargaining and decision-making procedures — create conditions where some actors are favored with respect to, and others more or less excluded from, certain issues and decision-making processes. Such rules may provide particular actors with the advantage of initiative. For instance, they give them chronological priority to make up the agenda or more favorable chances to build alliances and coalitions or to erode those of potential and actual opponents. (This point is well illustrated by different constitutional rules and practical models of parliamentary activity.)

The power to manipulate or to transform interaction conditions, and in general the institutional framework of social action, is referred to as *meta-power* (Burns *et al.*, 1985; Baumgartner, Buckley, Burns and Schuster 1976). This may be distinguished from power exercised *within* a given institutional order.[7] The exercise of meta-power entails the manipulation or change of interaction conditions, the matrix of rules, distribution of resources, and cultural orientations. These conditions, among other things, institutionally define the power of actors to exercise behavior control with respect to one another. Clearly, although an actor may have social power within an interaction framework or game (e.g., greater ability than others to realize his will or to select a preferred outcome over the opposition of others within that institutional context), he or she may or may not have the meta-power to manipulate or change the distribution of resources, the rules governing interactions among the actors involved, or to alter the "type of game" they play.

3. Conflict Resolution and Conflict Development Patterns

We are interested in process-level conflicts where one or more actors find the available or likely outcomes and options unacceptable. In general, a subset of the actors involved fails to realize — or, at least, anticipates, failure to realize — their interests or goals (these may include one another's goals to a greater or lesser extent). Specifically, *conflict solutions acceptable to the various actors involved do not appear possible within the existing game conditions or institutional framework.* Under such circumstances, the actors are expected to explore, individually or collectively, possibilities of trying to transform one or more components making up interaction conditions.

Two patterns of transformation are of interest here:

—One where the actors, possibly as a result of the initiative of one of those involved or of a third party, *cooperate in restructuring the game in order to resolve conflicts.*

—The other where the actors (possibly with the participation of outsiders) *try to structure or restructure game conditions in opposing ways,* each trying to increase his or her chances of gaining (or avoiding losses) at the expense of others in the situation.

Below we discuss specific properties of conflict resolution and conflict development patterns, and certain of the meta-processes through which conflicts are resolved and developed.

Conflict Resolution   The resolution of conflict occurs when the actors involved agree on (1) the structure of the game, including its dimensionality and (2) an acceptable solution within that framework, possibly entailing compromises to conflicts. The outcome of such a process is conflict settlement (at least in a given time frame of analysis). *Conflict resolution processes are identifiable as meta-level operations altering or transforming one or more components of game or interaction conditions* (p. 170). Two major types of restructuring are considered below for illustrative purposes: transformation of perceptions and evaluations and transformation of options (Baumgartner, Burns, DeVille and Meeker, 1975; Braybrooke, 1976; Burns *et al,* 1985; Burns and Meeker, 1976a, 1976b).

Transformation of Perceptions and Evaluations

1) Issue conflicts may be settled through *re-perception or re-conceptualization of options and relationships between options and their outcomes, or by perceiving new outcomes of existing interaction patterns.* In this type of settlement, the actors become convinced of a particular conceptualization of the interaction situation or action/outcome linkages to the effect that mutually satisfactory options, for instance, a compromise option, is perceived as best (see p. 173). Group ideology and social influence processes (e.g., those carried out through social relationships, especially authority relations) are of central importance in such conflict settlement processes. They can serve to structure and to coordinate individuals' perceptions and evaluations (or the cognitive models and value criteria underlying them) so as to bring into collective focus a specific option, e.g., a compromise solution.

2) Conflicts may be settled through re-evaluation of options, that is, *the transformation of preference structures.* New evaluations come into play in

several ways (in each case higher order or meta-strategies are utilized to achieve the desired resolution): (1) the actors consider additional dimensions of the problem or introduce new issues in such a way that the resulting complex of evaluations points to one option as best overall for the actors (of course, as we shall see later, the process may go in the opposite direction); (2) they linearly order the rankings R_1 and R_2, thereby permitting them to lexicographically order outcomes and resolving the conflict between a_i and a_j in Table 6.1 — for instance, R_1 is ranked over R_2 and hence a_i is preferred to a_j, possibly favoring actor A over B; (3) they use a weighting scheme with respect to rankings 1 and 2 with scales for rankings introduced so that a common utility scale is obtained, and conflicts are settled by finding the option with the highest value in such an evaluation system; (4) if no ranking or underlying dimension is of overriding importance or if a common scale is not easily determined or considered appropriate (e.g., for quantitative-qualitative or qualitative-qualitative attribute pairs), the actors may develop a compromise ranking in which intermediate elements for each ranking are judged preferable to those highly ranked on either attribute or dimension (see discussion in the following section).

3) Preference structures may be transformed through selective sanctions or incentives which alter the outcomes of acts and thereby restructure actors' preference orderings in such a way as to increase the likelihood of them agreeing on a specific option, e.g., a compromise solution.

Transformation of Options[8]

Decision-making as commonly viewed, entails *removing* options, because they are irrelevant, unrealizable, or have unacceptable consequences, or because they are inferior to other available options. *The discovery or development of new options is an equally important part of any collective or individual decision-making process.* Of special interest in this context are options with outcomes that settle a conflict or that make strategies of conflict settlement easier to apply.

Examples of the transformation of options are provided below.

1) A new option a_k is developed or discovered, which *transcends* the conflicting options a_i and a_j, for example, combining the chief attractions of a_i and a_j (see Table 6.3).

Such a solution requires that the dimensions underlying rankings R_1 and R_2 in Table 6.3 are either independent or positively interdependent. If such is the case, an optimal solution exists, and the problem is to find it.

2) A *compromise* option is formulated or developed, for example, with maxmin properties. a_k' may combine advantages of a_i and a_j, but is ranked

TABLE 6.3
Transcendant Solution to Conflict

Rankings of Options from A's and B's Perspectives			
R_1	R_2		
Options	a_k	1	1
	a_i	2	3
	a_j	3	2

lower in this respect by each actor. However, the option avoids, at least to some degree, the disadvantages of the options a_i and a_j for actors B and A respectively (see Table 6.4).

In case 1, an option better than either of the conflicting options is discovered or creatively developed. In a word, the immediate issue conflict is transcended. It may be impossible under the given conditions to generate or develop such multi-criteria, dominant options, if the dimensions underlying preference structures R_1 and R_2 are constrained by exogenous factors to be negativly interdependent or correlated. Hence, the compromise solution, a'_k of case 2 may be the best option (e.g., in the maxmin sense).[9] Acceptance of such an option often requires persuading the actors to restructure their preferences, as discussed above.

In sum, actors may settle conflicts by discovering or developing additional options, a meta-process expanding action sets. Conflicts are also settled through a combination of the transformation of options and the transformation of the evaluation basis (Braybrooke, 1976). For instance, a new option with dimensions absent in the other options under consideration is generated at the same time that goals and evaluations related to these dimensions are activated or introduced. This occurs in such a way as to make the option preferred collectively (see (1) in sub-section Transformations of Perception and Evaluations).

Structural Conflict and Conflict Development An institutional framework for structuring social action and, above all, for identifying and settling conflict typically presupposes (1) a certain agreement or acceptance of it on the part of those involved and (2) a certain minimum of mutual trust and readiness to cooperate in institutionalized activities.[10] A conflict process may erode the institutional order or make it into an issue.

Here we are interested in processes where the perceptions, especially evaluations, and action possibilities and predispositions of those involved in a concrete setting are transformed so as to develop or amplify a conflict. The development or amplification of concern here is where (1) there occurs increasing mutual distrust and antagonism and/or growing awareness of objective structural conflict conditions, and (2) this results in the actors trying to transform one or more components of the interaction conditions or the institutional order in opposing ways.

Corresponding to our discussion of conflict resolution, we discuss briefly the transformation of perceptions and evaluations and the transformation of options in conflict development patterns. The developments discussed typically occur in interrelated patterns and are separated here only for analytical purposes.

A. Transformation of Perceptions and Evaluations

In the course of a conflict process actors may re-perceive and re-evaluate the situation in such a way as to develop the conflict. For instance, they become increasingly aware of other differences separating them, above all differences which erode their commitment to or acceptance of a given institutional framework within which to negotiate and settle conflicts. Ultimately, this can result in the actors' perceiving their conflicts as unresolvable within that framework, and refusing to negotiate and interact (at least in any genuine manner) within that framework.

1) In a conflict process, the actors come to increasingly distrust one another. That is, they perceive one another as more and more likely to act in a purely self-interested or hostile manner, above all in seeking to manipulate or transform game conditions to self-advantage. Such a process may emerge as a result of actors' considering either additional dimensions of the options as a result or entirely new matters. Evaluations of these converge with or reinforce existing contradictive evaluations so that what may have been a single-issue conflict becomes a multi-issue conflict.

2) Actors in established or emergent hostile relationships are typically inclined to place a positive value on outcomes which are believed to be least valued by one another. Thus, even where there is no objective basis for additional issue conflicts, to the extent the hostile relations are activated or relevant, the actors would be predisposed to generate or create such

TABLE 6.4
Compromise Solution to Conflict

Rankings of Options from A's and B's Perspectives			
R_1	R_2		
	a_i	1	3
Options	a_k	2	2
	a_j	3	1

multiple issue conflicts in the concrete interaction settings in which they find themselves involved.

The developments referred to above in (1) and (2) often lead actors to re-perceive and re-evaluate the situation as an increasingly threatening conflict, and these very transformations contribute to erosion of conflict settlement institutions and to the spiraling tendencies characteristic of many conflicts (see Part 2).

3) In the course of substantive issue conflict(s), the actors become aware of structural conditions which emerge as points of contention between them. Such awareness may develop as a result of an issue conflict appearing unresolvable within an existing institutional arrangement. Through their communications, decisions, or other activities with regard to transforming interaction conditions, *they become conscious of their incompatible viewpoints on appropriate new arrangements for social interaction and for the identification and resolution of conflicts* (see Part 2).

B. Transformation of Options

In the case of conflict development, each actor tries independently to transform action possibilities in the game so as to gain a more favorable outcome for himself or to improve his chances of gaining in the situation. These efforts are oriented toward either (i) developing or gaining new action opportunities, allies, or control over new resources, which can be used against others and/or (ii) reducing or interfering with the action opportunities of others, cutting them off from material or human resources such as allies, or bringing about a redistribution of resources in his own favor (which of course would affect differentially their action possibilities vis-á-vis one another). Such independent and non-cooperative efforts to transform the action possibilities vis-á-vis one another restructure the game. This transformation is not in the direction of a conflict settlement mutually acceptable to those involved but toward widening the scope of the conflict and developing it further, e.g., through the development of action capabilities which enable the actors to more effectively deceive, outwit, or subdue one another (see related discussion below).

4. Factors Affecting Conflict Process Patterns

In general, the dynamic patterns of a conflict process depend on its social structural and normative context, including the social relations among the actors involved (these may themselves undergo change during the course of a conflict). Several of the principal factors which make one dynamic pattern more likely than the other are (Coleman, 1957; Burns *et al.*, 1985;

Deutsch, 1973; Kriesberg, 1973; Simmel, 1964):

— The type of social relations the actors have or develop, in particular, the extent to which they have solidary relations, the number and strength of cooperative linkages, etc.

— The normative and value context to a conflict, specifically, the extent to which the actors share a common vision or image of the appropriate institutional framework within which conflicts are to be settled.

— The social matrix in which the actors' social relations are imbedded, for instance, cross-cutting identifications, common allegiances and memberships, and above all, the likelihood of effective third party intervention and the imposition of normative guidelines.

We discuss briefly aspects of each of these interrelated factors which are most relevant to the theoretical formulations in this paper.

Social Relations

The social relationships among actors play a major role in their collective responses to an issue or conflict situation, *since such relations represent a potentiality or predisposition of the actors to interact in certain patterned ways.*[11] Above all, they affect the likelihood of conflict settlement or conflict development.

Cooperation in game transformations, enabling achievement of mutually satisfactory outcomes, is more likely to occur under conditions where the actors have solidary social relationships — such as those of close kinship, friendship, comradeship, or certain coordinating role relationships. These typically entail a *social interaction potentiality and normative context, which the actors to a greater or lesser extent may take as a given and can activate for purposes of conflict settlement.* The more solidary the relationships among them (as indicated by "mutual attraction," "mutual orientation and consideration," "community spirit," etc.), the more the actors would be inclined to expect mutual consideration from one another, to try to take one another's goals and preferences into account, and to seek mutually satisfying outcomes, other things being equal. In particular, they would be predisposed to cooperate in transforming interaction or game conditions compatible with their social relationships (see Conclusion). Such a readiness manifests itself concretely in the search for or development of options synthesizing their incompatible preferences in the situation or other conflict resolution strategies.

The communication and problem-solving processes involved in developing new, mutually satisfying options are easier to carry out and are likely to be more effective among actors who have solidary social relations, other things being equal. Reciprocally, *the more successful the coordination, the more positive and solidary the mutual or collective orientations of the actors tend to be, and the more likely they are to place high value on their solidary relations, and the social potentialities which these represent. Such reciprocal feedback spirals underlie the development and reproduction of many co-operative social relationships.*

The transformation of games to achieve a mutually satisfactory settlement of conflicts typically requires a certain minimum level of undistorted communication and possibilities of coordination in creative problem-solving, e.g., in restructuring game options. Alienative or hostile social relationships (in which actors are self-oriented or antagonistic) define a context of distrust in which actors are less likely than in the case of those involved in solidary relationships to expect effective cooperation. Because they expect indifferent or negative attitudes and behavior from one another, the incentive of each to behave in a generous or cooperative manner vis-á-vis one another is substantially reduced.

The social relational concepts, expectations, and behavioral predispositions of actors with alienative or hostile relations are incompatible or incongruent with expressions of a readiness to cooperate in game transformations and to jointly achieve conflict settlements. The model of their relationship implies that their interactions are likely to entail the "win/lose" syndrome; "solutions" to conflict can best, or possibly only, be achieved by means of superior power, deception, or cleverness (Deutsch, 1973: 359). *The transformation of options will then be characterized by attempts to achieve greater intelligence, deceptiveness and power vis-á-vis one another. Such activity tends to expand the scope of the conflict from immediate issues to conflict related to game conditions and strutural conflicts generally.*

We pointed out earlier that selective sanctions may serve to transform preferences so as to settle conflicts. Conflicting actors in alienative or antagonistic social relations typically carry out or threaten to carry out sanctions against one another in order to restructure one another's preferences in the situation. This process is characterized by two distinct patterns: 1) Because of the alienative nature of their social relations, the actors tend to be limited to trying to force one another to give in or to compromise by means of increasing the costs or risks of a refusal to accept one another's demands or preferences in the situation. 2) At the same time, each tries to convince the other that the sanctions of the other will not deter or compel him or her to give in or compromise, *since expressions of such willingness generally imply a restructuring of the game favorable to the opponent.* This combination of trying to influence one another through negative sanctions and to deny the effectiveness of one another's sanctions leads often to an escalation of such sanctions. In this way, game transformation strategies designed to bring about a "winning solution" can lock the actors into a spiraling conflict.

Alienative or antagonistic relationships fail generally to provide the necessary social capabilities for effective joint game transformation and conflict settlement. But failure to achieve mutually acceptable solutions as well as continuation of interaction patterns such as described above reinforce the alienation or hostile relationships.[12] *Such vicious circles underlie the reproduction of the relationships* (as discussed in section 5).

Ideological and Value Context

Conflicts may be distinguished in terms of their value context (which, of course, will reflect the social relations of the actors). Actors find themselves in agreement or in opposition to one another on grounds other than those underlying an immediate issue, although these evaluations may not initially manifest themselves or become activated in the conflict situation. Thus, actors often *experience* their opposition over a specific matter in the context of their agreement on other important matters, for instance, a normative model of suitable institutional arrangements, or the value of their solidary relationships and cooperative predispositions. In our earlier discussion of conflict resolution processes, the opposition of the actors in a concrete setting was assumed to occur in the context of agreement on major questions.

Of special importance, as we suggested earlier, is the extent to which the actors share, or come to share a common cultural or ideological perspective on appropriate game or more generally social structural conditions. Consensus in this respect — for instance, concerning appropriate power and status relationships, norms of equity and reciprocity, the use of persuasion rather than force to settle disputes, open communication and mutual respect, etc. — increases the likelihood that the actors will be able to reach agreement on transforming games and find mutually satisfactory solutions to their conflicts, other things being equal.

Conversely, actors may find themselves in disagreement about minor issues — or even in agreement about them — *in the context of disagreement about strategic structural conditions.* Nonetheless, they might be able to establish and maintain compatible preference patterns with respect to these minor issues and could cooperate to the extent that the more important issues, e.g., structural ones, dividing them *are kept out of the context.* The instability of this situation is apparent: either the major issues dividing them come into play through a conflict development process or, given their preoccupation with these, they would *inject* them into the interaction situation and into their evaluations and decisions in the situation.[13]

Third-Party Intervention

A third party may intervene to transform or to facilitate transforming game conditions, so as to either resolve or develop a conflict. The choice the third party makes in this regard depends on its interests and value structure in the setting. Also, he or she may intervene favoring one side at one conflict level and the other at a different level (see related discussion on pp. 168, 182-184). Thus, the state, in settling or regulating management-labor conflict, often supports workers about substantive issues at the same time that it acts to maintain the capitalist institutional order (see section 5 and Part 2). The analysis of the interests of third parties in intervening in a conflict is important, particuarly in complex multi-level conflicts, but such considerations would take us beyond the scope of this Chapter.

The greater the hostility or distrust among the conflicting parties, the more likely a mutually acceptable settlement of a conflict requires development of formal contractual norms and institutions by means of third-party intervention and regulation (Thibaut and Faucheux, 1965).[14] The conflict settlement role may be institutionalized as in many industrial societies where the state intervenes in and regulates labor-management disputes through the use of mediation, arbitration, as well as other strategies (see Chapter 6 of Burns *et al.* (1985)). For instance, the third party settles or regulates a conflict (1) by influencing actors' perceptions and evaluations through persuasion and control of communication and information flows; (2) by helping in the discovery or development of new options; or (3) by establishing and maintaining an institutional framework and rules on the basis of which the actors are to carry out conflict settlement activities themselves.

In general, a third party can serve as a channel of communication and a creative source of settlement options acceptable to the conflicting parties. By removing the onus of "willingness to cooperate and compromise" from actors in antagonistic or alienative social relationships, a third party may be able to break the vicious circle of mutual vehemence and distrust characteristic of such social relations (Simmel, 1964, p. 147; see discussion on pages 183-184).

Even with the intervention of a third party — certainly one with strictly limited restructuring powers — one or both of the protagonists may refuse to engage in productive communication or coordination efforts mediated by the third element. Often this is because such cooperation is seen as imcompatible with — and likely to change — the character of the relationship, to which one or both is seriously committed or bound by psychological and sociological constraints (see Footnote 12).

Third-party intervention may also be for purposes of creating or maintaining conflictive interaction conditions (Burns *et al.*, 1985). This would entail structuring the aggregate action and interaction possibilities of those involved in the situation, e.g., restricting the oportunities of actors to associate or communicate or to use collective decision procedures (as opposed to individual ones); or structuring the gains and losses associated with particular interactions to promote conflict or competition, e.g., the creation of payoff structures such as "zero-sum" or "prisoners' dilemma;" or it may entail promoting distrust among the actors or an individualistic self-interest ideology.

As we shall see in Part 2, state intervention in the Lip factory conflict operated both to create conditions conducive to the settlement of certain conflicts (between management and the established labor unions) and to create or exacerbate others (between the labor unions and the "counter-institution" of the workers, the Action Committee).

5. *Conflict Process Outcomes*

Conflict resolution efforts may result in the settlement of a conflict. The actors succeed in jointly transforming the game — possibly with the assistance of third-party intervention so as to achieve mutually acceptable outcomes.

Conflict development can also lead to conflict settlement. 1) In the course of the conflict development, there is a redistribution of meta-power so that a subset of actors sharing more or less a common vision of an appropriate institutional order is able to impose such an order. Within such an order solutions favorable to the dominant actors are realized (Baumgartner, Burns and DeVille, 1977). 2) Actors or events external to the conflict process contribute to game transformation so as to realize conflict settlement. For instance, a third party intervenes to establish a framework within which conflict settlements are possible — not necessarily to the equal satisfaction of all the participants; or external threat or intervention restructures perceptions and goals of the conflicting parties so that they settle or, at least, suspend the conflict for the time being. 3) Unacceptably high costs of continuation of the conflict lead to the transformation of outcomes and preference structures. Conflict settlement seems preferable to the continuation or further development of the conflict.

In the context of this Chapter we cannot systematically explore the various ways in which conflicts are settled or continued without settlement. And there remains the far more subtle question of outcomes which appear as conflict "termination" but where, for instance, conflict resolution has merely succeeded in deferring or displacing the conflict. To suggest the direction of such analyses, we discuss briefly the reproduction or maintenance of conflict through conflict resolution, on the one hand, and through conflict development (where no apparent settlement is achieved), on the other.

Reproduction of Structural Sources of Conflict Through Settlement of Issue-Conflicts

The settlement or regulation of specific process-level conflicts is often accomplished without dealing substantially with — and indeed possibly obfuscating — the underlying or ultimate source of conflicts. Here we have in mind contradictions linked to the structure of the system itself: institutionalized differences in power, function, and outlook, e.g., between management and labor or between developed and less developed countries (Galtung, 1964, 1971). In the case of management-labor conflict, the basic structural issue of differential control over resources and the unequal power of actors to realize their goals and values is displaced to specific issues of wages, working conditions, employment, etc. by virtue of legal and government structuring and regulation of "bargaining conditions and processes." Such institutionalized conflict settlement mechanisms often work to the disadvantage of those in subordinate positions who wish to substantially change their structural conditions but, in order to do so, are compelled to engage in what is *defined institutionally as disruptive or illegal conflict* (see Part 2 discussion).

Opposition of subordinates to their subordinate status cannot be resolved effectively by a compromise (p. 173) entailing "better treatment" or the promise by their superiors to stop misusing or abusing their power. But this is precisely a strategy dominant actors often utilize in offering what is graced with the normatively compelling label, "a compromise solution." In this way they try to maintain the essential structural arrangement. As Rapoport suggests (1974: 236):

Once the structure of the system becomes the real issue, offers of this sort will be seen as attempts to preserve the structure and will be rejected as long as the revolt can be sustained.

They (such structural conflicts) touch upon the very existence of the challenged institutions, not on the way they function. From the point of view of an abolitionist (whatever the institution he seeks to destroy) "improvements" only make matters worse because they render the offending institution more acceptable to some. There are, then, conflicts where refusal to settle by compromise is not always an "unreasonable" position, because the impossibility of compromise is inherent in the very nature of the conflict.

Conflict resolution addressed primarily to substantive issues and only secondarily to social structural issues plays an important role in the reproduction of structural sources of conflict or contradictions underlying many issue conflicts in society (DeVille and Burns, 1977). Resolution of such contradictions in any fundamental sense requires bringing about transformation of the social system *as a system*: an entire system of rules, resource distributions, social structural arrangements and related ideological frameworks becomes the point of contention. This typically entails far-reaching conflict development.

Reproduction of Social Conflict Systems

In the absence of a redistribution of meta-power resources, third-party intervention, or external threat, conflict development may lead to an *institutionalized social conflict system*. Such a system, as suggested earlier (pp. 177-179), *is characterized by minimal conflict settlement capabilities and the reproduction of conflict interactions through self-reinforcing multi-level processes*:

1) Communication and the exchange of information is obstructed. The use of secrecy and deceit are characteristic of the interactions between alienated or hostile actors. Indeed, the random or "mixed" strategy of game theory is precisely a device to keep an opponent from obtaining certain behavioral information.

2) Because the actors are inclined to deceive and take advantage of one another, mutual distrust is a characteristic feature of such relationships. Uncertainty in conflict situations — and the general problem of obtaining hard and fast information — tend to reinforce distrust. Trustfulness, in any case, is a risky orientation in such a context. Correspondingly, there is reliance on *established* expectations, orientations, and patterns of action — a social relational model to interpret and guide social action vis-á-vis one another.

Due to their reliance on such a social relational model vis-á-vis one another — even in circumstances where it may to a greater or lesser extent be invalid — the actors are likely to distrust peaceful overtures or expressions from one another of a willingness to cooperate. Any good faith in back of such overtures would appear highly ambiguous in view of the nature of their established social relations. Moreover, because of their expectations of negative attitudes and behavior from one another, the incentives to behave honestly in a generous or cooperative manner vis-á-vis one another is reduced substantially, thus limiting their capability, or the likely success, of jointly transforming interaction conditions (and their social relationship).

3) Involvement in social conflict relationships brings about the creation of new goals and values and the development and reproduction of conflictive action capabilities and related social and organizational preparations.

For instance, persons within conflict groups are intentionally or fortuitously socialized in assuming belligerent goals and attitudes toward their opponents ("the enemy"). Behavioral and technical preparations are made, entailing the acquisition of knowledge, skills, and "weaponry" essential to the performance of conflict acts in relation to one another. (In the case of modern societies in international affairs this also entails the establishment of organizations and networks of organizations for such purposes — the "defense establishment"). The internalized orientations and values, the conflict preparations and capabilities, and the social structures established for conflict action within the collectives reinforce the hostile orientations and predispositions. Such developments confirm in a permanent, highly structured manner the beliefs of each about the bellicose intentions and capabilities of the other.

4) Possession of "weaponry" and substantial capacity to do harm strengthen the patterns described above, for they introduce greater risks into the situation (Andreski, 1968: 9-10). Consequently, hostile communications or other negative actions are typically given exaggerated interpretations. When both actors respond according to such distorted assessments, the spiraling or escalation tendencies often characteristic of conflict processes are observable (see related discussion on pp. 177-179).[15]

5) *The properties of conflictive social relationships outlined above involve "feedback loops" to the effect that A's negative attitudes and behavioral predispositions reinforce and reproduce similar attitudes and predispositions in B and vice versa.*

In sum, the orientations and expectations of the actors in relation to one another make the joint transformation of games and settlement of conflict more problematic. Continuation of conflictive interaction patterns — or their likelihood — contribute to the reproduction and development of mutual antagonisms and predispositions to engage in conflictive behavior in relation to one another. The vicious circle operating to reproduce and develop social conflict systems is thus completed. Herein lies the social inertia and difficulties in transforming developed conflict relationships into more cooperative ones.

Although they may wish otherwise, the possiblities of the actors achieving mutually satisfying structural transformations and conflict resolutions are strictly limited, at least through any *internal* effort and development of their own (our earlier discussion on third-party intervention is, of course, relevant). Because of the likelihood of conflict development leading to an institutionalized social conflict system in which cognitive, evaluative, and interaction processes contribute to the reproduction of the system, the costs and resources required to restructure or transform the system typically multiply over time. A point in this development may be reached where the necessary resources for transformation and conflict resolution are apparently not readily available (we have in mind the development of the conflicts in Northern Ireland, Cyprus, and Lebanon).

2. The Lip Factory Conflict

Lip is the most disturbing social conflict ... because the continued social production after a robbery, in essence, of the stockholders, calls into question the principle of authority, of property, of responsibility, of respect for contracts vis-á-vis suppliers and subcontractors, which are at the very base of our economic system and commerical law.

Chamber of Commerce, Paris, 1974

The story of the Lip factory conflict in Besançon (France) is an interesting historical example of those dynamic processes at work in conflict situations that may lead to either conflict development or conflict resolution.[16] In our discussion of the Lip conflict, emphasis is placed on identifying and explaining the sequence of phases which characterize the conflict. To each phase corresponds a certain state of the conflict and certain processes which tend to transform the situation and to lead to a new phase (Kriesberg, 1973). Section 1 describes the background conditions of the Lip factory conflict. The various stages of the conflict will be discussed in the next section "The Phases of the Conflict."

1. The Historical Background[17]

According to French standards, the Lip factory had been and still was in 1973 a relatively large enterprise. Rather prosperous for a long time because of the recognized quality of its watches, its production was initially based on the craftsmanship of highly skilled workers. The internal hierarchy structure was minimal. The factor was controlled by successive generations of Lips, typically dominating but also highly paternalistic bosses. In 1960 Fred Lip opened a new plant, progressively increasing mechanization in watch production and adding two new sections, machine tools and precision mechanisms for weaponry. During that same period, increased structuring of the hierarchy and trade union activity took place.

In 1973 there were 1320 employees in the factory; 300 of them were unskilled workers, working on assembly lines, 391 were operatives, and 175 were clerical employees. In addition, there were no less than 339 foremen and surveillance personnel, 66 technical engineers and 12 division supervisors and corporate executives (Loureau, 1974: 19). Half of the total personnel and almost all of the unskilled assembly line workers were women. More than half of the employees were members of trade unions, which is about average for this type of factory in France. The two main French trade unions — the Communist C.G.T. and the Christian-Socialist C.F.D.T. — were both represented by their own locals, the latter having slightly more members than the former.[18]

By 1965 it was already clear that Lip was doing badly. Poor advertising and inadequate marketing, high product differentiation and large inventories had led to low profitability. More fundamentally, the Lip management failed to realize and respond to decisive changes on the world market: competition had increased because of the introduction of much cheaper watches produced through completely automated production processes in the U.S. and Japan. But at the same time, due to increased trade union activities, the Lip workers, in the midst of the 1968 general strike, won pay raises, a cost of living escalator and other fringe benefits, especially a pension fund. Faced with increasing financial difficulties, Fred Lip was forced to sell shares of his business to a Swiss watch trust, Ebauches. In 1971 when the Swiss group owned 43 per cent of the shares, and had a majority on the Board of Directors, Fred Lip sold out completely.

So far the story is a classical one: inability of an old family enterprise and its management to adjust or to adapt to basic changes both in production technology and related market conditions. Financial difficulties led to a change in ownership. Such a change, by modifying the power relations between management (presumably becoming stronger) and the workers (presumably weaker) then creates new conditions more conducive to the imposition on the workers of a reorganization scheme and technological changes that the previous management was unable either to conceive of or to implement. It is precisely at this point that the systemic conditions for a structural conflict to actually emerge or to manifest itself are satisfied (see pp. 175-176): (1) a mutually acceptable solution to an issue conflict does not appear possible *within* the existing social arrangement and (2) actors try to transform the situation at one another's expense, thus exposing or activating incompatible or contradictory visions of appropriate social structural arrangements and problem-solving strategies.

2. The Phases of the Conflict

Phase 1: A Traditional Labor-Management Conflict
The strategy of the new management, to be expected under the circumstances, was:

— Increased "rationalization" of the production of watches. In becoming an assembly plant of parts already manufactured in Switzerland, the Lip factory was to become an integral element of a large international venture.

— Related to this was the objective of eliminating the weaponry and machine tools division. These divisions were no longer fitting into the international division of labor centered around the production of watches, as envisioned by the new management.

These objectives were never disclosed explicitly to the workers, not even within the factory council.[19]

The implementation of such a strategy was to be gradual. Starting in 1971, the new management attempted to make a limited number of layoffs. But it was met with strong resistance on the part of the workers, forcing management to back down. The almost complete lack of information about the real intentions of management created considerable anxiety among all workers, each of them uncertain about her or his own future. This was a decisive factor in contributing to cohesion of the workers and successful mobilization of them by the unions in opposing the proposed lay-offs.

The first stage of the conflict is thus characterized by the simplicity of its structure: a single dimension — the employment issue. The strategies utilized by each party were the normal ones: exercise of managerial power legitimized by ownership rights of the Swiss group. Opposed to this power was the collective strength of the trade union locals. At this stage, no solution could be found. The fact that no solution satisfactory to both management and labor was achieved and that the outcome of phase one was perceived by the workers as a victory over management indicates: (1) the social relationship between the major actors had become and was likely to continue to be increasingly antagonistic; and (2) each of the major actors was likely to engage in separate efforts to transform the game to its own advantage under the influence of its perception of how the first stage had ended:

— On the managerial side, they would attempt to broaden as much as possible the prerogatives that are attached to their property rights.

— The workers would adopt meta-strategies appearing to offer the most success in increasing the unity of their movement and hence their collective power.

Phase 2: Workers' Control

In April 1973 the Swiss group asked its own director at Lip to resign and filed a bankruptcy report in court, which designated two provisional managers (Herman, 1974: 19). The two provisional administrators immediately stated that they could not guarantee either the employment of all personnel or the continuation of the enterprise as a whole. In response to this threat, the Lip workers reacted in three ways: setting up their own internal organization, challenging management's control of the production process, and extending the conflict beyond the walls of the factory. First, instead of relying solely on the existing trade unions, they formed an "Action Committee" with representatives from both unions and from non-unionized rank-and-file workers.[20] Secondly, following previous examples set by Italian workers, they organized production slowdowns, partial work stoppages designed to force the new management into discussion without having to go on strike and leave the factory. Finally, in an effort to over-come the artificial separation of the "place of work" and "place to live," they involved the population of Besançon by organizing support meetings in the city.[21] Similar meetings were also held in Paris, in Switzerland, and, later in the conflict, all over France. Still, no favorable decisions were forth-coming. Worse, in early June the company claimed effective bankruptcy and stated that wages and vacation pay would not be paid. On June 12, the Lip workers confined the two administrators and several supervisors in their offices (*Le Monde*, 1974a). Their major request was to be informed of management's plans. They quickly found the answer in the company's files: management planned to lay-off 500 workers (almost 40 percent of total employment) and, as we indicated earlier, the dismantling of the machine tool and weaponry divisions, and a transformation of the watch production division. The Lip factory would become essentially an assembly plant with most of the principal components of the watches manufactured in Switzer-land. A General Assembly of all the workers convened and voted to con-ceal the entire stock of watches "as guarantee of continued employment" and, later, to occupy the factory "to safeguard our tools."

In the second phase, the structure of the conflict has become increas-ingly complex. The rules of the game in the previous phase were those of a management-labor bargaining system. The primary issue was employment to be negotiated within the existing enterprise. These rules were modified now in two ways:

1.Shifts to meta-level strategies. The Lip ownership, first by filing a bank-ruptcy report, then by claiming effective bankruptcy, shifted from the pure management-labor bargaining setting to the judicial level. The owners were willing to actually accept a partial transfer of their power to the judicial system. Indeed, reliance on such a judicial process had two obvious advan-tages for them. First, it guaranteed that, within legal limits, the full exercise of their property rights would be protected by the judicial system. Second, if required by the situation, the state would be forced to support manage-ment in its efforts to achieve its objectives.

On the workers' side, the recourse to higher-level strategies took an opposing form: it was to use their collective strength to ignore or reject capitalist legality. Their first step into illegality (as defined by the capitalist

system) was to contest the owners' *legal* appropriation of the means of production by the workers' *real* appropriation of them (to use Bettelheim's terminology 1970: 137-138) To achieve this, the workers had to bring about
an institutional transformation.[22] Creation of the Action Committee — i.e.,
no longer exclusive reliance on the trade unions — and the important role
given to the General Assembly of workers were not only ways of attracting
non-unionized rank-and-file workers but also of diffusing responsibilities
— or, more precisely, enhancing collective responsibilities — of all the
workers for "illegal" activity.[23]

2. Complexification.   The conflict no longer had a single uni-dimensional
structure. Although the employment issue remained very much at the core,
the entire question of ownership and control — in particular, the crucial
issue of the relationship between owners' property rights and the workers'
right to information — came to be at stake. The strategy used by the
workers points up their perception that the distribution of power between
management and themselves depended crucially on their control both over
valuables (inventories, equipment, tools, etc.) and intangibles (information,
public and political support, etc.). It is for these reasons, that in order to
guarantee their employment, they had decided to "control by seizure" (but
not to claim ownership of) their tools, the factory, and the products of their
past labor which they felt had been "invested" in the enterprise. For this
reason, we have characterized this phase as being that of "workers' control".

The increased complexity of the conflict between phases one and two
entails a conflict development process. There are three reasons for this: (1)
The meta-strategies of management and workers to transform the game
were directly opposed to one another in a symmetric way. The managerial
use of judicial and legal processes was directly countered by the take-over
of the factory and the inventory appropriation, in other words, by the
workers' rejection of the norms imposed by the legal system. (2) The shift
from a single issue to a more complex set of issues did not lead to a more
likely compromise solution, since it did not improve the "trade-off structure of the game." The new issue of control and appropriation emerged
from and now came to dominate the initial one of employment. (3) Failure
to achieve any solution (or even the development of a useful trade-off
structure), the extension of the conflict to more fundamental issues, and the
almost total lack of communication between the conflicting parties amplified their antagonism (see pp. 177-179).

Phase 3: Self-Government

On June 18, the General Assembly of workers decided to resume production of watches but at a low rate (eight hundred a day instead of the
usual five thousand). Further, they decided to pay wages from the sale of
these watches and those confiscated earlier. The workers subsequently paid
themselves five times on a monthly basis.[24] To implement these decisions,
seven standing committees were created: Production, Sales, Finance,
Security, Public Relations, Food and Day Care, and Welcoming-of-
Visitors. These committees were open to all workers and reported to the
General Assembly which met regularly every day. Membership in these
committees rotated, with each worker taking a turn on each commission.
Work on the production line was organized in such a way that everyone
had a chance to participate in discussions.

An important qualitative shift occurred between Phase II and Phase III,
and it is important to note its precise nature. The decisions to resume production and to sell watches were made in order to meet the workers' financial needs and to allow them *to continue the struggle in complete independence from both the trade unions and the state, and, by so doing, to preserve
the unity of the workers and the integrity of the Lip movement.*[25] But at the
same time that they resumed production under their own management, a
typical slogan at Lip was "We want to have a boss." Self-management was
viewed as a spontaneous action required by the logic of the political
struggle and *not as an end in itself* (Martinet, 1974: 162). For example, the
sale of watches became not only important as a fund-raising activity but as
a means of legitimizing their action socially (if not legally), of gaining
public support and outside help, and of disseminating information about
the conflict throughout the country. It is essential to realize certain implications of the organizational structure (Figure 6.1) adopted by the Lip workers as well. Although the two trade unions and the Action Committee were
involved all along in the conflict, the question of representation had not
been raised thus far: the unity of the workers was realized in the General
Assembly despite the institutional segmentation between unionized and
non-unionized workers and, among unionized workers, between the two
locals. In particular, the Action Committee refused to legitimize itself as an
organization (institution) by refusing to be a representative body. As one of
its members put it: "The Action Committees does not exist by itself, it does
not have any structures. ... The Action Committee — it is us, it is everybody." (Anonymous, 1974: 19).

In early August 1973, the conflict intensified further and became even
more complex. On August 14, two months after the workers' takeover,
3000 riot police broke into the plant during the night and evicted the 50

TRADE UNION LOCALS

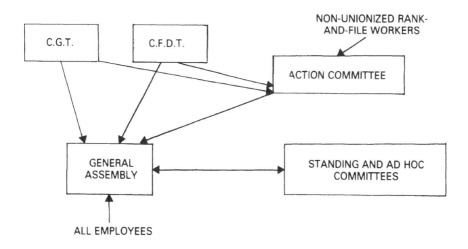

FIGURE 6.1   Self-government organization of the workers.

workers on guard! However, key parts of machines had been removed before the arrival of the police. The Lip workers declared, "The factory is where the workers are." Clandestine workships were established and production continued. But at the same time, while the government began to take an active part in the conflict by using the police, *it also initiated negotiations with the trade union representatives.* These talks culminated at the end of August with the "Plan Giraud,"[26] which proposed a lay-off of 160 workers, suppression of the machine tool division (where the unions were particularly strong), and elimination of most of the social benefits acquired by the workers since 1968 (Anonymous, 1974: 19). On October 12, in a secret ballot the General Assembly of the Lip workers rejected the Plan with 627 votes against and 176 votes in favor, and asked for a reopening of the negotiations.

The third phase of the conflict represents both the culmination of the conflict development process and the starting point of conflict settlement. On the workers' side, the strategy of control led to self-government, not only in terms of self-managing the factory but also, as a related consequence, in terms of maximizing their control over the cohesion of what had become their own movement and thus over the systemic conditions of the conflict. The reliance of management on the judicial process forced the government to intervene. Although the latter's use of brutal repression was only partly successful in disorganizing the workers, its ability to impose on the trade union organizations a *framework for negotiation* — even if this

proved unsuccessful in finding a rapid solution to the conflict — was nevertheless highly *successful as a divisive strategy, ultimately restructuring relationships within the workers' movement.*

The impact of the Giraud plan on the movement was recognized.
Though it entailed at least a theoretical guarantee of employment for most
of the workers, the plan was perceived by many workers as a subtle attempt
to divide the movement and to ensure, by dismantling the enterprise, that
such a movement would not emerge again. Developments confirmed these
initial perceptions: the fragile unity between the two unions broke down,
the C.G.T. urging the workers to adopt the plan and accusing the C.F.D.T.
of obstructing future negotiations concerning the employment issue.[27] Not
only did the Giraud Plan and its rejection bring out the tension existing
between the two trade unions but it also led rapidly to increased tension
between all union representatives (especially those at the national level)
and the Action Committee, the militants, and the General Assembly. For
the workers, the ultimate objectives were still the same: "no" to dismantle-
ment, "no" to lay-offs, employment security for everyone, and continued
payment of wages and fringe benefits.

The workers at Lip rejected the Giraud Plan because they believed that
they had the right to work and this right should not be denied to any of
them. They rejected the logic of negotiating conditions which compelled
them to condemn some of their fellow workers to unemployment by
accepting the plan. (Solidarity continued to remain high among them.) The
C.F.D.T. trade union leaders held a slightly different viewpoint. The
employment issue was also crucial for them but it was conditional on the
economic viability of the restructured enterprise. They were not satisfied
with the Giraud plan, because, although offering an immediate solution for
most of the workers, it did not address itself to the key issues of financial
feasibility of the enterprise and workers' control of it. The Giraud Plan was
a failure because it could not achieve any of these objectives. Neither the
Lip workers nor the unions (or at least one of them, the C.F.D.T.) were
satisfied.

The state of the conflict at the end of Phase 3 can be summarized in the
following terms:

1) It was no longer an obvious "two-person" game (see p. 168). It
involved four sets of social actors: the managers and owners, the judicial
system and the government, the trade unions (especially their national
representatives), and the Lip workers and their "counter-institutions." If
there were common interests among the first two and among the last two,
*there were also important differences in their perceptions of the conflict and
their objectives with respect to it,* as suggested in the discussion above.

2) The conflict settlement process began to take place because, among these four sets of actors, two of them — the government and the trade union representatives — had convergent perceptions of the possible trade-off structure among the various dimensions now involved in the conflict, and they had sufficient discretion to negotiate a compromise solution. These dimensions were:

— the employment issue

— the workers' control issue

— the issue of the financial feasibility of the enterprise and the question of how and by whom it was to be guaranteed.

3) Conflict settlement was possible because the actors generally agreed about (1) the societal level where the "bargaining" must take place (government organizing initiatives and proposals), (2) the basic dimensions (issues) that were involved in the conflict, and (3) ultimately the trade-off structure within which a compromise could be found (pp. 172-174).

Phase 4: Conflict Settlement

The ambiguities and ambivalence within the Lip movement emerged fully in the last phase of the conflict, as the gap continued to widen between the Action Committee and the trade union representatives. To revive the negotiations, the latter not only formulated "industrial plans" but directly contacted corporations, banks, and financial holding companies that might be interested in the project (Martinet, 1974: 103). The final negotiations, and the settlement that followed, were engineered by the trade union representatives under the direct supervision of their national leaders and the so-called modernist or "progressive" industrialist who were politically close to these union leaders and who were supported by government administrators.[28] The result was the Neuschwander Plan.

On January 29, 1974, the Neuschwander Plan was accepted by the General Assembly by 650 votes against 3, with 16 abstentions. If one casually examines the provisions of the Giraud and the Neuschwander Plans regarding lay-offs, one is struck by an apparent contradiction. In October the Lip workers had refused the Giraud Plan providing for the immediate rehiring of 900 workers. In January they accepted a plan that provided for the rehiring of only 300 workers.

One has to keep in mind that the Neuschwander plan entailed a compromise, but not simply between management and the workers. It was also a compromise between the trade unions, the institutional representation of the workers within the capitalist system, and the Lip workers themselves, unified by their struggle and expressing themselves in a counter-institution, the Action Committee.[29] A comparison of the two plans points this up.[30]

1. Financial and Economic Structure

Giraud Plan: Association of two small industrialists with the new corporation. No significant financial plan. Suppression of the machine tool division.

Neuschwander Plan: Creation of a financial holding company including the participation of two industrial giants in France (B.S.N. and Rhone-Poulenc) and the Swiss group Ebauches which would control two corporations, one for watch production, the other for machine tool and armament production. In addition, the French Government would support the project with an important subsidy for industrial development.

2. Employment, Wages and Other Social Benefits

Giraud Plan: Immediate rehiring of 989 employees, definite lay-off of 160 workers. Wages were fixed at their January 1973 level for at least six months; most of the fringe benefits acquired since 1958 would have been discontinued.

Neuschwander Plan: The text of the settlement states, "It is the objective of the new corporation, *in line with its economic development*, to ensure employment for all the workers. ..." (emphasis ours). However, only a plan for minimum rehiring was precisely stipulated: 300 workers before the end of March, 500 workers for September 1st, if the economic performance of the enterprise was satisfactory. Unemployed workers would receive continuing education and training. No wage ceiling. Certain of the existing fringe benefits would be lost. Simplification of the wage ladder.

3. Workers' Control

Giraud Plan: No worker control to guarantee the implementation of the plan.

Neuschwander Plan: To guarantee a fair implementation of the plan, a special "Commission for Employment and Training" would deal with all employment issues. Members of the Commission would be designated by the trade-union locals.

The conflict settlement process ends once the principal actors have more or less the same perception of the trade-off structure between the three key dimensions involved (see p. 193) and can thus find a compromise within that structure. Table 6.5 indicates these trade-offs.

The changes between the Giraud and Neuschwander Plans provide a good example of the restructuring of options and payoffs. The Neuschwander plan, in particular, illustrates conflict settlement through development of a compromise solution (see discussion on pp. 173-174 and especially remarks about compromise option a'_k). The financial feasibility consideration added a new dimension to the options considered. Both management and the workers could expect possible gains, as a result of government interventon with a subsidy for industrial development.[31] Because the issue of feasibility was of such importance for both sides in the conflict, this particular dimension — where the preferences were concordant — became more or less dominant.

The new plan offered a better guarantee of financial viability and economic development than the Giraud plan did, but it made the rehiring of all previously employed personnel contingent on economic performance. The unions and workers accepted a compromise on the employment-level issue in exchange for greater control over employment questions in the future. In this regard, establishment of the "Commission for Employment and Training" was of considerable significance. Although the text of the Plan was extremely vague in defining what exactly would be the powers of the Commission, most trade union representatives viewed that body as both controlling and deciding the employment question. In that respect, it was consistent with the entire logic of the negotiations: the revival of the enterprise depended upon genuine collaboration within certain limits between managers and workers.

The degree and quality of state intervention was of decisive significance in the dynamics and outcome of the Lip conflict. In the French context, especially in light of May 1968, primary reliance on repression would certainly have led to the development of social conflict (obviously extending

TABLE 6.5

Neuschwander Plan's Trade-off Structure (Compared to the Giraud Plan).

	Employment and Wages/ Cost Reduction	Financial Feasibility	Workers' Control
Unions and workers obtain	less	more	more
Managers and owners obtain	more	more	less

beyond the local Lip situation), with unknown, possibly uncontrollable out-comes. Certainly, state administrators, industrial interests, as well as the national labor unions realized the risks of such a development and sought alternative strategies of settlement. These additional parties to the initial conflict — rather than the Action Committee and the Lip management — dominated the game in the final phase and, of course, played an instru-mental role in shaping the eventual settlement (see p. 168). In finding the solution, the Neuschwander plan, not only was the conflict settled but it was accomplished *within a capitalist institutional framework*. Thus, while the settlement certainly succeeded in reducing antagonisms and the likeli-hood of social conflict development, it also contributed to the reproduction of underlying structural contradictions (by not addressing them). In par-ticular, the workers did not attain substantial control over their work environment and long-term fate.

As an epilogue, we should point out that the attempt to save the entire factory has been unsuccessful. After slightly more than fifteen months dur-ing which most of the workers who desired to stay at Lip were rehired, one of the financial holding companies refused to honor its financial commit-ments. Of course, the presidential elections had in the meantime confirmed the dominance of the conservative alliance of Gaullists and Republicans with the victory by Giscard d'Estaing. Bankruptcy application was again answered with the occupation of the factory and the illegal making and selling of watches. A long drawn out struggle followed ending in the for-mation of a number of small workers' cooperatives. The Lip workers, hop-ing that the presidential election in 1981 would bring the socialists to power, resisted for a long time a proposition to move into another, smaller factory in exchange for the town's and the state's financial support. But when even the new socialist government failed to support their demand for remaining in the Lip factory, the workers gave in and moved their coopera-tive ventures to the smaller locale. Even this move and the town's and the state's new financial support has not been enough to stave off renewed financial difficulties in 1983.

The Lip conflict points up certain of the key features of conflict develop-ment and resolution discussed in Part 1: (1) the notion of game transfor-mation, carried out by the actors directly involved as well as by external agents; (2) the relationship between the multi-level structure of the conflict situation and development and resolution processes; and (3) the role of the social structural context in affecting the course of the conflict (above all in the Lip case, the judicial system, the government, powerful industrial inter-ests, and national labor unions as well as other agents, such as the mass media, not treated in our limited analysis here).

Conclusion

The major aim of the theoretical formulation outlined and illustrated here is to provide a means with which to describe and analyze the dynamics and complexity of human conflict: its multi-level, multiple issue character, the involvement of different actors on different levels with different perspectives and interests, the formation of new collective actors and the fragmentation or collapse of others, and, above all, the developmental properties of many social conflicts.

Besides providing a language for the description and analysis of the complexity of conflict dynamics, our multi-level framework points toward certain general principles (Burns *et al.*, 1985):

1) Established social relationships are a major factor structuring conditions and activities on the process-level. On the one hand, if the relationships between actors are antagonistic, they will be predisposed to oppose one another in transforming a game, and mutually satisfying conflict settlements will be unlikely. This contributes to the reproduction of the antagonistic social relations. On the other hand, if actors have solidary social relations, the likelihood is increased that they will cooperate in transforming conflict situations so as to obtain mutually satisfactory outcomes. In other words, actors with solidary social relations have a capability and predisposition — within certain limits, of course — to transform conflict situations so as to settle conflict in mutually satisfying ways and, hence, to reinforce and reproduce their solidary relationships.

In multi-level terms, there tends to be compatibility between structural-level and process-level conditions. This is an important factor in *the reproduction of social relations (at structural levels) through social interaction processes (at the process level)*. Thus, "zero-sum" and "prisoners' dilemma" type games tend to be unstable in a social structural context of solidarity and are likely to be transformed into more cooperative games or at least games where the most mutually satisfying outcomes are likely. In other words, there is a reduction of the incompability or incongruence between the actors' solidary social relations and oppositional features (such as incompatible goals and preferences) at the concrete interaction level.

2) Although social relationships are a major factor structuring social interaction conditions and processes, there are additional structuring factors, such as material and cultural conditions, operating in concrete interaction settings to shape and regulate interaction patterns, often in contradictory ways. Incompatibilities or contradictions may arise between the social relationships and the actual interaction conditions and processes

experienced in concrete social settings. The interaction conditions and processes are shaped by forces from outside of the relationship as well as from activities within the context of the relationship which have unintended consequences. Actors' inability (because of physical or social constraints) or unwillingness (due to payoff incentives in the situation) to transform a game situation so as to resolve conflicts to their mutual satisfaction tends to erode solidary social relations. The interaction conditions and processes contradicting the social relations alter or interfere with the processes and conditions which work to reproduce the social relationships. As a result, the relationships are subject to transformation into a different type or quality of social relation.

NOTES

We are grateful to the following persons for their helpful suggestions and criticisms on earlier versions of the paper or parts of it: Bill Behn, Martin Carnoy, Trygve Gulbrandsen, Marit Hoel, Tord Höivik, Helge Hveem, Björn Hvinden, Louis Kriesberg, Marc Lagneau, Benoit Millot, Bruce Roberts, John Shippee, and Björg Aase Sörensen.

1. See Chapters I and II in Burns et al. 1985.

2. In this context we want to emphasize that social conflicts are not 'games'. The occasional use of game theory terminology reflects our wish to draw on the valuable research and conceptual development found in the game theory tradition.

   Traditional game theory and its various off-shoots in the social sciences conceptualize and analyze games as closed systems (Baumgartner, Burns, Meeker, and Wild, 1976). Research in this tradition has contributed substantially to more effective analysis — within a single level, often uni-dimensional utility framework — of the structure of issue conflicts and related resolution processes. Two major tasks remain, to which this paper is in part addressed: (a) to ground interaction analysis in a theory of human action which, above all, emphasizes the transformational protentialities and tendencies of such action; and (b) to specify and analyze the material, social structural, and cultural context of conflict situations or games and the role of that context in structuring conflict patterns and outcomes. But at the same time, social activities, partially determined by this context, constitute a fluid and dynamic force maintaining or changing it.

   In our framework games are viewed as potentially open, multi-level dynamic systems, and emphasis is placed on the relationship between conflict and social change, in particular, the relation of conflict activity to structure maintaining and structure changing processes in social development.

3. An institution or institutional arrangement is a system of organized or structured social action.

4. In terms of traditional interaction analysis, conflict and exchange would be defined here as 'process-level' interactions, in which case the institutional arrangements and other contextual factors are taken as given (Keohane and Nye, 1973; Baumgartner and Burns, 1975; Baumgartner, Buckley, Burns and Schuster, 1976; Baumgartner, Burns, Meeker and Wild, 1976). Structure-level processes may themselves be structured by higher-level processes (see Table 6.2 and Footnote 7).

5. It is assumed here that the actors are able to reduce their complex evaluations of the options on different dimensions to a suitable index (see Burns and Meeker, 1976a). The

discussion on the transformation of preference structures in conflict situations points up that additional evaluations may come into the picture in the course of conflict resolution or conflict development (see pp. 172-176).

6. It is beyond the scope of this paper to analyze systematically situations where the actors involved perceive no way to restructure the game or where a dominant actor, either within the set of conflicting actors or external to it, simply imposes an institutional framework within which a solution satisfactory to a subset of the actors is achieved.

7. Power analyses focus typically on differences in resources, skills, and strategies among actors who interact *within* a matrix of rules, resource distributions, structural constraints, and action opportunities. The institutional structure remains in the background or is taken for granted. Power relationships are analyzed in terms of interpersonal or inter-group relationships in which one actor has the capability to get another to do something, usually against the latter's will. Actors maneuver their resource strengths and weaknesses in an effort to maximize their returns and minimize their costs. However, such an approach captures only a part of the power activities of groups, organizations, and states. It is inherently morphostatic, since the existng institutional framework is taken for granted (Baumgartner, Buckley and Burns, and Schuster, 1976; Baumgartner, Burns and De-Ville, 1977).

8. Braybrooke (1976), who has developed independently a framework sharing a number of features in common with that presented here, emphasizes that the transformation of options is characteristic of the political process. But then so is persuasion which results in re-conceptualization and re-evaluation.

9. There may be a lack of 'complete' information in this case, e.g., information about a possible trade-off function between underlying dimensions. The use of such information to resolve conflicts is referred to in 2, pages 173-174.

10. Note that the resolution strategies referred to on pp. 173-174 entail the actors agreeing to such strategies.

11. The social processes producing and reproducing social relationships are not of central concern in this paper, but see pages 182-185 (Baumgartner, Buckley, Burns and Schuster, 1976).

12. Typically, there are complex interactions between changes in the activities of actors and their orientations and behavioral predispositions in relation to one another. They may find themselves induced or compelled to interact in ways incompatible with their relational model and past predispositions. The resulting contradictions between their social relational model and their actual interaction patterns in concrete settings result in: (1) a denial or reinterpretation of reality, or possibly, a 'reaffirmation' of the relational model through such social devices as ceremony, ritual, symbolic acts, etc. By such means, experiences from social interaction which clash with the relational model are transformed into perceptions more or less compatible with it, thereby maintaining the conception of the relationship in the face of contradictory evidence; or (2) whenever contradictions cannot be resolved through denial, reinterpretation, or reaffirmation, the relational model is restructured, that is, significant aspects of the social relationship are reconceptualized.

13. Of course, we are assuming here, as throughout the paper, that none of the actors, or a viable combination of them is sufficiently dominant (in meta-power terms) to impose an institutional framework and, further, that no external agent imposes and maintains such a framework.

14. Agreements under such conditions must essentially be guaranteed by an external agent, in contrast to the case where actors with solidary relationships feel that their agreements are binding and are supported through endogenous social exchange and control processes.

15. Richardson (1960), among others, has formulated quite simple, but nonetheless representative, models of conflict interaction in which, for instance, rising hostility and conflict escalation feed one another.

16. The social and political significance of the Lip conflict goes beyond simply illustrating conflict theory. It touches crucial contemporary issues — self-management and socialist democracy, among others — that we can only discuss indirectly here (see the next chapter).

17. Anonymous (1974), Herman (1974), Loureau (1974), and Piaget (1973) are the sources of this account together with articles in *Le Monde, Le Nouvel Observateur, Politique-Hebdo, The New York Times, The Guardian,* and *The Industrial Worker* (Special Supplement, November 1973).

18. The C.F.D.T. (Confédération Francaise Démocratique du Travail) no longer has any explicit Christian reference. The establishment of the C.F.D.T. in 1964 had the precise objective of eliminating it. It is important, however, to realize that the C.F.D.T. is still characterized to a large extent by its unique blend of members of Christian origin and non-communist leftists.

    C.F.D.T. and C.G.T. (Confédération Générale du Travail) are frequently able to actively cooperate on concrete issues and to engage together in concrete actions. But their respective ideological traditions are a persistent source of antagonism between them. The organizational structure of the C.G.T. is based on the concept of democratic centralism as a result of the union's close relationship to the French Communist Party. The C.F.D.T., in contrast, is more democratic in its internal representation and delegation system, due to its traditional blend of Christian and leftist members.

19. The factory council is a legal requirement in France. Its effectiveness is a function of the willingness on the part of management to provide meaningful information to, and to allow discussion of serious issues within, the council. The Lip factory council never played an important role in the events described here.

20. The intention behind the establishment of the Action Committee was not to substitute itself for the unions; neither was it an attempt to destroy the unions. Rather, it involved efforts to make working class institutions (the unions) continuously subject to questioning (Anonymous, 1974:251). For example, the worker-members of the Action Committee demanded to control the negotiations taking place between union representatives and the government negotiator (Loureau, 1974:107). Union representatives were intensively questioned in the General Assembly by Action Committee members. (See Footnote 22).

21. The environment of Besançon was in this respect particularly favorable, because of the economic importance of the factory in an area where all other factories were much smaller. Hence, the lack of job opportunities for the workers and the concern of a large part of the population about the conflict.

22. For the Lip workers, their ability to freely self-organize their struggle did not lie in the destruction of existing institutions. Rather, it rested on *the conflictive but constructive tension between the Action Committee and the Unions* (Anonymous, 1974:252).

    The creation of a counter institution (see Footnote 20) has consequences going beyond the critique of the institution against which it is directed. *It tends to de-structure the entire institutional system and the related norms and rules upon which a particular social organization of society is based.* The existence of the Action Committee enabled the workers' movement to transgress capitalist legality: takeover of the factory, seizure of the watch inventories, resuming production and selling of watches, making wage payments themselves. (Even the sale of watches entailed by-passing state laws, since the value-added tax was of course not included in the price!) These actions violate the basic rules of capitalist society. From this negation emerged a positive new consciousness:

workers realized, '*we* can produce and *we* can sell the product of *our* labor' or, 'the factory is where the workers are' (emphasis ours). *The entire concept of a capitalist enterprise is called into question.*

23. This prevented the usual arrest of the leaders. It is important to note that the trade-union leaders, especially from the C.F.D.T., were instrumental in the creation of the Action Committee.

24. According to an Action Committee proposal, everyone would have received the same flat wage rate. This last proposition met considerable resistance from the trade-union leaders and, although constantly debated during the conflict, the 'equal wage proposal' never materialized (Herman, 1974:21; *Politique-Hebdo*, 1973:9). As B. Millot has suggested in a personal letter to DeVille, one possible explanation of the failure of the equal wage proposal may have been the fear of trade union leaders that many workers would not join the movement due to the 'permanent' level of their personal expenses and consequently their inability to adjust themselves to the new income level implied by such an egalitarian proposal.

25. The discretionary use of strike funds has always been a way for higher-level union leaders to control and orient local conflicts in a way that would not jeopardize their own power. Workers could get unemployment compensation from the state social security system provided they were declared legally fired, which is precisely what the Lip workers were fighting to avoid.

26. Henri Giraud of the Institute of Industrial Development was the negotiator nominated by the government.

27. It is beyond the scope of this paper to explain the differing ideologies and political attitudes of the two unions: for instance, they hold opposing positions on self-management (the C.G.T. is against it), or the role of unions in capitalist societies (the C.F.D.T. is in favor of an active political role for unions while the C.G.T. prefers leaving most political initiatives to the Communist Party).

28. José Bidegain, chief negotiator, is the undisputed leader of the 'progressive' wing of the National Association of French Industrialists (C.N.P.F.). Claude Neuschwander, who ultimately became the new director, and is a marketing specialist, has close and friendly relations with several leaders of the United Socialist Party (P.S.U.).

29. The term 'counter institution' (or 'anti-institution,' 'non-institution') is taken from Loureau (1974:125-133).

30. For a more detailed description of the two plans, see Anonymous (1974) and *Le Monde* (1974a, 1974b).

31. Such government intervention has frequently assured a solution *within* the framework of the capitalist system and may be perceived by the workers as advantageous to them. This corresponds to Shorter and Tilly's general findings in the case of France between 1830-1968 (1974:31-32):

> If an official within the government hierarchy, or indeed a mere justice of the peace, could be persuaded to take a hand in the strike, the chances were vastly improved that the strike would end either in victory for the workers or in compromise — also a happy result; and the chances were greatly lessened that the strike would end in failure or indeed in the workers' dismissal. Government intervention had not always benefitted strikers, for during the July Monarchy, exactly the opposite relationship prevailed. The government stepped in to repress conflict, and its intervention substantially lessened the chances of success.

REFERENCES

Andreski, S. (1968) *Military Organization and Society.* New York, Pantheon.

Anonymous (1974) *Il était une fois la Révolution.* Paris.

Baumgartner, T., Buckley, W., and Burns, T.R. and Schuster, P. (1976) "Meta-power and the Structuring of Social Hierarchies," pp. 215-286 in T.R. Burns and W. Buckley (eds.), *Power and Control: Social Structures and Their Transformation.* London and Beverly Hills, California, Sage.

Baumgartner, T., and Burns, T.R. (1975) "The Structuring of International Economic Relations." *International Studies Quarterly* 19: 126-159.

Baumgartner, T., and P. DeVille (1977) "The Oil Crisis and the Emerging World Order: The Structuring of Institutions and Rule-making in the International System." *Alternatives: A Journal for World Policy,* 3: 75-108.

Baumgartner, T., and DeVille, P., and Meeker, D. (1975) "A Systems Model of Conflict and Change in Planning Systems." *General Systems Yearbook* 20: 167-183.

Baumgartner, T., Meeker, D. and Wild, B. (1976) "Open Systems and Multi-level Processes: Implications for Social Research." *International Journal of General Systems* 3: 25-42.

Bettelheim, C. (1970) *La Transition vers l'Économie socialiste.* Paris: Maspéro.

Braybrooke, D. (1976) "The Transformation of Issues." In *Foundations and Applications of Decision Theory,* Edited by C.A. Hooker. Dodrecht-Holland, Reidel.

Burns, T.R., W. Buckley and T. Baumgartner, (1985) *The Shaping of Society* London: Wiley.

Burns, T.R., T. Baumgartner and P. DeVille (1985) *Man, Decisions and Society,* London: Gordon and Breach

Burns, T.R. and Meeker, D. (1976a) "A Systems Theory of Multi-level, Multiple Objective Evaluation and Decision-making." *International Journal of Systems* 3: 105-125.

Burns, T.R. (1976b) "Conflict and Structure in Multi-level Multiple Objective Decision-making Systems" In *Foundations and Applications of Decision Theory,* Edited by C.A. Hooker, Dodrecht-Holland, Reidel.

Coleman, J.S. (1957) *Community Conflict.* Glencoe, Ill., Free Press.

Deutsch, M. (1973) *The Resolution of Conflict: Constructive and Destructive Processes.* New Haven and London, Yale University Press.

DeVille, P. and T.R. Burns (1977) "Institutional Response to Crisis in Capitalist Development." *Social Praxis,* 4(1-2): 7-42.

Galtung, J. (1964) "A Structural Theory of Aggression." *Journal of Peace Research 1.*

Galtung, J. (1971) "A Structural Theory of Imperialism." *Journal of Peace Research* 8:81-117.

Herman, P. (1974) "Workers, Watches and Self-Management." *Working Papers for a New Society* 1: no. 4: 18-25.

Keohane, R.D. and Nye, J.S. (1973) "World Politics and the International Economic System." Pages 115-117 in C.F. Bergsten (ed.), *The Future of the International Economic Order,* Lexington, Mass., D.C. Heath.

Kriesberg, L. (1973) *Sociology of Social Conflicts.* Englewood Cliffs, N.J., Prentice-Hall.

Le Monde (1974a) January 30, page 30.

Kriesberg, L (1974b) January 31, page 28.

Loureau, L. (1974) *L'analyseur Lip.* Paris: Union générale d'editions.

Martinet, G. (1974) "L'avenir depuis vingt ans." *Le Nouvel Observateur,* No. 518, October 14.

Piaget, C. (1973) *Lip.* Paris: Stock.

Politique-Hebdo (1973) August 23, pp. 9ff.

Rapoport, A. (1974) *Conflict in Man-Made Environment.* Baltimore, Md., Penguin.

Richardson, L.F. (1960) *Arms and Insecurity.* Pittsburgh, Boxwood Press.

Shorter F. and Tilly, C. (1974) *Strikes in France: 1830-1968.* London, Cambridge University Press.

Simmel, G. (1964) *The Sociology of Georg Simmel.* Edited by K.H. Wolff. New York, Free Press.

Thibaut, J. and Faucheux, C. (1965) "The Development of Contractual Norms in a Bargaining Situation under Two Types of Stress." *Journal of Experimental Social Psychology* 1: 89-102.

7

Yugoslav Postwar Development Patterns and Dialectics: Self-Management, Market, and Political Institutions in Conflict

Thomas Baumgartner   Tom R. Burns
Dusko Sekulić

1. Introduction

SELF-MANAGED work organizations are, in general, those where workers (shop-floor workers, technicians, and administrators) have the right to control the means of production, the resources of the organization in which they work, its organizational structure and processes, and its products, without undue interference from state, party, or other interests. Workers — either directly, as in small enterprises, or through their delegates, as in larger enterprises — decide on economic plans, determine salaries (above a government set minimum), make investment and development decisions, distribute the organization's income and other benefits such as apartments and vacation time, select their top administrators, and resolve internal dilemmas and conflicts.

In our view the emergence and development of self-management values and institutions must be examined in their specific historical and social structural context. This chapter attempts to to do this in the case of Yugoslavia. We focus particularly on such factors affecting the development of self-management as: Yugoslavia's international relationships, market institutions and participation in the international division of labor, and a communist political movement determined to build socialism as well as to maintain the dominant leadership of the party.

In the following section we describe briefly the background and development of Yugoslav self-management institutions. This provides a basis for the discussion in sections 3 and 4 concerning socio-economic developments in Yugoslavia following the establishment of self-management. The limitations of self-management institutions operating under market allocation rules and the technical division of labor are pointed up. In particular, we indicate several of the ways in which economic and technical conditions and forces constrain and distort the actual practice of self-management as well as interfere with the realization of socialist values such as equality and solidarity: by inducing an emphasis on technical and economic values rather than on social and political ones, by fostering unequal accumulation and uneven development rather than equalization, and by failing to provide socially integrating values and institutions. Section 3 focuses on micro-organizational features of self-managed enterprises; due to the technical division of labor and differential involvement in work processes, different categories of participants develop differential capabilities and knowledge. Section 4 takes up macro-level aspects: uneven accumulation and development patterns by region, sector and enterprise in Yugoslavia. These processes of social differentiation lead to corresponding as well as opposing developments within the political and socio-cultural spheres. Opposition is manifested in conflict and struggle between those seeking to maintain (and reproduce) — and those struggling to change — existing institutions, the 'rules of the game', and patterns of development. Such processes are related to qualitatively different phases and dialectical shifts in societal development, discussed in section 5. These developments and shifts are generally not controllable or subject to planning through self-managed enterprises.[1]

2.   The Development of Self-Management in Yugoslavia: A Brief Overview[2]

The triumph over the German Occupation by the Popular Liberation Movement under the leadership of the Communist Party (later renamed the League of Yugoslav Communists (LYC)) set the stage for the development of contemporary Yugoslavia. The movement supporting the liberation was very heterogeneous (made up of different social groups with different motives and interests). The party was the only major actor which dominated and integrated these different groups. Other forces participating in the liberation movement lacked the power and legitimation to overcome the suspicion and opposition of others and to integrate the whole. Organized social actors outside of the liberation movement, who might have been capable of playing a key role, had either lost in the internal struggle (e.g. royalists or Chetniks led by General Draza Mihailovic and various 'home guards')[3] or had associated themselves with the Germans. With the victory of the movement, they disappeared from the scene. This left the Communist Party, which at the outbreak of the war had been an illegal group, insignificant in number but with growing influence, in charge.[4]

In addition to the fact that all serious internal rivals for power had disappeared or been removed from the scene, the party had a number of other advantages in consolidating and developing its power (Dubey, 1975:26):

— The prestige and legitimation it had acquired from its courageous and successful leadership of the partisan resistance against internal and external enemies during the second world war.

— The fact that it could represent and draw support from all sections of the country, and had no special bias or commitment toward any particular linguistic, regional or religious group.

— The active support of the Soviet Union, together with the tolerance (following what had eventually become close military collaboration in the war years) of England and the US.

In sum, the party was the only well-organized social actor enjoying both widespread internal as well as external legitimation. It alone was capable of acting in all spheres of Yugoslav social life, political/military, economic, and socio-cultural. Efforts at organizing new forces within the liberation movement (and after the war within the new political system) were successfully prevented by the party. The monopoly of power in the post-war period was consistent with the ideological principles of the 'ruling party' and the 'dictatorship of the proletariat.'

Thus, the party was prepared, both organizationally and ideologically, to initiate institution building and transformation, a type of structural power which we refer to as meta-power (Burns et al., 1985). Such power is based on control over key institutional spheres and processes which can be used to mobilize resources and to maintain or change societal institutions (e.g., private property relations).

The dynamics of post-war Yugoslav society can be described and analyzed in terms of the interests and capability of the Communist Party to structure and restructure institutions in response to:

— changes in the environment of the country (e.g., international political and economic developments);

— intended changes within the society;

— unintended consequences of changes introduced within the system.

The development of Yugoslav self-management and related social institutions can be divided into four periods (see, for example, Gorupić and Paj, 1970; Bošnjak *et al.*, 1978):

— 1947-52: planned economy managed by the state administration;

— 1953-64: construction of the system of worker and social self-management and its institutional definition in the Constitutions of 1953 and 1963

— 1965-71: self-management with full-fledged market allocation and the emergence of challenges to the top political leadership, the so-called laissez-faire period.

— 1972-80: attempts to re-establish political and ideological constraints on the functioning of self-managed enterprises and autonomous economic and political processes.

The system institutionalized immediately after the second world war was characterized by a Soviet model of socialist development with substantial centralization and bureaucratization.[5] The first two years of the five-year plan beginning in 1947 showed an impressive increase in output. Then, disagreements with the Soviet Union broke out, culminating in the break in mid-1948 and the 1948 Cominform resolution expelling Yugoslavia from the 'community of socialist nations.'[6]

This international event marked a dramatic external change in the economic, political and even military conditions of Yugoslavia. In particular, the break with, and the economic boycott by, the Soviet Union and other Cominform countries made fulfillment of the 1947-52 plan impossible for at least three reasons (Dubey, 1975:28):

— There was a rapid reduction, literally to zero, in exports to and imports from what had previously been — and had been expected to remain — the principal trading partners. Imports from the socialist countries, which had been 56 percent of the total in 1947, had ceased altogether by 1950.

— Both 1950 and 1952 were years of drought and exceptionally poor harvests.

— The new external threat motivated the Yugoslav government to increase its defense expenditures substantially (approximately by a factor of 3 during the period 1947-52), so that by 1952 it reached as high as 20 percent of national product).[7]

Between 1948 and 1952 there was virtually no growth.[8] At the same time, the political-military situation for Yugoslavia was extremely tense.[9] The weakness of imperative central planning, particularly in the face of enormous problems of adjustment created by the break with the Cominform countries, became increasingly apparent. Longer term planning was given less and less attention, and the actual practice became to formulate annual plans only.

The economic and political difficulties led to pragmatic efforts at institution restructuring and innovation. At the enterprise level, changes were made in December 1949 with the introduction of the first workers' councils as consultative bodies in a number of enterprises. Dedijer (1971) writes that the political leadership recognized that the economy could only be rescued if the workers were mobilized and granted broader rights, and if rigid bureaucratic forms were broken down.

Although the initial response of the Yugoslav leadership was a defensive one — 'they had not committed wrong' — gradually they took the initiative. The defects and limitations of the Soviet system became matters for extensive discussion and analysis. There arose a debate in Yugoslavia concerning the nature and problems of the transition to a fully socialist society, matters which for many communists had been settled by the 'successful' example of the Soviet Union. New concepts and principles were developed which were essential to the task of mobilizing socialists and legitimizing the Yugoslav position.[10]

The political elite introduced self-management institutions into Yugoslavia to a large extent in response to inter-system competition and threat. This institutional innovation was intended to provide a source of legitimation and an institutional basis on which to oppose the Soviet Union (1953 Program of the League of Yugoslav Communists).[11] The innovation was initiated with economic units and was only later extended to socio-political and territorial units, in particular, communes. All of this led, through experimentation, reformulation of concepts and further innovation to an alternative strategy and model for socio-economic development and construction of a socialist society. The strategy combined normative and socio-political features along with purely economic ones.

The system of participatory socialism with market allocation was worked out and tested between 1953 and 1971. Already in 1950 elected workers' councils emerged as advisory or consultative bodies (520 enterprises by late 1950). These councils had no formal decision-making power. However, they had the right to propose measures on any matter concerning the management of the enterprise and the director was obliged to take their views into account. With the introduction of such bodies, the direct external influence of state agencies began to be challenged and the director's powers, instead of being exclusively controlled by the state, became subject to the influence of workers' collectives through the councils. Yet, the director, with his direct command over the technical staff and the hierarchical management pyramid and his role in representing the enterprise to the outside world, had an effective monopoly on the knowledge and information possessed by the enterprise. As central administrative planning of the economy was gradually done away with, greater knowledge and greater initiative was demanded of the technical and management staff of the enterprise in order to operate successfully in a competitive market. Thus, there emerged duality of influence (or competing organizational principles) — a duality which continues to exist and to generate conflicts (see later discussion):

— the new democratic self-management bodies and processes;

— the traditional, hierarchical management organization with the existing enterprise-internal structure of management unaltered.

The control of all state enterprises was formally vested in the workers' councils in 1952. These were regarded as the trustees of the fixed capital which was provided to the enterprises by the state. At the same time all production decisions became the responsibility of the enterprises themselves. Although initially the director of each enterprise was still appointed centrally, by late 1952 the appointment was vested in the local authority (the commune) and in the following year this was replaced by a system of appointment by a committee representing the workers' council and the commune (municipality). (Gorupić and Paj [1970] describe the shifts of authority and the main conflicts of interest.) The federal ministries which had devised and administered the plan were abolished and replaced by secretariats with much smaller staff and greatly restricted functions. In December 1951 a law on 'Planned Management of the National Economy' established as of 1952 a system of annual plans. (A second five-year plan was not initiated until 1956.) It introduced the practice of what was known as planning of 'basic proportions' in which the amount and broad allocation of investment was determined, while the decisions regarding quantity and quality of output and, to some extent, its price were left to enterprises. Before 1952 the investment allocations of the plan were implemented through the budget. This arrangement was abolished with the Law on Planned Management.

The development of the system after the 1953 constitution — which gave self-management a legal and constitutional basis and thus greater legitimation than simply a major government policy could provide, as in the preceding phase — followed the general principles and patterns of development already initiated in the previous phase: self-management, decentralization, liberalization, and increased reliance on market mechanisms.[12] The increasing reliance on such mechanisms was not the result of a conversion to a capitalist model of development, but reflected reasoning about effective conditions in which self-management might best be realized. In general, the Yugoslav leadership tried to work out the practical implications of the management strategy that it had adopted (Dubey, 1975).

As central administrative planning was weakened or done away with altogether, enterprises were given increased autonomy at the same time that their responsibility for business performance was increased. They were expected to operate successfully in a competitive market. In particular, they gained increased control over the distribution of income. This is indicated by the increase in the proportion of enterprise income at their disposal in the form of net personal incomes, depreciation and enterprise funds. This proportion increased from 43 percent in 1959 to 55 percent in 1964 and 62 percent in 1966. (Also, the proportion of depreciation and enterprise funds to total net income increased from 17 percent in 1959 to 27 percent in 1964 [Dubey, 1975:34].) Other developments indicating increased self-management took place as well. For example, until 1958 the directors of enterprises were appointed by a committee on which the enterprise had one-third representation. After 1958, half the members of the committee were from the enterprise. Eventually, the workers' councils were given the power to appoint directors from lists approved by the selection committee.

Parallel with the development of enterprise autonomy, there was progressive decentralization of the powers of the federation to republics and local governments. The basic idea was that self-management of enterprises should entail increasing self-government by communities. At the same time republic and local governments were to play a role in the 'supervision' of enterprises in their territory, at least in the initial stages. That is, instead of centralized state control at the federal level, enterprises were to face decentralized government regulation at the commune level.

Corresponding to this development there occurred a redefinition of the party role, to make it more an ideological and educational weapon than a decision-making or administrative body. This entailed movement away from total regulation to a separation of party and state, and the ongoing separation of state and economy. The renaming of the party as the League of Yugoslav Communists in 1952 was indicative of this change. This was not meant to imply that the importance of the party should decline. As its program stated in 1958: 'the working class cannot give up the weapons of its class struggle, the dictatorship of the proletariat and the leading role of the League of Yugoslav Communists,' because of the existence of 'antagonistic forces' which endanger the existence of socialism (Dubey, 1975:50). The process of decentralization, however, was implemented also within the party organization. The report of the Eighth Congress of the

LYC (1964) commented that the independence and initiative of the organizations within the LYC had increased, so that instead of being 'agents for passing on views and executors of tasks assigned, they were becoming participants in the adoption of conclusions and decisions' (Dubey, 1975:51). The process of decentralization in Yugoslavia was marked by internal debate and struggle within the party. A struggle within the party in the early 1960s between those in favor of greater self-management and those for greater centralization resulted in the success of the former. This set the stage for the very substantial reforms from 1965 until 1969.[13] Dubey points out (1975:36):

While significant progress toward decentralization and self-management had been made by 1964, it was much less than would appear at first sight. There continued to be a large degree of central control of the economy, and particularly of investment, in the interests of coordination and stabilization or ensuring what was termed the 'basic proportions' of development. The emphasis placed on achieving greater regional equality was another reason for central intervention in investment allocation. There was also a large degree of control of prices and wages. The state continued to control the prices of 70 % of the products and thus exercised a strong influence on the pattern of decentralized resource use.

... there was also some resistance to the ideas of the new economic system and its implications, which slowed the process of decentralization and self-management. Such views were increasingly voiced in 1961 and 1962 when there was a reduction in the rate of growth. This was attributed to the significant increase in enterprise autonomy that occurred in 1961, and a return to the old system of income distribution in enterprises and greater state influence in investment allocation was demanded. The ideological opposition was defeated. The constitution of 1963 and the Eighth Congress of the League of Communists of Yugoslavia in 1964 reaffirmed the basic principles of Yugoslav development.

The economic reform of 1965 consisted of a number of measures adopted during 1964-67 which were designed to achieve three major objectives: (a) to give greater autonomy to enterprises and limit the role of the state in the economy by reducing taxation on enterprises and leaving investment decision to them; (b) to correct, by major price adjustments, the long-standing distortions in relative prices, and thus improve the pattern of output and investment; (c) by devaluing the dinar, approximately halving customs tariff rates, and liberalizing imports and the foreign exchange regime to integrate the economy more closely with the world economy and exert pressure on Yugoslav enterprises to increase efficiency (Dubey, 1975). The measures were adopted over a number of years. The reduction in taxation of enterprises occurred in 1964, the devaluation and principal price adjustments in July 1965 and the liberalization of the foreign exchange regime in January 1967.

In the period following 1965 steps were taken strengthening the autonomy of enterprises and self-management structures as a whole. The basic law of 1965 on enterprises formally established the concept of organizations as free associations of responsible work partners (as opposed to wage earners) managing the organization directly or through delegated bodies. The primary autonomous organization for this purpose became the 'work unit' (or, after 1974, 'basic organization of associated labor') — such as a production unit or professional services section. The share of industrial commodities under price controls also decreased from 1965 to 1970 from more than 70 percent to 43 percent. A law of 1968 on the assets of enterprises provided wider scope for inter-enterprise cooperation. Amendment XV to the Constitution, passed in 1969, gave enterprises freedom in creating and designing their own inner self-management structures (for example in the authority, number and interrelationships of different self-managing bodies). With the passage of Amendment XV, the only structural legal requirement was the establishment of a workers' council. Other and additional self-management bodies were to be regulated by the statutes of each enterprise (Hunnius, 1973:277). Thus, enterprises were given the right to define for themselves the role of individual as well as collective executive bodies. The practical result was to enhance and to legitimize the existing powers of managers and technicians within enterprises. In general, there was decreasing interference in enterprise affairs from political authorities, e.g. communal bodies. For instance, the influence over the choice of enterprise director shifted completely in 1968 to the enterprise's workers' council.

A major change instituted in this period related to the role of the banks and financial institutions in Yugoslavia. The classical concept of statist socialism insisted on state monopoly over investment. Self-management (developed in the theoretical works of Yugoslav economists and politicians, not necessarily consistently) implied self-financing of enterprises.

The Law of Banking and Credit of 1964 gave state investment funds to the banks, thus making them more or less autonomous systems providing services to enterprises rather than acting as agents for the central or other government bodies. From this time dates the process of strengthening the banks, although the banks were still partially connected with centers of political power, and partially with managerial elites. But eventually they became independent centers of power. The growing importance of banks can be seen from data about the source of financial investment.

In 1961 (before the economic reform), 61.7 percent of investment was in the hands of political organizations, 37.4 percent in the hands of enterprises and 1.0 percent in the hands of banks. By 1970 43.3 per cent of investment was controlled by banks, 50.1 percent by enterprises, and only 6.4 percent by Political-territorial organizations.[14] (A detailed discussion of investment policy in this period is found in Bendeković, (1975).)

TABLE 7.1
Investment in fixed assets in the social sector by source of finance (in percent)

	1952	1960	1970	1975	1980
State	78	62	7	3	2
Work organisations	22	37	50	53	50
Bank credits	—	1	43	44	48
Total	100	100	100	100	100

Source: Razuoj Jugoslavije 1947-1981. Savezni zavod za Statistiku, Savezui zavod za društveuo planiranje, Beograd, 1982 page 69.

This development of the banking system was regarded as a crucial factor in the mobilization of savings and their allocation to the most efficient use. The shift from public to bank financing, where banks are typically more oriented uni-dimensionally to profitability considerations, is one indicator of the depolitization of the economy during this period. This translated into more clear-cut pressures on enterprises from their managements to be profitable. In general, economic accountability and stress became more pronounced, and the mandate to take action to deal with 'unprofitable' enterprises more securely established.[15]

Although economic concerns were important from the beginning, there were also strong ideological aspects of giving self-managed enterprises greater autonomy and control over their resources. Over time, economic considerations came to dominate: enhancement of productivity, exploiting the advantage of modern technology, and participating in the international division of labor (see section 5). Self-managed enterprises operating under market allocation rules were to provide institutional conditions to facilitate innovation and productivity, to reward individual and collective (enterprise) efforts and skills, and to produce goods and services at higher quality and lower prices (Zukin, 1975:23).[16]

The establishment of a system of self-managed enterprises operating under market allocation of resources is the identifying feature of Yugoslav institutional development. By the end of the 1960s the self-managed enterprise was an autonomous body with the status of a legal person, with freedom to contract for capital goods, raw materials, and workers. The assets of the enterprise were social property,[17] but it could mortgage or dispose of them. The enterprise was free to determine what to produce, how to produce it, how much of it to produce, and in principle, the price of its products.

The management of self-managed enterprises was carried out by a workers' council elected by all the workers (the work collective), a managing board, and a director, who was appointed by the workers' council. The workers' council elected its executive body, the managing board. This was usually — but not necessarily — from its own membership. The board had from 3 to 17 members (the director ex officio) elected for one-year periods; if a member was elected twice in succession, he or she was then ineligible for the next two years.[18] The board had important functions including the supervision of the director's work, ensuring the fulfillment of the plans of the enterprise, and the drawing up of the annual plan (Gorupić and Paj, 1970; Pateman, 1970).

The director, together with the 'collegium' of department heads, was responsible for the administration of the enterprise and the execution of the workers' council's decisions. He also had the power to sign contracts in the name of the enterprise, to represent it in dealings with external bodies and to ensure that the enterprise operated within the law.

The management of the enterprise, including decisions on basic policy, was formally the responsibility of the workers' council and the managing board, while the responsibility for implementing decisions and for organizing production was given to the director alone.

The workers' council met collectively. Each member served for two years (but members were subject to recall by the electorate). Half of the council members were elected annually. To ensure wide participation, no person could serve more than two terms consecutively. The workers' council decided on the internal relationships in the enterprise, adopted economic plans and accepted annual financial reports, decided on the utilization of funds and the distribution of the enterprise earnings between personal income and investment. The workers' council also decided matters concerning employment and dismissal of personnel.

When an enterprise failed to operate successfully and was unable to meet the income payments to its members, it was usual to appoint assignee management, normally chosen by the commune. Such assignee management is limited in the first instance to one year, though this can be continued where necessary.

From 1950 until 1980, Yugoslavia has undergone dramatic transformations: the decentralization of the state apparatus from the federal level to republics, communes, and enterprises, the development of a new type of work organization, self-management,[19] the introduction of market institutions, the transformation of imperative planning into indicative planning and then, more recently, the attempt to establish new types of planning and coordinating institutions, the incorporation of the Yugoslav economy into the international division of labor, the partial separation of the party from the state apparatus, and the renaming of the party as the League of Communists with a stress on its educational, ideological, and persuasive role and a de-emphasis (until recently) of an administrative/decision-making role in societal regulation and development.

All of the most important decisions about the development of Yugoslav institutions have been taken initially by a small group of party leaders. Moreover, the introduction of self-management institutions and values into Yugoslavia entailed more of a discontinuity than a continuity with earlier institutional development. The concept and ideology of self-management was not a factor in the thinking and experience of the party leadership. The self-management concept cannot be found in any document of the Communist Party before, during the war or during the first years after the war. The party's concept of socialism was based on the model of the Soviet Union: a 'people's democracy' with substantial central planning and government control of all important societal activities and developments.

Moreover, the concept of self-management was not present in the ideology or thinking of any other group which participated in the liberation movement. In sum, one can say that the introduction of self-management was discontinuous, 'an imposition on societal development', since (i)until 1948 the party leadership with the power to shape and reshape institutions nevertheless oriented Yugoslav society toward a Soviet type of model; this was completely consistent with the guiding ideology of this group; and (ii) other groups, which might offer any opposition to this development, had no concept of self-management.

Self-management as an ideology and way of organizing society was not the result of a movement (and groups supporting this movement). But one should bear in mind that the liberation movement was necessarily a decentralized movement, and stressed active participation and local initiative. The experience and success of this movement was a part of the ideology and cultural heritage of post-war Yugoslavia.[20] It provided a potentiality, both in structural forms and ideology. These could be activated to deal with societal problems, such as the crisis facing Yugoslavia after the 1948 break with the Soviet Union. That this potentiality of Yugoslav society was activated and managed by the political leadership is not disputed. But they did not create the potentiality, they simply used and transformed it.[21]

The very institutions established or restructured by the political elite may produce effects and lead to developments which they did not intend, and which compel them to take further action. At the same time, decisions and values institutionalized early in the process constrain to some extent the possible institutional responses of the elite in later phases. Due to a lack of knowledge, competence, or because of preoccupations with other spheres of action, the political elite may fail to regulate certain institutional areas which permit actors within these areas to establish and develop social power. Such power, e.g., in the case of Yugoslavia, the power of the managerial-technical elite in the economic sphere may, under certain conditions, be translated into power in other spheres of social action and into meta-power and the capability of not only shaping social institutions to its advantage, but challenging or competing with, and even undermining the legitimation of the initial holders of societal meta-power, the political elite. Typically, however, emerging power groups lack linkages throughout — or possibilities to penetrate — all major institutional areas. In the Yugoslav context, nationalist movements provide a quick and ready way to establish such linkages, and for this reason, they appear in the Yugoslav context as a potentially serious threat to the existing social order (see section 5).

3.   Management/Labor Relationships and Other Micro-Organizational Features of Self-Managed Enterprises

The reproduction of inequality in capitalist enterprises and in the capitalist system as a whole depends, in part, on the unequal distribution of managerial/technical skills, organizational capabilities and knowledge. Such distributions also affect the extent to which self-managed enterprises maintain or develop social hierarchy, which limits or undermines the realization of self-management values and institutions.

Productive activity has multiple consequences (products), entailing benefits and costs. These tend to be distributed unequally even in self-managed enterprises because of the technical division of labor (hierarchy and segmentation) and the differential involvement of enterprise members in planning and work processes. That is, even if 'all of the workers' in self-managed enterprises control some products of their labor, e.g., the distribution of net income, they do not control all of the socially important or strategic products of productive activity.[22] The technical division of labor, and economic structures and processes generally, structure a variety of socio-cultural as well as political consequences.

Through the functions they perform in the social division of labor, managerial and technical groups (top and middle management, accountants, engineers, economists, and shop-floor supervisors) acquire and develop valuable knowledge, skills, social linkages and status. Those in operative and laboring functions cannot acquire such resources or acquire them only with the greatest of difficulty. For instance, information acquired through management and technical processes serves as a basis for many self-management decisions. Managers can filter and decide on the distribution, the way of presenting and timing information. This control — in many instances monopolistic control — over information enables them to play a dominating role in self-management processes, and to determine or heavily influence self-management decisions and plans (Obradović, 1972, 1976). As Županov has pointed out, 'a skillful manipulation of information can limit collective decision-making to a mere voting for the decisions made in advance by management' (cited in Obradović, 1976:27).[23] Also, the knowledge, skills, and contacts which managers and technicians acquire in the performance of their functions are resources often transferable to political and socio-cultural spheres of social action. Such transference can then feedback to reinforce the division of labor (however, there may be opposing movements, see section 5). In general, Yugoslav self-management during the 1960s consistently showed oligarchic patterns of power and influence, often to an increasing degree — and therefore, conditions and developments incompatible with the self-management norm of a democratic distribution of power within work organizations (Obradović, 1976).

Of course, the actual situation is more complex. The intensity of participation tends to vary with level and area of decision-making. It is most intensive in areas of immediate concern to workers, such as matters of income and social welfare. Managerial and technocratic influence is greatest at the level of the whole enterprise and the problem areas of enterprise organization and planning, selection of technology, solution of technical and economic problems, marketing considerations, etc.[24]

The influence of managers and technicians tend to be reinforced if workers select leaders and authorize decision-making powers to those who have technocratic credentials and orientations because they believe this will ensure the viability and success of their enterprise in a dynamic market system. In this way they may satisfy short-term income goals on the basis of good economic results of the enterprise. But this achievement may be at the expense of the development of their own managerial and technical knowledge and capability. Stephen's study (cited in Pateman, 1970) of a shipyard in Split found that although the proportion of manual workers on the workers' council rose from 61.5 to 72.4 percent from 1955 to 1967, in 1967 only 2.7 percent of the representatives were semi-skilled and 2.9 percent unskilled. Split workers explained the low representation of the least skilled as due to generally low educational levels and the desire for the 'best men to hold office'.[25] In general, market institutions and competition contribute to reinforcing the power and prestige of the managerial and technical elite because they are expected to make the enterprise succeed and grow.

In sum, the technical division of labor is not only an organization of production. It entails social differentiation and power/dependence relationships, both within enterprises as well as, to a certain extent, outside of them. It tends to keep many workers relatively ignorant and only peripherally involved (or able to be involved) in the major technical and economic decisions of the enterprise. It also contributes to differentiation in orientations and values.

Yugoslav studies on self-management not only found that managers and professional personnel enjoyed greater initiative in enterprise decision-making and planning but that they were more prepared than workers to take risks regarding the consequences of decisions (e.g., trying new productions, production processes or organizational forms). Županov (1969), in a study of ten Croatian factories in 1966, found that the majority of workers favoured the continuation of price controls.[26] Only the managerial group was in favor of the elimination of price controls, and even in this group one-third wanted controls to continue. In response to the question of whether an unprofitable enterprise should be kept going with government support in an attempt to improve it or be closed down, the majority of workers opposed shut-down. White-collar employees and supervisors were approximately evenly divided in their opinion while the majority of managers and staff were in favor of closing down unprofitable enterprises.

The high level of influence of managers and technicians in enterprise decision-making and planning is certainly welcomed from the viewpoint of the maximization of production (and thus also income) growth (Drulović, 1973).[27] But the loss of relative influence in self-management institutions, especially on the part of unskilled and semi-skilled production workers, has at least two negative consequences.

First, those who already have above average education, knowledge, and experience in crucial power areas are structurally and functionally favored to acquire even more of these valuable capabilities. Second, to the extent that the better educated and trained personnel are also those who occupy administrative and managerial positions in the enterprise, managerial control over the enterprise increases at the the expense of control by the total work force of the enterprise. This development will be reinforced if the language of the specialists and their shared understandings dominate in the meetings of the various councils and committees, thus reducing the effective participation of those workers who lack access to this language and models of shared understandings and interpretations.

In this way, a dynamic process of (re-)institutionalization of managerial and technical control may take place and be reproduced in self-managed enterprises. The active participation of unskilled and uneducated workers decreases, and their influence in the councils and committees declines, as indicated by Table 7.2. Between 1956 and 1968 there was a marked increase in the proportion of chairmen of workers' councils elected from among white collar workers (from 24.6 to 44.5 percent), without an increase in the proportion of such workers in the labor force. The share of skilled, semi-skilled and unskilled workers' decreased (especially the latter two categories).[28]

In sum, studies of self-managed enterprises in the 1960s showed that the enterprise director, management generally, and technicians exerted a substantial degree of discretionary control over enterprises, despite the fact that the workers' councils were legally the legislative bodies of the enterprises and chose the director and other organs of management. This pattern is only in part the result of the differential possession and acquisition of managerial skills, the unequal access to and control of information, and the dependence of common production workers on managers and technicians for enterprise viability and success. Equally as important has been management's necessary and often automatic access to and close links to influential social actors in other spheres (local politicians, party leaders, etc.) and higher-level institutions (federal and republic planners and inspectors, bankers). This provides managers and technicians with informational advantages as well as external persons and arguments which they can refer to in legitimizing their choices and decisions. They have also the possibility of calling on these persons and organizations, through party, trade union and government channels, to influence the opinions and judgments of enterprise workers. The problem is not only one of external contacts. Many of the roles in different social spheres, at least at the local level during the 1960s, were occupied by one and the same person (Hunnius, 1973:287). The cumulation of decision-making positions in socio-political organizations, commune assemblies, and self-management bodies in enterprises was often complemented with the rotation of single-office holders in such a way that the same group of cadres exchanged the different positions (Hunnius, 1973:272).[29]

Actors occupying these cumulated positions and participating in office rotation are typically the better educated and higher skilled as well as the more active persons.[30] They will be able to absorb, assess, and act upon the information which usually comes to their attention in their functions within the different spheres.[31] Both position in the structure of relationships and access to important information provide these actors with strategic power resources. Situated at the interlinkages of the different spheres, they are in a position to use their knowledge in such a way as to have a predominant influence within and between spheres. In this way, social power tends to accumulate in their hands. The widespread acquisition and development of decision-making abilities and knowledge in organizational and managerial matters is inhibited.

In addition to the substantial power and initiative of managers and tech-

TABLE 7.2

Membership of workers' councils and boards of management in enterprises (percent)

Qualifications	Labor force of the economy			Membership of workers' councils						Membership of managing boards*				
	1955	1970	1978	1956	1960	1965	1970	1972	1979	1956	1960	1965	1970	1972
Manual workers														
Highly skilled[1]	6.2	7.6	6.8	14.3	15.1	16.7	17.2	17.4	11.8	17.9	19.3	19.7	18.2	17.8
Skilled	29.2	29.9	28.0	38.0	40.5	37.8	33.7	32.3	26.6	33.1	34.9	31.0	20.4	22.6
Semi-skilled	19.5	14.9	13.1	13.7	13.4	10.8	9.1	8.9	7.5	9.5	8.9	6.8	3.4	4.0
Unskilled	24.3	27.1	18.2	10.5	7.8	8.0	7.4	6.7	6.0	5.6	4.5	4.3	2.2	2.5
Non-Manual Workers														
Higher education	3.2	4.3	11.2	3.5	4.1	5.9	10.1	11.6	19.4	8.1	11.0	13.8	27.2	25.3
Secondary education	8.3	9.9	16.8	11.8	12.0	13.0	16.0	17.0	23.4	15.7	15.0	17.4	22.9	22.3
Lower grade education	9.3	6.3	5.9	9.2	7.0	7.3	6.4	5.9	5.3	10.7	6.4	6.9	5.6	5.5

Sources: Statistički godišnjaci Jugoslavike, 1971, 1972, 1973. This data concerns the economy and therefore excludes 'non-economic' activities classified in Yugoslav statistics as culture, health, schools, government and social agencies (the level of education of the labor force is higher in these areas). The enterprises covered here are those which have elections for workers' councils. Enterprises with less than 50 employees do not have elections; anyone is automatically a member of self-management organs. Approximately 25 percent of the labor force is engaged in such small enterprise.

1. While the percentage of manual workers participating in worker councils and managing, boards has declined over time (76 percent to 65 percent, 66 percent to 47 percent, respectively) the proportion of highly skilled workers participating has increased in the workers' councils and held its own in the managing boards. One might conclude that there is a tendency for representative and management functions to be carried out by an elite group of 'workers' consisting of managers, technicians and other non-manual workers with higher and secondary education, and highly skilled workers.

2. One cannot directly infer differentials in influence or control among different categories of workers from this data. 'Control' is a complex matter relating to social processes in different spheres and at different levels.

* No newer data exists for the composition of managing boards. Anyway, there role has changed, making the interpretation of intertemporal comparisons difficult.

nicians in self-management processes within enterprises, the economic elite gained increased freedom from interference from their socio-political environment.[32a] One indicator of the relative autonomization from political and ideological regulation has been the tendency to professionalize management concepts and roles (Županov, 1969). (This is not to imply, however, that the economic elite did not also play strategic roles in political and ideological processes [see section 5].) In one survey Županov found that the actual role of general manager was perceived by half of the respondents as a 'professional role' and by the other half as a 'political role'.[32b] But almost all respondents agreed that ideally the role of the manager should be professional and not political. Consequently, a majority of respondents were against the principle of rotation of personnel in enterprise positions, since they felt that this principle should be applied only to political functionaries. The general opinion was that the manager should behave in accordance with the role of professional businessman, if the different roles which the general manager must play at one and the same time (professional businessman, keeper of legacy, political functionary, leader of the collective, and executive organ of self-management bodies) come into conflict.[33]

This section has addressed itself to the nature of social relations of production under Yugoslav self-management operating under market allocation of resources. The means of production are not privately owned and sanctions based on property concepts are not available to managers. Nevertheless, the social division of labor (hierarchy and segmentation) and the technologies utilized (e.g. assembly lines, scale, and corporate structure) operate to develop and reproduce unequal power and control relationships and uneven accumulation of knowledge, capabilities, and social linkages among actors engaged in production.[34]

4. Self-Managed Enterprises and Market Processes of Unequal Accumulation and Development

Capitalist enterprises operating in market systems accumulate and develop unequally (see Chapter VII in Burns *et al.*, 1985). Self-managed enterprises — acting as collective entrepreneurs, transacting with one another under market rules — tend also toward the differential accumulation of resources, capabilities and social power.[35] In the absence of institutional limits on such accumulation, enterprises develop unequal capabilities to shape or take advantage of action opportunities (e.g., the development of new products and production processes and movement into new markets) or to avoid or overcome negative conditions (e.g., a recession, loss of a market, major technological changes requiring reorientation of production, etc.). Especially noteworthy are differential accumulation and development of capital, management knowledge and skills, technology and overall development capabilities (e.g., to conduct research and development), different standards of living for workers, and different levels of legitimation and capability of influencing political conditions.

Such uneven development capabilities support further differential accumulation and vice versa. The outcome is the emergence of advanced and backward enterprises, sectors, and regions. The former are inclined to use their powers to assure the persistence of market conditions and rules advantageous to their interest. In this way, differential accumulation and uneven development may be maintained and reproduced.

The differential accumulation and uneven developments occur at different societal levels:

— Between regions (see Tables 7.3 and 7.4).

— Between sectors, e.g., between agricultural and industrial production and in industrial production between advanced and traditional sectors. (These differences are, of course, associated with those between regions, because of the different production profiles of various regions.)

— Between enterprises, e.g., monopolistic or oligopolistic enterprises versus small enterprises in highly competitive markets; or expanding enterprises versus those stagnating or declining.

There have been and continue to be substantial disparities in the levels of economic development and standards of living between different republics and autonomous regions. These have been recognized as a major political, economic and social issue throughout the postwar period (Dubey, 1975:12).[36] Although there are less developed areas within even the wealthier republics, the differentials between the republics (and autonomous regions) have been at the center of attention, both because of their magnitude and because they are associated with political units with differences in language, nationalities, religion, and culture.[37]

The per-capita income of the underdeveloped regions (Bosnia Herzegovina, Kosovo, Macedonia, Montenegro) remains substantially lower than the national average (see Table 7.3). They also continue to be relatively backward according to social indicators used in any assessment of standard of living and socio-economic welfare (percentage of illiterates, population per hospital bed, infant mortality). Moreover, although they have shown significant progress in the quality of life as indicated by the proportion of illiterates in the population aged 10 or more (reduction from 2/5 to 1/5) and infant mortality (halved), the per-capita income differences with the

TABLE 7.3a

Index of per capita incomes

Regional Differentiation	1953 Actual	Actual	1971 (1966 Prices) Same population growth[1]	Same GMP growth[2]
Developed regions	100	100	100	100
Underdeveloped regions	65	50[3]	57	56
Bosnia-Herzegovina	74	53	60	65
Kosovo	42	28	37	29
Macedonia	60	56	62	55
Montenegro	60	58	64	53

Source: Dubey (1975).

1. Population growth assumed to be the same as for yugoslavia as a whole (17.4) in developed and underdeveloped regions. The column indicates the impact of differences in economic growth on relative per capita income.

2. GMP assumed to be the same for Yugoslavia (240.9) in developed and underdeveloped regions. The column indicates the impact of differences in growth of population on relative per capita incomes. (GMP = Gross Material Product which excludes public services.)

3. Even though there has been a rapid improvement in the standard of living in the less developed regions since the second world war (that is, the regions of Bosnia-Herzegovina, Kosovo, Macedonia, and Montenegro), they have been losing ground relative to the developed regions. (See also Table 7.3b.)

TABLE 7.3b

Relative Percapita GDP of Underdeveloped and Developed Regions

	1952	1956	1960	1964	1968	1972	1976
Underdeveloped	100	100	100	100	100	100	100
Developed	160.0	162.6	180.5	181.8	195.6	194.7	205.4

Source: M. Bazler, S. Bolčić, Č. Ocić, J. Tomić-Jurišić: Jedinstveni objektivizirani kriteriji za odredjivanje stepena razvi jenosti republika i autonomnih pokrajina, Institut ekonomskih nauka, Beograd, 1978

more developed regions have continued to grow (see Tables 7.3 and 7.4).

Similarly, personal incomes for labor with similar skills differ by a factor of 3 to 4, both across economic sectors or branches and across enterprises within sectors. These differences are a function of differences in efficiency, in capital endowments, and market structure. Capital intensive — and rapidly expanding — sectors and enterprises can afford to pay much higher

TABLE 7.4
Selected developed indicators

	Bosna-Herzegovina	Kosovo	Macedonia	Montenegro	Underdeveloped regions	Developed regions	SFRY (Yugoslavia)
Per capita GMP, 1971	441.0	196.0	424.0	430.0	394.0	807.0	663.0
Growth rate of GMP							
1953-71 (1966 prices)							
Total	6.3%	6.6%	7.6%	7.6%	6.7%	7.4%	7.3%
Per capita	4.9%	4.2%	6.3%	5.3%	5.3%	6.8%	6.3%
1971-1980							
Total	5.5%	5.5%	5.8%	6.9%	—	—	5.7%
Per capita	4.2%	2.6%	4.3%	4.8%	—	—	4.8%
Gross fixed investment as % of GMP (1953-1969) (1966 prices)	29.9%	29.1%	43.8%	52.6%	35.0%	24.4%	26.6%
Shares of industrial production							
1953 (1966 prices)	11.6%	2.6%	3.1%	0.6%	17.9%	82.1%	100.0%
1970 (1966 prices)	12.1%	2.0%	5.0%	1.5%	20.6%	79.4%	100.0%
Share of agriculture in GMP (1966) prices							
1953	39.6%	51.8%	46.5%	38.5%	42.3%	39.2%	39.9%
1970	19.5%	26.2%	26.3%	15.1%	21.5%	19.5%	19.9%
1980 (1972 prices)	11.7%	21.0%	16.6%	9.6%	—	—	13.4%
Fixed assets per worker in industry (thousands of 1966 dollars)							
1952	43.6	52.4	44.2	71.3	45.7	51.4	50.2
1970	109.8	124.1	84.2	152.5	108.2	85.9	91.3

TABLE 7.4 continued

Share of fixed assets in industry							
1962	12.80%	1.89%	2.88%	1.29%	18.86%	81.14%	100.0%
1970	17.4%	3.25%	4.86%	2.74%	27.99%	72.01%	100.0%
Percentage of illiteracy (10 years or older)							
1953	40.2%	54.8%	35.7%	30.1%	40.4%	19.1%	25.4%
1971	22.7%	32.2%	18.0%	17.2%	22.7%	11.7%	15.2%
Population per hospital bed							
1950	503.0	820.0	467.0	264.0	484.0	261.0	304.0
1970	253.0	364.0	185.0	165.0	236.0	153.0	174.0
1980	215.0	362.0	195.0	124.0	—	—	167.0
Infant mortality per 1000 live births							
Average 1950–54	134.0	154.6	138.8	88.6	135.7	101.0	115.7
1971	53.6	89.6	81.9	34.6	68.2	31.6	48.9
1981	28.4	663	55.4	20.7	—	—	31.3

Source: Dubey (1975:191) and Razvoj Jugoslavije 1947-1981, Savezui Zavod za statistiky, savezn; zavod za društreus planirauje, Beograd, 1982.

wages (personal incomes) by distributing part of the return to capital and favorable market situation as wages.[38] (But this also creates pressures for increasing personal income in other sectors or in other enterprises.) High income levels are also found in branches where one or a few firms dominate. And, of course, personal income levels tend to vary between enterprises which do well and those which do not. The largest firms have been growing more rapidly than others, and consequently, their share of the aggregate economic activity of the economy has increased steadily.

Sacks (1976:383-84): reports[39]

In every year the largest firms' share of total assets is greater than their share of total employment, indicating that they are more capital-intensive than the average industrial firm. This fact explains why their share of sales is greater than their share of employment. It also means that each worker in these firms 'controls', through his workers' council, a disproportionate share of the real wealth of the sector (and an even larger share of the real wealth of the entire economy).

As Tables 7.3 and 7.4 indicate, there are strong tendencies toward a 'dual economy' and uneven development generally in the Yugoslav system. This is particularly likely in the case of Yugoslavia since it launched its self-management system in the context of *already substantial social differences and uneven development.* These conditions have been a principal source of social movement and opposition to institutional conditions within Yugoslavia (section 5).

5.   Phases and Dialectical Shifts in Yugoslav Development

Yugoslavia has experienced several phases of socio-economic development in the post-war period (see page 207). The period of Yugoslav development up until the early 1950s stressed ideological and political features of development, although, of course, there was considerable attention given to economic and technical matters. Beginning in the early 1950s a phase of economic/technical preoccupation emerged and reached its height in the period 1964-71. In the earliest phase the party, and the party's top leadership dominated. After 1964, the economic-technical elite and professional politicians with local and regional constituencies predominated. The top leadership of the LYC appeared to be fragmented and on the defensive. The third phase (1972-1980) reemphasized political and ideological principles and reestablished the dominance of political institutions and objectives, particularly at the national level, over economic-technical aspects.

The phases are differentiated by the emphasis given to particular dimensions, goals, norms and standards of evaluation, and support or opposition to particular patterns of social action and structural developments. Each phase exhibits particular institution structuring, restructuring and innovation tendencies, for instance:

— An ideological-political phase where political institutions and values are given priority, that is, there is an emphasis on socialist norms and values (especially those opposed to wage and other economic inequalities and uneven development), solidarity, societal integration, and political and ideological control of economic institutions (and therefore with less stress on productivity, economic-technical expertise, specialization, and differentiated incentive systems).

— A technical-economic phase where economic institutions and values are given priority, with an emphasis on economic productivity, capital accumulation, efficiency, technocratic expertise, professional qualifications and performance, (differentiated) material incentive systems, and economic objectives and standards generally.

Shifts from one phase to another are typically associated with conflicts among groups associated or identified more with one set of goals, norms, and institutionalized patterns of social action than others.[40] There is a struggle over societal development, for instance, with respect to maintaining or changing characteristic structures and processes. A given phase generates certain consequences, intended and unintended. Different socio-political groups react, either opposing or supporting and reinforcing existing trends. Overall effective support reinforces the characteristic pattern of that phase. Effective opposition tends to bring about a phase characterized by a set of goals, norms, standards of evaluation, and patterns of social action which were secondary or neglected in the preceding phase.

What is of particular interest here are assessments by and initiatives of the dominant political leadership in Yugoslavia, and its use of meta-power in restructuring institutional arrangements, rules of the game, and other features which identify a phase of development. The third phase (1972-1980) was initially characterized by a shift away from an economic/technical emphasis to a more ideological/political one — this has involved the LYC leadership in substantial restructuring and innovations in institutions. This development was related to both problems of socio-economic performance and its social consequences and to matters of power in the society. We discuss these two interrelated aspects separately.

Socio-economic Aspects

The period 1965-71 of increasing autonomy of enterprises and of the economic sphere from political control led to both desirable and undesirable consequences:

— relative rapid growth, the increase in production averaging 7 percent per year during 1964-72;[41]

— the fixed assets per worker have risen sharply since 1964, having been fairly stable until 1964; the capital output ratio, declining until 1965, has tended to increase particularly in industry;

— exports' share of GNP continued to grow;[42]

— substantial increases in personal income;[43]

— relatively large and increasing unemployment;[44]

— substantial emigration abroad to West European countries (approximately 700,000 Yugoslav workers abroad, 45 percent of them of peasant origin);

— during 1968-70 there emerged serious inflationary pressures and increasing balance of payments deficits;[45]

— increased differences in income levels and in the accessibility to collective goods and services by various social groups and communities;

— uneven development and growing inequality generally between enterprises, sectors of the economy, and regions of Yugoslavia:

— increasing, pluralism, above all nationalistic tendencies.

Although some of the economic indicators were positive, several key ones, such as rates of inflation and unemployment and increased socio-economic differentiation, were substantially negative. Self-management institutions, particularly enterprises operating relatively autonomously under market allocation, generated socio-economic consequences which were inconsistent with some of the leading norms and values of self-management socialism (as discussed in sections 3 and 4). The oligarchic tendencies (section 3) and uneven accumulation and development patterns (section 4) indicated that economic objectives, activities, and institutional arrangements to increase productivity and income, profitability, and growth operated to some extent in opposition to values and institutions relating to democratic participation, equality, and solidarity. Moreover, serious social and political problems emerged during 1970-71.

Socio-political Aspects

The power and legitimation of the political leadership, which had established the institutional set-up in the first place, appeared to be threatened by the emergence of intra-societal competing groups and social movements opposed to the particular development tendencies and features of the institutional set-up in Yugoslavia. This situation was one aspect of the emergence of pluralistic centers of power in Yugoslavia, associated with economic and political decentralization. These various developments, summarized below, were interrelated and in this sense should be viewed as part of a system development, a dynamic totality.[46]

— Decentralization of the economy and development of the open market facilitated the increased autonomy of enterprises from political and ideological regulation. The managerial and technical elite came to increasingly dominate self-managed enterprises. At the same time, this elite penetrated political (as well as socio-cultural) circles. The emergent elites of managers and technicians in the different republics stressed economic growth and rationality, professionalism and meritocracy, and institutional arrangements to advance these and related values. These new elites could also challenge the top political elite in the context of economic policy-making, as well as in a variety of settings which could be seen to be relevant to the maintenance of its own creative dominance.

— Non-egalitarian developments were increasingly apparent in the economic sphere and had, of course, socio-cultural and political implications: (i) personal accumulation and enrichment, increasing variation in standards of living, life styles and life chances; (ii) the economic power and conglomeration of some enterprises and sectors increased while others lagged behind; (iii) regions and republics accumulated and developed unequally.

— General problems of coordination and societal integration became increasingly prominent. This was manifested either in immobilization in the face of serious problems such as inflation or balance of payments difficulties or in the vigorous pursuit of self-interest. Decentralization of the political system brought into play pluralistic factions of the republican and local level politicians (e.g. much greater *informal* autonomy, than previously, of the republics and republican parties and the orientation of professional politicians more to particular interests of their republics, regions, and special groups). This development was reinforced by uneven development of republics and regions, the enormous socio-economic gaps between the wealthiest and poorest regions, and their competition for economic resources and economic advantages.

— There emerged social movements, for example, students reacting to economic inequality and the apparent lack of democracy,[47] nationalistically oriented circles[48] strove to enhance or protect their national interests vis à vis other national interests in Yugoslavia. In some instances, ties developed between the emerging managerial and technical elite and nationalistic/ cultural elites. Such developments are especially dangerous since nationalistic tendencies could prevail over other tendencies and loyalties such as Party orientation.

Because the concept of self-management is a legitimizing feature of Yugoslav socialist ideology and the value system of the society (Denitch, 1977:153-57), every group appeals for its proposals to, or grounds its arguments in, self-management and the development of self-management institutions and values. Of course, operationalization of the concept of self-management — its concrete interpretation and application — differs for different groups.[49] During the period of liberal development, the economic technocrats interpreted self-management in terms of increasing enterprise autonomy. This autonomy, combined with an oligarchic distribution of power within enterprises, meant freedom of the oligarchy from external political and ideological regulation. It was also this group which argued for and sought to legitimize economic rationality connected with economic growth and qualitative restructuring of the economy in accordance with the demands of a dynamic market.

The 'self-management faction' within the political leadership initiated the Constitutional Amendment XV (1969), which gave enterprises freedom in creating and designing their own inner self management structures (see page 212). In many enterprises this meant a strengthening of the managerial bodies including that of the director (Hunnius, 1973:277). New executive bodies, such as directors' boards and business boards, were created where managers and technicians played a clearly dominant role. In such ways the power and status of the technostructure within enterprises was not only enhanced but increasingly legitimized.

These developments were paralleled by changes in the economic system especially concerning the bearer of investment. The growing power of banks and financial institutions is indicated by the data in Table 7.1. Of course, this development was compatible with the stress on economic values and norms (as opposed to more socio-political and solidarity values).

On the broader socio-political scene, the increasing influence of managers and technicians was observable in the 'House of Producers' (which was one of the important houses within the parliamentary structure preceding the 1974 Constitution). In matters of economic policy, programs, and institution formation and adaptation, expertise was a decisive factor. On all levels (federal, republic, and commune parliaments) economic managers and technicians penetrated and played a dominating role in legislative bodies.[50]

The Yugoslav economy and political system became increasingly pluralistic — later referred to as laissez faire. This was also characteristic of cultural and intellectual life during this period. Moreover, the increasing pluralism within the polity was linked to the growing power of the economic technocracy. In the beginning this pluralism was limited to the different factions of the political elite, but later it broadened. Some factions of the political elite connected themselves to new groups striving for power, in particular the managerial/technical elite (see note 50).[51]

Decentralization of the economy, self-management institutions operating under market conditions, economic competition and inequality, and political decentralization resulted then in the emergence of pluralistic centers of power in Yugoslavia — where initially, there were no autonomous centers of power to speak of. The increasing pluralist tendencies and conflicts characteristic of the late 1960s and early 1970s threatened the existing distribution of meta- or structural power. Meta-power relationships themselves could have been restructured in terms of the emergence of legalized or legitimized pluralism within the political sphere in combination with the ever-growing influence of the managerial/technocratic elites. The influence of the latter rested not only on the autonomization of the economic sphere but on their penetration of, and alliances with actors in, the political and socio-cultural spheres. Although such interpenetration existed earlier, it was then primarily based on political criteria and objectives. The growing influence of the technocratic groups rested, above all, on their claims of assuring economic efficiency and potentialities for socio-economic development.

The dominant political leadership took action to halt the growing pluralism and the apparent threat to its domination over the system (and possibly, threat to the system itself).[52] These steps were taken ostensibly to deal with other problems, for instance the increasing inequality within enterprises and between sectors and regions of Yugoslavia, uneven development generally, the dominance of market institutions and economic considerations over self-management and political institutions and values, and the particularistic, above all nationalistic, interests and distortions incompatible with Yugoslav socialist ideology and the viability of Yugoslavia as a society. The most significant actions of the political elite were to restructure as well as to introduce new institutions.[53] This was accompanied by the removal of persons, or shifts in personnel, from key positions (which often commanded the most attention in newspaper accounts).[54] Key instances of such restructuring were:

— Dehierarchization of enterprises, increased power to basic organizations of associated labor (BOAL), with the enterprise consisting of a contractually integrated cluster of BOALs to deal in external relationships and to appear in the market.

— Attempts, through increased involvement and influence of political actors and communes as well as through contractual institutions, to control self-managed enterprises and their development in accordance with broader societal interests and to constrain some of the economic and related imbalances and distortions discussed earlier. This meant, of course, reduction in the autonomy of enterprises, above all their politicalization.

— Introduction of institutional devices in the 1974 Constitution to increase coordinating, planning and integrating capabilities: social compacts, self-management agreements, delegation system, integrated economic, social, and physical planning.[55] Also, self-managed interest communities were established in the spheres of health, education, culture, research, and sport. Transport and electric power 'networks' were set-up. A central planning office charged with revitalizing planning, which had been neglected at the federal level from the 1960s on, was created.

— Steps were taken to enhance differences in power between political and economic/technical elites, that is, to re-establish and maintain the domination of the political over the economic sphere, above all through party and labor union activity.[56]

— Purges of 'nationalistic elements' at the same time that republics and autonomous provinces were given more economic autonomy.

The concept of self-management was redefined or reinterpreted in the process. The intent was to increase the influence of workers, particularly the less skilled workers, and to decrease or limit the influence of managers and technocrats. In particular, the power of workers' councils was formally increased at the same time that the new institution of the 'assembly of all workers' (of a BOAL) was introduced and given special rights. Also, to increase the competence of workers in management processes, they were given access to specialized units providing accounting, financial analysis, and other services. At the macro-level, the new institution of legal defender of self-management, and the new parliamentary system based on the principle of delegation was established. Directors were not to be elected to self-management bodies. Similarly, they could not be elected to the new Chambers of Associated Labor, corresponding to the former 'House of Producers'.

Enterprise autonomy has been de-emphasized. Mechanisms to promote political and ideological influence and regulation over enterprise decision-making and development have been re-activated or established (e.g. concerning income distribution). However, this de-autonomization is not to be accomplished through state regulation but through new institutions which are considered compatible with self-management, such as self-management agreements and social compacts.[57] The contractual nature of these institutions is designed to compel different actors to coordinate their actions and interests as well as to regulate one another's development. That is, they should protect the global interests of the larger collectivity or society from narrow 'enterprise egotism'. Compacts and self-management agreements are the tools and expression of the new planning system (Kalogjera, 1977). This planning system is unique in its attempts to protect the independence of the different basic social units of the economic, political and socio-cultural spheres from interference and pressure by the state (especially the federal and even republican state administrations). In a word, it is an institutionalized form of planning designed to be compatible with self-management institutions (Bošnjak *et al.*, 1978).[58]

The LYC and labor unions have been formally given more prominent roles in socio-economic and government processes. The increasing role of the party does not automatically mean greater influence of workers. The party functions as an integrator of the interests and demands of many groups, not only those in whose name it claims to speak. Moreover, the social composition of the party indicates that every second manager is a member of the party, every fourth professional, but only every eleventh worker and sixteenth peasant.

Not all the results of the period of pluralistic development were undone. The autonomy of the republics and autonomous provinces has been increased to a certain extent and justified in terms of the right to self-management at the republic or province level. However, this autonomy and pluralism is purged of any nationalistic trait and, in practice, is very much limited to economic matters. The political elites in the republics (and provinces) can advocate the economic interests of their respective regions and they retain enlarged economic independence from the federal leadership. The integration of the federal level is henceforth to be based on common economic interests and the political/ideological motivation of solidarity. But political democratization is limited. The LYC is the only societal actor able to influence decision-making at all levels and in all spheres.

The success of the LYC's multi-faceted strategy of institution restructuring and innovation was helped by its judicious use of the widespread unease about increasing income inequalities, uneven development, and the difficulty or inability to solve collective action problems and to check nationalistic tendencies. The consistency of the reforms with these criticisms helped them assure widespread support. The justification of the reforms was helped by its consistency with one of the basic ideological tenets shaped during the post-liberation period, decentralization and self-management.[59]

Although the structural changes which have been introduced are supposed to increase the power of workers inside as well as outside enterprises, workers do not apper to make up a relatively autonomous movement on the global level, which could assert itself vis à vis other societal groups, above all the party. The characteristic feature of worker action is its local nature. Thus, strikes tend to be limited to small numbers within factories. They do not occur in a branch or in a territory — this would require a broader organization or societal movement than presently exists. On the other hand, democratization appears to have been strengthened at the enterprise level by increasing the power of basic organizations of associated labor (BOALs) and workers' assemblies as opposed to enterprise level self-management organs and management bodies. At the same time, these changes are likely to weaken the social power of the managerial and technical elites (and their values, standards, patterns of activity and leadership, etc.) in relation to the political elite, in that they are constrained in the use of their expertise and of economic power materialized in social capital and property (Rusinow, 1977:328). Thus, 'democracy' at the marco-level — and understood here as increased participation, at least of different elite groups in political processes — would appear to be weakened.[60] The principle is a well-known one: atomization of social units, in this case production units, contributes to maintaining the power of a political elite.

6.   Concluding Remarks

The arrangement of multiple institutions in a society — in the case of Yugoslavia, self-management, social ownership of the means of production, market allocation, and a decentralized polity with a single revolutionary party — makes up a dynamic totality. Conflicting social values and patterns of social activity are pursued through multiple and partially incompatible institutions. The operation of one institution limits or undermines the intended operation and development of another. For instance, institutional activities and development (or pressures for development) relating to the market economy interfere with or undermine the activities and development of other institutions, such as those associated with democratic participation and self-management. The result is that the latter are encapsulated and remain underdeveloped. In this sense one may speak of contradictions and opposing tendencies among societal institutions.

Societal development entails institutional innovation, the shaping and reshaping of social institutions. The outcomes of such processes cannot be fully predicted. Invariably, there will be unintended consequences and unanticipated developments. Therefore, institutional change — whether motivated by system maintaining or system transforming interests — involves some degree of social experimentation. This is particularly so in the case of Yugoslavia since, as Dubey (1975) suggests, the Yugoslavs have had no clear-cut societal model to follow. Rather, they have been engaged in the process of developing and testing such a model. The workability and compatibility of concepts and institutions have had to be tested and judged through praxis, and alterations made on the basis of performance results and experience. Basic laws and even the constitution have been changed frequently. Periods of rapid and qualitatively distinctive changes (e.g., 1953, 1961, 1965 and 1971-72) have been followed by periods of consolidation.

The analysis in this chapter suggests that a system of self-managed enterprises does not entail in itself the full democratization of work. Nor does it imply the liberation of political power (or workers' control over political power). The system has failed thus far to provide workers with the structural power to shape the institutional environment and rules governing self-managed enterprises, above all the regulation of political power.

A more complete or extensive work democracy would entail extending workers' control *beyond the enterprise* to cover the environments within which the enterprise functions — that is, the economic and market institutions and above all the political and socio-cultural spheres. Such control is a necessary but not a sufficient condition. It must be exercised in such a way as to produce conditions and processes compatible with the further development and reproduction of self-management institutions.

The description and analysis presented in this chapter does not, however, conclude with a blueprint for final solutions.[61] It is unlikely that even the best of the societal models would tell us what the emerging institutional arrangement will or even should entail, at least not in any detail. But the process of development can be understood as a continuing process of social learning, institutional innovation and experimentation, critical assessment in terms of democratic socialist values and ideology, and further restructuring and experimentation.[62]

Epilogue

The economic crisis in Yugoslavia has deepened in the 1980s (50-199 % inflation, balance of payments crisis, shortages, and increasing unemployment). The external shocks of oil price increases and world recession have been major factors in provoking the crisis, but socio-political cleavages and the lack of effective central economic policy-making explain Yugoslavia's inability to respond coherently and effectively to the crisis and the depth of the crisis.

1) The 1974 constitutional reform was to improve coordination between enterprises, communes and socio-political organizations. At the same time, it strengthened the autonomy of republics and provinces in economic matters. Given the national cleavages and the aspiration of the less-developed regions, every republic and province has tried to control its own infrastructure (railways, airlines, electricity, banks) and to build up its own frontline technologies (oil refineries and related petro-chemical companies, automobile assembly lines, electronic and appliance companies, and so forth). Productivity growth began to decline in Yugoslavia just when adaptation to a changing world economy would have required making optimal use of limited resources. The decentralized nature of the self-management system has also contributed to blocking the growth of new industries. Individual enterprises cannot mobilize sufficient resources for effective R & D. At the same time, when a new product or product line is available for marketing, many enterprises produce the same equipment at a high cost. The lack of consolidation, while exemplary for free market enthusiasts, prevents achievement of scales of production and more effective resource utilization. For instance, non-optimal domestic production of solar technologies has prevented Yugoslavia from greater exploitation of a domestic, alternative energy source.

2) Political response to the economic crisis failed to come in time and has been far too weak in any case. A period of political immobilization set in shortly before the end of Tito's reign (1981) and has continued since. The national institutions such as the collective, rotating presidency with unanimity rules, established by Tito to assure a peaceful future for Yugoslavia, have been unable to take decisive actions. They simply reflect the deep cleavages in Yugoslavia rather than transcending them.

The recourse to the inflationary settlement of conflicting claims on resources is quite natural in the context of a weak and divided political leadership (see Part One), a shrinking resource base, and still rising expectations and demands (especially from the less developed regions, which are also major centers of political opposition and conflict).

Policy responses and tough measures to deal with the crisis have not come from the political leadership. They have been imposed by *actors external to the system*: international banks and the IMF. The deflationary measures imposed will not resolve the underlying social and political cleavages and, indeed, are likely to intensify tensions and conflicts.

Whether the leading politicians come up with new institutional innovations in the near future remains to be seen. Yugoslavia's situation is not entirely hopeless. Its strategic position between East and West power blocs insures that the USA and other Western countries will come forward with additional loans if this is necessary to prevent socio-political struggles and conflicts over income distribution from becoming uncontrollable. But this is a temporary solution, not a resolution of Yugoslavia's problems. At the same time, the increasing role of external, economic agents in Yugoslavia's policy-making means that the possibilities to pursue her experiment with a "third way" are more or less reduced. In becoming increasingly dependent on external agents, Yugoslavia runs the risk of losing autonomy and the freedom to innovate and restructure (see related discussions in Chapters 4 and 5).

NOTES

1. It is our hope that the following description and analysis, even in its present tentative form, will contribute to the discussion and clarification of the creative potentialities in, as well as constraints on the development of self-management institutions in Yugoslavia.
2. This section draws on the following sources: Dubey (1975), The International Institute for Labor Studies (hereafter, IILS) (1972), and Rus (1977). Other materials used are Bošnjak et al (1978), Hunnius (1973), Zukin (1975), and Rusinow (1977).
3. That is, each of the two main political causes which had existed before 1945 — the maintenance of a regime dominated by old Serbia and its ruling group before the war and the establishment of a fully independent Croatian State during the war — had been not merely defeated but totally discredited.
4. At the outbreak of the war, the party was an illegal organization with 6,455 members and 17,800 members in SKOJ (the party youth organization) (Bilandžić, 1973).
5. Up until 1948 the Communist Party of Yugoslavia was recognized as highly 'bolshevized' (Deutscher 1972:577-78; Stojanovic, 1973).
6. The break with the Soviet Union and Cominform must be viewed in its international context, the growing tensions between the Soviet Union and the USA, and the emerging Cold War. 'Deviationism' not only threatened to undermine Soviet domination over other Communist countries in Eastern Europe, but to weaken Eastern Europe as a buffer area which the Soviet Union sought to establish. There were also disagreements between the Soviet Union and Yugoslavia about questions of socio-economic development, about a suitable rate of Yugoslav industrialization, Yugoslavia's place in the international socialist division of labor, and the economic (and ultimately political) relations with the Soviet Union. Boris Kidrić, one of the leading postwar economists, recalls (cited in Bon, 1975:42-43):

    Their purpose was to keep Yugoslavia as an agricultural and raw-material producing appendage, which is why they opposed our setting up basic industries that would help us become independent. We were offended by their opposition to our economic plan and our industrialization program ... They called us megalomaniacs and said that our industrialization program was an Utopian dream.
7. For three years, from 1949 through 1951, the combined percentage of G.M.P. (Gross

Material Product) committed to investment and defence expenditures exceeded 40 percent (Dubey, 1975:28). *Note:* These figures reflect only basic wage incomes and do not take into account overtime and family earnings. Nor do they reflect differences due to profit-related wage bonuses, enterprise-owned apartments with nominal rents, company cars, expense accounts (allowed for much coveted foreign travel), and other enterprise allocated consumables).

8. Even if the harvest fluctuations are averaged out over the periods 1947-49 and 1951-53, the average rate of growth in national product was only about 4 percent. Dubey (1975:28) points out that this was low in relation both to later achievements and to the rate of growth in the immediate postwar years (although higher than the interwar average).

9. Yugoslavia feared an invasion. Border incidents with Hungary, Bulgaria, and Romania increased. Besides the external threat, there was the threat of the Soviet Union exploiting national divisions within Yugoslavia. Also, there were factions within the Yugoslav Communist Party sympathetic to the Soviet Union ('Stalinists') who might have gained widespread support within the party. (These elements were particularly strong in some units, for example, the Montenegran Communist Party.) Eastern European countries sent radio broadcasts to 'loyal communists' to replace the 'Tito group'. Propaganda was also directed at officers in the army.

   At the same time, trials were conducted in Eastern Europe during this period, in which 'Titoist plots' of the most unlikely sorts were revealed. Dedijer (1971:212, 130-31, 140-45) describes various forms of pressure in addition to tshe economic ones. (The most systematic description of the conflict is given in Randonjić, 1975.)

10. As Zukin (1975:53) stresses, the Yugoslav communists were compelled to find a way to define their continuing revolution as socialist, and also as totally divorced from the leading exemplar of socialism at that time, that is the Soviet Union. This called for finding criteria to define their revolution and development strategy as distinct and genuinely socialist as well as opposed to the Soviet Union as a model. Official Yugoslav arguments after 1948 held the Soviet Union to be etatist or state capitalist and *not* socialist. Early articles questioning the socialist character of the Soviet system are Baće (1949) and Pijade (1949).

11. In any description and analysis of Yugoslav post-war institutional development, it is essential to stress that the Yugoslav Communist Party had a popular base — and a military capability of its own — in contrast to parties in other Eastern European countries. (The partisans had liberated Yugoslavia without the Red Army.) This enabled the Tito leadership to develop a type of national communism (as in the case of China, also) with opportunities and motivation for self-reliant innovation and experimentation, which has been possible only to a very limited degree in other Eastern European countries (with the exception of Albania and to a much lesser extent Romania). That is, the high level of innovation in developing and changing social institutions has to a large extent been a function of national independence and self-reliance of the leadership as well as of its internal support and legitimation (Ionescu, 1976:31):

    > This kind of leader is trusted by the people to be able to take on another power that might threaten national integrity — both Tito and Mao turned easily against the Soviet Union with the support of their people ... They could change their policies without relinquishing their leadership.

12. In 1953, in the course of rewriting the 1946 Federal Constitution, the government tried to clarify the semi-autonomous status of enterprises as well as the rights and duties of the workers. Zukin (1975:59-60) writes:

    > A federal government proclamation of that time stated officially that enterprise auto-

nomy — as far as plans, profits, and wages are concerned — was an essential component of workers' self-management. However, the state maintained certain controls to
ensure that the enterprise would fulfill its financial obligations to the government, to
its workers, and to its own continued functioning. The 1953 proclamation also upheld
the right of work collectives to manage economic organizations directly and through
workers' councils, assemblies of agricultural cooperatives and other representative
organs which they themselves elect and recall.

13. In 1966, A. Ranković ,who was vice-president of Yugoslavia and head of the secret
    police and who had supported centralization tendencies, was ousted from the party
    leadership. Zimmerman (1976:68-69) writes:

    If we are to believe the accounts of the victors, Ranković was opposed to the whole
    proposed direction of Yugoslav policy being advocated by the adherents of market
    socialism. Thus, he apparently concluded (correctly) that the economic reforms were
    fraught with important political consequences. Those economic reforms ... envisaged
    judging enterprises primarily by efficiency as measured by market criteria. To achieve
    efficiency, the dinar was to be devalued and the goal was set of convertibility by 1970.
    The country's borders, furthermore, were to be opened both to the in-migration of
    capital (especially under the aegis of Yugoslav-foreign joint ventures) and to the out-
    migration of workers. Ranković evidently feared that, as a result of the economic
    reforms, Yugoslavia would be integrated into Western Europe and into the capitalist
    international market, the problems of internal political control would be increased,
    the Yugoslav citizenry would be exposed to Western influences, and a more Western-
    oriented foreign policy would ensue — all of which ranković opposed. Instead, he
    appears to have stood for an entirely opposed line: the continuationo of 'political' fac-
    tories, the discouragement of foreign investment and close ties with the socialist states.
    Finally, his behavior conjured up fears, most notably in Croatia, that his dominance in
    post-Tito Yugoslavia would bring about a return of Serbian dominance ...

    The victors were not content, however, to limit themselves to the purging of Ran-
    ković and his cohorts. Ranković's ouster was followed by a series of institutional alter-
    ations designed to prevent a similar occurrence (use of the secret police to try to
    strengthen his position) and to provide an institutional context in which economic
    reform and political decentralization might flourish.

14. Also, the character of state investment changed (see Table 7.5).

TABLE 7.5

Investment in fixed assets financed by different levels (in percent)

	1953	1955	1960	1962	1964	1966	1970	1972
Federation	97	73	60	51	19	40	55	10
Republics	2	14	11	15	22	20	20	70
Communes and districts	1	13	29	34	59	40	25	20

Source: Dubey (1975).

15. Nevertheless, the picture remained quite complicated. The allocation of funds continued
    to be influenced by considerations other than simply the 'profitability' of projects.
    Government policies and viewpoints of founding members of banks, who were also the

chief borrowers, exercised considerable influence.

There were also strong tendencies toward concentration. In 1966 there were 111 banks, which were reduced to 64 by 1970. These mergers resulted in the emergence of some very large banks with practically a national field of operation. Banks came in for increasing criticism as being too powerful in determining the allocation of funds and being a serious obstacle to greater autonomy of workers' self-managed enterprises.

16. The stress on economic objectives and on institutions such as monetary and financial institutions — in order to facilitate the rational allocation of resources and to increase productivity and income — is motivated in part by genuine interest in raising the material standards of workers and the society as a whole. Thus, as suggested later, there may arise a genuine dilemma here between economic gains and gains indemocratic participation and equality.

17. Social ownership means neither state ownership nor workers' ownership, but diffusion of ownership among producers, consumers, and collectivities in Yugoslav society. Thus, ownership as a socio-economic category is not vested in any particular holder. No societal actor holds the rights of social ownership, not even the Federation. However, the law recognizes a special property right which it refers to as the 'right-to-use'. Under this, workers are vested with management of the means of production and the right to dispose of the products (IILS, 1972:133). That is, the authority to manage property is delegated to more or less autonomous enterprises and institutions which, in turn, are managed by the workers directly or through their elected organs of self-management (see Footnote 21) (Hunnius, 1973:274).

The Yugoslav property concept appears to facilitate a shift from emphasizing the rights of 'property owners' to stressing the duties as well as rights of 'property users' vis à vis other social actors. This contributes to generating a broadly based social network regulating and integrating the resource, information and value flows between and among different spheres of social activity. Such a regulatory network and social integration is difficult, if not impossible to achieve under capitalist institutions with their restrictive interpretation of property rights and assignment of costs and benefits.

18. In the case of an enterprise consisting of less than 30 persons, there would be no elected workers' council. The whole working community acted as a council. This arrangement was also legally permissible in any working community with no more than 70 persons. In the case of enterprises with more than 70 persons, the workers' council had to consist of a minimum of fifteen persons, with no maximum specified.

When an enterprise had less than 10 working members, there was no managing board, but above that number a managing board consisted of a minimum of 5 persons, again without any maximum. Prior to 1974 the director of the enterprise attended meetings of the workers' council and was a member of the managing board.

19. It is worth reminding ourselves of Yugoslavia's limited resources initially, that it undetook this experiment not as one of the rich lands of the world, but as one of the poorest and least developed in Europe (see section 4).

20. This contrasts with the development of 'soviets' in the Soviet Union which were supported by a social movement. The process of centralizing and bureaucratizing society was carried out over the opposition of, and struggle with, parts of that movement: Kronstadt, workers' opposition, etc. Such self-governing movements did not exist in Yugoslavia. (For a discussion concerning the 'imposed nature' of self-management in Yugoslavia, particularly in relation to the shaping and dynamics of the social system, see Golubović [1971].)

21. This argument attempts to go beyond the issue of imposed versus emergent basis for Yugoslav self-management institutions. The key elements in the argument are: (1)

Yugoslav society, on the basis of the historical experience of the liberation movement, acquired certain social structural potentialities and corresponding cultural elements; (2) the political leadership activated and transformed these in the face of a serious challenge to Yugoslavia, and their position in it, acquiring legitimation for the struggle against Stalin and the Cominform; and (3) although the leadership was instrumental in activating and reshaping these potentialities and cultural elements for its purposes, the latter nevertheless led to developments and movements not entirely under its control. Thus, both the continuity and discontinuity of self-management in relation to earlier developments can be identified. This corresponds to a certain extent with the argument of Rus (1977:2) that self-management was a continuation of the liberation movement. Although the initiative for self-management originated from above, it was not simply a system of 'imposed democracy', because it had its own real social base in the liberation movement:

> Thus, self-management was not only the voluntary act of the political elite, which could in this way acquire legitimization for its struggle against Stalin and the Cominform, but was at the same time a transformation of the liberation movement, based on *political* participation, into a labor movement, which would now be based on the economic participation of those employed.

22. Wage, income and consumption differentiation illustrates this point. Basic wage differentials, taken as averages, are low both within enterprises and even nationally (see Table 7.6). The spread in average incomes between different skill levels at the national level is less than 1 to 3. Wage incomes differ in most enterprises by a factor of 1 to 4 (only about 7 percent of Yugoslav enterprises had a spread of 1:6 in 1970) (Vušković, 1976:31). This is little compared to capitalist societies. But the cumulation of regional, sectoral and skill differentiations leads to much larger spreads, up to 1:15 (Vušković, 1976:33).

In addition, income is only one criterion of social differentiation. It does not indicate consumption of educational services which appears to be the major intergenerational transmission mechanism of position and status in communist societies where private ownership of the means of production has been largely abolished. Also, other bases of social differentiation, relating to political and cultural aspects of social life, contribute to substantial differences among employees.

TABLE 7.6
Average personal incomes by level of skill or education (unskilled workers = 100)

Non-manual	1966	1968	1970	1972	1974	1976	1978	1981
University	274	274	293	274	269	255	273	261
Advanced	201	198	211	200	197	189	203	198
Secondary	162	159	166	158	161	154	163	160
Lower-grade	126	125	128	122	128	121	125	123
Manual								
Highly skilled	187	179	193	187	186	176	184	187
Skilled	137	131	137	135	141	132	140	146
Semi-skilled	114	110	116	112	116	111	113	121
Unskilled	100	100	100	100	100	100	100	100

Source: Statistički godisnjaci Jugoslavije 1983.
Note: Figures are for the whole socialist sector (including aducation, health, banking and political sector). These figures reflect only basic wage incomes and do not take into account overtime and family earnings. Nor do they reflect differences due to profit-related wage bonuses, enterprise-owned apartments with nominal rents, company cars, expense accounts (allowed for much coveted foreign travel), and other enterprise allocated consumables.

23. Ignorance about self-management institutions themselves is widespread. Large numbers of workers have been found unable to give account of problems treated by self-management bodies. As many as one-fifth were found to be unfamiliar with the formal self-management structure of the company, and an equal number of them could only state a few things about it (Tanić, 1972).

The lack of knowledge and often interest is partly a result of the system having become 'too complicated for most of the workers who have to operate it', although knowledge varies according to the type of worker and type of factory (Riddell, cited in Pateman, 1970).

24. One of the most systematic interpretations of the bases of managerial influence within Yugoslav work organizations is given by Županov (1971a). Participation in discussions at work unit levels is twice as great as in discussions at the enterprise level (43 percent compared with 20 percent) (IILS, 1972:144). A survey in Slovenia in 1968 (in 111 industrial and mining enterprises) showed that workers were interested in the following issues: 72 percent in personal income matters, 61 percent in the business results of the enterprise, 40 percent in welfare facilities, 34 percent in development of the enterprise, 16 percent in the organization of production and work relations, 10 percent in personnel policy, 5 percent in the work of self-management bodies, 2 percent in irregularities in the enterprise, 1 percent in retirement income (IILS, 1972:152).

25. Highly skilled and skilled manual workers make up more than 50 percent of the membership of workers' councils and 46 pecent of the membership of boards of management (see Table 7.2). This strengthens the trend toward intensive industrialization and rationalization of work (IILS, 1972:145):

They tend to strive for occupational advancement and so to draw nearer to the technical intelligentsia; they also tend by their roles, attitudes, ideology, and social perceptions, to influence other workers and the non-manual employees.

26. The majority of prices were controlled until the 1965 reforms.

27. This viewpoint ignores the sources of growth and its impact on working conditions and work environment, a theme we shall return to later. Increased productivity and higher incomes, benefiting many, may be purchased at the expense of some workers' health and welfare. Greater influence of less skilled workers could lead to preferential improvements of their workplace conditions instead of, possibly, wage increases for all.

28. Without a more precise definition of 'worker', one is unable to conclude from this that there is not 'workers' control' or self-management. It is 'white collar' workers and highly skilled workers who appear to exercise disproportionate influence over self-management processes. In other words, the split between skilled and unskilled workers may be greater than that between skilled workers and managers and engineers.

29. On the other hand, the accumulation and rotation of offices and positions in different spheres of social life (especially political and economic, but probably including the socio-cultural) by individual actors facilitates the coordination of decisions in the different spheres.

30. Salaried workers (39 percent) along with students, soldiers, etc. (20 percent) dominate the League of Yugoslav Communists, while workers remain a minority (34 percent) — and an even smaller minority of its leadership (Horvat, 1969).

31. Nor does the establishment of quotas or the banning of leading managers from self-management and social management bodies (as under the 1974 Constitution) solve the problem. For this does not in itself improve the ability of production workers to participate in fact and effectively in key decision-making processes. However, it does explicitly define a conflict between manager/cadre groups and shop-floor workers. This has effects of its own.

32a. Županov (1972) suggests that self-management operates as 'collective entrepreneurship', where self-management has come to imply autonomy from the environment. At the same time, workers' influence on decision-making and planning is acknowledged ideologically but in practice is depreciated in the name of efficiency.

32b. Because of the *potential* ideological and socio-political context in which managers operate, their role is not as clearly or as exactly defined as in capitalist systems. Obradović (1976:30) points out in the case of Yugoslavia:

> His power is rather high, but *illegally so*. He has to be versatile and find the legal rationale for all his actions. According to J. Županov, ... he manipulates various interests and groups watching closely the rationale of his behaviour in the institutional, legal, and ideological sense. In many actions he is relying on organizations outside the company. In the first place on the banks and socio-political organizations, sacrificing there a part of his autonomy.

One interpretation of the success of strikes in Yugoslav work organizations suggests that strikes make the illegitimate power exercised by management obvious: the strike is oriented against management. But management is institutionally defined as simply the executive organ of self-management bodies. The strike points up a lack of worker control due to weak or ineffective self-management bodies.

Such a paradoxical situation gives legitimation to political bodies outside the enterprise to intervene because 'something is wrong with self-management' (much as near-bankruptcy or bankruptcy brings outside intervention in the case of enterprises operating under capitalist institutions). This intervention is made against the management and in the name of workers (the legitimate holders of enterprise power). To avoid such intervention management tends to quickly meet the demands of striking workers. The success of strikes in Yugoslavia is an indicator of management concern about and eagerness to maintain autonomy. (Županov, 1971b).

In this context, it should be pointed out that approximately 80 percent of the strikes last less than 1 day and 35 percent 3 hours or less. The strikes typically involve small numbers (a few hundred), who are usually production workers (79.6 percent)(this data comes from a study of Jovanov, 1973). That is, only exceptionally are technicians and members of the administrative staff involved. Major factors underlying Yugoslav strikes the low economic status and unfavourable market position of an enterprise (Obradović, 1976:31). The highest frequency and intensity of strikes are in the metal, metallurgy, and textile sectors.

33. The stability of social hierarchization in the economic sphere depends to a large extent on parallel or corresponding conditions within the socio-cultural and political spheres, for example, legitimation to support managerial/technical elitism and autonomy. The outcome of struggles and developments in these spheres determines whether or not a compatible — and even reinforcing — context for economic structure and processes will obtain (see discussion in section 5).

In other words, ideological and legitimation processes must address and resolve the substantial gap between reality and ideal, the divergence between the actual perceived distribution of power and aspirations for the normative or ideal one, democratic participation. Thus, some theoreticians (e.g. Bilandžić) argued that self-management should be something analogous to parliamentary democracy. Practically, this means that workers and their representatives would not be involved in day to day operations but only elect competent managers who are to fulfill their responsibilities and programs. At the same time, Rus (1972) found some evidence that the ideal distribution was adapted to be more compatible with the real one during the course of the 1960s. Initially, workers felt that all members of the enterprise should participate equally in decision-making. However, by the end of the 1960s workers had come to more and more accept the oligarchic status quo and no longer sought equal participation (Rus, 1972; Zukin, 1975). This can be interpreted as a lowering of democratic aspirations under pressures from market rules and forces (for a discussion of the consequences of tension between ideal and reality in social systems, see Sekulić, 1975).

34. Self-managed enterprises operating under conditions of market competition cannot regulate effectively technical innovations and system change with a view to developing self-management institutions. Technologies and other instruments of production (e.g., assembly lines), division of labor, and development strategies and paths are selected for their comparative advantage in market competition, and not for their contribution to , or compatibility with, self-management institutions and values.

The pressures to adopt more capital intensive technologies, to increase enterprise size (see section 4), and to adopt new organizational forms (such as divisionalization) adapted to modern market conditions and development are not as much a matter of worker choice as 'given' by the conditions and forces of markets. Participating in the world economy and the international division of labor generates particularly intense pressures — pressures that do not originate in or are not subject to regulation by Yugoslavia — toward efficiency, larger industrial units, more advanced technologies, and higher degrees of professionalization. These tendencies move decision-making and planning upward and away from shopfloor workers (Hunnius, 1973:314-15). And differences in function, outlook, and power within enterprises are amplified. Expressed in another way, the democratization of the internal structure of work organization, motivated and guided by ideological and political goals, comes into conflict with external arrangements and developments associated with market competition and forces.

35. In spite of 'social ownership', advantaged enterprises retain control over 'their' positive gains, while disadvantaged enterprises have in practice very limited rights to the benefits others gain, nor do they receive substantial compensation for relative losses. 'Solidarity transfers', e.g., through the 'fund for aid to under-developed republics and autonomous regions' are defined in monetary terms, rather than in terms of a multi-dimensional concept of costs and benefits suggested here. They have quite a limited regional impact on the actual process of differential accumulation and uneven development.

36. The major poblem facing the political leadership of Yugoslavia — and a problem for the federation as a whole — was and continues to be the backwardness of substantial regions of Yugoslavia as well as the diversity of, and long-established conflicts among, the Yugoslavian peoples. Yugoslavia has been and remains a complex multi-national society with pockets of extreme underdevelopment among some of its sub-populations and with enormous socio-economic and cultural gaps between the wealthiest and poorest regions.

The most socio-economically underdeveloped regions of Yugoslavia, Bosnia-Herzegovina (with 1 percent of the total Yugoslav population), Macedonia (8 percent), Montenegro (3 percent), and Kosovo (6 percent), lie in general to the south of the River Sava. These regions were either part of the Ottoman Empire or buffer zones in the defence of Europe against Ottoman expansion. The more developed northern and western republics and provinces, Slovenia (8 percent), part of Croatia (22 percent) and Vojvodina (10 percent) were under Central European influence and formed part of the Austro-Hungarian Empire. Prosperity was greatest in Slovenia and in a small number of urban areas in Croatia (including Dalmatia) and in the rich agricultural areas of the Vojvodina. Little industrial development had taken place in Serbia (26 percent). In general, one should bear in mind the substantially different socio-economic structures inherited by the Yugoslav revolution, ranging from industrial capitalism in the north to feudal structures in the south. This suggests the structural bases of many political conflicts (Bičanić, 1973).

37. An atomized self-management society has difficulty dealing effectively with collective action problems and societal coordination, since self-managed enterprises and other work organizations do not produce social integrative mechanisms within themselves. In practically every sphere where coordination is required at levels above self-managed enterprises, other work organizations, and local socio-political units (communes), there have been substantial problems. In capitalist societies, the state has become a key institution in the efforts to provide integrative and stabilizing mechanisms, but this solution has become increasingly unacceptable ideologically in Yugoslavia (see section 5 concerning efforts to develop functionally equivalent institutions).

The point here is that the differential accumulation of material as well as socio-cultural and political resources by different groups, enterprises, as well as political/administrative units of communes, regions and republics, is, in the long-run, incompatible with socialist objectives and, moreover, threatens the basic cohesion of a multi-national society such as Yugoslavia and the reproduction of its self-management institutions. The likelihood of realizing social cohesion and collective commitment of societal actors to the maintenance and development of a self-management society is increased to the degree that inequalities and patterns of uneven developments do not become extreme, that inequalities which do occur are generally viewed as temporary and correctable 'dysfunctionalities' (not fixed or basic characteristics of the institutional set-up or society), and that most social groups, if not all, have opportunities to exercise meaningful control over the system so as to re-negotiate and to correct felt injustices.

38. Personal income differences arising due to varying capital endowments contradict the notion that all capital is supposed to be socially owned (Dubey, 1975).

39. Typically, corporate size increases effectiveness in competition with other enterprises, particularly in international markets where multi-national corporations play a major role. Sacks (1976:387) has shown that Yugoslav firms in general grew substantially in size during the period 1958-71. Early in this period there were indications that they were already large by international standards. This evidence is consistent with Sacks's hypothesis that firms in a market socialist system find competitive advantage in large size, but unwillingness to establish new enterprises may also be a factor.

40. Zimmerman (1976) stresses the intense and articulate dispute about 'the proper organization of Yugoslav society'. 'This not only entailed a confrontation of different interests and methods, but a confrontation of different, broader concepts of problems of the socialist society' (Marko Nikezić, former foreign minister and 1971-72 president of the Serbian Party, quoted in Zimmerman [1976:72]).

41. The growth of industrial output averaged over 10 percent per year, agricultural output fluctuated declining by 5 percent in 1970 and increasing 9 percent in 1971. Overall, from 1947 to 1972 the social product increased 4.8 times with a yearly rate of growth of 6.6 percent. The lowest rate (2 percent) occurred in the first period covering the break with the Soviet Union, and the fastest rate of growth (8.5 percent) was in the following decade: the economy changed over to a decentralized market economy and to self-management of work organizations (Rus, 1977).

42. The percentages (1966 prices) are indicated in Table 7.7.

43. The rapid economic development, based on high rates of investment, was achieved in part at the expense of personal incomes preceding the 1965 reforms. Thus, the growth of personal income of the employed for the entire economy was for this reason significantly less than the growth of the social product through 1963. Only from this period onwards did personal spending grow parallel with the growth of social product (Rus, 1977:17).

TABLE 7.7
Exports as percentage of GNP

1952	1961	1965	1970	1980
10.3	14.3	18.2	20.7	23.2

Rus suggests that because of this development, conflicts within enterprises decreased, whereas strikes had grown in number from 1952, reaching their peak in 1965 (Jovanov, 1973). Rus writes (1977:17):

Where earlier management together with political organizations within enterprises strongly insisted on as great as possible investments and as low as possible salaries, the situation today tends toward negotiating and compromise. The reason that greater social unrest did not appear in the earlier periods despite relatively low incomes, may be found, among other things, in the relatively greater equality of personal incomes for various categories of workers.

44. The growth of unemployment is indicated in Table 7.8. This data must be viewed in the context of the rapid growth of the economy. The number of employed increased 2.5 times in the last 20 years. Every year, on the average, 124,000 new work places were opened, so that the total number of employed grew in the period from 1.7 million persons to 4.2 million (Rus, 1977). But this growth was insufficient to keep up with the rapid growth of employable adults (due both to population growth and rapid urbanization).

TABLE 7.8
Growth of unemployment in Yugoslavia

	1957	1960	1965	1970	1975	1980	1982
Total number	116,000	159,230	236,969	319,586	590,135	785,499	862,474
Percentage of unemployed in relation to all employed	2.7	5.4	6.5	8.3	11.4	13.5	14.1

Source: Statistički godišnjak Jugoslavije, 1983.

45. Inflation (see Table 7.9) has been a chronic problem of the Yugoslav system and reflects (1) the operation of a market system in the context of (2) the power and motivation of workers of individual enterprises to raise wages and pass the costs on in the form of higher prices and (3) the provision of easy credits by the banking system to make this possible on a continuing basis, thereby reducing the chances of 'zero-sum conflicts' (Černe, 1971).

46. For instance, economic competition and unequal accumulation and development patterns stimulated nationalistic tendencies in the context of a policy decentralized to the republican level. This was particularly manifest in Croatia's relation to Serbia. At the same time, economic competition tended to increase the influence of the managerial/technical elites (Bilandžić, 1974).

TABLE 7.9
Inflation rates

	1956	1965	1970	1975	1976	1980	1981	1982
Rate of inflation in percent calculated on the basis of retail prices	3.3	39.1	10.7	26.0	9.0	30.0	46.0	32.0

Source: Statistički godišujak Jugoskivije, 1983

47. Belgrade University was occupied in 1968. The Zagreb University strike, which took place in 1971 (see later discussion), was coupled with a demand for a Croatian currency and had clear nationalistic overtones. Non-party and Croatian nationalist types had won earlier in the year leadership of the Student Federation at Zagreb University and at republican level and led the strike. Their inability to mobilize workers in factories to strike limited its overall impact and averted the chances of civil war (Rusinow, 1977).

48. This was particularly manifest in the expansion, and increasing political importance, of *Matica Hrvatska*, a Croatian cultural organization which had played a 'distinguished and aggressive role in developing Croatian national consciousness during the 'Slav awakening' and the bitter nationality struggles of the last decades of the Habsburg monarchy' (Rusinow, 1977:276-77). In less than a year's time during 1970-71, a membership drive resulted in growth of the organization from 2,323 members in 30 branches to 41,000 in 55 branches. Political publications were also initiated (Rusinow, 1977).

49. That is, the interpretation of self-management and relative stress on different features of it vary among these groups.

50. The rising influence of the technocracy was also connected to increasing conflict within the political elite. Some argue that the conflict was limited to a narrow circle at the top of the party (Bilandžić, 1974). The subject of the struggle was the further development of the economic system. The main factions were apparently those supporting the development of greater centralization and state regulation and opposition to the market economy, on the one hand, and, on the other, the self-management faction and economic technocrats supporting the view that all alienation of surplus value from the producer is contrary to self-management. The technocratic faction and, indirectly, the self-management faction supported the autonomy of self-managed enterprises and their internal technostructure.

51. The development was different in the different republics: in the case of Serbia, de-etatisation of state capital (Table 7.1) led to a concentration of power in the hands of Belgrade banks and foreign-trade companies. The technocratic elite in the economy was tied to technocrats or technoratically oriented members of the political leadership of Serbia. In highly developed Slovenia, where the influence of financial viewpoints and groups was strong, the official party policy advocated the 'shareholders' model' of self-management. (This is the notion that inputs into the enterprise are not only work but capital, that within the management of the enterprise, holders of capital should be represented also, and that capital owners should enjoy income [Županov, 1975].) Moreover, in Slovenia, there emerged claims for national autonomy. In the case of Croatia, such expressions took extreme forms (see footnotes 47 and 48), including demands for the admission of Croatia to the United Nations and for the formation of a National Bank of Croatia whose governor would be sent to Washington for credits (Zimmerman, 1976:66; Rusinow, 1977). The emerging nationalistic movement in

Croatia was supported not only by the traditional intelligentsia but by technocrats concentrated in the largest enterprises and banks in Croatia who felt disadvantaged vis à vis Serbia and the Federation as a whole.

It was argued that the 'surplus value of Croatian labor' was being 'expropriated' by Belgrade banks, Belgrade-based foreign trade enterprises and bureaucracy. Although Croatia produced 27 percent of the Yugoslav social product, 30 percent of its industrial production and 36 percent of its foreign currency earnings, Croatian banks controlled only 17 percent of Yugoslavia's total bank assets. Serbian banks controlled 63 percent. The three largest banks in Yugoslavia among the top ten were in Belgrade. Four of the ten largest foreign trade enterprises were also located in Belgrade and together had an annual turnover at that time of 23, 500 million (old) dinars, compared to the 2,000 million of Zagreb's one large firm in this sector (Rusinow, 1977:323).

Such analyses underlay the demands in Croatia for separate republican foreign currency regimes, so that each republic could keep what was earned or remitted in its territory, buying and selling as needed in a free all-Yugoslav (in fact inter-republican) currency market (Rusinow, 1977:297).

52. Zimmerman (1976:74) contrasts the position of Tito, Stane Dolanc, and Kardelj with Nikezić's (see footnotes 47 and 48):

For them [Tito, Dolanc, and Kardelj] the lessons of the Zagreb [University] strike were dramatically opposed to those derived by Nikezić. For Nikezić, the need was for a policy approved by the masses and for greater democratization; for Tito and Dolanc, the main danger was liberalism. Their policy prescriptions were those typically associated with the Leninist tradition. Democratic Centralism must be observed: 'We have forgotten that ... ' Tito declared, 'and that fact is one of the basic causes of the situation in our country.' In the words of the now famous September 18, 1972 letter by Tito and the LYC Executive Bureau: 'There has been a fair amount of wavering, inconsistency, and deviation from the principles of democratic centralism.' Moreover, 'Cadre policy has also been neglected', Tito said. As the letter expresses it, 'The League of Communists must consolidate its role and influence in the field of cadre policy ... Responsibility for constructive social and state affairs [must] be entrusted to people who will perform these duties in the interest of the working class and the development of socialist self-management.' To ensure such an occurrence, the party, in the words of the letter, must be 'transformed into the kind of organization of revolutionary action that is capable of translating its stands and policy into life more efficiently.' 'We have never believed,' Tito declared, 'that organized democratic institutions in the state and society represent separation or disassociation of the League of Communists from the obligations and the responsibility to act as an ideo-political force in an organized manner: ... Communists in all institutions should imple-ment the LCY policy.' Finally, opportunism must be fought: 'The toleration of views and political conduct that are at variance with the ideology and policy of the League of Communists' must be terminated.

53. The dominant political leadership's ability to introduce such reforms and to rewrite the Constitution and change basic laws, thus restructuring the institutional set-up and changing the 'rules of the game', indicates its meta-power capabilities with respect to Yugoslav society.

54. The Croatian 'nationalist leaders' were dismissed in 1971. Stane Kavčić, prime minister of Slovenia in 1972, one of the major political figures most committed to efficiency, market solutions and decentralization (along with close economic ties to Europe, which also came under criticism during this period) was removed in 1972. Marko Nikezić, former foreign minister and in 1971-72 president of the Serbian Party, a prominent advocate of extending democratization, resigned in 1972 and was removed from the

party in 1974. (In 1971 he had emphasized, concerning the Croatian developments, the importance of 'freeing ourselves from our own Communist conservatism which, being unable to respond to the changed needs of society, would try to master the difficulties of the present stage by returning to the old norms and relations, to a renewal of ideology and a renewal of the party and so forth' (cited in Zimmerman, 1976:73; also, see Rusinow, 1977).

15 of the 52 members of the party presidency at the 9th Congress were no longer members by the time of the 10th Congress. Eight resigned under attack for serious deviations and seven had lost their party membership (Rusinow, 1977:336). Removals were not only carried out at the top political levels. Rusinow (1977:330) reports that in Belgrade alone some 200 enterprise directors were replaced in the two year period between mid-1972 and mid-1974, many of them after losing party membership.

Neutralism and professionalism in all walks of life were vigorously attacked, at the same time that central party control over newspapers and weeklies was greatly enhanced (Zimmerman, 1976:76). Zimmerman reports that the mass media were particularly promising sources for the discovery of 'technocrats, anarcho-liberals, and nationalists.'

55. Self-management communities of interest are required by law in the fields of education, health, research and cultural activity, on the community and republican levels. They are planned for and administered by delegates from production organizations which finance social services and by delegates who are employed in the corresponding social services. Collectively and on an equal basis both sets of delegates decide about yearly and middle-range plans of work for the social service, as well as about financing the realization of these plans. In this way, work organizations, through their delegates, have a direct influence on the financing and development of social services.

56. The reforms altered or re-established certain power relationships in the economic sphere as well as between the economic and political spheres. For instance, members of the managerial and technical elite have been blocked from participating in the Communal and Associated Labor Chambers. At the same time, delegates to these chambers have been 'deprofessionalized' through the requirement that they keep their ordinary jobs during their term of office (the lack of time and experience would tend to enhance the opportunities for party members to exercise influence).

Directors of enterprises are to be elected from a list of one to three candidates proposed to the workers' council by a commission. (Directors are now referred to as 'individual management organs' to avoid the 'bourgeois-technocratic connotations' of director (Rusinow, 1977:329)).The commission is composed of an equal number of enterprise representatives and of communal assembly appointees. This represents a return to the pre-1964 system which had commune participation in the nominating commission. This sytem had been criticized earlier as unjustifiable political interference in workers' rights (Rusinow, 1977:129). Also, the 10th Party Congress reaffirmed the party's right to 'intervene' in decision-making and selection of officers by the commission.

In general, during the 1950s leading economic actors consulted politicians before making important decisions. Then, during the liberal phase, the opposite occurred. Assemblies after 1963 tended to be dominated by the managerial-technical elite and by professional politicians with regional and local constituencies (such politicians tended to be oriented more to 'special' and even 'nationalistic' interests than to Yugoslav party and party discipline interests). Now, once again, political leaders oriented to the top leadership appear to be preeminent.

57. These institutions were introduced in the 1974 Constitution as a major new technique for coordinating and regulating social relationships and exchanges by agreements or

contracts. They are intended to serve as functional equivalents to state planning, compatible with self-management principles of social organization in that they negate both the lack of social control over the liberal market and hierarchies of state planning. Social compacts are contracts between government organs, economic chambers, trade unions, and other collective actors, and concern such matters as price policy, the policy of personal incomes, employment policy, and planning. Self-management agreements regulate relations between and among work organizations, whether these relations concern cooperation in production, the business integration of enterprises into a larger company, the creation of banks on the part of work organizations, the instituting of economic chambers, or even penetration (by Yugoslav enterprises) in foreign markets. Economic relations between work organizations which bear on the policy of salaries and on personnel policy in work organizations are also regulated by such agreements.

58. Proposals to return to centralized planning and control would, in our view, be a step backward. Such centralized controls would inhibit the development of democratic relations among those engaged in production. Democracy must be learned, practised, and maintained through everyday processes. Moreover, centralized controls fail to realize and utilize for the collective good the potential interest of producers in their work and in the operation of their work units. They also discourage the development of conscientious, responsible attitudes toward work and social ownership. Finally, such solutions only exacerbate problems of status differentiation and hierarchization in society. Even problems of uneven development may be left unsolved.

59. Self-management has been institutionalized as a societal value and pattern of social relationship and activity. This has constrained and biased possible restructuring and institutional innovation that could have been effectively initiated by the political leadership. This is another way of saying that the meta-power of the political leadership was, in part, constrained by conditions which they had helped bring about. And these constraints provide a certain logic and continuity to current Yugoslav development.

60. In other words, destratification of power within organizations may be closely connected to stratification of power in the global system (the establishment or maintenance of meta-power). But at the same time there are immediate social welfare benefits in the form of the equalization of personal incomes within and between organizations. For example, the introduction of social compacts concerning income distribution contributes to bringing about destratification of incomes within and between enterprises and branches. There is still a basic dilemma between the power to liberate and the liberation of power. On the one hand, a political leadership itself acts to establish and develop self-management and participatory democracy at the same time that the realization of these goals and values ultimately implies a negation to a greater or lesser extent of the power of the leadership.

61. As we see it, a major task for societal analysis is to identify contradictions and conflicts occurring, or likely to occur, in a particular institutional arrangement. On the basis of this examination, one may be able to develop concepts and strategies to deal with the same dilemmas and to contribute to producing and developing desirable societal structures and processes. For instance, one aim here would be to indicate areas where constraints and regulatory processes could be imposed on market and other key social institutions in order to facilitate the development of self-management institutions and values. Among the areas for the exploration of such social control are the following: (1) the design and use of technology which is compatible with genuine self-management. Along such lines, Fusfeld (1978:8) proposes (i) technologies that rely on decision-making abilities of workers at all levels, in place of the present pattern of routinizing individual work; (ii) technologies that facilitate shifting of individual workers and groups between jobs; (iii) technologies that bring workers together into small groups. (2) The regulation of market

forces and developments which work in opposition to, and dominate, self-management forms and processes within enterprises. (3) Exploration of the effects of size on self-management practices and specification of optimal size for effective self-management practice. (4) Indication of limits to the division of labor (and the types of division of labor) compatible with full development of self-management. (5) The establishment of learning and socio-cultural conditions and processes in family, community and work as well as in the usual cultural and educational institutions in such a way as to be compatible with the full development and reproduction of genuine self-management. (6) The establishment of political institutions and the effective practice of politics in ways compatible with the development of self-management.

62. Ionescu (1976:33) suggests that a major dilemma facing all Eastern European societies hinges on the contradiction between socio-economic forms which are emerging and the established political forms:

The real object of the contradiction is the necessity to adapt Leninist structures to the technological revolutions that have swept the industrial world since the second world war. By now it is universally clear that the industrial-technological society, with its built-in corporate structures and therefore with its essential need for expanding pluralization, can no longer live within the narrow Leninist boundaries or parameters.

REFERENCES

Baće, M. (1949), 'O nekim pit anjima kritike i samokritike u SSSR,' Kommunist, 3, No. 6.

Baumgartner, T., W. Buckley, T.R. Burns and P. Schuster (1976), 'Meta-Power and the Structuring of Social Hierarchies,' pp. 215-88 in T.R. Burns and W. Buckley (eds.), Power and Control. London: Sage Publications.

Bendeković, J. (1975), 'Analiza sistema investiranja u SFRJ Poslije 1965,' Ekonomiski Pregled, 26, Nos. 3 and 4.

Bičanić, R. (1973), Economic Policy in Socialist Yugoslavia. Cambridge: Cambridge University Press.

Bilandžić, D. (1973), Ideje i praksa društvenog razvoja Jugoslavije, Beograd: Komunist.

Bilandžić, D. (1974), 'O kriznom razdoblju u razvoju samoupravljanja u Yugoslaviji,' Pogledi, No. 11-12.

Bon, E. (1975), 'Viewpoints on the Yugoslav Model of Socio-Economic Development.' Unpublished manuscript.

Bošnjak, V., T.R. Burns, S. Saksida, and D. Sekulić (1978), Dialectics of Societal Planning and Change: Studies of Planning, Conflict, and Democracy. Unpublished manuscript.

Burns, T.R., T. Baumgartner and P. DeVille, 1985 Man, Decisions Society. London: Gordon and Breach.

Černe, F. (1971) 'Komparativna motivno-funkcionalna analiza nåseg kolektivno-samoupravnog sistema,' in: Samoupravni ekonomski socijalistički sistem, Beograd: Savez Ekonomista Jugoslavije.

Dedijer, V. (1971), The Battle Stalin Lost. New York: Viking.

Denitch, B. (1976), The Legitimation of a Revolution: The Yugoslav Case. New Haven: Yale University Press.

Denitch, B. (1977), 'Notes on the Relevance of Yugoslav Self-Management', pp. 141-60 in: M.R. Haug and J. Dofny (eds.), Work and Technology. London: Sage Publications.

Deutscher, I. (1972), Stalin. Harmondsworth, Middx.: Penguin.

Drulović, M. (1973), L'autogestion à l'épreuve, Paris: Fayard.

Dubey, V. (1975), *Yugoslavia: Development with ˹ecentralization: World Bank Report.* Baltimore and Boston: Johns Hopkins University Press.

Fusfeld, D.R. (1978), 'Workers' Management and the Transition to Socialism'. Paper presented at the First International conference on the Economics of Workers' Management, Dubrovnik.

Golubović, Z. (1971), 'Ideje socijalizma i socijalistička stvarnost,' *Praxis,* No. 3-4.

Gorupić, D. and I. Paj (1970), *Workers' Self-Management in Yugoslav Undertakings,* Zagreb: Ekonomski Institut.

Hoi vat, B. (1969), *An Essay on Yugoslav Society,* New York: International Arts and Sciences Press.

Hunnius, G. (1973) 'Workers' Self-Management in Yugoslavia,' in G. Hunnius, G.D. Garson, and J. Case (eds.), *Workers' Control.* New York: Random House.

International Institute for Labor Studies (1972), *Workers' Management in Yugoslavia.* Geneva: International Labor Office.

Ionescu, G. (1976), 'The Modern Prince, Its Princes, and its Condottieres,' *Studies in Comparative Communism,* 9:27-34.

Jerovšek, J. (1969), 'Struktura utjecaja u općini', *Sociologija,* No. 2.

Jovanov, N. (1973), 'Odnos štrajka kao društvenog sukoba i samoupravljanja kao društvenog sistema,' *Revija za Sociologiju,* No. 1-2.

Kalogjera, D. (1975). 'Samoupravni sporazumi i društveni dogovori — mechanizmi samoupravne integracije udruženog rada,' *Ekonomski Pregled,* No. 3-4.

Kalogjera, D. (1977), 'Planning under the System of Workers' Self-Management.' Paper presented at the 2nd International Conference on Participation, Workers' Control and Self-Management, Paris.

Obradović, J. (1972), 'Distribution of Participation in the Process of Decision-making on Problems Related to the Economic Activity of a Company in Zagreb,' *Participation and Self-Management,* **12**:3-17.

Obradović, J. (1976), 'Sociology of Organization in Yugoslavia,' *Acta Sociologica,* 19:23-35.

Pateman, C. (1970), *Participation and Democratic Theory.* Cambridge: Cambridge University Press.

Pijade, M. (1949), 'Veliki majstori licemjerja,' *Borba,* 22, 29 September, 5, 6 October.

Randonjić, R. (1975), *Sukob KPJ sa Kominformom.* Zagreb: Centar za aktuelni politički studij.

Rus, V. (1972), *Odgovornost in moč v delovnih organizacijah.* Kranj: Moderna Organizacija.

Rus, V. (1977), 'Yugoslav Country Context,' Unpublished manuscript.

Rusinow, D. (1977), *The Yugoslav Experiment: 1948-1974.* Berkeley: University of California Press.

Sacks, S.R. (1976), 'Corporate Giants under Market Socialism,' *Studies in Comparative Communism,* 9:369-88.

Sekulić, D. (1975), 'Motivacija i socijalna akcija,' *Revija za Sociologiju,* No. 3.

Stojanović, S. (1973), *Between Ideals and Reality.* New York: Oxford University Press.

Tanić, Z. (1972), 'Dimensions and Factors of the Aperception of Self-Management,' *Prva medjunarodna konferencija o participaciji i saoupravljanju, Zagreb.*

Vušković, B. (1976), 'Social Inequality in Yugoslavia,' *New Left Review,* No. 95, January-February, pp. 26-44.

Zimmerman, W. (1976), 'The Tito Succession and the Evolution of Yugoslav Politics,' *Studies in Comparative Communism,* 9:62-79.

Zukin, S. (1975), *Beyond Marx and Tito: Theory and Practice in Yugoslav Socialism.* New York: Cambridge University Press.

Županov, J. (1969), *Samoupravljanje i društvena moć.* Zagreb: Naše Teme.

Županov, J. (1971a), 'Samoupravljanje i društvena moć u radnoj organizaciji,' in J. Jerovšek (ed.), *Industrijska sociologija*. Zagreb: Naše Teme.

Županov, J. (1971b), 'Industrijski konflikti i samoupravni sistem,' *Revija za Sociologiju*, No. 1.

Županov, J. (1972), 'Employees' Participation and Social Power in Industry,' in: *Prva medjunarodna konferencija o participaciji i samoupravljanju*, Zagreb.

Županov, J. (1975), 'Evolucija i involucija samoupravnog poduzeća — jedan nacrt za tipološku analizu,' in *Proizvocne organizacije i samoupravni sistem*, Grupa Sistem i čovjek Zagreb.

8

Institutional Conflict and Power: Capital, Market and Other Constraints on Self-Management

Thomas Baumgartner   and   Tom R. Burns

Introduction

THE DEVELOPMENT of self-management entails the extension of workers' control over the means of production, the production process, products and their future development, and, above all, the institutional context of production. This definition necessarily relates the concept of self-management — and more generally of economic democracy — to the socio-political and institutional context. From such a *holistic perspective*, the larger context in which production takes place is of utmost importance.

This chapter is concerned with the process of extending workers' control over the social context of self-management institutions.[1] Toward this end, we sketch a framework with which to analyze ways in which self-management institutions interact with, and are constrained and contradicted by other key social institutions, for example, financial ones.

Part I presents the key notions of our theoretical approach and its implications for an institutional analysis of self-management. Part II discusses the problem of finance and financial institutions in relation to self-managed enterprises in terms of this framework. In Part III we suggest several general policy and strategic implications of the analysis.

It is our hope that this analysis, even in its preliminary and tentative form, will contribute to a clarification of constraints on the development of self-management institutions as well as the potentialities and strategies for further development. It should become apparent from our discussion that we evaluate social institutions and their development in terms of a democratic socialist model. For our purposes here it is enough to say that, among other things, this means the establishment and reproduction of democratic participation and solidarity in social life, and the achievement of human control over social relationships and a balanced relationship between human society and nature.

Part I   Conflict and Mutual Constraint among Social Institutions

The arrangement of multiple institutions in a society makes up a *totality* and generates within it opposing or contradictory tendencies. The operation of one institution often limits and undermines the intended operation and development of another. In this sense one may speak of conflict and contradiction among societal institutions. Section 3 below focuses on ways in which economic and, particularly, market institutions may constrain self-management. This discussion is preceded by a brief introduction to our concept of self-management in Section 1 and a presentation of several key notions in our analytical approach.

1. Self-Management

Self-management entails a distribution of power and control which allows human actors — individuals and groups — to exercise decision-making control over their activities and the environments constraining them.[2] This conceptualization has several interrelated features:

1) Actors have the capacity to structure the production relations and processes in which they are involved. Production is here broadly conceived to cover all spheres of human activity, i.e., economic, political and socio-cultural.

2) They have control over the products of their production processes, including the spin-offs and spill-overs impinging on actors in the production processes and spheres other than the ones in which their activity is located.

3) They exercise control over their "social units of production", the basic cells of the social system.[3] This implies, in particular, control of their development.

4) They have the capacity to *participate* in the control over the economic, political, and socio-cultural environments which influence and constrain the activities of their units of production.

One major implication of this formulation of self-management is that *such a system is not expected to be free of conflict.* Self-control over as many aspects of the social system as possible will inevitably bring individuals and groups into conflict with one another, especially in modern, complex social systems with substantial interdependencies. The further development of self-management requires the identification of such contradictions and the design of structures and processes which (1) have conflict resolving and consensus shaping capabilities, and (2) are compatible (or coherent) with the fundamental properties of self-management societies. The discussion in the remainder of this chapter is an effort to respond to this challenge.

2. Analytical Points of Departure

Our approach to the analysis of self-management and its development within a societal totality is based on the following notions:

1) Societal development entails institutional innovation, the shaping and reshaping of social institutions. Its outcome cannot be fully predicted. Invariably there will be *unintended consequences and unanticipated developments*. Institutional change — whether motivated by systems maintaining or transforming interests — involves therefore some degree of *social experimentation*. This is particularly so in the case of Yugoslavia since there was no clear-cut societal model to follow. Rather, Yugoslavs have been engaged in the process of developing and testing such a model. The workability and compatibility of concepts and institutions have had to be tested and judged through praxis. Alterations have had to be made on the basis of performance results and accumulated experience (Dubey, 1975).

2) Different societal values are pursued through distinct but typically interrelated institutions. This *institutional arrangement* tends to generate conflicts among groups engaged in different institutional activities, and also within specific institutions to the extent that opposing groups interpenetrate them. As a consequence, the *reproduction and development of desirable structures and processes, such as self-management, are not guaranteed.*

Yugoslav societal dynamics can be interpreted in terms of the relationships and struggles between different groups. It can also be understood in terms of conflicting social values and patterns of activity which are pursued through multiple, partially incompatible institutions making up an institutional arrangement: self-management in the economic and increasingly in the political sphere; commodity production for markets and participation in the international division of labor; social ownership of the means of production; and a single, revolutionary party seeking to transform Yugoslavia into a socialist society.

This arrangement produces unexpected and unintended developments. For instance, it has generated growing pluralism and conflict, increasingly uneven socio-economic development, and potential threats to the leadership of the League of Yugoslav Communists (LYC) in the period 1965-72. These developments were inconsistent with basic notions about the appropriate organization and development of Yugoslav society held by the dominant leadership of the LYC, provoking it into using its power to undertake institution restructuring and innovation. The result was, for example, the 1975 constitution and the 1976 planning law (see preceding Chapter).

3) A major task of societal analysis is to identify the conflicts and contradictions occurring, or likely to occur, in particular institutional arrangements, and to specify and analyze the dilemmas they present. On this basis, one explores concepts and strategies which deal with dilemmas and which contribute to developing desirable societal structures and processes.

3. Constraints on Self-Management Socialism through Market Allocation

This section is concerned with constraints on the effective development of self-management socialism, i.e., democratic participation, equality and solidarity, in the context of economic market institutions.[4]

1) A system of self-management operating under market rules tends to result in differential accumulation and uneven development defined in material as well as social and political terms. At the micro-level, within enterprises, this entails social differentiation and hierarchization due to the technical division of labor in work and management processes. Unequal resource accumulation and uneven development occur at the macro-level between enterprises, sectors, and regions. The preceding chaper has presented already some evidence of these tendencies in Yugoslavia.

2) Non-egalitarian developments and conditions within the economic sphere typically generate parallel and reinforcing developments within the political and socio-cultural spheres. Thus, emphasis on professional expertise to enhance economic performance, as opposed to stress on egalitarian values, tends to reinforce the political importance of professional expertise. Experts are in a position to bring their economic orientation to bear on political and socio-cultural decisions and developments. Such effects in non-economic spheres can in turn reinforce processes of economic hierarchization and uneven development. The overall effect, if not opposed or regulated, is to weaken democratic and egalitarian principles in society as a whole.

Such differentiation processes may however generate opposing developments, leading eventually to struggle over institutional restructuring. Some groups with vested interests seek to maintain existing institutions, the "rules of the game", and patterns of development generated by them. Others will seek to change them. Such processes and conflicts underlie the dialectical shifts and discontinuities in Yugoslav post-war societal development analyzed in the preceding chapter. This point is that such shifts may not be controllable or subject to planning through self-management, or, indeed, through other social institutions.

3) Institutions of market allocation tend to generate social inequality and uneven societal development. At the same time, the system of self-management enterprises provides minimal social integration at the regional and national levels. This institutional combination — along with weak Yugoslav-wide institutions — both provokes, and fails to effectively regulate, the powerful nationalist tendencies among some ethnic groups inside Yugoslavia.

In general, an atomized self-management society cannot deal effectively with the requirements for macro-level coordination and related collective action problems. In practically every sphere where coordination is required at levels above self-managed enterprises and local socio-political units (communes), there have been problems in Yugoslavia. The introduction after 1972 of a variety of new institutional devices such as 'self-management agreements' and 'social compacts' can be understood easily in light of this observation. But we have pointed out in the preceding chapter that these reforms failed to provide a mechanism through which the republics and regions could coordinate their economic and development policies. It is this failure that partially explains the high inflation and deep economic crisis which Yugoslavia has experienced thus far in the 1980s.

4) Self-managed enterprises operating in markets, especially international ones, fail to select and regulate technical innovations and system developments so as to reinforce and improve self-management institutions. Technologies (e.g., assembly lines) and division of labor (e.g., segmentation and hierarchy) are selected for promise of success in market competition, not for their compatibility with self-management institutions. Yet, they limit the realization of self-management, understood as participation and control of decision-making, by enhancing the internal power of managers and technicians, especially when combined with related values of "economic rationality" and "technocratism."[5]

Enterprises operating in the context of markets also find it advantageous to grow in size (Sacks, 1976). However, the larger the enterprise, the more difficult it is to practice self-management (Hunnius, 1973:314-315). Of course, decentralized management is possible, and the institution of the Basic Organization of Associated Labor (BOAL) has been introduced for this purpose. But increasingly there are functions of *meta-management* and *strategic planning* in enterprises with multiple divisions from which the majority of workers are excluded because of limits on the number of persons who can participate effectively.[6] Developments of this type are not a matter of workers' choice. They are in part "given" by the pressures of market processes and institutions. Yet, these developments tend to amplify differences in function, outlook, and power within enterprises, and thus work against the full development of self-management institutions.

5) Self-managed enterprises operating in markets compete with one another for resources. Competitive rather than cooperative, social relationships among societal collectivities are produced and reproduced, even though there is no private ownership of the means of production. Economic criteria dominate — and ultimately must dominate — in the calculus of decision-making and action to the detriment of criteria and values related to self-management and social ownership. Market principles and processes tend to determine the allocation of societal resources and socio-economic development.

Of course, the stress on economic rationality and the allocation of resources is motivated by a desire to raise the material standards of workers and to provide the material base for further societal development. Nevertheless, there are dilemmas here in that economic institutions and processes may operate contrary to essential norms and values of self-management socialism such as democratic participation, equality and solidarity. This dilemma and issues related to it are examined in the next part of the chapter which deals with the relationship between self-management and financial institutions.

Part II   Financing and Financial Institutions in Relation to Self-management

Workers' participation and self-management are emergent forms of production in many countries. This development will take a variety of forms and will have to function in a range of institutional contexts. But regardless of its specific form, it tends to come into conflict — albeit to differing degrees — with other established institutions operating or impinging on economic activity and organization.

Of particular interest to us are the ways self-management institutions interact with capital, financing, and financial institutions. This focus is motivated by three considerations. For one, capital accumulation and financing have been practical problems in the Yugoslav self-management system as well as in cooperative sectors of capitalist systems. Secondly, system performance, particularly in terms of capital accumulation, have been a major issue in assessments of the relative merits of capitalist and self-management systems.

We limit ourselves initially to a discussion of key arguments for introducing capital charges and external sources of financing — the latter case leading to the establishment of a bank-like financial sector in relation to self-management enterprises and economic systems. Section 1 raises questions about these arguments. Section 2 reviews the theoretical debate with respect to capital accumulation in worker-managed enterprises. In section 3 we discuss several empirical findings which have been offered to support the theoretical arguments, and in section 4 we draw attention to problems of social power and control which tend to be overlooked in connection with the implementation of external financing.

1. Self-Management and Economic Theory

A specific theory of the Yugoslav self-management system is only beginning to emerge (Horvat, 1971, 1976).[7] The evaluation of self-management, both in theoretical and practical terms, is therefore still dominated by the thinking of neoclassical economics. Vanek's classic works in this field offer a useful point of departure to question the application of neoclassical concepts, assumptions, and procedures to self-management economies. Of particular concern to us are the proposals for the remuneration of enterprise capital and for the external financing of self-management enterprises. Our approach differs from Vanek's in several ways:[8]

— He utilizes traditional capital/labor production functions. We stress the complex character of production processes and the importance of institutional context for their organization.

— He utilizes traditional utility functions and a uni-dimensional incentive structure (maximizing average net income). We insist on the importance of institutional context which may provide for (and allow expression of) multiple goals and interests of workers and other actors in the system.

— He proposes the institution of external financing based on the supposition that ownership can be separated from control. We feel such "technical neutrality" of institutions is the result of abstracting from questions of social power and control.

— He finds support for his theoretical arguments about a self-management system by examining cooperatives within capitalist systems and by comparing Yugoslav economic performance to that of other countries. This neglects the consideration of contextual and historical factors which could explain the results, or which, more seriously, should disallow the implied use of the *ceteris paribus* assumption.

We do not claim that this type of micro-economic analysis is totally incorrect. But we suggest that it is not well suited for evaluating a (still emergent) self-management system, and, in particular, for supporting *the creative task of searching for, designing, and evaluating appropriate structural and institutional solutions in the future.* This is because neo-classical theorizing:

— *neglects* structural and institutional factors, especially the mutual interaction between them and the outcomes of economic processes.

— is built *on definitions* of actors, processes, inputs, and outputs which are uni-dimensional, i.e., economic. But self-management, if it makes any sense at all, is based on complex, multi-dimensional definitions and inter-actions. Workers are worker *and* employer at the same time. While working they both work *and* consume work. They bear risks and make decisions with respect to them.

— assumes that market *processes transcend efficiently collective action problems*, the solutions to which are essential to any social system.

— neglects conflict and power processes which inevitably link econ-omics with politics and the socio-cultural. Yet, self-management is a system set up to deal explicitly with conflict and power.

The next three sections illustrate and elaborate the above points.

2. The "Perverse" Behavior of the Self-managed Firm in Neo-classical Theory

Since Ward (1958), much has been made of the fact that self-managed firms according to neo-classical theory are expected to behave perversely:

— They reduce output and employment in reaction to an increase in output prices.

— And they accumulate less than capitalist firms, and their production methods tend to be more capital intensive.[9]

Self-management economic systems would therefore be inflationary, would lack growth, and would provide little employment. Vanek (1975b), and in some sense even Meade (1975), suggest that if not stopped, self-managed firms would self-extinct through a vicious circle of (1) labor-shedding to maximize average net income with the given capital stock and then (2) of desinvestment to align rates of time preference and marginal capital productivity.[10]

Analysis of the first point has shown that more realistic assumptions about self-management production imply almost "normal" enterprise behavior, and that, under current forms of wage determination, behavior similar to that of a capitalist firm is predicted (Horvat, 1971:35-36). Steinherr and Thisse (1978) show that the self-management firm also behaves "normally" if workers exhibit socialist solidarity and take into account not only their personal income gains, but the losses of those being laid off. Similarly, workers will not vote for contraction, even in the absence of socialist solidarity, if they take into account the risk that they themselves might be among the workers to be laid off in the interest of average net income maximization.[11]

To solve the second problem, Vanek (1975a, 1978) proposes to turn the worker-managed firm into a "quasi-capitalist" labor-managed enterprise by linking capital use to charges for depreciation and use. To prevent the financing of accumulation through an almost exclusive reliance on bank credit,[12] Vanek suggests the introduction of workers' financial claims equivalent to the value of assets accumulated out of each worker's retained net income. The power implications of such a solution are discussed in Section 4. What is of interest here is the assumption about utility functions underlying the analysis.

Neo-classical utility functions are strictly defined. They contain one argument, income. The social utility function is the additive result of individual functions, all of them with the same structure and independent of each other. In practice, and certainly in Yugoslavia since 1972, "utility functions" in self-management systems are likely to differ from the hypothetical function in neo-classical theory, both on the individual and the national level.[13] Workers are no longer institutionally constrained to be simply suppliers of labor and recipients of income. They can have and express interest in work conditions, the long-term survival of the firm, and the welfare of their commune which depends in part on the performance of their enterprise.

Furthermore, it is not correct to deduce the behavior of the self-managed firm in a full-fledged self-management system from the postulated behavior of a self-managed firm in *social isolation* or as an *alien exception within a capitalist system.* Yet both Vanek (1975b) and Daurès and Dumas (1977) make this error, which, of course, is understandable within a theoretical edifice based on a pure market model.[14] But the self-management system implies the participation of social actors in enterprise decision-making to solve collective action problems and to deal with the many externalities occurring in any system. But this means that the *utility function at the enterprise level is the end result of a complex social information, influence and decision-making process through which the utility functions of a large number of societal actors with different interests and obligations are reconciled.*[15]

Of course, irrespective of all such divergence between neo-classical assumptions and the real features of a self-management system, one should question the value of institutional arrangements and social control mechanisms designed solely to compensate for an inadequate performance (compared to a capitalist firm and system) judged in terms of rates of accumulation and factor proportions. Supposedly self-management socialism means more than this as Vanek (1978) takes pains to stress.

3. The Comparative Economic Performance of Yugoslavia

Empirical support for the two theoretical propositions about the perverse economic behavior of self-managed enterprises (see page 261) rests on two cases: Producer cooperatives in the capitalist system, and a comparison of the Yugoslav self-management economy with capitalist, centrally-planned socialist, and Third World economies. Vanek (1978) makes use of both cases. The discussion below focuses on the Yugoslav case, but indicates certain problems in assessing the performance of producer cooperatives and worker-managed enterprises in alien institutional contexts.

Cooperatives often have to operate in an unsupportive environment. Suppliers, customers, and financial institutions may not know how to evaluate and deal with these "non-capitalist" entities. More frequently, they are hostile to such alternative institutions. Both factors severly limit the economic opportunities of cooperatives, making the achievement of even normal performance levels so much more difficult (Horvat, 1975b).

Producer cooperatives and self-management experiments are in many instances successors to failing or bankrupt capitalist firms. They are from start saddled with weak products facing shrinking markets, low market shares, outdated production technologies, non-existent research and product development capabilities, and hence lack new products with which to launch a revival. They lack financial resources, access to supplier and customer credit. Financial institutions justify their reluctance to help alternative institutions by stressing their low profitability and high risks, all arguments consistent with the capitalist logic of the system.

Such factors explain the general *inability* of self-managed enterprises to perform at par with capitalist enterprises *in a capitalist system.*[16] It explains, of course, also any *unwillingness* of worker-owners to attempt to redress the situation through internally financed accumulation out of their labor income. The initial emergence of a producer cooperative has often been the result of a refusal by capitalists to invest their *own* funds. Thus one must seriously reconsider the interpretation that Vanek (1978:12) gives to the research of Jones:[17] The relative *small scale and under-capitalization* of producer cooperatives are due to the *initial and continuing contextual conditions* with which the enterprises have to contend. They are not the result of the "rational behavior" of worker-owners postulated by the neo-classical model. It is the unsuitable, even hostile environment which explains the lackluster economic performance of such enterprises, not necessarily the workers' "unwillingness" to invest.

In general, it is not appropriate to *generalize* from the experience of a social organization under circumstances where it is "extraordinary" in, or incompatible with, the historically given society. Nor is it appropriate to reach conclusions and make proposals about the behavioral effectiveness of such social constructions in one social context and apply them to a very different one.

Let us examine more closely the case of Yugoslavia. In order to test the relative effectiveness of self-management, Vanek (1978:8-11, 17ff) provides interesting data of Yugoslav economic performance in a comparative perspective. Several key findings can be summarized in the following way:

— Yugoslavia has an accumulation rate some 10 points above what could be expected for a country of its level of development.

— Its total productivity growth (up to 1970) is about double what it is for the U.S. and peripheral European countries.[18]

— However, its growth rate is not significantly different from what is predicted from a world sample of 70 countries.[19]

The high accumulation rate should, in Vanek's view, contribute to a high growth rate.[20] Vanek explains in part the Yugoslav gap between expected and actual growth rates in terms of an overvalued exchange rate and the lack of proper capital charges.[21] Both together, Vanek argues, account for about 5 points of the missing potential growth rate.[22]

The high accumulation rate, despite the faulty capital pricing policy, is explained by Vanek in terms of non-economic factors: The application of political persuasion, the high social consciousness of workers, and the influence of socio-political actors exerted through the institution of social contracts.[23] Vanek suggests that these institutional mechanisms are somehow less respectable and legitimate than those of capital charges and private property claims to assets accumulated out of labor income. This is a dubious argument in view of Yugoslavia's development goals and ideology. A more serious question concerns the effectiveness and stability of the accumulation patterns and behavior over time. This is, however, a general question, which also concerns the sustained effectiveness of purely economic and financial institutions in a given historical society.

Vanek's analysis raises also a question about the treatment of contextual factors when making inter-systemic comparisons. The productivity growth rates for Yugoslavia, presented to show that self-management in Yugoslavia has had the expected liberating effect, are compared to U.S. data for a much longer period, going back to 1925 and even 1869. The comparability of these data is highly doubtful:

— The different periods used include different business cycle histories. In particular, the U.S. data includes the effects of the 1930 and even earlier depressions. The Yugoslav data reflects an international environment of exceptional vigor.

— The history of technological advance is different for the different countries. In particular, Yugoslavia started out from relative underdevelopment and drew on a stock of knowledge accumulated during the long period reflected in the U.S. data. The comparison favors Yugoslavia which drew on resources accumulated during the U.S. period, an accumulation probably costing the U.S. some productivity growth.

— Is it permissible to characterize the post-1950 period in Yugoslavia as one dominated by *a single stable* self-management system and to attribute to it the responsibility for the favorable productivity growth? Horvat (1971, 1976) and the preceding chapter show that the Yugoslav system has evolved through a series of stages characterized by substantially different institutions, processes and values.

Furthermore, Horvat (1971:17) suggests that this history has been quite costly in terms of lost material growth. Could this possibly explain the "unexpected" underperformance of the Yugoslav system? We suggest that the Yugoslav data about productivity and material growth cannot be taken as a reflection of the performance potential of a stable self-management system. The Yugoslav economic history since 1950 is neither defined by *one* self-management system, nor by a period in which any one system could be said to have been *stabilized*. Nor can it be validly compared to the histories of other countries unless it can be shown that development out of underdevelopment is the same as the development of a mature system, and that the growth impetus coming from the international system has been the same for the different countries and the periods considered. The Yugoslav self-management system is still too much of an experiment to provide an indication of what self-management as a system could mean in terms of economic performance.

4. External Financing: The Problems of Institutional Power and Coherence

The preceding sections have presented arguments suggesting that the neo-classical policy and institutional proposals — capital charges and titles of individual ownership — rest on shaky theoretical grounds. Below we discuss the power implication of such institutions and regulatory mechanisms.

Vanek (1971, 1975b) proposed two possibilities for realizing individual ownership rights: The institution of cooperative shareholders and/or lenders and the mediation between savings and loans by a financial sector paying and charging interest. The second solution is the only one to guarantee some stability to enterprises. Vanek proposes a state bank as the financial intermediary for producer cooperatives in a capitalist system, and the use of bank, insurance, trade union and individual funds in a complete self-management system.[24]

The proposed solution appeared straightforward to Vanek (1978:7-8). The first-order difference between systems hinges on the question of control exercised by workers or capitalists. Vanek considers the question of ownership in the sense of "right to an income" of a secondary nature, differentiating worker-owned from labor-managed systems. The question then becomes one of determining *the exact nature of rights and powers which go with this right to receive an income.* Certainly no one pretends that owners of bonds and providers of loans and credits in capital systems do not have some right of control over the affairs of the debtor even though these instruments give formally only the right to an income.[25] We would argue that *a right to an income* provides in most instances *a right to some form of control* over the borrower, if only to assure that proper management is exercised, thus guaranteeing the future income stream. Vanek poses the wrong question. Self-management always implies management *within constraints.* Violation of these constraints leads to intervention of an outside actor exercising some type of control. In Yugoslavia, communes have *the right and duty* to intervene into management of an enterprise if it proves unable to fulfill its financial obligations, thus very much filling the role of bankers and creditors in capitalist systems.[26]

The challenge, as we see it, is to design institutions which preserve a dynamic balance between the concept of "self-management" and the desired and necessary control rights of outside actors. Of course, providers of external funds may prefer to exercise as much control as possible and to intervene as soon as threats to the financial viability of the enterprise appear. The question about the appropriate structure of the financial system as well as other systems in society with respect to self-management institutions is a central one.[27] The on-going debates in Yugoslavia about these matters indicate their centrality. They involved questions of the distribution of income and welfare and of the power to determine future developments of the social system. The latter should be the focus of analysis and societal planning. A purely economic approach in the neo-classical tradition is too narrow a basis for such an analysis.

Part III   Policy and Strategy

We have suggested ways in which market pressures and financial institutions may distort and constrain the actual practice of self-management in Yugoslavia. An important task in support of self-management development is the determination of constraints and regulatory institutions which might contribute to the development of self-management institutions and values. Section 1 below points to areas which deserve future attention. Section 2 points out, however, that dilemmas and contradictions are rather natural and cannot be completely eliminated through such institutional structuring.

1. Economic Democracy

Several areas can be identified where new or additional policies and regulatory institutions could provide an appropriate and facilitating context for the development of self-management structures and processes.

1) The design and use of *"appropriate" technologies* should favor egalitarian participation in decision-making and production and develop the workers' capacity for such participation. For this purpose, new technologies should allow for (Fusfeld, 1978:8):

— the development and use of decision-making abilities of workers at all levels, replacing the present pattern of routinized work;

— shifting individual workers between jobs;

— bringing workers together in small, self-organizing and semi-autonomous work groups;

— flexibility in task definition and organization so that the same machinery can be used for specialized learning as well as enriched routine production activity.

2) The division of labor — especially between skilled/unskilled, productive/administrative, and routinized/creative work should be limited, so as to *minimize hierarchization.*

3) *The optimal size of organization* compatible with the effective exercise of self-management should be determined. This would enable the institutionalization of rules to limit enterprise growth and concentration and to optimize the conditions for direct participation in decision-making. The search for and development of efficient small-scale technology would be a particularly important effort to improve the trade-off between minimal economic and maximal participatory size for enterprises.

4) The *regulation of market forces* should maintain within acceptable limits differentiation inside and between enterprises. This would entail, besides limiting accumulation and concentration processes, establishing new institutions to complement, and in some instances to replace, the market.

5) *Alternative institutions* should be developed to regulate the dilemma between consumption and accumulation, and between external financing and enterprise autonomy (but limited ability to grow). This could help overcome tensions and conflicts characteristic of self-management systems.

6) *Appropriate educational processes* in family, community, and at work, as well as in the usual cultural and educational institutions, should be established to support the development and reproduction of self-management in the economic sphere.

7) *Compatible political institutions* and the effective practice of politics should be established to reinforce the exercise of enterprise self-management.

The problems of enterprise size and the convergence between self-management practices in the economic, socio-cultural, and political spheres are central to the realization of economic democracy. Successful self-management at the micro-level depends to a large extent on the existence of relatively small, decentralized decision and production units. Otherwise, direct participation is reduced; concrete and direct experience in acquiring relevant knowledge and in decision-making is likely to be diminished; specialization, if not hierarchization, in decision-making and planning sets in. The institutionalization of the Basic Organizations of Associated Labor (BOALs) in Yugoslavia seems to bear this out (see preceding Chapter but consult also Chapter 11).

The development of norms and rules to assure a constraint on the differential accumulation of resources is therefore of prime importance.[28] These rules should ensure that production and administrative units do not grow substantially beyond the mean size for a given industry and technology. This means that the rules may be adjusted as new technologies allow efficient production in smaller-sized enterprises. At the same time, specialized institutions for resource accumulation may have to be designed for those industries where economies-of-scale imply large enterprises in relation to existing markets.

It is important that these rules and institutions induce self-management units to accumulate for their own growth up to the limit specified. At the limit, units would then either *split up into at least two independent units or continue to accumulate for the benefit of other enterprises.*[29] The institutions and rules facilitating the division of enterprises which reach upper limits of optimal size should be carefully framed so as to assure an equitable division of material, human, knowledge and power resources providing the impetus for growth.[30]

The concepts and institutions of social property, social compact, and self-management agreement also provide regulatory instruments to control enterprise size and uneven developments (see preceding Chapter). Agreements can be used to concentrate service production — including administrative tasks like bookkeeping — in independent units providing services on a contractual basis. This would favor deconcentration not only because it hives off administrative work from traditional enterprises, but also because most service activities can be performed effectively in rather small units. Social compacts with a wide range of organizations in different spheres give political and social actors the instrument with which they can assure a certain evenness in enterprise growth and community development.[31]

Of course, this discussion raises the question about the extent to which economic democracy through self-management in the economic sphere implies in fact the "liberation of political power" or workers' control over politics, or vice versa. Clearly, economic liberation in the limited sense of control over the production process and its products does not necessarily provide the power to shape the institutional environment and rules governing self-managed enterprises. But it provides important enabling conditions for the following reasons:

— Self-management of enterprises contributes to the articulation of self-management concepts and norms in social life. They may be extended to the macro-political sphere as part of a global process of participatory democratization.

— Workers are likely to acquire competence and confidence to participate and exercise influence in the political and socio-cultural spheres to the extent that self-management in enterprises functions effectively.

— Workers may be able to bring about restructuring of the institutional context within which enterprises operate through their participation and representation in political organizations and labor unions.

— Producers have some leverage on the structuring of the economic environment through their control (within general allocative rules) of revenue and transfer payments to the political, administrative and socio-cultural subsystems.

— Democratic socialist ideology, and its activation in political and socio-cultural production processes, provides a favorable context for regulating market institutions.

In sum, more complete economic democracy entails extending workers' control beyond the enterprise to its environment — in particular the economic market institution and the political and socio-cultural spheres. But such control is only a necessary, not a sufficient condition. It will also be necessary to exercise power to produce conditions and processes compatible with the development and the reproduction of self-management.

2. Contradictions, Dilemmas, and Institutional Development

Conflicts inherent in the values and activities of different institutions, which are part of an institutional arrangement, pose societal dilemmas. In this chapter we have concentrated on the dilemma between self-management institutions and values, and the unrestrained operation of market and financial forces. Effective control of market forces requires restricting the unequal accumulation of resources and power by enterprises, communes, regions and republics, and constraining the exercise of power by the state or dominant actors of market institutions. This may limit economic development, at least in the short run.[32] Thus there may exist a dilemma between the development of self-management and the achievement of high standards of living.

A related dilemma is that between effective democratic participation and effective instrumental performance. If participation of workers in management and planning functions — and its cultural and educational aspects — is to be maximized, a short term in office is necessary. But if members of workers' councils and other self-management bodies are to be effective decision-makers and participants in long-term planning, then the opposite organizational principle, i.e., long office terms, would be appropriate (Pateman, 1970:97).[33] In part, this dilemma is the result of the existing uneven distribution of knowledge and capabilities between managers and workers. Effective and high-quality participation — to the extent it leads to learning — should attenuate this dilemma. Increased familiarity of workers with enterprise and societal conditions and problems should facilitate the assumption of decision-making positions within self-management institutions even with relative frequent office rotation.[34]

A major dilemma in the Yugoslav system is that between localism and local autonomy, and social integration implied by social ownership and socialist solidarity. The tension between the autonomy of enterprises and the interests of the wider community poses a particularly serious problem for the poorer communes (Hunnius, 1973:288). Such communes may feel compelled to make heavy demands on the enterprises within their jurisdiction in order to achieve or to maintain acceptable standards of living of their citizens. This may hurt the development of the enterprises. In general, self-management as an institutional device stresses very particular interests, whereas social ownership, the state, and the leading party, as institutions, may stress universal interests. This dilemma is one which continues to challenge theory and practice of self-management.

Finally, there is the dilemma between the power to shape economic democracy and the democratization of power. On the one hand, a dominant political group has acted to establish and develop self-management and "participatory democracy". On the other hand, the realization of these goals and values implies negation of the power of that group.[35]

3. Conclusion

The readiness to socially experiment and to explore the possibilities and meaning of the socialist vision is one of the most characteristic features of contemporary Yugoslavia. This has enhanced its development capabilities by allowing it to deal creatively with changes in its international environment. It also has enabled Yugoslavia to transform in constructive ways internal conflicts and contradictions. Flexible organizational and institutional structures allowed the generation of new options, the transformation of perceptions and value structures, and, ultimately, changes in the "rules of the game" and the institutional set-up.[36]

Contradictions between, on the one hand, hierarchical developments within enterprises, and uneven economic developments generally, and, on the other hand, egalitarian social movements within the socio-cultural and political subsystems can be expected to continue. Yugoslavia will therefore have to maintain its dynamic and flexible character. It appears as essential that normative commitments and political constraints continue to be extended into the economic sphere to (a) counteract and to minimize hierarchical developments and to (b) minimize tendencies of uneven development as a whole.[37] Otherwise, social cohesion and collective commitment to the reproduction and development of socialist institutions could be threatened. In that case, the openness and "continual flux" of the Yugoslav system — which presently appear as basically positive features — could become its greatest weakness.

NOTES

1. The preceding Chapter describes and analyzes the historical process through which self-management institutions have been introduced, extended and restructured in the concrete historical case of Yugoslavia.
2. See the preceding Chapter for a further discussion. This conceptualization is to a substantial degree convergent with the definition of a socialist society given by Horvat (1975a:127-129).
3. Social units of production include enterprises as well as political groupings and the many formal and informal groups which are 'units of production' in the political and socio-cultural spheres.
    The next Chapter uses a similar conceptualization to analyze international exchange relations between developed and under-developed countries using key concepts such as unequal exchange and uneven development.
4. See Baumgartner (1978) who discusses the reproduction and transformation of industrial democracy measures, including self-management institutions, in more formal modelling terms.
5. Rus (1977:21)points out that the traditional 'scientific division of labor' is one of the main obstacles to the full development of self-management. Workers come to rely on the greater knowledge, skill, and presumed ability of the technical and managerial personnel for the sake of enterprise viability and success.
6. The expansion of Yugoslav enterprises into foreign countries obviously sharpens this problem. Size therefore will remain a critical problem. The underaccumulation of self-managed firms cannot, therefore, be evaluated only negatively.
7. The dynamic and experimental nature of the Yugoslav system makes this a difficult and uncertain undertaking. Such a theory has to be based on an agreed upon interpretation of the system and its institutions. This has been a problem in the past (see Horvat, 1971 and 1976) and seems still to be one today if the Yugoslav debate about capital charges is a valid indication (see Ocić, 1977).
8. We refer mostly to Vanek (1970, 1971, 1975b, 1978). But see also Nutzinger (1975) and Daurès and Dumas (1977).
    The implied criticism of Vanek's work cannot detract from its valuable contribution to the development of self-management theory. The establishment of a school of analysis implies that all future work must start by considering critically the initial undertaking.
9. See Vanek (1975b, 1978:11-14), Nutzinger (1975), and Furubotn and Pejovich (1973).
10. Both Vanek and Meade (1975:415) are assuming physical capital to be 'putty-putty', an

assumption critized a long time ago by Joan Robinson and found to be severly wanting in the analysis of the problem of technology transfers to the developing countries.

11. The Steinherr and Tisse results do not, of course, exclude contraction through retirement and normal labor turnover. However, the latter is low in the Yugoslav context (and not only for the negative reasons given by Furubotn and Pejovich (1973)). Retirement could only result if everybody believed that the higher price remained high in the long run.

12. This has been largely the case in Yugoslavia (Nutzinger, 1975; Furubotn and Pejovich, 1973).

13. The analysis of Steinherr and Thisse (1978) implies inter-dependence of individual utility functions. This leads to innumerable difficulties in constructing a neo-classical aggregate utility function.

14. Similarly, time is used as a simple periodization factor, not as a concrete, historical and social phenomena linking firms to their environment and each other, forcing them to act and react in a changing system.

15. Decision-making influence in Yugoslavia has so far differed substantially from the pure model implied by neo-classical analysis. (See the data and references to studies by Obradović, Županov, and Rus in the preceding chapter.) This suggests that Yugolav micro and macro data cannot really be used to simulate a pure self-management system of the type analyzed by Vanek.

16. Self-managed firms which emerge out of prosperous enterprises through the benevolent action of their owners do rather well. Examples are IPG in the US (Zwerdling, 1977) and Porst in Germany (*Business Week*, Dec. 11, 1978).

17. The misinterpretation of the Vanek-type analysis occurs because the neo-classical production function analysis rests 'on an idealized economy ... [where] ... full employment of resources prevails' (Vanek, 1978:12). Unfortunately, producer cooperatives find themselves in the real world where most points on the production function surface are unattainable for them.

18. However, Spain (1959-65) has a higher and Romania (1953-65) the same productivity growth rate as Yugoslavia (Balassa and Bertrand, 1970:343).

19. Employment in manufacturing and services is about 4 and 26 points below the predicted values in the absence of imperfect capital pricing.

20. Vanek's sample of countries includes a large number of underdeveloped countries. Data on their growth performance and most other economic variables are notoriously unreliable, making the calculation of expected growth rates rather speculative.

21. The growth-depressing impact of the lack of proper capital charges is estimated by relying on the concept of imperfect capital markets. The degree of imperfection is measured by the difference between a real rate of interest and an estimated 'actual' marginal product of capital. The latter is calculated with the help of regression analysis and seems to ignore the problem of imperfect factor markets in developing countries and the even more general problem of the role of social power in determining profit rates. It seems doubtful that one can estmate 'true' capital productivity by relying on data from different economic systems with vastly different power structures and institutions.

22. Our interpretation of micro-level behaviour suggests the need to take other factors into account to explain the non-realization of material growth.

23. The latter influence cannot have been strong during the period from which data has been drawn to support Vanek's argument. The institution of social contracts has been introduced in the 1970s.

24. Daurès and Dumas (1977:96) propose government rule-making to specify the use of net income. This is, of course, the Yugoslav solution of 1972 (Furubotn and Pejovich, 1973:294-297).

25. The extent of control is influenced by the importance of loans for enterprise accumulation and by the structure of the banking system. Both developed in ways highly favorable to the exercise of control rights by banks in the pre-1972 period in Yugoslavia (Horvat, 1971:70; Nutzinger, 1975:193-194; Furubotn and Pejovich, 1973:279; Dubey, 1975).

26. See Drulović (1973) and Milenkovich (1977) on this point of intervention. Horvat (1971:37) points out that everybody participating in the debate on ownership agreed that social ownership implied only a limited right.

27. The neo-classical analysis brushes this problem aside. Meade (1972:394), for example, argues that it does not make any difference if finance capital is provided through a competitive market and many private savers, or a central state lending institution charging a market-clearing interest rate. He obviously misses the major question. The concepts of power and control should be strategic ones in this analysis.

28. Two remarks are in order. For one, regulation through limited intervention by planners and politicians is inappropriate to a self-management system. In any case, it could not ensure consistent results. Secondly, the limit to growth of enterprises observed in self-management systems (see part II) is in this sense positive. Norms and rules should make sure that (a) an enterprise bumping against its size limit does not stop investing to achieve qualitative growth, and that (b) some accumulation is still taking place to favor the formation of new enterprises.

29. An enterprise's growth path would then look like that in the figure below.

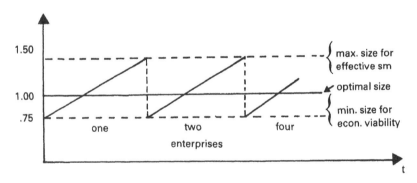

FIGURE 8.1

30. Here we think especially about the need to evenly allocate enterpreneurial talent. It is precisely the uneven possession of dynamic managers which accounts in part for the tendency of uneven development among Chinese agricultural communes (Peemans, 1976:35ff).

31. Such a rule and norm system may have to vary according to the stage of development and the nature of the system's structure. Development towards 'evenness' from a situation and a history of substantial inequalities — as in the case in Yugoslavia — demands different constraints than the reproduction of a more or less evenly developed socio-economic structure.

32. The tolerance of hierarchical developments on such grounds as improved technical and economic performances is likely to be revealed as a cost-efficient solution in the short term only. They are inefficient in the long-term perspective as they inhibit and undermine broad-based socio-economic development. The short duration of strikes in Yugoslavia indicates one of the benefits of taking the long view.

33. Some forms of participation appear to be efficient in realizing economic objectives and stimulating worker responsibility and morale while being inefficient in actualizing ethical and humanistic objectives (Rus, 1977).
34. Self-management can be expected to produce a general consensus about enterprise development. This would reduce the inefficiency of reorientation which goes frequently hand in hand with a rotation of office holders.
35. Eastern European countries experience a major contradiction between emerging socioeconomic and existing political forms (Ionescu, 1976:33):

    The real object of the contradiction is the necessity to adapt Leninist tructures to the technological revolutions that have swept the industial world since World War II. By now it is universally clear that the industrial-technological society, with its built-in corporate structures and therefore with its essential need for expanding pluralization, can no longer live within the narrow Leninist boundaries and parameters.

36. Creative conflict is in part a function of social cohesion and of the commitment of social actors to the maintenance and development of society. These are likely to persist as long as inequalities do not become extreme and are seen as temporary and correctable 'dysfunctionalities', and as long as most — if not all — social groups have opportunities to exercise meaningful control over the system so as to be able to renegotiate and correct felt injustices (see Burns et al, 1984; Chapter 5 also deals with such conflict developments).
37. Major actors in the society — labor unions, the party, local and national leaders — appear to be committed to further self-management development. Interests within enterprises, including managers and technicians, are opposed to the return of capitalism as such, and the private sector lacks political and socio-cultural influence (Hunnius, 1973).

REFERENCES

Balassa, B. and T.J. Bertrand 1970 "Growth Performance of Eastern European Economies and Comparable Western European Countries." *American Economic Review*, 60 (Proceedings): 314-320.

Baumgartner, T. 1978 "An Actor-oriented Systems Model for the Analysis of Industrial Democracy Measures." In R.F. Geyer and J. van der Zouwen (eds.), *Sociocybernetics*, Vol. 1, pp. 55-77. Leiden, Martinus Nijhoff.

Burns, T.R., T. Baumgartner and P. DeVillé 1985 *Man, Decisions, Society*. New York, Gordon and Breach.

Daurès, N. and A. Dumas 1977 *Théorie économique de l'autogestion dans l'entreprise*. Montpellier, Ed. du Faubourg.

Drulović, M. 1973 *L'autogestion à l'épreuve*. Paris, Fayard.

Dubey, V. 1975 *Yugoslavia: Development with Decentralization*. Baltimore, Johns Hopkins University Press.

Furubotn, E.G. and S. Pejovich 1973 "Property Rights, Economic Decentralization, and the Evolution of the Yugoslav Firm, 1965-1972." *Journal of Law and Economics*, 16:275-302.

Fusfeld, D.R. 1978 "Workers' Management and the Transition to Socialism." Dubrovnik, First International Conference on the Economics of Workers' Management.

Horvat, B. 1976 *The Yugoslav Economic System*. White Plains, IASP.

Horvat, B. 1975a "An Institutional Model of a Self-Managed Social Economy." *Eastern European Economics*, 10 (1972). Reprinted in J. Vanek (ed.), *Self-Management*. Middlesex, Penguin.

Horvat, B. 1975b "Why are Inefficiencies of Private Enterprise Tolerated?" *Economic Analysis*, 9:181-201.

Horvat, B. 1971 "Yugoslav Economic Policy in the Post-War Period: Problems, Ideas, Institutional Developments." *American Economic Review*, 61 (3, Supplement).

Hunnius, G. 1973 "Workers' Self-Management in Yugoslavia." In G. Hunnius, G.D. Garson and J. Case (eds.), *Workers' Control.* New York, Random House.

Ionescu, G. 1976 "The Modern State, its Princes and its Condottieres." *comparative Communism*, 9:27-34.

Meade, J.E. 1975 "The Theory of Labor-Managed Firms and of Profit Sharing." *Economic Journal*, 82:402-428.

Milenkovich, D.D. 1977 "The Case of Yugoslavia." *American Economic Review*, 67 (Proceedings):55-60.

Nutzinger, H. 1975 "Investment and Financing in a Labour-Managed Firm and its Social Implications." *Economic Analysis*, 9:181-201.

Ocić, C. 1977 "The Associated Labor Act: Some Macroeconomic Implications." Paris, 2nd International Conference on Participation, Workers' Control, and Self-Management.

Pateman, C. 1970 *Participation and Democratic Theory.* Cambridge, CUP.

Peemans, J.P. 1976 'Modèle d'accumulation et de transformation des rapports sociaux: Remarques sur les problèmes de la stratégie de développement en Chine." Louvain-La-Neuve, Institut pour l'Etude des Pays en Développement.

Rus, V. 1977 "Yugoslav Country Context." Ljubljana, Institute of Sociology.

Sacks, S.R. 1976 "Corporate Giants under Market Socialism." *Studies in Comparative Communism*, 9:369-388.

Steinherr, A. and J.F. Thisse 1978 "Is there a Negatively Sloped Supply Curve in the Labour-Managed Firm?" Louvain-La-Neuve, Institut des Sciences Economiques, Working Paper Nr. 7812.

Vanek, J. 1978 "Self-Management, Workers' Management, and Labour Management in Theory and Practice: A Comparative Study." *Economic Analysis*, 12:5-24.

Vanek, J. 1975a "Introduction." In J. Vanek (ed.), *Self-Management.* Middlesex, Penguin.

Vanek, J. 1975b "The Basic Theory of Financing of Participatory Firms." In J. Vanek (ed.), *Self-Management.* Middlesex, Penguin.

Vanek, J. 1971 *The Participatory Economy.* Ithaca: Cornell University Press.

Vanek, J. 1970 *The General Theory of Labour-Managed Market Economies.* Ithaca, Cornell University Press.

Ward, B. 1958 "The Firm in Illyria: Market Syndicalism." *American Economic Review,* 48:566-589.

Zwerdling, D. "At IPG, it's not Business as Usual!" *Working Papers*, 5 (Spring): 68-81.

Development and Underdevelopment

9

Wealth and Poverty Among Nations:[1] A Social System Perspective on Inequality, Uneven Development and Dependence in the World Economy

Thomas Baumgartner   and   Tom R. Burns

1. Introduction: A Perspective on the World Socio-Economic System

WHEN OPEC asserted control over oil at the beginning of the 1970's, many hoped, even believed, that a turning point in the history of world capitalism had been reached: A number of underdeveloped countries acting together would overcome the strategic resource and financial constraints which had previously blocked the realization of many of their own development ambitions. Oil revenues would make them independent of Western capital markets. Control over oil would provide them with the power to renegotiate the international economic and political order in their own interest and on behalf of all Third World countries (Baumgartner *et al.*, 1977).

Recent history suggests that this transformation, if it is underway at all, will take much longer and will be much more of an undertaking than was originally thought. Some of the reasons for this can, in our view, be identified and analyzed through the use of a social systems framework which entails a holistic, transdisciplinary approach and consideration of key societal processes and dynamics (Burns *et al.*, 1985).

In the following pages, a theoretical model is outlined. The model focuses on production, exchange, power and conflict relationships between rich and poor countries, the social frameworks within which their interactions take place, and the development tendencies between and within the groups of rich and poor countries. The model is used to specify and analyze some of the major processes and conditions (1) which produce and maintain (reproduce) inequalities in wealth and power between 'developed' and 'less developed' countries (indicated by DC and LDC respectively),

279

and (2) which produce and maintain some of the differences among LDCs in the Third World.

Our point of departure is the organized system of inequality between developed and underdeveloped countries and their economic agents. The industrialized, high-income countries of the First World and the less developed, low-income countries of the Third World are not only unequal in their resource control, their access to and ability to develop advanced technologies, the skills and technical know-how of their labor forces, and their strategic opportunities and development capabilities.[2] Also the international socio-economic framework, the "rules of the game" for internationalized markets, within which production and exchange take place is biased against most Third World countries. Finally, governments as well as economic agents of DCs and LDCs have unequal capability to structure and restructure the international framework.

Participation in such a framework, as we discuss in more detail later, leads to or reinforces inequalities in wealth, power and capabilities for socio-economic development: DCs and LDCs have, for instance, unequal possibilities to take advantage of opportunities for profit and economic growth, or to avoid losses and negative effects of an economic downturn or transformation. Inequalities in wealth and capabilities for future growth and development tend to be reproduced.

Even "legislation" for equal opportunity or "fair exchange" would not, in our view, be sufficient to prevent the reproduction of the inherited and historically produced differences among nations of the world and their economic agents. Of course, specific normative and socio-political regulations and substantial transfers of resources could prevent or correct the development of extreme inequalities. However, these controls are almost totally lacking on the international level. Nor do they exist within Third World countries to the same extent as in DCs. Also, DC governments and their economic agents tend to have greater powers than LDC governments to shape and reshape economic environments in advantageous ways. Moreover, the former are typically better able than the latter to adapt to changing environments in terms of developing new technologies, new organizational arrangements and better conflict resolution capabilities.

The conditions and development tendencies characterizing the world economic system result in not only the production of greater wealth, but also the production of relative poverty and a system of uneven development and dependence among nations.

2.   A Social Systems Model of the Reproduction of Wealth, Inequalities, Uneven Development, and Dependence

This section presents a framework for the specification and analysis of the relationship between inequalities in wealth and power and the maintenance and reproduction of such inequalities.

A social systems model is formulated to represent and analyze processes and conditions which result in the unequal distribution and accumulation of resources and capabilities, and thereby contribute to the reproduction and extension of inequality and uneven development.[3] Economic exchange in this context becomes unequal exchange, development becomes uneven development, and interdependence becomes unequal dependence, or, simply, dependency.[4]

2.1 Premises

The following seven premises underlie the formation of the model and later analyses:

1) The social process of economic production and exchange generates multiple outcomes. These include effects in the sphere of economic production and exchange (spin-offs) as well as in other spheres of social action (spill-overs).

2) Actors or classes of actors have qualitatively and quantitatively different linkages to the products and their spin-offs and spill-overs because of their differential possession of property rights (and control rights in general) and because of their positions and roles in the division of labor.

3) The distribution of benefits and costs of production and exchange is unequal. The result is an unequal accumulation of capabilities, resources, and social power among the different actors or classes of actors.

4) Differential accumulation leads to the uneven acquisition of development capabilities. Actors acquire differential abilities to shape or to take advantage of productive opportunities and to avoid or overcome traps and vicious circles.[5] Thus, reproduction and elaboration of power differences are supported.

5) Systems of social production both reflect and produce unequal power structures. Such systems are human constructions, and therefore they are artificial. They require continual reproduction and structuring activities in response to changes in their environments as well as in

response to their internal developments. When characteristic societal relationships and processes are maintained, we speak of *social reproduction*. The reproduction of the economic sphere depends not only on replacing the means of production and on reproducing the labor force. It also entails suitable structuring and restructuring of the political and socio-cultural contexts for economic production and exchange. For instance, the social process of reproducing an institutional framework, even if the latter is limited to a particular sub-system or sphere of social action (e.g. the economic subsystem), depends on the developments in other spheres of social action. In general, the reproduction of institutions depends on compatible or corresponding developments in other spheres of social action and, in this sense, is *context dependent* (Burns *et al.*, 1985; Baumgartner, 1978).

6) An institutional arrangement generates not only particular intended outcomes. There are also various unintended spin-offs and still-overs which can either help to reduce the arrangement or operate to undermine or transform it. Also, these developments are often the unintended consequence of the policies and actions of dominant groups (DeVille and Burns, 1977).

7) Actors or groups of actors adversely affected by the operation or development of an institutional set-up may socially articulate, through communicating with one another, their disadvantages and deprivation, e.g. in terms of norms and values about fairness or equity, or on other ideological grounds. Some may also mobilize to carry out social action to change the institutional set-up, or at least certain (for them) undesirable features of it. These activities usually bring them into conflict with those having an interest in, or commitment to, system reproduction. In other words, conflicts arise concerning the maintenance or transformation of the institutional set-up. Such conflicts can interfere with reproduction processes, thereby setting the stage for social transformation.

2.2 The Structure of the Systems Model

The model presented in Figure 9. 1 can be read in two different ways with slight modifications. The model represents, in both cases, *a system of unequal exchange and uneven development based on the production of and exchange between two classes of enterprises*. The case represented in Figure 9.1 describes the international system where DC enterprises exchange *in international markets* with LDC enterprises.[6] The other case (see note to Figure 9.1) represents a production and exchange system *within a LDC*, where local subsidiaries of foreign multi-national corporations (MNC) interact in domestic markets with nationally-owned, MNC-independent enterprises.[7]

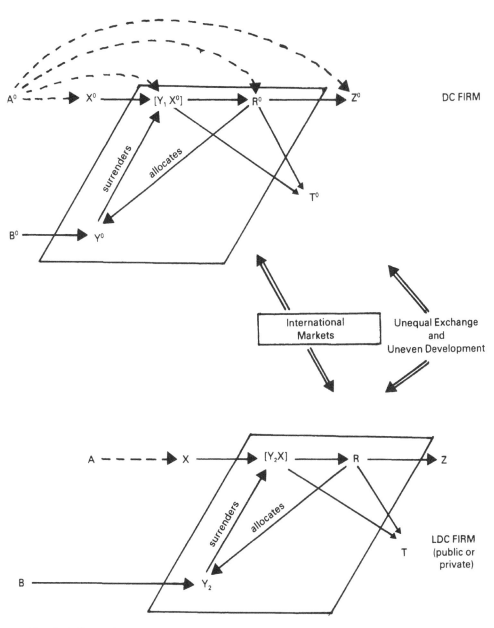

A, A⁰— Capitalists and managers
B, B⁰ — Workers
X, X⁰— Capital
Y, Y⁰ — Employment
T, T⁰ — Taxes
Z, Z⁰ — Spin offs, spill overs
R, R⁰ — Revenues

FIGURE 9.1   International division of labor and exchange between DC and LDC enterprises.

Below we refer to certain characteristic features of the production and exchange system represented in Figure 9.1:[8]

1) *Production.* DC enterprises produce advanced technology, capital goods, and processed consumer goods with high valued added. LDC firms tend to produce incompletely processed raw materials and agricultural products and consumer goods with low-valued added, based on the use of cheap labor or labor intensive processes. Demand development tends to favor the producers of processed raw materials and food, and of complex, high value-added consumer products and capital equipments.[9] Technology developments seem to go in the direction of making products and production processes less material and energy-intensive.[10] As indicated below, center producers enjoy therefore better pricing and profit opportunities which favor their quantitative and qualitative growth.

2) *Capital.* The quantity and quality of capital is unequally distributed between DC and LDC enterprises (X^o and X respectively).

3) *Labor.* The labor allocated between DC and LDC enterprises (Y_1 and Y_2, respectively) usually differs qualitatively. That is, DC enterprises have, or are better able to attract, human resources and to develop them to a greater extent through education and knowledge production than LDC enterprises.

4) *Revenues.* DC and LDC enterprises have different levels of revenue (R^o and R) and gains per unit of input (of capital and labor). Specifically, DC enterprises usually achieve a greater surplus revenue and a higher rate of return on investment than periphery enterprises.[11] The different levels of revenue and returns on inputs result in unequal allocation in the two cases: (1) to capital owners; (2) to reproduction and development of production; (3) to labor income necessary to maintain and reproduce labor power; (4) to transfers and taxes (T^o, T) paid to public institutions; (5) to transfers of resources to socio-cultural processes.

5) *Wages.* DC enterprises are more likely to offer higher wages, better working conditions and fringe benefits, and employment security than periphery enterprises. This could be represented as a spin-off from employment Y_1 and Y_2.

6) *Capital accumulation.* LDC enterprises typically fail to either accumulate substantial surpluses or to attract capital (loans, equity capital, etc.) to the same extent as DC enterprises.

The features specified in the model above contribute to the analyses of inequalities in exchange, resource accumulation, and development potentialities:

— Differentiation in power and control relations with respect to advanced capital (X^o), higher quality labor (Y_1), and more advanced production processes.

— Differentiation in functioning, in that advanced and backward production processes entail different quantities and qualities of capital and labor.

— Differentiation in gains and losses whereby control over advanced production generates more advantageous spin-offs and spill-overs (R^o, T^o, Z^o), for instance in terms of developing forces of production.

These differences may be examined in our framework at different levels and with respect to different categories of actors and collectivities: (1) between different classes (owners/managers and workers); (2) between MNC and DC enterprises, on one hand, and LDC enterprises, on the other; (3) between advanced and backward sectors within LDCs; and (4) between regions and countries which are characterized by different production profiles and combinations of actors.

In the following we shall focus on the relationship between DCs and LDCs and their economic agents.[12] We will show in what sense one can say that *sectors, enterprises, owners, managers and workers of developed countries enjoy structural advantages relative to those in less developed countries, and gain in part at their expense.*

3.   Theses about Center-Periphery Systems

Below we present eight theses about the shaping and reproduction of wealth and poverty among nations. These follow from the model presented in the foregoing section which specifies a structured system of inequalities in wealth and power, a division of labor, and exchange in the international economic system. The theses are formulated in terms of the relationships, transactions, and development tendencies among center and periphery countries (DC resp. LDC) and their respective enterprises.[13]

By center-periphery relations are meant those in which there are at least two classes of interacting actors: dominant and subordinate. Such actors, and intermediate categories of actors, are typically differentiated in terms of their power and meta-power across a wide range of interaction situations. The dominant actors not only have the ability to realize preferred outcomes and to impose, at least in part, their will over the opposition of others in specific, socially structured interaction contexts. (Bargaining or transactional power among actors may be understood in such terms.) But they also have the capability to manipulate or change the distribution of resources (or distribution processes), the institutional set-up (hence to basically change the "types of games" and the "rules of the game" and conditions of social action and transaction generally), and the legitimizing cultural and ideological orientations in social relationships. Such capability is referred to as *structuring or meta-power*, a fundamental concept for understanding and analyzing social reproduction and development.[14]

Thesis 1: The Center is less dependent on its trading environment than the Periphery

Enterprises differ in their degree of dependency on their exchange relationships. They therefore differ in their bargaining power in relation to one another. The same holds also for countries.

Much of the work utilizing the concept of "dependency" has identified it with the state of being subject to non-reciprocated influence. This means that in concrete, often structured exchange situations B is said to be dependent on A when A controls valuables which B needs or values, and which are not readily available through alternative channels or means. There are multiple bases for dependency conceived in this way as reversed power. The greater the peripheral actor's *need for the goods and services provided by center actors, and the fewer the opportunities to satisfy these needs outside of the relationship, the weaker the bargaining power of the peripheral actor.* An actor is likely to be compelled in this situation to accept unfavorable terms of exchange (e.g. terms of trade).

We indicate below several general factors which tend to maintain or increase dependence of LDCs on DCs in their relationships, and hence result in low bargaining power for LDCs and their enterprises.

High concentration on one or a few trading partners, markets, and products Peripheral countries and enterprises tend to produce and supply *few* products, most of which are raw materials, agricultural products, or finished products with a low degree of processing. The center countries and enterprises typically produce and supply *a variety* of highly processed consumer and capital goods.

Center countries and enterprises have alternative sources for many of the valuables the peripheral countries produce and supply, either from other peripheral countries or from one another. Also, they can often substitute for raw materials, at least over the long run, by using their know-how and technology to develop substitutes. Peripheral countries and enterprises lack a significant capability for producing *alternative* goods for sale to the center.[15]

Low flexibility in product range, product processes, and organizational set-up   Flexibility depends on a highly differentiated, yet well integrated system. In such a system, one can always find somewhere the knowledge and capability to identify new opportunities and to start up new productive activities. A rich infrastructure is obviously a precondition for the realization of a flexible production structure.

LDCs, and especially their less developed regions, sectors and enterprises are poorly equipped with infrastructures (transport, communication, energy, financial and capital markets) and support structures in general (education and training, advisory, repair and maintenance services, etc.). Dependence on imported equipment increases the significance of these structural weaknesses (see Chapter 10).

This low flexibility is of course one of the reasons why it is so difficult to overcome the narrow production range and the small numbers of exchange partners discussed above. Efforts to diversify the economy or to substantially increase the rate of growth require in many instances the import of foreign advice and capital at a faster rate than exports can be increased. This often causes balance-of-payments problems, deterioration of the terms of trade, and pressures to cut back on imports. In other words, *this strategy runs up against the balance-of-payments constraints on development possibilities.*[16]

Foreign indebtedness   Less developed countries are capital-importing countries. Use of foreign capital to build up domestic production or export industries requires eventually an export surplus.

Generally, foreign capital donors and their experts advise further expansion of production along the lines of existing specialization and traditional exports. This strategy promises ready export expansion and therefore ability to service the contracted debt. But it also depends for its success on the creditor country's (or countries') willingness to buy up these exports (Streeten, 1972). This export strategy tends to reinforce the LDCs narrow range of produced goods and services, lack of flexibility, and weak bargaining power, especially as DCs have been able, through the development of technology to limit imports of, or in some instances to find substitutes for, raw materials, foodstuffs, and simple products coming from LDCs.

On the whole, underdeveloped countries producing primary goods find it more and more difficult to increase the exports of their traditional products (Streeten, 1972:212), except in times of war when LDCs provide highly welcome additional production capacity enabling the pursuit in the DCs of a "guns as well as butter" strategy. In this context it should be noted that the resultant cyclical demand and supply pattern itself has a negative impact on peripheral development.

In general, the capital-importing strategy for development entails the substantial risk that debt accumulation will decrease LDC flexibility and market bargaining power, and thereby will increase dependence, especially when debt service reaches or exceeds the gross inflow of new capital.

Thesis 2:   The Center exerts an agglomerative pull on strategic resources

The relative market advantage, profitability and development potential of enterprises in market economies depends on a variety of factors: control over the production process, over essential material and human resources, and over technology, knowledge and patents; political and economic support from governments; and legitimacy based in part on success in producing wealth. Typically, DC enterprises have greater access to or control over these factors than LDC enterprises and, therefore, in general promise more secure profits and growth than LDC enterprises.

As a result, center enterprises are in a better position to maintain and develop a total agglomerative pull, attracting and gaining access to qualitatively superior and quantitatively sufficient physical, financial and human resources, as well as community and government support in the form of favorable legal and tax conditions, and transportation, training and education, research and information facilities.

In addition, center enterprises tend to pull input prices up for the qualitatively better factors of production to the disadvantage of periphery enterprises who can draw on fewer economic resources to finance increased costs. The resultant cost differentiation in favor of periphery enterprises is less than the quality and productivity gain experienced by the center.

These processes increase the development potentialities and chances of success of center enterprises in competition with periphery enterprises in international as well as more local markets.

Such agglomerative pull can also be observed on the international level between LDCs and DCs. This is particularly important in the case of education and qualified manpower, where there is a veritable brain drain from LDCs. Many of the best qualified and most entrepreneurially-minded people leave LDCs. They try to reach DCs where they can improve their standard of living and develop and use their capabilities. Of course, substantial numbers of the most capable people are exiled for political, tribal or racial reasons, and find their way to DCs where not only do they escape physical repression but find substantially better opportunities for careers and professional development.

Thesis 3:   The Center acquires better development potentialities than the Periphery and their respective economic agents

Center enterprises not only have access to and utilize qualitatively better factors of production than peripheral enterprises (see Thesis 2). They are also less dependent, having more bargaining power and hence benefit more from exchange transactions than peripheral enterprises (Thesis 1). *Exchange under these conditions becomes unequal exchange, because it maintains and reinforces the unequal accumulation and development of the forces of production.*[17]

Exchange between the center and the periphery is unequal to the extent that the production of raw materials and minimally processed goods for export results, in the periphery, in (1) *less* stimulation of internal markets; (2) *fewer* possibilities or pressures to develop a more highly skilled labor force; (3) *less* development of new or indigenous technologies and resources for advantageous exchange in a *developing* world market; and (4) *fewer* gains in system capabilities and structural advantages in the economic and political context of international relations.

This differentiation is not merely a matter of the production and trade of agricultural goods and raw materials as opposed to manufactured goods. It is, for one, a question of the socio-economic and political context in which production and exchange take place. The food producing and exporting developed countries such as the U.S., Denmark, and New Zealand are cases in point. On the other hand, some primary goods, such as petroleum currently, provide strategic leverage and exceptional gains on international markets to some LDCs.

The differentiation between DC and LDC enterprises is reflected in different rates of resource accumulation. DC enterprises achieve higher capital-intensity in production, higher wages and salaries, higher returns on investment as well as greater revenue resources generally available for allocation to capital investment and to system reproduction and development. Especially noteworthy are the differential accumulation and development of management knowledge and skills and technology development capabilities (R & D activities). They can also devote more resources to legitimation processes such as welfare and tax payments, workers' education, work redesign, workers' participation in management and other conflict resolution reforms.

In sum, DC enterprises are generally in a better position than LDC enterprises to compete for and invest in new capital, human capital, R & D and support structure development (such as transportation systems, training and research facilities, etc.), which contribute to maintaining or improving their wealth, advantageous terms of exchange, and development potentials. The LDCs and their economic agents tend to lose out, or at least find it impossible to catch up. Of course, a few, by virtue of finding niches and effectively managing their systems, may achieve significant 'upward mobility'.

Thesis 4: The transfer and creation of development capabilities tends to be blocked

In general, the uneven accumulation of development capabilities generates the differences in meta-power which allow center actors not only to reproduce and develop productive relationships locally. It above all allows them to maintain conditions on the global level which are conducive to the reproduction of uneven development and dependence relationships between DCs and LDCs and their economic agents.

The differentiation between advanced production and backward production, and between center and periphery countries, has both a history and a future. Below, we briefly discuss the processes that tend to block the diffusion or movement of information, skills, technology, or other productive factors which are essential in future economic development. Such blockage contributes to the reproduction of inequalities in wealth and power between DCs and LDCs and their economic agents.

The DCs or their economic agents control more advanced technologies (through ownership, patents, generalized and specific expertise) than LDCs or their agents.[18] And what is even more important, *they control the capabilities to generate or develop yet more advanced technologies.*

The LDCs, as pointed out earlier, have fewer resources to produce their own innovations or to produce the base to generate future innovations. At the same time, the DCs may provide technology and knowledge, but not the *basis* (capital in the most general sense), to generate new knowledge and technology in the future.

Thus, even if there were to be a substantial transfer of industrial technology to LDCs, *the DCs would remain in an advantageous position in terms of their capability to develop yet more advanced technologies in the future* — through their extensive research and development systems, substantial numbers of scientists and engineers, and advanced educational systems.

The classic pattern is for center countries (or their enterprises) to provide outputs from the operation of advanced production systems rather than to provide or assist in the acquisition of capabilities (knowledge, skills technology research and development base) to produce such outputs themselves. The technology, e.g. industrial technology, now being supplied to some LDCs tends to be of low strategic value in the emerging international market situation: e.g. automobile production, not to speak of shoe and textile productions, as opposed to computer technology, knowledge production, etc.

The argumentation here should not be understood as a plea for the unrestrained transfer of technology to the LDCs. Much transferred technology is too capital-intensive, or too 'modern'. Rather we argue that whatever the nature of the technology transferred — inappropriate or appropriate for development purposes — DC enterprises and governments can assure that:

— only technology is transferred which *has been* of strategic importance to the power and well-being of the center;

— the satisfactory operation of modern technology has to rely on back-up services located in the center;[19]

— complete systems (like the full nuclear fuel cycle) are never transferred;

— the technology creation process remains located in and under the control of the center. This means among other things that scientific training is still predominantly located in DC. It also means that efforts to create 'appropriate technologies' tend to be located in the DCs.

Thus one can conclude that the transfer of technology is tailored in such a way that it does not lessen the degree of dependency, but simply changes the content of the dependence-maintaining mechanism.

Thesis 5: The Center is able to propagate the wrong development model for the periphery

Streeten (1972:464) has argued that,

There is overwhelming evidence (now) that industrialization is not a safe escape from poverty and dualism, but can follow along high-cost, inefficient lines that reinforce dualism, increase inequality, raise unemployment and worsen balance of payment crises, thereby aggravating the ills against which it was to be a remedy. ... *What is needed is the building up of an indigenous technical capability, combined with the human attitudes and social institutions and the national integration that can implement the benefits of such a capability.* ... Dependence results not from being hewers of wood and drawers of water. ... Dependence derives from the absence of an indigenous range of technological and organizational inputs to respond to investment and trade opportunities." (our emphasis)

The tragedy is that both the center countries and the elites in LDCs believe in the development model which is based on past DC successes.[20] They ignore or fail to examine carefully the extent to which the socio-cultural conditions in the DCs several decades ago can be compared to the conditions existing in the LDCs today.[21]

The Japanese succeeded in their adoption of and adaptation to the Western development model exactly because they closed themselves off from intensive interaction with the West until they had established an indigenous development process based on their long and undestroyed socio-cultural tradition. *Adoption of Western technology took place under carefully controlled conditions, conditions set by the Japanese themselves and not by the Western countries or their economic agents.*

In contrast, Third World countries have not in general, dissociated themselves from the world economic system, or have not found it feasible to do so. In addition, for many LDCs, colonial intervention by some DCs largely destroyed the potential base for an indigenous Japanese-style development process. Rodney (1972) aptly titled his book "How Europe Underdeveloped Africa". He shows how the socio-cultural and political conditions, which hinder development today in large part of the Third World, were consciously produced through the application of colonial power.[22]

The tragedy of the DC domination of the production of a development model is that it:

— excludes explicit and systematic consideration of socio-cultural and political dimensions;

— assumes (in a strangely Marxist way) that the build-up of the material base of production will generate the appropriate socio-cultural and political super-structure;[23]

— almost completely eliminates from DC aid packages support for the creation of better socio-cultural and political conditions. This is not surprising as such activity does not create orders for DC industry or DC aid bureaucracies; pay-offs are uncertain and far in the future; and the consequences are likely to be revolutionary, threatening the power structure which supports the "working relationship" and situation of dependence.[24]

DC ideology justifies the unequal exchange and development outcomes of the development model. The strength of this ideology rests not only on the proven success of DC economic development but also on its characterization as objective or scientific theory. The ideology of 'free trade' is used to keep commodity exchange as well as the flow of finance capital as unrestrained as possible, to the advantage of those nations which have accumulated the most resources and have developed the greatest productive capabilities. The ideology derives its legitimacy from the theoretical argument of 'comparative advantage' which suggests that maximal national well-being is best assured by the existing international division of labor. The proof of this proposition is based on a model which uses strict economic assumptions far removed from economic reality and which above all abstracts from the socio-cultural and political context of production and exchange. But it is exactly this reality (see Thesis 1) and this context which explains why "free trade" is not freely generated and takes the form of unequal exchange.

It is taken for granted — the assumed, structured way things are done — that what happens to one country, its gains or losses, "belong" to it. Given this ideology, DCs retain control over — or have rights to — "their" positive gains from trade while LDCs trading with them have few or no claims or rights to these positive effects.[25] Nor do they receive compensation for relatives losses, for example, in terms of system development capabilities (see Thesis 3).

Thesis 6: World institutions are structured to create conditions for unequal exchange

DC governments supported by other DC actors often explicitly act to shape and regulate economic exchange processes.[26] This involves reserving the right to use domestic policies which facilitate and develop domestic production activities with positive ramifications *within* their own systems. A corollary to this is that they try to prevent, or at least to limit, the extent of those production activities and developments which would have negative societal ramifications. LDC governments are typically less effective in doing this, in part because their economies are more subject to external shocks and the impositions of international banks.

DC governments attempt to shape international institutions and structural contexts such that an "invisible" and "neutral" hand guides international economic exchange to ensure that it is unequal exchange. International institutions such as the Bretton Woods institutions (IMF, World Bank) have been established and are maintained to "manage" the international exchange system. They tend to operate to protect common interests of the center countries and also permit the coordination of their policies, even at the same time that these countries compete with one another. This assures a certain degree of cohesion within the dominant group. The center countries apply sanctions particularly to the weaker, peripheral countries who try to challenge the "taken-for-granted" way of doing things. Typical instances of this type are:

1) The use of international organizations to impose sanctions on those LDCs which violate DC rights of ownership and control. Nationalization of assets without proper compensation — as defined by the DC actors — is

answered with a refusal to grant development credits (World Bank and other development banks) and adjustment credits (IMF).

2) The creation of GATT (the General Agreement on Trade and Tariffs) with the predominant focus on problems of trade liberalization of *industrial goods* (predominantly exchanged by the DC) in the various tariff reduction rounds. *The explicit toleration of a national protection of agricultural production, the implicit acceptance of non-tariff barriers (quotas, administrative rules) to limit industrial imports from low wage countries, and the acceptance of tariff discrimination by free trade zones and common markets, above all those in Europe, are further reflections of this fact.*

Even newer institutions dealing with international trade problems such as UNCTAD — where LDCs are significantly represented — have for example established consensus decision rules which considerably lessen chances that resolutions are passed involving real concessions on the part of DCs. If such resolutions are passed at all, the lack of any real enforcement power on the part of such international organizations guarantees that their implementation must depend on the goodwill of the center countries which typically is lacking.

3) The IMF and related monetary institutions maintain the international monetary system. They provide the framework for determining international reserve currencies according to the trading needs of the major industrialized countries. Exchange rate systems are set up and changed according to the prevailing views of major industrialized nations. They enforced relatively stable exchange rates as long as they felt it was necessary and the costs were bearable. LDCs had to fend for themselves. Of course they have had to in the past, and are still forced to, accept the impositions of international banks. In times of economic crisis, this implies adopting deflationary policies which are politically destabilizing (see Chapters 3 and 5).

Thesis 7: LDCs have a low capacity to control effects of the activities of MNCs and related interests

DCs and LDCs have unequal capabilities to structure and restructure their internal environments. LDCs have a relatively low capacity to prevent foreign private actors and governments from structuring internal processes and relationships which inhibit and distort capability development.

This is largely the case because LDC governments are relatively weak politically and administratively and are unable or unwilling to exercise systematic coordinated control over strategically important economic structuring processes. In addition, political and economic structuring conditions partially lie in the hands of external actors. They, together with local actors linked to the external agents, can intentionally or unintentionally affect domestic social organization and capability development.[27]

Distortions and disruption of economic processes can occur because of the investment and productive activity of powerful multinational firms which attract resources away from processes relating to internal development, thus stifling such development (see Thesis 2). Foreign investment and economic activity may adversely affect the distribution of income. It can discourage investment in areas and sectors that might lead to significant spin-offs and spill-overs advantageous for development.[28] Finally, it may lead to the emergence of domestic interest groups which depend on and support the external ties and the economic and social activities which, although rewarding from their narrow perspective, may inhibit national socio-economic development. Such interest groups are often successful, not infrequently thanks to external support, in confusing or weakening "national will", if not in suppressing more "nationalistic" elites or movements (see Thesis 8).

In Latin America, a number of countries with substantial resources have been unable to protect their societies from foreign economic penetration, disruption, and domination. The result has been that their economies have been structured and driven here and there by the decisions and operations of powerful, autonomous foreign firms and their satellites which have little or no commitment to goals of national development — nor are they subject to rigorous pressures to develop such commitments.[29]

Thesis 8: *DCs limit and avoid international redistributive institutions*

The absence of normative (ideological) and socio-political arrangements to correct the unequal distribution of resources and development capabilities tends to maintain and reproduce uneven development conditions and processes, and along with it, center-periphery relationships.

Streeten (1972) pointed out that if uneven development occurs within a DC, where certain growth poles enrich themselves at the expense of, or without spreading substantial benefits to, the regions left behind, powerful national movements may succeed in establishing economic policies and regulatory institutions to remedy the situation. Tax and subsidy policies, social services, regional policies and public works all contribute to compensate those who are losing out. This reaction presupposes a certain degree of national cohesion, consensus and responsiveness to the development of unequal distributions of income and wealth beyond some point.

Yet many DC governments, and above all the US government in its Latin American backyard, oppose social movements in LDCs which aim to establish radically redistributive domestic institutions and to regulate international relationships so as to reduce unequal exchange.

Internationally, there is no government to impose taxes, disburse subsidies, direct public works or provide social services for the victims of the international division of labor. The economic institutions which do exist at the international level tend to be dominated by DCs and their refusal to consider international redistribution. Of course, the lack of LDC influence over international economic institutions reflects their fragmentation, their lack of collective power. The success of OPEC so far has only been sufficient to wring from DCs a grudging acceptance to consider negotiating new economic and political world orders. Concrete measures and reshaping of institutions are likely to be a long way off.

4.   Conclusion

What we have tried to suggest here is that there are institutionalized conditions as well as deliberate structuring activities which maintain and reproduce inequalities in wealth and economic power in the world system, in particular between DCs and LDCs and their economic agents. The various processes described — unequal exchange, resource accumulation and acquisition of unequal development capabilities, foreign private and state structuring of internal conditions in LDCs, and DC dominance of the structuring of international economic institutions — contribute as components of a global process to the reproduction of differences in wealth and power among nations in the world today.

Current inequalities are the necessary conditions for the reproduction of center-periphery relationships *in the future*. Center-periphery relations tend to be reproduced to the extent that DCs are able to use their advantageous position to maintain (or gain) control over the most strategic future resource combinations — which of course are subject to change. To maintain their positions, they must improve their development capabilities at a rate sufficient to counterbalance gains and improvements in periphery countries. The processes blocking LDCs from gaining possession of resources which are technologically or economically superior to those of the DCs are an important element in the reproduction process.

The problems of unequal wealth and economic power among nations of the world are *systemic problems*. They will not be solved through market and production processes, exchange and accumulation. Instead, they must be solved, at least in part, by the restructuring of the international economic system. Such restructuring will not simply "happen". It will require actors and movements with new visions and demands.

NOTES

1. We are grateful to Hayward Alker, Jr. and Philippe DeVille for their contributions in developing some of the ideas presented here. We wish to thank especially Felix Geyer and J. van der Zouwen for detailed editorial suggestions, which went substantially beyond mere questions of language and style.
2. Not all of these differences are found in every instance. The oil-producing and exporting countries point up the possibility for some Third World countries to have some strengths among a variety of weaknesses.
3. The model presented draws heavily on the work of Amin (1973), Andersson (1972), Brown (1974), Burns et al (1985, Chapter VI), Emmanuel (1972), Galtung (1971), Myrdal (1968) and Wallerstein (1974).
4. Many of the specific factors and processes discussed below have been described and analyzed in classic works on problems of underdevelopment, distorted development, and dependency, e.g. Amin (1973), Frank (1978), Galtung (1971), and Senghaas (1975), but from entirely different perspectives.
5. See Chapter 3 for a discussion of the concept of vicious circles and its application to the study of inflation processes.
6. The LDC enterprise may even be a subsidiary of the DC enterprise. In this case, exchange is often intra-corporate exchange.
7. This dual LDC model might have to be replaced with a three-actor model in the case of the Newly Industrializing Countries (NIC) such as Mexico or Brazil. NICs have modern, capital-intensive, high-technology firms which are in many aspects the same as subsidiaries of MNC. The difference is that the former cannot draw freely on the resources of a world company nor can they rely on a large volume of intra-corporate sales or on political support from the government of a MNC-home country.
8. The reader should translate for himself the international model into the national one by replacing DC and LDC enterprises by MNC and indigenous enterprises repectively.
9. Due to the tendency, known as Engel's law (a low income-elasticity of agricultural products as compared to that of manufactured products), differential development of demand is likely to occur over time, favoring, other things being equal, the producers of manufactured processed goods, for which demand grows relative to supply, producers are more assured of substantial returns for such goods than their trading partners, the peripheral (i.e. LDC) enterprises with whom they exchange primary commoditities and simple, manufactured goods for which demand remains relatively more constant.
10. The developments in the 1950s and 1960s were historically exceptional.
11. Note that productivity increases may have substantially different consequences in the different contexts of A^0 and A. In the case of A^0s, they would be reflected in increased profits (and also possibly increased wages). Such productivity increases may not lead to substantial gains in profits, wages, growth potential etc., in the case of peripheral enterprises. This is often the case in agriculture where productivity growth may lower prices.
12. Burns et al (1985, Chapter VII) presents a similar analysis of the owner/manager and worker relationship in capitalist countries.

13. Wallerstein (1974) presents a historical analysis of the emergence of center-periphery world systems. The analysis of Cardoso and Faletto (1969) of Latin American dependent development can be in part assimilated to our analysis. See Targ (1976) for a relevant review of the literature.

14. Such forms of social power partially determine the bargaining power positions and relationships associated with particular, more or less institutionalized interaction contexts. For a more detailed presentation and illustration of the concepts of meta-power, see Burns *et al* (1985).

15. Given commodity concentration, fluctuations in export earnings for a key export (and low-processed raw materials and agricultural products tend to suffer such fluctuations) result in severe economic dislocations and distortions. This, in turn, can lead to hindrances to economic growth as well as to political tension and disorder (see Chapter 5).

16. LDC's often find themselves forced to engage in certain productive activities, e.g. the production of goods they have traditionally produced and that they are *currently* capable of producing in the international division of labor, in order to maintain their balance of payments, to pay-off external debts, or to import necessities or 'luxurious goods' for their elites, etc. As Hirschman (1969) has pointed out, very few countries would ever consciously wish to specialize in unskilled labor and in a backward production sector, while foreigners with a comparative advantage in entrepreneurship, management, skilled labor, and capital took over or developed the advanced sectors instead of the inferior 'local talent'. But this is precisely the situation in which most LDCs are compelled to operate.

17. Unequal exchange has several meanings, referring for example to the actual goods and services exchanged, the indirect consequences of exchange, and the long-term structural and power consequences of exchange (see Amin (1973), Andersson (1972), Emmanuel (1972), and Galtung (1971), among others). In general, exchange is a process which entails a *complex social interaction with a variety of intended and unintended consequences.*

18. Chapter 11 deals in detail with the questions raised here on links between technology and development.

19. Different levels and qualities of cultural development (at least in relation to certain forms of technology) make for unequal capability among LDC to use technologies developed at the center. Of course, some countries, initially on the periphery, have demonstrated a general capacity to assimilate and develop imported technologies.

20. We cannot take up in this context the distorted forms of DC development: the destruction of the natural environment, wastage of non-renewable resources, pollution, dequalification of work, forced labor mobility, social disruption, etc.

21. Mexico seems to fail to make this analysis. Its present 'oil-fired' development push is more likely than not to end once more in suffering and disappointment (see Chapter 10).

22. This does not necessarily mean that African pre-colonial conditions would have been sufficient to allow the realization of a Japanese development path.

23. Always assuming of course that the DCs seriously wish the development of the Third World and the reduction of the income and wealth gap between the center and the periphery. We do not know to what extent DC systems require such inequality for their functioning.

24. The rule of non-intervention into domestic affairs, while positive in some sense, becomes here a very conservative force, providing a ready excuse for not considering such a development effort.

25. The institution of private property differentially links actors to the positive and negative

spin-off and spill-over effects of production and exchange activities. Property rights assure differential control not only over money accumulation and strategic physical resources, but knowledge, technology and technology development.

26. The detailed argument and empirical support for this thesis are given in Baumgartner and Burns (1975) and Chapter VI of Burns *et al* (1985).

27. Apart from the most obvious interventions of DC governments and their economic agents to maintain colonial or neo-colonial regimes, there are a variety of subtler ways in which — through investment, joint ventures, aid, etc. — distortions and negative cumulative processes may be intentionally or unintentionally generated.

28. A case in point is the tendency of DC enterprises to introduce capital-intensive, labor-saving, physically and socially disruptive production capacity, which is at the same time completely dependent on foreign support structures.

29. In our view, the long-term development objectives of LDCs are inconsistent with corporate global strategies and operational models. LDCs, on the other hand, should seek to (1) increase the productivity and competitiveness of domestic industry; (2) assure mass-produced goods for low income groups; (3) develop the capabilities and skills of their human resources; (4) acquire appropriate technology and an indigenous R & D capability; and (5) decrease dependence on foreign technology and related industrial support structures. Center corporations, on the other hand, are interested in selling goods and services at a profit and maintaining equity ownership, managerial controls, and flexibility. These corporations also have a vital interest in the long-term control and development of their global human resources and physical assets (Johnson, 1970).

REFERENCES

Amin, S. 1973 *Le développement inégal.* Paris: ed. de Minuit. (Am. transl., Unequal Development. New York: Monthly Review Press, 1977).

Andersson, J.O. 1972 *Utrikeshandelns teori och det ojämua utbytet.* Abo: Akademi.

Baumgartner, T. 1978 "An Actor-oriented Systems Model for the Analysis of Industrial Democracy Measures." In R.F. Geyer and J. van der Zouwen (eds.), *Sociocybernetics*, Vol. 1, pp. 55-77. Leiden: Martinus Nijhoff.

Baumgartner, T. and T.R. Burns 1975 "The Structuring of International Economic Exchange." *International Studies Quarterly*, 19:126-159.

Baumgartner, T., T.R. Burns and P. DeVillé 1977 "The Oil Crisis and the Emerging World Order." *Alternatives*, 3:75-108.

Brown, M.B. (ed.) 1974 *The Economics of Imperialism.* Middlesex: Penguin.

Burns, T.R., T. Baumgartner and P. DeVillé 1985 *Man, Decisions, Society.* New York: Gordon and Breach.

Cardoso, F.H. and E. Faletto 1969 *Dependencia y Desarrollo en América Latina.* (Am. transl. Dependency and Development. Berkeley: University of California Press).

DeVillé, P. and T.R. Burns 1977 "Institutional Response to Crisis in Capitalist Countries." *Social Praxis*: 5-46.

Emmanuel, A. 1972 *Unequal Exchange.* New York: Monthly Review Press.

Frank, A.G. 1978 *Dependent Accumulation and Underdevelopment.* London: Macmillan.

Galtung, J. 1971 "A Structural Theory of Imperialism." *Journal of Peace Research*, 8:81-117.

Hirschman, A.O. 1969 "How to Disinvest in Latin America and Why." *Essays in International Finance*, Nr. 76, Princeton University.

Johnson, H.G. 1970 "The Multi-national Firm as a Development Agent." *Columbia Journal of World Business*, May-June.

Myrdal, G. 1968 *Asian Drama.* New York: Twentieth Century Fund.

Rodney, W. 1972 *How Europe Underdeveloped Africa.* London: Bogle-L'Ouverture Publications.

Senghaas, D. 1975 "Multinational Corporations and the Third World. On the Problem of the Further Integration of Peripheries into the Given Structure of the International Economic System." *Journal of Peace Research,* 12:257-274.

Streeten, P. 1972 *The Frontiers of Development Studies.* London: Macmillan.

Targ, H.R. 1976 "Global Dominance and Dependence, Post Industrialism and International Relations Theory." *International Studies Quarterly,* 20:461-482.

Wallerstein, I. 1974 *The Modern World System. Capitalist Agriculture and the Origins of the European World Economy in the 16th Century.* New York: Academic Press.

10

Dependent Development: The Case of Mexico

Philippe DeVille

1. Introduction

The main objective of this chapter is to present some conceptual and methodological considerations which might be useful in designing models of dependent development.

In Section 2, we will argue that, in order to operationalize a multi-level systems approach to dependent development, modelling techniques which focus on the notion of causal *structure* could be used. The central proposition for this paper is that several properties of the causal structure of complex models can provide an operational methodology appropriate to the theoretical approach of dependency in a multi-level systems framework.

Section 3 will illustrate the usefulness of this methodology for the analysis of the Mexican economy in the light of the recent oil discoveries. Such discoveries could indeed be considered as a substantial external shock for a dependent economy like Mexico. This section raises the issue of how oil production and revenues for oil exports are expected to solve Mexico's important problems. In other words, the case of Mexico allows us to analyze the morphostatic and morphogenic capabilities of a dependent economy facing such an external shock.

2. Modelling a Multi-Level System of Dependent Development

2.1 Dependency: A System Approach

Dependency can be defined as non-autonomous societal reproduction that, within a global political economy, distorts societal development. Such an approach to dependency seems to me quite far apart from the more usual and supposedly more operational definition of dependency as a state of being subject to non-reciprocated influence. To clarify these differences will help to make my own position on dependency more precise, and to derive more easily its implications in terms of modelling methodology.

When talking about "non-autonomous societal reproduction", we should first outline briefly how to conceive a social system[1].

A social system could be defined as a set of relationships defining and linking interaction subsystems both among themselves and with their external environment. Institutional fragmentation in modern societies is such that specific sets of processes (decision-making, information-gathering, transaction mechanisms) can be formally constructed and identified as representing the political, economic or cultural spheres and could be viewed as such interaction subsystems. What needs to be strongly emphasized is that these subsystems embody the specific *forms* of the social relations among the actors of the system and that they are structured among themselves in a hierarchical way. In *any* social system, economic as well as cultural or political transactions, all being the products of human action in a social setting, are manifestations of social relations.

But a *concrete*, historically determined social system characterizes itself by a specific hierarchical structure among these subsystems.[2] Some periods of history have been marked by the dominance of the religious or the political spheres in many societies; others by the dominance of the economic one.

However societies evolve through time: social systems are complex and dynamic entities in which multiple processes and subsystems interact with each other and with their environment in compatible or in contradictory ways. The issue here is the relative strength between identity-preserving (structurally morphostatic) and identity-changing (structurally morpho-genic) processes in a social system: such strength clearly depends upon the power distribution among actors who have an interest either in systems preservation or in system transformation.[3]

This quick summary of some basic propositions of an actor-oriented social system theory sheds some light on our definitional approach to dependency. In a synchronic perspective, dependency is viewed as a *situation* wherein necessary and sufficient conditions for a society's *reproduction* are not internally controlled (*non-autonomy*), while in a diachronic perspective it is viewed as a self-restructuring *process* characterized by *externally* induced deformations.

On the one hand dependency is not simply a state, a situation in which a social system is subject to "non-reciprocated influences": to accept such a definition would imply that we recognize every social system as being to some extent dependent.

So defined, the concept becomes non-operational. And the whole question of "dependency" as a state restricts itself, in that case, to the determination of the *degree* of non-reciprocated influences which would justify the assertion that dependency is the main feature of a country as a socio-economic system. The use of quantitative indicators (flows of trade, financial links with "Center" countries) follows this line of reasoning and leads to endless and hopeless discussions of "where to draw the line". On the other hand, "dependencia" theorists have correctly emphasized the importance of the internal social structure of dependent societies, but they have not provided so far a completely specified model which can articulate, in a coherent way, the linkages between the internal and external factors structuring the dependency situation and its peculiar (morphostatic) self-reproduction patterns. These patterns entail the simultaneous perpetuation of characteristic social relations and processes, allowing externally induced transformations to take place.

2.2 Modelling Dependency: Methodological Considerations

The preceding remarks indicate the necessity to develop a formal model of a multi-level system, which could function as a general script or framework within which we could progressively specify the structure and the reproduction mechanism of dependency.[4]

2.2.1 Multi-level systems: higher order processes and constraints.

We start from the evidence that, once the pure "black box approach" is left behind, prediction of social events requires explanation of social processes. Causal modelling is then a necessity. However, there has been a long tradition of critical discussion of the use of causal modelling in the social sciences, especially when expressed in mathematical forms.[5] But many of the criticisms are misdirected in our opinion: either they are based on purely ideological oppositions to or misconceptions of the mathematics involved, or they are actually related to measurement and statistical estimation procedure.

Causal modelling of a complex system takes the form of building a multiple equations model. At this stage it is not necessary to specify what kind of model: it could be for example a macro-economic model of a developing country's economy.

Let us single out any equation from this model of the type:

$$x_{1t} = a_o + a_1 x_{2t} + a_2 Z_{1t} \qquad (1)$$

x_1 is the dependent variable, x_2 and Z_1 are the independent variables, the former being supposed to be endogenous to the complete model, the latter being exogenous to the model.[6] Here the analyst clearly has to make a first critical choice: to determine the boundary between the "explained" and the "unexplained" part of the model. Such a choice, which concerns the determination of the vector $Z = (Z_1, \ldots, Z_n)$, could be made for two basically different reasons. First, we could recognize that in principle there might be some causal relations going from the x_{it}'s to the Z_{it}'s, but that the lack of precise knowledge about these relations makes it preferable for the subsequent statistical estimation of the model to use directly the observed values of Z_{it} instead of the estimated values that could be obtained through the "correct" specification of the model. It is quite clear that this reason is only related to the problem of the empirical estimation of the model and not to any theoretical considerations: it is actually equivalent to leaving out unexplained — although they have been identified — higher-level processes which may affect equation (1).[7] But, and this is the second possibility, we can also argue for *theoretical* reasons that in principle there are no (or extremely limited) causal effects from any of the x_{it}'s on any of the Z_{it}'s. In this case, equation (1) states that there is a "non-reciprocated" influence of Z_{1t} on x_{1t}.

Moreover, x_{2t} being defined as endogenous to the model and thus as a function of at least one of the x_{it}'s, x_{1t} might have a reciprocal influence on x_{2t}. In such a case the time patterns of x_{1t} and x_{2t} are determined by the interactive structure of the model, but are constrained by the time pattern of Z_{1t}.

Let us imagine that x_{2t} is a variable controlled by the actors within the system, then equation (1) suggests that they are able to control x_{1t} only to the extent that $a_1 \neq 0$ and that they can "offset" influences imposed by the exogenous behavior of Z_1. One could say that Z_1 *dominates* x_{1t} conditional upon the relative magnitude of a_1 and a_2.

The importance of the parameters a_1 and a_2 leads us to the second issue traditionally raised in causal modelling: the existence of "stable" parameters which presupposes a stable *causal structure*. An important feature of multi-level modelling is to make explicit the determinants of the causal structure of the processes like the one described by equation (1). To clarify the issue, let us rewrite equation (1) in the following way:

$$x_{1t} = a_o + a_{1t}x_{2t} + a_{2t}Z_{1t} \tag{1'}$$

Suppose that we can identify, based on theoretical considerations, the causal determinants of a_{1t} and a_{2t}.[8]

$$a_{1t} = \gamma_1 Z_{2t} \qquad (2)$$

$$a_{2t} = \gamma_2 x_{3t} \qquad (3)$$

One can see that to allow for explicit determination of the value of the parameter a_{1t} in equations like (1') is equivalent again to take into account higher-order processes that were left unexplained so far. Equations (2) and (3) state that the causal structure of (1') is *constrained* by exogenous variables like Z_{2t} or endogenous variables like x_{3t}.

Again it should be emphasized that systems like these involve substantial problems as far as numerical solvability and statistical estimation are concerned because of the implied non-linearities; but they do not raise — in my opinion — substantial conceptual or even epistemological issues. On the contrary, one cannot be but amazed by the potentialities of such a modelling approach.

The existence of exogenous variables in the equation describing the process itself and in the implicit equations determining the parameters (the causal structure) of this process allows us to introduce the notions of constrained *processes* and *constrained structures*.

These two different types of constraints should be interpreted carefully. Indeed, although both of them refer clearly to higher-order processes which affect the lower level process described by equation (1), their respective meaning is however different. A constraint on the process itself (symbolized by the presence in (1) of the exogenous variable Z_{1t}) limits its domain of validity since it restricts the admissible values of the couple $\{x_{1t}, x_{2t}\}$. To illustrate this point, let us suppose that equation (1) describes the relation between the pay-offs of a multi-objective bargaining "game". It could be, for example, a trade-off function between two pay-offs like a "Phillips curve" (a commonly used negative relation between the unemployment rate and the rate of inflation). The value of Z_{1t} clearly determines together with a_{1t} and a_{2t} what is the "price" that has to be paid in terms of inflation (here x_{1t}) by the actor mainly interested in minimizing unemployment (x_{2t}). To determine who has the power or control over z_{1t} is crucial: to the extent that z_{1t} is outside the realm of influence of all the actors participating in the game underlying equation (1), the process is said to be *externally constrained*. In the opposite case, it is going to be *internally constrained*.

A *constrained structure* has rather different implication because it affects the reaction function between x_{1t} and x_{2t} through the coefficient a_{1t}. The coefficient reflects the "intensity" of the relation between x_{1t} and x_{2t}.[9] Clearly such intensity might not be invariant through time which is another way of saying that a_{1t} is itself a function of variables as indicated by equation (2). Again, I would like to suggest the possible broad range of interpretations of this formalization in a multi-level systems perspective.[10] In the example described above, a_{1t} determines the intensity of the trade-off between x_{1t} and x_{2t}: it could be hypothesized, at least intuitively, that such intensity could depend upon the power differential existing among the actors involved in the game: the greater a_{1t}, the smaller would be the relative power of the actor concerned mainly to minimize x_{2t}. As in the case of the constrained process, the structure could be either externally or internally constrained.

In the latter case, Z_{2t} could then represent a "meta-level" linkage coming from a higher level. Controllability of Z_{2t} by a specific actor would be the outcome of the meta-power relation: the impact of Z_{2t} on a_{1t} would be the extent to which this meta-power relation can restructure the game and consequently its payoff function (1).

From this discussion, we can derive so far the following conclusions:

1) causal modelling, if correctly and carefully used, can be used to model multi-level systems of the kind described for example by Baumgartner (1978).

2) the precise analysis of the global causal structure of a multiple relations system, which involves meta-level linkages and complex feedforward or feedback processes, is of crucial importance for understanding the hierarchical structure among the different levels implied by the model.

2.2.2 Dependent, non-autonomous versus autonomous systems. The point of departure is the basic proposition that to be subject to "non-reciprocated" influences from the outside is not a sufficient condition for a socio-economic system to be characterized as "dependent". This simply expresses the commonsense idea that absolute freedom does not exist in this world, but that real freedom is the ability to make choices under constraints, the capacity to undertake purposeful actions to achieve self-defined objectives. In other words, in a dependent system we should find more than the constrained structures or processes that we discussed in the preceding section.

The question actually is how a socio-economic system submitted to external constraints deals with them internally. In face of these ever-present external constraints, could we define the formal conditions of *autonomy* for a social system? This requires examination of the *internal* structure of the constrained system.

Again let us suppose that we have a-priori defined a social system and its environment.[11] We have thus defined the external constraints (the exogenous variables) whatever the way they do operate on structures or on processes.

A social system is a complex set of interrelations among different social actors. In a most general way, such a system could be represented as a system of equations like:[12]

$$h(x,z) = 0 \qquad\qquad (4)$$

where $x = \{x_{1t}\}$ and $z = \{z_{1t}\}$ are respectively the vectors of endogenous and exogenous variables. I am not making any specific assumption about the nature of the x_s' the z_s' and the functions h.[13] The only requirement is that the h functions are either pure identities (isomorphisms) or causal relations. This latter requirement implies that the existence of a variable x_{1t} or z_{1t} in the argument of a function determining x_{jt} presupposes a causal relation from x_{1t}, z_{1t} on x_{jt}.[14]

The causal structure of the model is the hierarchical ordering among the variables x_{it}'s which is determined by the set of relations $h(x,z) = o$. Three possibilities arise. First, the structure might appear totally recursive: in this case there is a hierarchical ordering over the entire set of the x_{it}'s. Second, the opposite case, the structure might be comprised of a single set of simultaneous equations; there is no hierarchical ordering among the variables. These two cases can be represented by the two graphs of Figure 10.1.

The third case is the intermediate one: there are subsets of $\{x_i\}$ that constitute simultaneous equations subsystems. In such a case there is a hierarchical ordering among variables and/or among sets of variables.[15] These properties can be used now to define the formal characteristics of an autonomous versus non-autonomous system. An example will help to illustrate the argument.

Let us image a simple economy which produces only for exports and

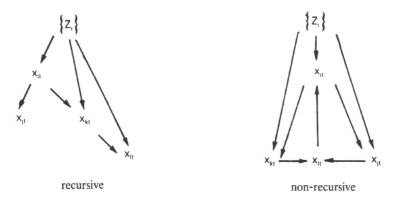

recursive   non-recursive

FIGURE 10.1   A recursive and a non-recursive structure.

consumes only imported goods. Such a simple system could be described by the following equations and graphs:

$$Y = F1\,(\bar{X}, \bar{p}_c); \quad F1_{\bar{x}} > 0, F1_{\bar{p}x} > 0^{16} \tag{I.1}$$

Domestic production Y is a function of export demand $\bar{X}$ and the price of exports $\bar{p}_x$, both determined outside. Export demand and export prices affect positively domestic production in real terms.

$$R = \bar{p}_x\,\bar{X} \tag{I.2}$$

National income R in nominal terms is equal to export revenues.

$$N = F2\,(Y); \quad F2_Y > 0 \tag{I.3}$$

Employment N is determined via the existing technology by domestic production.

$$Y \xrightarrow{\;+\;} N$$

Domestic production increases affect positively employment.

$$W = \bar{w}\,N \tag{I.4}$$

Since our economy is supposed to be a labor-surplus economy, capitalists are able to impose a wage rate $\bar{w}$ irrespective of the amount of employment; the two combined determine labor income W.

$$R - W = P \tag{I.5}$$

The national income identity implies that labor income plus profits P is equal to national income.

$$M = F3\,(P, W, \bar{p}_m); \quad F3_W > F3_P > 0, F3_{\bar{p}m} < 0 \tag{I.6}$$

Real final demand which consists of imported goods M depends on the distribution of income and on the externally determined price of imported goods, $\bar{p}_m$.

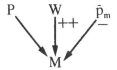

Real final demand is positively influenced by labor income, less so by profits. But it is negatively influenced by import prices $\bar{p}_m$.

The causal structure of this model can be described by the following graph:

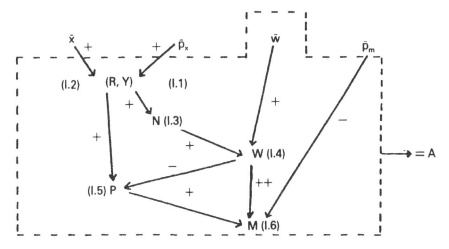

FIGURE 10.2   The total dependency case.

As is immediately apparent, the system is entirely recursive: if we consider our economy as a subsystem defined by the subset $A = (\bar{w}, R, Y, N, W, P, M)$, we can see that, with the exception of $\bar{w}$, all the relevant variables of A depend directly or indirectly on the *external* constraints $\tilde{X}$, $\bar{p}_x$ and $\bar{p}_m$. For a given $\bar{w}$, production, employment, distribution of income and real demand depend ultimately on these external constraints. One could argue that this is the case of a totally dependent, non-autonomous system, although the actors within this system might well make rational choices through optimizing procedures that result in the behavioral rules described by F1, F2, and F3. But non-autonomy depends not only on the particular causal structure among the elements of A, but also on the assumption related to $\bar{w}$. In other words, the existence of an *internal* constraint like $\bar{w}$ is a crucial element in determining the subsystem A as being dependent.[17]

To see this point, let us modify the model in the following way: suppose that now, in our simple economy, the labor force gets organized and, through bargaining processes with the capitalists, is able to affect the determination of the wage level: the smaller the unemployment, the stronger its ability to ask for better wage conditions. Assuming that the total available labor force is given ($\bar{N}_s$), this requires adding one more relationship to determine the wage levels:

$$w = F4\ (\bar{N}_s - N);\ F4\ \bar{N}_s < 0,\ F4_N > 0 \tag{1.7}$$

($\bar{N}_s - N$) is by definition unemployment. For a given level of employment, an increase in the labor force implies an increase in unemployment which will tend to decrease the wage level. Alternatively, for a given level of the labor force, a decrease in employment will have the same effect. This could be graphically represented in the following way:

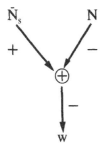

But the wage level affects the profitability of the production process and thus the employment prospects.

We should now rewrite (I.3) as:

$$N = F2\ (Y, w);\ F2_Y > 0,\ F2_w < 0 \tag{I.3'}$$

Given that export prices are externally given, an increase in the wage rate decreases the profitability of the production process and consequently we assume it will induce capital-labor substitution.

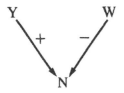

The causal structure of the model appears now as follows:

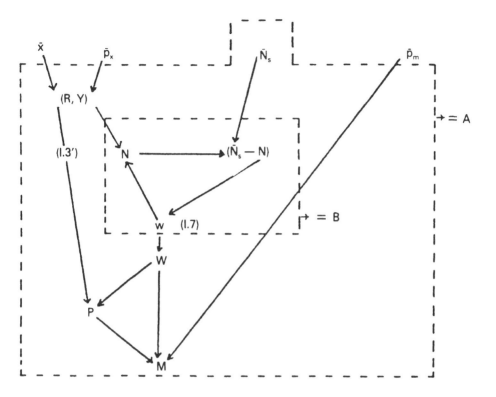

FIGURE 10.3   The relative autonomy case.

In formal terms, the crucial difference appears to be the simultaneous determination of N and w: they form a *separable* smaller subsystem B within A.

The separability of B within A implies that there exists now within A an internal self-determination process for the employment level, the wage rate and consequently the distribution of income, although the range of possibilities for this self-determination mechanism is constrained by the external factors $\bar{x}$, $\bar{p}_x$ and $\bar{p}_m$.

These examples have no other pretence than to outline some of the conceptual issues involved in defining dependency. But it seems to me that, however simple they are, they capture the essentials. In the "total dependency" scheme, the causal structure among the variables contained in A clearly implies that the necessary and sufficient conditions for a society's reproduction are *not internally* controlled (see above Section 2.1.) and that "its self-restructuring process is characterized by *externally* induced deformations". However, this last sentence deserves additional comments.

To use the word "deformations" makes sense only if we have some conceptual standards against which we could define "deformations". In other words, this last part of our definition appears clearly to be normative. Indeed, these standards are often based upon the a-priori assertion that externally controlled reproduction distorts or thwarts more desirable self-structured development. Our analysis so far suggests again a more precise interpretation of what should be meant by "externally controlled reproduction" and, by way of consequence, how "distortions" could be defined.

We have already seen that "externally controlled production" implies two conditions:

1) a specified set of external constraints which directly affect essential "core" variables of the system.

2) an internal causal structure of the system which does not include collectively and internally controlled self-correcting mechanisms.

It follows that "distortions" cannot be defined objectively: distorted development can only be specified in comparison to the development pattern that would have existed for the system if it had not been subjected to condition (2) above. This is exactly what our simple example has shown. In the "total dependency" case, the existence of the specific wage determination mechanism (working internally, but exogenously determined because of the labor surplus) is the explicit manifestation of the internal power relations which enable the *external* constraints to feed through the entire system. Removing this assumption transforms the system into the "relative dependency case": the different power relations implicit in the new wage determination function manifest themselves through, for example, a collective bargaining process and allow for an internally controlled (although possibly conflictual) self-determining (from the sub-system's point of view) mechanism. Such a mechanism does not free the sub-system from its external constraints, but enables it to effectuate internal choices within these constraints.

There are in my opinion two important consequences of what has just been said:

1) purely single-level quantitative indicators are not sufficient to diagnose dependency: at best, they can only give indications, in a purely deterministic way, of the importance of the external constraints.[18]

2) it is meaningless to attempt to forecast *dependent* development, since autonomous development cannot be objectively defined, such "autonomy" depending upon the social structure, the decision-making processes and the value systems of the actors involved.[19] And all these elements are always subject to possible structuring processes.

This last remark leads us into the question of the relation between the internal structure of the sub-system and its morphogenic (structure-changing) or morphostatic (structure-preserving) capabilities.

2.2.3. Self-preserving or self-transforming dependent systems. The preceding section has emphasized the importance of the internal causal structure in determining the dependent versus the autonomous nature of a sub-system. In contrast to the recursivity characterizing the structure of the former, the latter implies a system of simultaneous internal determinations of the crucial variables and processes. But what are the dynamic properties of these *structures?* Do they tend to be stable (self-reproducing) or on the contrary unstable (leading to contradiction)? In the latter case, are these contradictions or conflicts internally resolved or are their "solutions" externally imposed? In other words, are these structures self-restructuring or not?

These questions related to system dynamics are obviously quite complex and cannot be dealt with by means of the simple models and methodology developed so far in this paper. We can only advance some tentative propositions to clarify the issues of process stability versus structural stability.

Since, in our approach, dependency does not depend so much on the existence of external constraints but rather on the causal structure within the constrained sub-system itself, the dynamic stability of a dependent system will depend upon the existence of positive (reinforcing) or negative (restructuring) feedback processes on the causal structure of the sub-system A itself. The examples given in the previous section can illustrate this point.

In the "total dependency case", the self-reproducing nature of the dependent sub-system A is conditioned by the maintenance of the internal wage determination rule $\bar{w}$. Capitalist power relations, imposing a minimum wage over an unorganized labor force, will be perpetuated to the extent that capitalist control over the determination and use of the surplus P will lead to an accumulation process congruent with the reproduction of rule $\bar{w}$.

In the simple model described above, the problem does not arise. The increase in productive capacities will lead to an increase in the production of exports. But suppose now that we are in a more complex system where part of domestic production is sold on the domestic market as consumption goods. In such a case, the increase in productive capacities to be profitable requires an increase in final demand. This will consequently require an increase in real wages sufficient to absorb the increased production through additional consumption expenditures but not exceeding the increase compatible with the maintenance or the improvement of the profitability of the

productive process. If this condition is met, we will have a positive reinforcing feedback mechanism preserving the overall structure of the system.
But other, more complex linkages might exist too: for example, the profitability of the productive process not only determines the accumulation of
physical capital but also the maintenance of system-preserving institutions.[20] A detailed description of these linkages, however, would entail a
complete description of the multi-level internal structure of A and its
corresponding hierarchy. But the general proposition would be the following: whenever, as in the total dependency case, the internal structure is
such that no conflict resolution process, no arbitrage procedure exists
between conflicting but unequally powerful social groups, the structure will
tend to be inherently relatively stable and the system will exhibit relatively
little self-transforming morphogenic capabilities.[21]

In the "relative autonomy case", where conflict resolution processes or
arbitrage procedures do exist, matters are quite different. Sub-system B
within A could be viewed as a decision-making process whose outcome
depends upon the relative power of the actors involved if such a process is
essentially a conflictual one; for example, if it is either objectively a zero-
sum game or is subjectively perceived as such. The structural stability of A
will then depend upon the respective actor's abilities to restructure B
directly or indirectly. But such restructuring might generate meta-level contradictions which can affect the overall linkage structure of A with its
external constraints.

Suppose for example that the wage bargaining process leads to wage
increases which affect the profitability level P negatively. Employers might
react by adopting less labor-intensive technology. For a given level of
exports and therefore of production, this will tend to restore profitability;
but, since labor productivity increases will create at the same time more
unemployment, the relative bargaining power of labor will decrease. Such a
dynamic process might lead sub-system A back toward the dependency
case where wage determination is ruled by capitalists alone.

This negative feedback process is, of course, not the only possible outcome. One could also imagine a positive feedback process which would
reinforce the relative autonomy of A. Wage income increases might make
the development of import-competing local productions more profitable.
By creating additional locally controlled employment and relaxing the
balance of payments constraint, these processes will contribute positively to
autonomy.

To summarize, relative autonomy will tend to persist and to reinforce
itself, if the following conditions are met:

1) the more cooperative the strategies adopted by the social groups and

the greater their shared commitment to relative autonomy. (This may be found in authoritarian regimes which are genuinely nationalistic and even prepared to alter internal power relationships and institutions in the interest of achieving relative autonomy.)

2) the more important the internally structured games and their related internally controlled conflict resolution processes or arbitrage procedures.

3) the more balanced the distribution of power among social groups across these games. (Social cohesion based upon truly democratic processes is probably the most essential protection against dependency; dictatorial rule, even with some nationalistic overtones, is typically an institutional structure allowing for the maintenance and reproduction of dependency.)

3. Mexico's Recent Development Prospects in the Light of its Oil Discoveries[22]

The objective of this section is to suggest, on the basis of the preceding formal discussion of dependent systems, which key structures and processes have to be looked at in trying to assess the possible impact of Mexico's recent oil discoveries on its own relative economic autonomy.

3.1. The Mexican Autonomy and the Oil Issue

After the revolution and especially from the thirties onward, Mexico's development has been aimed at freeing its economy from dependency. Starting in 1934 with the strongly nationalistic Cárdenas administration, Mexico has built a development strategy based on the following key elements:

— gaining control over the foreign controlled export sector: heavy taxes on companies exporting minerals and nationalization of foreign petroleum holdings in 1938;

— creating public development banks and strongly increasing federal government expenditures;

— following an import-substitution strategy to promote the development of domestic industries stimulated by the growth of internal demand.

However, the lack of growth, of external demand and of foreign capital — due in part to the nationalization measures and the general distrust of the Cárdenas Administration — forced Mexico to rely mainly on inflationary financing and corresponding devaluations of the peso when recessions in the United States put pressures on the current account of the balance of payments.[23]

After the 1954 devaluation, the inflationary financing strategy was progressively abandoned for a strategy emphasizing internal price stability, and foreign borrowing to finance a now persistent current account deficit under a fixed exchange rate system with an overvalued peso. The import-substitution strategy was continued, but with more emphasis on intermediate and equipment goods. The social consensus upon which this strategy of "stable growth" was based gradually eroded when the industrialization process seemed unable to resolve serious problems of resource allocation, income distribution and social equity. A protectionist import substitution strategy coupled with constraints on real consumption to favor capital accumulation tended to shift production to high capital-intensity production processes at the expense of agriculture and more labor-intensive industries; hence the rise in unemployment and the worsening of income distribution. In addition, the heavy reliance on foreign capital increased the burden of servicing the external debt and weakened the efforts to generate internal savings in the forms of either additional exports or domestic financial savings.

Such economic distortions were also accompanied by changes in the balance of power among social groups, especially with the trade unions becoming more aggressive in demanding real wage increases, greater social benefits and sustained growth to promote employment creation. This is why the Echeverria Administration, pressured to accelerate growth and social spending and to redistribute income in favor of the less privileged classes, found itself forced to rely again on inflationary financing. The rapid exploitation of the new oil fields as of 1974 "marks" the beginning of the Mexican oil boom, concurrently with the rise in oil prices imposed by OPEC.

But, at the end of 1976, the Mexican economy was nevertheless in a deep crisis which culminated with the devaluation of the peso by nearly 100 %. President Echeverria's third world oriented political attitudes had occasioned a loss of confidence amongst the Mexican industrial and financial sectors resulting in a very low rate of investment and a huge flight of capital. When Lopez Portillo's term began in 1976, one of his main tasks was to regain the confidence not only of the Mexican capitalists but also — and even most important — of foreign investors and international agencies. The oil discoveries and a rather conservative economic policy allowed this to happen. This is one of the reasons why the transition period from Echeverria to Lopez Portillo is very important in understanding how the "oil priorities" were defined, and how oil became the lifesaver of Mexico, not only in economic matters, but also in political affairs.

As is well known, Mexico has become a very important oil producer and exporter over the last 5 years. An examination of the main oil activity indicators during these years will give an idea of the increasingly important role played by this sector in the Mexican economy. The size of the total proven reserves (oil and gas) has increased more than eight times between 1974 and 1980: from 5.8 billion barrels in 1974 to 60.1 billion in 1980; probable reserves are of the order of 38 billion barrels and potential reserves are 250 billion. The level of proven reserves places Mexico as the 6th most important oil-producing country in the world.

Oil production increased in the same period from 639.3 thousands of barrels per day to 2.12 million barrels per day in June 1980. By September 1980, Mexico occupied the 5th position in world oil production. Exports have shown a similar impressive performance. In 1974, they accounted for 34.1 thousand barrels per day; they increased to 681.0 thousand barrels per day in the first quarter 1980 and then again to 950.0 thousand barrels per day in June 1980. Oil revenues amounted to 62 million dollars in 1974 and to 3900 million dollars in 1979; the share of crude oil in total exports increased from 4 % in 1974 to 45 % in 1979 and some forecasts suggest that this figure could be 70 % in 1982.

Given the magnitude of these figures it is thus not surprising that the Mexican government has considered oil as the long-awaited remedy for Mexico's most important problems. When those huge reserves were confirmed, oil became the element upon which most of the country's development plans and policies were centered. From the beginning, the official position concerning oil exploitation has been conservative and prudent, in part for historical reasons and in part due to the desire of avoiding the negative effects of an overly fast oil exploitation: i.e. amongst others, insufficient absorption capacity and inflation.

Despite the relatively conservative production and export policies adopted by the government, oil now plays the key role in Mexican development. The best example of this is to be found in some of the statements of the "Plan Nacional de Desarrollo Industrial 1979-82" (National Plan for Industrial Development), Mexico's development cornerstone, which sets up "... the guidelines and details of the country's future growth in the short, medium and long-run in areas such as production, employment, utilization of productive capacity, investment, exports and imports". (Secretaria de Partrimonio y Formento Industrial, 1979).

Among these statements we have for example:

The National Plan for Industrial Development .... rests upon a pivot. The pivot is a platform of oil production that guarantees an adequate equilibrium between internal consumption and exports,

as well as:

In the case of Mexico the possibility of overcoming the crisis resides in the financial potential offered by the oil export surplus ... these resources will allow the country a bigger financial self-determination (p. 24).

3.1. A Simple Multi-Level Model of Mexican Development

The preceding historical survey indicates what might be some of the key elements and processes that should be clearly identified to form the basis of a multi-level systems approach to Mexico's development: they are structured as a set of interlinked games.[24]

Game A: The income distribution game

Actors: — Local managers
   — Foreign capital
   — Federal government
   — Trade-unions

Variables and Processes	*Linkages to or from*
— Distribution of income	— Balance of payments
— Wage rate	— Social spending
— Return on capital	— Socio-political stability
— Employment levels	— Inflation rate
— Investments	

Game B: The resource allocation game

Actors: — Local managers
   — Foreign capital
   — Federal government
   — Trade-unions

Variables and Processes	*Linkages*
— Export-oriented or import-competing production (open sector)	— Balance of payments
	— Real consumption levels
— Locally oriented protected sector	— Employment

Game C: The financial game

Actors: — Federal government
— Foreign capital
— Bank of Mexico
— Mexican financial intermediaries

Variables and Processes	*Linkages*
— Exchange rate policy	— Investments
— Credit expansion	— Public debt
— Capital flows	— Balance of payments
— Money creation	

Game D: The government spending-social policy game

Actors: — Federal government
— Bank of Mexico
— Trade-unions

Variables and Processes	*Linkages*
— Public, especially social spending	— Money creation
— Taxation	— Distribution of income

This obviously crude and incomplete set of games, focusing only on the essentials, still allows us to propose a characterization of historical periods. Each period exhibits a specific hierarchy of these games.

Phase 1. Import-substitution, inflationary finance 1938-1954

This phase could be considered as a strategy trying to promote a nationalistic capitalist industrialization process as much as possible independent of the external constraints the Mexican economy was faced with. Such a "relatively autonomous" strategy was made possible by a very large consensus between the state and private capitalists to promote such a development through inflationary finance, which enabled them to control the distribution of income in real terms in favor of the accumulation process. This is illustrated by the specific recursive nature of the various games with the important feedback loop (1) which symbolizes the overall control by the public authorities over the various levels of the system. We note in passing that talking about a recursive structure as such, regarding the system depicted in Figure 10.4, might be misleading. The feedback loop

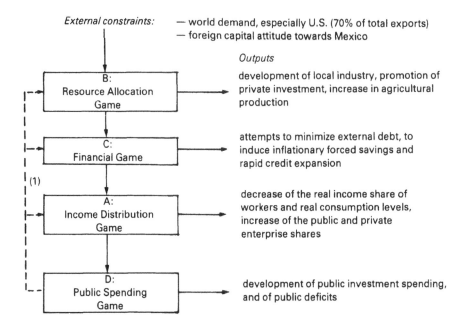

FIGURE 10.4   The hierarchy of games: Phase 1.

(1) clearly implies that the system is completely simultaneous. However, within a totally simultaneous system, it is possible to find recursive structures by decomposition.

Phase 2. Import-substitution, External Financing 1954-1970

The sluggish demand for exports, the worsening of the terms of trade, and the corresponding deterioration in the balance of trade — partly due to the U.S. recession of 1953 — clearly showed that the strategy of inflationary finance had reached its limits. The only way to further maintain the overvalued peso would have been to take strong internal deflationary measures, which would have required a drastic reduction in public spending and public deficits. Facing a growing dissatisfaction from organized labor about the inflationary effect on real incomes, such a deflationary strategy was politically and economically not feasible. The 1954 devaluation was thus not only a necessary shortcut measure but also a prerequisite for an overall change in strategy. The stabilization program which followed was "inspired" by the recommendations of the International Monetary Fund: it called for a decrease in the rate of growth of the money supply through fiscal discipline, better allocation of public investment and imposition of controls over banks to regulate credit expansion. This latter aspect was especially important since it allowed to shift partly the burden of financing public deficits from the Central Bank to private banks.

Gradually, stability of exchange rate and prices was achieved. The high and now safe returns on Mexican capital assets increasingly attracted foreign capital. The result was a stable external balance, despite now persistent current account deficits, but at a price of a growing private and public external indebtedness. Considerations of external balance became dominant.

This shift in policy could be regarded in some sense as a step backward from a relatively autonomous strategy. As indicated in Figure 10.5, financial considerations prevailed over an internally controlled pattern of resource allocation (game C now dominates B) and the fiscal discipline imposed by the new policy would tend to dominate the income distribution game (D dominates A). Latent contradictions became more acute and obvious: rising unemployment, stagnation of purely locally oriented productive activities (especially agriculture), rising external debt.[25]

Phase 3. Overall Inflation, Internal Recession and the 1976 Crisis, 1970-1976

The social tensions inherited from the previous period led to increased

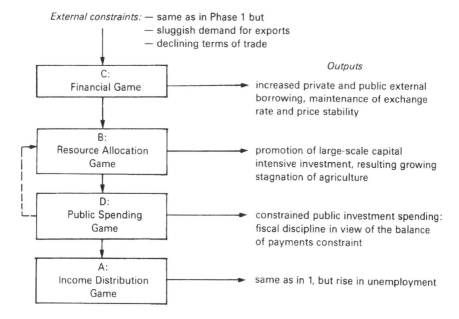

FIGURE 10.5   The hierarchy of games: Phase 2. Import-substitution, external financing 1954-1970.

social spending by the Echeverria Administration without restructuring the overall public spending and taxation patterns. This resulted in a new spurt of domestic inflation which, combined with very unfavorable external constraints (rise in import prices and worldwide recession) led to the 1976 crisis with its 100 % devaluation of the peso and subsequent socio-economic instability.

Phase 4. Is Oil the Life-saver? (1976-????)

The preceding discussion suggests the necessity to recognize the mutual interdependence between:

a) the internal resource-allocation strategy

b) the distribution of income issue

c) the problem of financing the industrialization process

as a prerequisite for the design and implementation of an autonomous strategy of development. Accordingly this implies rejection of strategies that would give absolute priority to one of these issues at the expense of the others. In today's Mexico, there is indeed a great danger in the belief that the enormous amount of export revenues eliminates the financing constraint on the development process and would allow the country to follow a Phase 2-like strategy, but with "internal" financing. Its proponents will argue that such a switch from external to internal financing will alleviate the balance of payments constraints and consequently will give much more autonomy to the country in deciding its resource allocation, public spending and income distribution policies.

The reliance on oil export revenues to finance the development process does not eliminate the external constraint: it simply changes its qualitative nature. The expansion of the oil export sector, because of its essential characteristics, i.e., capital-intensive technology, low creation of jobs and its emphasis (because of its feedforward and feedback linkages) on the modern sectors of the economy, will not necessarily bring about an improvement in the distribution of income. It could even lead to a deterioration of the *relative* distribution of income in the country as a whole and between regions. If this happens, the consequences could be extreme industrial concentration, accelerated development of certain favored regions at the cost of some others' backwardness, neglect of the traditional sector, especially agriculture, and eventually even social instability.

The problem for Mexico is thus to set up a social control mechanism (which could take the form of a democratic and decentralized planning system) which can regulate the internal impact of the expansion of the oil sector so as to simultaneously achieve progress in terms of a balanced pattern of economic development and of a substantial improvement in the distribution of income and wealth.

The issue is thus not only to model in a conceptually correct way the linkages between these various games but also to create social processes (institutions, rules ...) to bring about clearly the interactive structure between these games.

This simple interactive scheme, which is given for illustrative purposes only, suggests the various policies that could enhance Mexico's autonomy with respect to its development strategy:

1) commodity taxes and subsidies to provide the necessary adjustments between the productive structure of the economy and the desired distribution of income, in order to maximize social welfare;

2) government consumption and investment policies to sustain a balanced growth pattern of the productive structure, especially for the agricultural sector;

3) redistribution of assets and wealth to improve the distribution of income;

4) appropriate monetary and credit policies to improve competitiveness;

5) direct taxes on household and business incomes to improve income distribution;

6) exchange rate and commercial policies to help increase the contribution of the traditional export sector to the balance of payments;

7) income policies and its related bargaining institutions to maintain a socially acceptable and economically feasible distribution of value added;

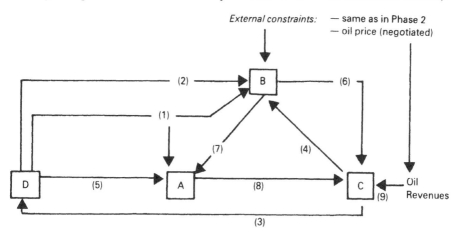

FIGURE 10.6   An interactive structure to promote automony.

8) reorganization of credit institutions to facilitate access to safe financial savings for low-income groups etc.;

9) planning of future oil production and export targets.

These measures are suggested not only to illustrate how a complex set of interrelated policy instruments can be used to promote balanced growth and improved equity. But, since these measures are directed to conflicting issues and interests, they also suggest the need for internal collective decision making processes for their implementation.

NOTES

1. For a more detailed discussion of these concepts, see Chapter II in Burns *et al.* (1985).
2. Such a conception of social systems finds its roots clearly in the Marxian tradition.
3. See Burns *et al.* (1985).
4. The following is based in part on our recent research on the causal structure of macroeconomic models: see DeVille (1981).
5. Chapter IX in Burns *et al.* (1985) discusses these methodological issues.
6. The choice of a linear equation model is made for the sake of clear, direct exposition. The only *necessary* assumption is that there is a causal relation between x_2 and x_1.
7. The presence of a constant term like a_0 implies that we recognize the existence of unidentified higher-level processes: in a linear form, like e.g. (1), a change in the intercept is a change in the values of x_{1t} independently of the values taken by x_{2t}.
8. Such a simple multi-level formulation can be found in Chapter 9 of Burns *et al.* (1985).
9. In mathematical terms, for a simple linear equation like equation (1), a_{1t} is the partial derivative of x_{1t} with respect to x_{2t}. It measures the change in x_{1t} induced by a given change in x_{2t}.
10. For another interesting interpretation of a_{1t} along the same lines, see Leroy (1981). In this paper, the author suggests that the magnitude of a_{1t}, being in his example the price coefficient of a supply or demand equation, could be interpreted as a multiplicative function of two implicit variables, v, 'tastes or values' and the 'capacity to transact or not to transact', p: $a_{1t} = p.v.$
11. It must be emphasized that this is no trivial or easy task and that it raises substantial epistemological issues in the field of general systems theory. See for example Pask (1978).
12. For the formal developments of this approach, see Gilli (1979).
13. In particular, this does not exclude constrained structures the way we defined them in the preceding section, once it is realized that such a model can always be reduced to (4) although it is going to be non-linear in the variables.
14. This is of course a very strong requirement for an empirically estimated model but not for an a-priori theoretical specification.
15. This method was already used by H. Aujac in the early sixties to identify dominanat branches in the production structure on the basis of an input/output analysis. See Aujac (1960).
16. $F_{i_j} = \delta F_i / \delta j$ for $j = \dot{x}, \dot{p}_x$ etc.
17. The reader should compare our simple model with those presented in Chapters 3, 4 and 9.

18. To caricature the point, if exports as a percentage of GDP would be a crucial indicator of dependency, Kuwait as well as Belgium would be considered as being among the most dependent.

19. We can always try to make single-level forecasts of development, but not to forecast its dependent nature.

20. Law enforcement agencies would be a common example.

21 The stability of totalitarian regimes would be an illustration of the proposition.

22. I want to thank Alvaro Baillet for providing me with the essential information contained in this section. Among other sources, see also Thompson, (1979).

23. During this period devaluations took place in 1938, 1948 and 1954.

24. For a more developed example of the same approach, see Chapter 3. The word 'game' should not be taken literally. It refers to a collective social decision-making process involving different social actors.

25. Particularly important in this respect has been the relative deterioration of the agricultural sector, which, combined with an increasingly unemployed urban proletariat, put pressures on food prices and caused demands for subsidies, which were opposed to the adopted fiscal restraint.

REFERENCES

Aujac, H. (1960). La hiérarchie des industries dans un tableau des échanges interindustriels. *Revue Economique*, 2.

Baumgartner, T. (1978). An actor-oriented systems model for the analysis of industrial democracy measures. In R.F. Geyer and J. van der Zouwen (1978), Vol. 1, pp. 55-74.

Burns, T.R., T.Baumgartner, & P. DeVille 1985 *Man, Decisions, Society*. Gordon and Breach: London.

Burns, T. R., T. Baumgartner, & W. Buckley 1985. *The Shaping of Society*. Wiley: London.

DeVillé, Ph. (1981). Marché du travail et contraintes macroéconomiques. *Rapport CIPS*.

DeVillé, Ph., and Burns, T. (1977). Institutional responses to crisis in capitalist development: a dialectical systems approach. *Social Praxis*, 4, 4-29.

Geyer, R.F., and J. van der Zouwen (1978) (Eds.). *Sociocybernetics*. Nijhoff, Leiden/Boston/London, Vols. 1 and 2.

Gilli, M. (1979). *Etude et Analyse des Structures Causales des Modèles Economiques*. Peter Lang, Bern.

Leroy, R. (1981). Le marché du travail: une approche hors paradigme. *Revue Economique*, Vol. 32, 2, 237-270.

Pask, G. (1978). A Conversation Theoretic Approach to Social Systems. In R.F. Geyer and J. van der Zouwen (1978), *Sociocybernetics* Vol. 1, pp. 16-26.

Thompson, J. (1979). *Inflation, Financial Markets and Economic Development; The Experience of Mexico*. JAI Press, Greenwich (CT).

11

Technology, Underdevelopment, and Social Systems: Problems of Technology Transfer

Thomas Baumgartner   and   Tom R. Burns

1. Technology and Development

"Technology" has become in the late 1970s a new key factor with which to explain underdevelopment and misdevelopment. The policy implication is that a massive injection into underdeveloped countries (UDC) of know-how and technology from the developed countries (DC) would enable socio-economic development to take off in the 1980s. This technocratic development model belongs both to the socialist and capitalist worlds (Corm, 1978). It also has the support of Third World governments.

Two weaknesses characterize this technocratic concept of development. First, modern technology is foremost a product of developed countries and reflects their *current* needs, structures and institutions. Yet this technology development is increasingly under attack within the developed countries themselves. Future evolution of the world economic system will certainly entail substantially different socio-economic and technological developments. Secondly, the naive belief in the benefits of high technology ignores the complex interplay between technology and social organization. DC technology may simply be inappropriate in most instances for UDC socio-economic and societal development.

The feasibility and desirability of DC technology transfer must be judged on the basis of a wider societal analysis. The creation, transfer and adaptation of technology is inseparable from the socio-cultural, economic and political institutions characterizing the societies in which it is produced and into which it is introduced. *Technology is more than equipment* or a socially neutral instrument for the fulfillment of a given task or the achievement of a particular goal. Technology is always part and parcel of a *social-*

technical system, where its use depends on the presence of infrastructures and where beliefs, values, and norms guide the selection and use of technology in production and in organizing production.

A technology may be appropriate for a given system only to the extent that it fits in with existing socio-cultural structures. In particular, it should be compatible with the institutions and cultural traits which are essential to the development model or vision pursued. The introduction of inappropriate technology may hinder, quite unintentionally, the realization of development goals. Thus, it may give rise to or reinforce social relations typical of the system of origin and totally different from the relations envisaged in the development ideal.

Below we investigate several problems related to the role of technology in socio-economic development. The arguments are based on a series of theoretical and empirical investigations, which take as a point of departure a model of development oriented toward increased satisfaction of basic needs, self-reliance and democratic participation. We criticize the ideology that socio-economic development can be achieved or driven by technology transfers from the developed countries to the underdeveloped ones without regard to the substantial incompatibilities between DC technologies and most UDC institutional and cultural frameworks. Technology transfer in these circumstances tends not only to create dependency on the international level. It leads on the national level to internal distortions and, in many instances, undesirable developments.

A major thesis, which follows from the above, is that further UDC technology and technology development should not be inspired by DC experience and development models, but should be more grounded in indigenous and independent reflections. Self-knowledge at the societal level is essential to successful learning and development.

Part 2 deals with the use of DC technology and current patterns of technology transfer which maintain dependency at various levels. Part 3 sketches an approach to technology and society based on the concept of a dynamic socio-technical system. We end by pointing to several implications of such a compatibility analysis of DC technology and UDC social systems, among them the necessity for underdeveloped countries to start to develop their own technologies, not only in terms of hardware, but also and above all social technologies.

2.   Technology in the International System

The demand for the massive transfer of DC know-how and technology to UDC is based on the belief that the establishment of current DC industrial structures in UDC will end underdevelopment and dependency. This is the argument of those who point to the success of the Newly Industrializing Countries (NIC) in industrializing and in partially reducing their dependency. They conclude that there is therefore no need for a New International Economic Order (NIEO). It is also an implicit claim of those proposing a NIEO to improve UDC access to DC technology. Underdeveloped countries could in this way accelerate industrialization and reduce dependency. The argument is questionable in both of these cases as we suggest in the following three sections.

1. End of Technological Dependency?

Some have suggested recently that the successful industrialization and export performance of a number of underdeveloped countries prove after all that the reduction in, if not the overcoming of, dependency is achievable through adoption of industrial technology and integration of UDCs into the world market. Our view is that most (although not necessarily all) NICs still lack the necessary capabilities to assure an end to economic and technological dependence. The drive to industrialize with imported technology has for the moment ended in a monumental debt crisis for most countries that had chosen this path.

Certain marginal changes in the dependency structure of the 1950s have occurred. There is now oligopolistic competition among foreign multinational corporations (MNC) in specific industries in newly industrializing countries.[1] Some indigenous firms have transformed themselves from dependent suppliers of MNCs in the home market to their challengers in world markets. But these and other developments do not demonstrate that such structures have evolved in today's *leading* manufacturing and service sectors. Isolated structural changes in specific, *mature*, but not highly advanced industrial sectors (such as steel, textiles, car, and even simple machine tool production) scarcely reshape in any radical way the structure of dependence. Such developments simply reflect the operation of the product cycle on the international level. Dependence is, in the final analysis, a complex set of relationships between the developed countries and the underdeveloped ones. These are based on structural differences in technological, financial, educational, political, and social institutional capabilities. In general it is a dubious argument to conclude that through the restructuring of one or a few industrial sectors *per se* a complex relationship such as dependence is transformed (as Moran (1978) for example has suggested).

The global political economy of the technologically leading production sectors, those which are likely to play a major role in socio-economic development during the coming decades, remains highly oligopolistic, if not monopolistic. These sectors are and remain dominated by producers located in the DC. The pattern in these sectors resembles strongly the pattern in the leading sectors of the 1950s and 1960s. New industries such as computers, electronics, telecommunications, data processing, nuclear power, and large civilian and military aircrafts are indicative of *the relatively unchallenged position of the DCs at the forefront of industrial and technological development.* The monopolization by developed countries of research and development activities in such areas as biogenetics, laser technology, and alternative energy technologies suggests that not much will change between DCs and UDCs over the long run. Interestingly enough, research programs, such as the French solar energy program, seem to be designed explicitly to allow DC firms to capture UDC markets.

The designs for a new international division of labor proposed by prominant politicians in the developed countries are fully consistent with this dependence maintaining development. For example in 1977, Tindemans, the prime minister of Belgium at that time, pointed to the shift from developed to underdeveloped countries of such traditional industries as textiles, clothing and shoes, basic materials industries such as steel, aluminium and petro-chemical feedstocks, and mass produced consumer durables (cars, appliances). This demonstrated, he suggested, that the developed countries were prepared to accept the NIEO. Maintenance and further development of Belgian and DC wealth would be assured by a concerted effort to develop new, high-technology industries in the developed countries and by providing the UDCs with all the equipment needed for their industrialization efforts (reported in Le Monde, March 9, 1977).

This and statements by other DC leaders suggest that the developed countries, at least some of them, might be prepared to accept a NIEO with large technology flows to the UDCs as long as it serves to institutionalize mechanisms maintaining their monopoly over new, strategic technologies, that is, those that will have important economic, social and political impacts, shaping future developments.

The benefits of the "third industrial revolution" are to be largely reserved for the DCs. The bimodal distribution of agricultural and raw material production, on the one hand, and manufacturing, on the other, characteristic of the colonial and neo-colonial periods, will be replaced in the future by one where DC control the major, new technologies while the UDC specialize in the old, established industries. The content of the dichotomy changes, but the dichotomy remains!

It is symptomatic of the DC approach to the NIEO that, when in 1977 the UDCs challenged for the first time the DC control of GATT tariff negotiations, a proposal was advanced for creation of a new GATT-like organization with only DC membership (Leddy, 1977). This organization would negotiate a new trade regime among developed countries entailing free trade in manufactured goods and reduced protection for agricultural products from within the zone. In this way, developed countries would maintain control over trade liberalization among themselves, thereby preventing underdeveloped countries from gaining direct influence over matters essential to their welfare. This is one more instance of the DC strategy to establish exlusive institutions to protect their own interests just at the time when international political developments threatened to transform those multinational institutions, such as GATT, which had traditionally assured DC dominance over UDCs.

One important aspect of this dependency situation is the prominence given to the development model of the developed countries. This model suggests that know-how, skills and knowledge, in combination with ever more sophisticated and complex technologies have been the basis of the developed countries' success. This model has dominated UNCSTED proceedings and continues to inspire present development efforts. It deserves therefore careful analysis to determine to what extent it might contain in it the genetic core of dependency.

2. Technology Transfers and the Structure of Dependency

The challenge to the old international division of labor has been substantially reenforced by events since 1971. The shift of power relationships in the world oil market revealed some vulnerability of the traditional DC world dominance. It provided a few UDCs, the OPEC countries, with the strategic means to try to institutionalize a NIEO. DCs have been compelled to develop new strategies for maintaining their dominance over UDCs. The loss of control over oil forced a shift in traditional principles of strategic resource control.

The DC strategy has been to restructure dependency mechanisms so as to make exercise of control, and hence of exploitation, as indirect as possible or as obscure as possible. Technology, based on knowledge development fits this requirement very well. Both the developed and the underdeveloped countries have come to see in the massive transfer of technology the solution to their respective problems, although for different reasons and from different positions of power. Underdeveloped countries see it as the key to development while developed countries see it as the key to accelerating technological progress.

The strategy of transferring technology contains a contradiction. It can serve to erode the current DC advantage in the world economy. In order to maintain their dominance, developed countries must maintain the technological gap, that is, develop new technologies at a rate equal to or faster than the underdeveloped countries can acquire and absorb existing technologies. Research and development of technology is increasingly costly just at the time when the economies of developed countries experience problems of stagflation. Selling technologies becomes therefore almost a precondition for developing new ones. Selling old technologies helps generate the cash flow to finance technology development. Selling new technology helps reduce the costs per unit of research and development effort (see Ernst in Ernst (1980)).

The DC strategy in this situation entails selective transfers of technology and know-how while making sure that the impetus for the direction of technological change remains under DC control. The elements of this strategy can be seen at three different levels.

a) The level of every-day exchange processes

Technology is preferably transferred in the form of equipment, production processes, and complete plants which require for their continued and efficient use:

- the continuous delivery of key inputs and spare parts by the original supplier or producer located in a DC. Contracts sometimes restrict the buyer's right to purchase inputs and spare parts on the market or to develop the local capability to produce them.

- access to repair and maintenance facilities and their experts located in DCs (Bennaceur and Gèze in Ernst (1980)).

- the long-term presence of expatriate technicians, managers and consultants.

Especially the third control tactic is reminiscent of the establishment of management dominance over workers. Lasch (1977:18) writes:

... as management extended control over production, it appropriated the technical knowledge formerly controlled by the crafts and trades, centralized this knowledge, and then parcelled it out piecemeal in a confusing, selective fashion guaranteed to keep the worker in a state of dependence.

Of course, UDCs may eventually gain the rights or possibilities to carry on these activities for most of their established industries. But here too there will be a product cycle. New industries will again depend on the same outside support facilities as the traditional industries did originally.

b) The structural level

Only industries and industrial activities are transferred to the under-developed countries which contribute to maintain a structure of specialization according to the DC preferences. These are:

• basic raw material processing and transforming industries of the industrial take-off period which are heavily polluting or which provide poor working conditions: steel, textiles, etc.

• mass production of standardized consumer durables where significant labor alienation has shown up in DCs: household appliances, cars, electronic assembly, standard machine tools, etc.

• routinized white collar work such as key-punching of data and standardized laboratory testing.

The newest, emerging industries are concentrated in developed countries, or if established in underdeveloped countries are likely to be kept under ownership and management control by DC multinational corporations. This explains IBM's decision to close its production plant in India and leave the country rather than accept Indian majority ownership. The new industries kept in developed countries are of course relatively non-polluting, and they provide good working conditions and use substantial amounts of trained, skilled and educated manpower.

Similarly to this sectoral division and specialization pattern, we find emerging a division of labor along functional lines. Developed countries concentrate on and try to preserve for themselves:

— the design and production of whole plants and large production systems;

— the top-level managerial and planning functions, R & D activities (which therefore are oriented towards DC needs and problems), the acquisition; manipulation, storing and control of information (Hymer, 1972; also several papers in Ernst, 1980).

And finally we find that DCs expend considerable effort and resources to develop production techniques and processes which would reduce (1) dependence of developed countries on UDC resources, and (2) competition from the underdeveloped countries for such resources. Examples of this type are:

• the development of synfuel production capacities and the search for oil and gas in the far north.

• efforts to develop processes to extract the alumina in common clays (abundant in the U.S.) and to exploit seabed minerals. The U.S. and other DC successfully prevented the establishment of an international authority with UDC control with responsibility for managing and exploitation of these resources.

• the selling and construction of nuclear power plants in UDC despite their questionable economics and their oversized capacity. This would not only establish technological dependence (see section a)) but would also lessen UDC demand for oil.

c) The Level of Social Technology and Conceptual Development

Here DCs have, at least until now, enjoyed a near total monopoly. They are still able to define the problems and issues to be dealt with in international forums and to provide "solutions", "strategies", and "institutions" to UDCs which have been conceived in response to DC needs and problems:

• DCs tend to define development problems and provide development strategies which assume integration of the underdeveloped countries into the world economy.

• Through their financing capabilities, DCs dominate world economic organizations and institutions. These define and impose the execution of "correct" economic policies in exchange for financial support. Exercise of this dominance is in part based on the ability of the DCs to define problem areas and solutions. In this way they have so far managed to limit the application of Keynesian thinking and policy to national economies. But they have insisted on a monetarist policy with respect to world liquidity creation, at least when it concerned the UDCs.

The applicability of Keynesian policies to the world as a whole is obvious. There are large unsatisfied needs in the UDCs while there is unused capacity in the DCs. The resistance to such a revolution is also understandable. DCs would have to accept the establishment of a world government authority, progressive income taxation at the world level, and the redistribution of income to the poorer world regions and classes.

• Information, measurement and accounting systems, decision-making criteria, even the time-frame for the evaluation of projects and development strategies are developed in DCs in response to their requirements. They are then imposed on UDCs irrespective of different needs and characteristics, and even negative effects. The case of the national income accounts is one of the best known instances of this type (OECD, 1974:21-33).

— DCs recuperate and redefine concepts defined by UDCs to help solve UDC-specific problems. "Intermediate technologies" and the concept of "basic-needs oriented development" are in danger of being refunctioned as props for stagnating DC economies. For example, the concept of intermediate technology is seen by medium and small-sized DC enterprises as an opportunity to break into export markets and become suppliers to projects funded by international development agencies.

— DCs dominate education, training and knowledge production processes. When UDC pressure leads to consideration of UDC based efforts, DCs tend to develop institutions of their own to control and influence the emerging UDC institutions. The U.S. International Development Cooperation Agency founded the Institute for Scientific and Technological Cooperation to support education and training of Third World scientists in their own countries and the U.S. as well in response to one of the demands formulated at UNCSTED.

• The definition and determination of technology development is under DC control, reflecting DC needs. The electronics revolution matches perfectly the resource availability in DCs: it is materials saving, but it uses skilled and educated manpower for design, development, and maintenance. The operation of the equipment may favor the use of low-wage, unskilled labor. Bennaceur and Gèze (in Ernst, 1980) point out that future, complex, automated factories will enable DC firms to maintain control of production capacity even if these are located in UDCs and even if DC agents do not possess ownership. This technology allows DCs to respond to UDC demands for national ownership of plant without, however, sacrificing final control, which is based on expert knowledge.

The far-reaching consequences, that technologies developed in developed countries but applied in underdeveloped ones can have, are best illustrated by the technique of national income accounting. Ravignan (1979) has pointed out that the exclusion of most non-market activities from the income accounts has led to a neglect of what are relatively unimportant or non-existent sectors in developed countries, but which are dominant in many underdeveloped countries: Namely the self-sufficient peasant sector and household non-commercial production in the urban sector. Not only has this led to a serious disregard in development theory and practice, and in government policy-making, of peasant production and its potentialities (leading to the well-known food shortages). It has also concentrated attention on the male workforce to the deteriment of women who carry out a great part of agricultural work.

O'Brien (in Ernst, 1980) points out that the national income accounts, the balance-of-payments statistics and the input-output tables are all based on definitions formulated in developed countries. They presume well-integrated national economies and a certain closure of the national economy against the international one. The reality of underdeveloped countries is however just the contrary: Fully developed national markets often do not exist, while the MNC-controlled segments and the economy of the capital cities are tightly integrated in the world economy.

The accounting system and the economic theory used has also an impact on the measurement of productivity. This is of fundamental importance for the evaluation of the usefulness of DC technologies for UDC purposes. A sentence like "... labor-intensive technologies are, at least at the present time, economically inefficient ...", made by Jacobsson (1979), raises more questions than it answers. Efficiency and productivity comparisons in neo-classical economic theory make only sense in market systems where prices clear markets. The existence of widespread un- and underemployment in underdeveloped countries is however an indication that wages do not clear the market. The existence of fractured UDC-internal linkages also produces a non-coherent price structure. Productivity measures based on market values are therefore extremely suspicious, especially if comparisons rely on productivities from countries with different disequilibriums.[2]

3. Technology Production and Comparative Strengths

Maintenance of the world dependency structure requires that developed countries continually create new technologies, at least as long as the massive transfer of technology is the dominant development strategy. Obviously, underdeveloped countries lack the conditions and capabilities to compete with developed countries on this dimension. The distribution of research and development facilities, of educated and trained manpower, and of managerial and organizational know-how to realize successfully large-scale innovation is all favoring continued technological dominance by developed countries. At the same time, they possess differentiated and complex production systems. This gives them great flexibility to reorient towards and accelerate development trends which maintain world stratification and unequal exchange favorable to their continued dominance (Emmanuel, 1972; Kindleberger, 1956:229).

We have already mentioned plans of DC politicians to concentrate on the development of high technology industries in developed countries. Others, among them Kates (1978), the former chairman of the Canadian Scientific Council, advocate openly the need for an accelerated development of technology to safeguard economic well-being of developed countries in the face of the emerging new international economic order. The outcome of the combination of a UDC strategy of transferring technology with a DC strategy of accelerating technology development will be a *technology race*. As in the case of an armaments race, both sides are likely to be loosers. Technological progress may of course lift underdeveloped countries to higher levels of productivity. But this welfare gain is highly spurious. The gap between underdeveloped and developed countries would continue to exist.

Rapid technological change may increase overall production but only at the price of a continually high rate of *"creative" destruction of capital*, compensated by a high rate of accumulation, a low rate of consumption increase, and a continual pressure for labor mobility and dequalification. This is a prescription for maximizing, not for minimizing human suffering (Adler-Karlsson, 1978).

4. Selfcentered Development and Technology

Repeated failures of underdeveloped countries to absorb and usefully exploit DC technologies are currently explained by their high prices and their unfavorable terms of exploitation. The multinational corporations are also accused of subjecting UDC technology choices to the needs of the companies' world strategies and the requirement that underdeveloped countries integrate their production into the world system. These and related explanations have led to particular demands from underdeveloped countries in the NIEO debate: Better terms of technology acquisition, national control rather than MNC control over the selection and use of technology,[3] and *selective delinking* from the world market, possibly going as far as to choose a strategy of *selfcentered development* (Senghaas, 1977, and in Ernst (1980).

The core idea underlying these various demands is always the same: Reproduction in underdeveloped countries of the industrial system and the technologies which have contributed to the socio-economic development and wealth of the developed countries. Selfcenteredness and delinking are concerned primarily with *methods* through which technologies are acquired and use is made of them, not with the *type* of technologies on which development is to be based. They are strategies which strive to duplicate the industrial structures of the developed countries, in part by providing "infant industry" protection through the use of tariffs, quotas and controls during the initial phases of building up an industry. This "Listian strategy" takes its inspiration from the German and Japanese success stories of the late 19th and the 20th centuries respectively (Senghaas, 1975, and his contribution in Ernst (1980)). The tragic histories of German and Japan suggest the great risks of such a strategy.

This development strategy leaves many questions unanswered. For example, does the Listian development conception imply that an underdeveloped country must repeat the historical sequence of "stages of growth" (Rostow, 1960) experienced by German and Japan? The answer is probably not. It would take too long a time. Since the end result is already known, leaping over stages of development is an obvious temptation. The Chinese development experience suggests that a country to a certain extent can skip stages but there would appear to be definite limits to what extent particular stages can be skipped (Green, 1978:712). The exact development sequence which a country should follow is undoubtedly a function of country-specific factors, such as its socio-economic structures and its political institutions. The chosen development goals also certainly play a role. It is not the imitation of a given development experience which will bring success but the application of some of the principles which have guided successful development in the past as Bagchi (1978:225) points out in his discussion of the Chinese development model.

Nobody of course advocates starting out on self-centered development with the technologies of the 19th century. But it was those technologies which permitted even small countries to follow a Listian strategy. The question is if today's technologies are appropriate for such a small-country strategy of development. (Many underdeveloped countries are rather small). It is doubtful, therefore the proposals for UDC cooperation and specialization. This however may turn out to be a major problem. It is far from clear if underdeveloped countries are willing and able to choose cooperation and if they are sufficiently *similar* to permit the use of the same technologies.

Listian development, where it succeeded, relied on a strong central state, the dominance of capital over labor, and a compensating nationalism which led both Germany and Japan into aggressive expansionism and a century of devastating wars. One or another element of this strategy is also found in several newly industrializing countries (Argentina for example). It is therefore highly questionable if a Listian strategy can be combined with a development strategy based on self-reliance, democratic participation, and cooperation among neighboring countries.

Lastly, one may question if contemporary DC technologies fit sociocultural structures and values currently existing in underdeveloped countries as well as 19th century technologies seem to have fitted German and Japanese structures and values. The Listian strategy would have to be reformulated if, as we argue, there exists today a great mismatch. Sachs (1977:9-10) suggests that such a strategy might have to be combined with the development of indigenous technology before it would succeed.

The problems relating to the compatibility of DC technologies and UDC structures and values are indicated by the many failures of technology transfers. Such failures are also observable in the case of transfers from state-socialist countries, including China, to the Third World. The rapid decay of the Tanzara railway in Tanzania due to lack of maintenance, unavailability of spare parts, and inability of management to control its rolling stock suggest both a failure in the Chinese concept of transferring its technology as well as local inability to handle this technology. Green (1978:711) hints that this and other failures of Chinese aid has been the result of overlooking the much greater lack of skills and of experiences with small-scale industry in African countries compared to China.

It is from this perspective that one should look again at concepts of intermediate technology and authochtonous technology development. New technologies generate development only if they stand in an "essential tension" (Kuhn, 1963) to the existing values, structures and institutions. Such technology has both to be close to them, yet also to some degree be conflicting with them, if creative development is to occur.

The judicious interplay between different levels of technology, urban and rural uses of technologies, transfers of second-hand plants and machinery (and workers trained on them) from old and established manufacturing centers to agricultural areas, the local adaptation of imported technologies, the building up from repairing of machinery to building and using it, suggest that the Chinese have understood part of the problem, at least within the context of their culture and their socio-economic system (Bagchi, 1978:225-228; Lövbraek, 1976-218-220). But these processes take time and the warning against skipping stages is fully appropriate here. But it is unlikely that the present DC technologies are appropriate, in the sense understood here, for most underdeveloped countries. Instead of looking towards the general transfer and adoption of DC technologies, the Third World should adopt a selfcentered development strategy which fully takes into account the technological dimension and its interplay with cultural and institutional factors.

3. Toward a Paradigm and Strategy

We have suggested that technology must be viewed in a wider societal analysis. The creation, transfer, and adaptation of technology cannot be separated from the socio-cultural, political and economic conditions, the social structures and institutions characterizing the societies in which they are produced and used.

Section 1 provides a general argument about the social dimensions imbedded in technology transfers from the developed to the underdeveloped countries. Section 2 outlines the method of compatibility analysis with which to analyze the relationship between technology and social systems and discusses some of the ways in which system structures and conditions may block or subvert effective introduction and use of technology. Section 3 uses this method of compatibility analysis to model the dynamic interplay between technology and social systems by looking at the introduction of tractors into a Ujamma village in Tanzania. We conclude in Section 4 by presenting strategic implications of the approach.

1. Capitalist Technology and Social Relations

Yugoslavia has experienced difficulties in developing its self-management system in the face of modern technologies and the production structures they imply (see Chapter 7). The Yugoslavs turned to the organizational structure of the Basic Organization of Associated Labor (BOAL) at the beginning of the 1970s in order to combat increasing hierarchization within enterprises and a renewed emergence of technocratic dominance associated with concentration of managerial functions. The BOAL was formed wherever possible of the smallest possible production unit, in most cases of the workshop. Yet, 1980 has seen again a growing tendency towards "deboalization". It is increasingly felt that modern technological conditions do not permit self-management of workshops and the regulation of their interactions through contractual cooperation. A higher-level control and coordinating unit was felt to be required, most often encompassing an entire plant. In this way, Yugoslavia has come full circle. The chances are high that the problems of the late 1960s will be again the problems of the early 1980s.

The contradiction between technology and a set of institutions is quite understandable. Technology always embodies and reflects the power relations of the system from which it emanates. Technology and its accompanying development strategies are in general designed to be compatible with and support existing social relations (Hettne, 1978; Lippit, 1978).

Production implies of course task specialization. But this specialization, together with the related work organization, work rules, and worker-management relation has been pushed in such a way as to fragment to a great extent the working class and to undermine control of the work process by the workers (Marglin, 1974; Braverman, 1975; Shorter and Tilly, 1974). In both capitalist and socialist industrialized countries one finds much the same production technologies as well as organizational and information techniques, factory organization, task specialization, and worker-management relations (Haraszti, 1976; Rosanvallon, 1976:128-129).

The technology developed for this factory system fixes workers to individual work stations with limited possibilities for interaction. Hunnius (in Burns *et al.*, 1979) suggests that technologies for some forms of job enrichment will extend this division to the after-work time with possibly serious implications for the collective struggle of workers. Shorter and Tilly (1974) show how the French trade union organizations and their goals changed with the changing nature of the capitalist system. They also show how the internally democratic structure of trade unions gave way to an organizational scheme mirroring factory power relations.

DC technology enforces a strict division between shop (including office)-floor work and managerial tasks including such specialized functions like accounting, purchasing, planning and, of course, the giving of orders. This separation has been one of the most important aspects of Taylorism. Yugoslav experiences indicate that this specialization poses a serious threat to the realization of workers' control and decision-making within formal self-management institutions, especially in poorer and less industrialized regions (Shawcross, 1977:34; Chapter 7).

The cumulative effect of work rules and work organization is to limit workers to the execution of orders and induce them to appeal to superiors for any decision which surpasses narrowly defined tasks. This situation intimates that workers are like children who have better rely on the managers in the know. Such a system of course supports and justifies the monopolization of control by managers and owners over surplus disposal and the use of many of the spin-offs and spill-overs of production.

Both aspects, the unequal acquisition of managerial and decision-making abilities and the formation of hierarchical structures in the economic sphere of production support the unequal distribution of abilities and capabilities and the legitimation and acceptance of similar inequalities and hierarchies in the socio-cultural and political spheres. This parallellism reenforces the centralization of power and control and forms a web of mutually supporting power processes (Burns *et al.*, 1985).

Chinese decision-makers seem to have been particularly sensitive to the possible contradiction between a certain type of technology and forms of societal development. Grow (1975) suggests that the industrial sectors which had been built up in China before the break with the Soviet Union on the basis of Societ technology and experts were also those organized fully according to the Soviet model with hierarchical authority patterns. Wheelwright and McFarlane (1970), Dean (1972), and more recently Watanabe (1980), all argue that the potential links between technology, enterprise organization, and social and political structures were one of the factors which turned the Chinese against the Soviet model of development and the unquestioned use of Soviet technology and turn-key plants.

Watanabe (1980) quotes a Chinese economist, Xue Muquiao, who argues that the planned productivity levels of all the Western technology presently imported into China will only be realized, if a number of elements of Western management, both on the enterprise and the national level, are also introduced into China at the same time. Watanabe also fears that the introduction of this Wetern mass production technology brings with it the social controls and stratifications we know from the developed countries. They could create an explosive mixture in combination with the existing bureaucratic organization of economic and social life.

Tsurumi (1977:151-152) suggests that not only the transfer of technology but also the method of transferring it has implications for socio-cultural development. The strategy of adopting and imitating foreign technologies puts special demands on and strengthens central authorities. Domestic technology creation and the adaptation of foreign technologies to local conditions require and reinforce a wide distribution of skills and technology-production capabilities.

The preceding discussion implies that if *self-reliance* and *democratic participation* are major development goals, then it is inappropriate to rely in many, if not most instances, on the mechanical transfer of technologies from the developed countries. Rather, one should develop one's own technology, or engineer a suitable transformation of DC technologies, in order to build into the production process, in very concrete terms, development goals and values. Here as elsewhere the dictum of Cherns (1978:5) is applicable: "A participative organization can be successfully developed only through a participative process of design."

2. Technology and Social Systems: The Method of Compatibility Analysis

Technologies are tools used in social action to produce certain products or to solve certain problems. Concepts, standards, and norms guide the organization of the product process and the relationships among the actors engaged in them. Thus one can speak of a *socio-technical system.*

Technology in this perspective is more than equipment. It is one component linked to other components in the system in order to accomplish tasks or to solve problems. Technology involves tools and machinery. It also involves skills, knowledge, and know-how. These relate not only to the concrete production processes. Managerial and planning tasks are invariably linked to production. In addition, and not least importantly, production involves a cognitive framework made up among other things of underlying assumptions, concepts and principles about reality. And it involves social organization.

A socio-technical system has therefore multiple features. Two classes of them are of special interest:

• *Instrumental Aspect.* A component, e.g. a technology, is defined and evaluated in terms of its contribution to solving a specific problem, such as manufacturing a machine, removing earth, harvesting rice. It is because of its instrumental character that it may be desirable and even possible to transfer a technology from one social context to another.

• *Socio-structural Aspect.* A component is also defined and evaluated in terms of its contribution to shaping or maintaining important and characteristic social relations. For this reason, actors in dominant positions try to propose, filter, and accept technologies which are compatible with their positions of power.

Instrumental considerations, in particular productive gains, often dominate the evaluation and decisions leading to the adoption or introduction of a technology. However, social structural aspects, and the indifference or opposition of particular groups, often dominate the practical utilization of the technology in concrete production settings.

In general, proposals to transfer technologies should, therefore, address the question of appropriateness or fit between the technology and other components that make up the socio-technical system in the technology-importing country.

The compatibility of a technology with a social system refers to the ways in which the technology in practice would relate to the actors involved; the ways it would affect their ways of acting and thinking about things; and the ways it would alter existing material and social conditions. One may therefore legimately ask how appropriate the material, social and cultural structures of a social system are for a transferred technology, if the system's *infrastructures* have been shaped and developed to match quite different, more traditional and indigenous technologies.

Technologies may be misutilized because some components in the socio-technical system are inappropriate or are missing. In such a case learning of some kind will inevitably take place. Such learning, unfortunately, may have negative effects. Learning does not only involve learning to operate a given technology more efficiently, or to make suitable adjustments or adaptations in the socio-technical system. Learning can entail starting to mistrust the technology or its advocates. This may ultimately lead to active or passive resistance to the new technology and its supporting agents. DC industrialization itself has suffered from such negative developments. (Nuclear power is, e.g., a recent instance).

Compatibility analysis of a technology and the social system into which it is introduced requires a social systems framework. Such a framework also provides the basis for assessing social and economic impacts of new technologies. We propose here in a preliminary way some of the elements of the framework.

The introduction and use of a technology entails shaping a socio-technical system, or reshaping an already existing one. The system is the context within which social actors will use the technology in production processes.[4] This context consists of certain material and technological conditions as well as of cultural and institutional infrastructures. The method of comparability analysis considers in what concrete ways the introduction and use of technology will relate to, and interact with, the infrastructures and conditions in the *concrete production setting*. We discuss below key elements in such an analysis:

i) technology and material infrastructures: Complementary technologies may not exist or may be inappropriate, thereby blocking the effective use of a transferred technology. Material conditions, including climatic and geographic factors, obviously play an important role in the problems of technology utilization. Serious constraints on effective use also arise when transport and communication systems are underdeveloped and repair facilities do not exist.

ii) cultural infrastructure: The cognitive frames and value forms in a given culture may prevent effective use of the technology. Essential activities, such as attention to care and repairs of machinery may be given a low value in society. Or lack of even elementary experience with the type of technology introduced may make it difficult in the short to medium term to learn appropriate cognitive models for using and maintaining the technology.

iii) organizational and social infrastructures: Established or customary ways for actors to relate to one another or to be organized *in practice* may prevent the effective utilization of the technology. Persons with traditional or ascribed authority, but lacking real knowledge or expertise, may dominate social initiatives and the formulation of work rules and forms. Those with technical knowledge or enterpreneurial drive may lack sustained influence or opportunities to bring about the restructuring and adaptations necessary to make effective use of the technology.

iv) external support structures and institutions: The socio-technical system for production does not operate in isolation, but it depends on external conditions and networks. Certain external agents and institutions may be critical to the success or failure of technology utilization. We think here about educational and research services, advisory organizations and training institutions. Political and legal support, and government infrastructures may be only weakly developed and are unable to help in bringing about or organizing necessary social and legal changes for the effective use of technology.

The problem is often not one of ill will or laziness, but of scarce educational, managerial and administrative resources. these are allocated to other problems, including those associated with other production systems. This implies that before the introduction of a new production system, for example, of commercial, large-scale farming in a self-reliant peasant society, one must investigate the demands it is likely to impose on already scarce support structures and institutions.

The above is only a rough sketch of the method of comparability analysis based on social systems theory. The utilization of such analyses can, in our view, contribute to realistic perspectives on technology transfer or technology development in relation to historically given socio-cultural systems. The following section provides an illustration of one of the ways in which the introduction of a technology into an unsuitable socio-technical context can set in motion a number of negative, unintended developments. The developments negate to a large extent the objectives behind the introduction of the technology.

3. The Social Dynamics of Technology Introduction

Edquist and Edqvist (1979) combine systems and actor-oriented approaches in the analysis of technology choices. The choices of technology, especially in the case of imported technology, is in most cases made by actors in positions of power or at least in possession of emergent power. But the actual use of this technology has inevitably to involve actors with relatively little or no power at all. The effective use of a given technology depends on both of these actor categories. The following example illustrates the problems which can arise in such a situation, here the introduction of tractors into a Tanzanian Ujamma village.[5] Two sets of actors are directly involved. The villagers, the future users of the tractors, and the state officials, those that decide to introduce the tractors. Both groups have specific but quite different interests, experiences and expectations about what the tractors should and can do. Both groups therefore interpret the events subsequent to the tractor introduction in their own and not necessarily convergent ways. In the end, those in power have come to a much more negative attitude towards the users, while these have reconfirmed

their distrust of those in power. The social relations have worsened, pre-
cluding the future use of self-reliant and democratic patterns of decision-
making and development.

The two sets of actors, the village peasants (wajamaa) and the state
officials concerned with the planning and administration of agricultural
modernization, have a different relationship to the Tanzanian socialist
development model. The wajamaa approach the process of agricultural
modernization with their long experience of traditional peasant agriculture
with its self-interest and self-sufficiency orientation. The tractor, or the
machine in general, is perceived as a useful device (instrumental dimension) "which does the work for us", or which, within the structure of village
socialism, "gives us time to work on our own fields" while the tractor does
the labor in the collective village fields (social structural aspect). That is, in
the context of their traditional way of thinking and doing things, the tractor
is not used in ways *intended* by the planners and administrators.

The state administrators and agricultural specialists represent the
'modern', rational sector of the system. They are somewhat disdainful and
suspicious of peasants and their motives and behavior. (Of course, this distrust is requited by the peasants). But they have a certain unreflected belief
that the peasants will know a good thing when they see one and that they
are after all imbued by a basic socialist orientation and a tribal inclination
towards collective production. The specialists and administrators see the
tractor as a vital and economically efficient complement to human labor.
They expect it to help realize rapid productivity gains and to facilitate
thereby the development of a self-reliant peasant sector with egalitarian
income and power distributions.

The administrators provide the tractors free of charge to the village, i.e.,
we have here a case of 'give-away-mechanization'. The peasants react first
as expected. They use the tractors to prepare and seed the collective fields.
But the next steps fail to fit to expected behavior. The peasants' subsequent
effort is devoted completely to their own individual fields because they
assume that the tractors by themselves would take care of the collective
fields from now on. After all, the tractor was supposed to increase productivity. Thus weeding and thinning, absolutely essential tasks in a tropi-
cal climate, are neglected in the collective fields. But these tasks are
performed very intensively in the individual fields as the peasants have now
much more time available for them. The result at harvest-time is of course
that the collective fields do very badly indeed, especially in comparison to
the individual fields which yield a bumper crop.

This result leads the administrators to change their view of the peasants.
In part it means simply reactivating deeply held beliefs and prejudices. The
public officials come to see the peasants as irreponsible, self-interested ego-

ists on whom one cannot rely to utilize properly the scarce resources given to them. They change their strategy. Instead of relying on a strategy of self-reliance, they will start to intervene into the organization of peasant labor and will assure the care of the collective fields through command and coercion.

The peasants too modify their perceptions and behavior. First, faced with the failure of the tractors to perform as expected and confronted with a partly unsatisfactory harvest, they expect the state and its representatives to come up with a solution to their problems. It was the state who gave them the tractors in the first place. Secondly, the failure discredits the ujamaa idea. Given the good harvest on the individual fields, peasants will be inclined to return to completely individualistic agriculture. Thirdly, modernization is discredited. This reenforces the always latent conservatism of peasants developed through long experience. Fourthly, the subsequent intervention of and commandeering by the state officials reawakens negative views of the state developed through the colonial experience. The rapport of trust and cooperation between experts and peasants, so important for development, is destroyed.

The peasants try to turn their undivided attention to their individual fields and evade the control of planners, administrators and experts. Thus the vicious circle of deteriorating social relations between the two groups is maintained.

Such a dynamic interaction may lead to higher-level changes. Confronted with failures in the ujamaa program, the state may have to change its development strategy. Given the elite orientations, this is likely to lead to a reduction in the level of experimentation and in efforts to pursue self-reliant, basic-needs oriented development. Instead large-scale, capital-intensive plantation agriculture in the form of state farms may become the only attractive option.

4.   Strategic Considerations

We have presented three arguments why it may be inappropriate for underdeveloped countries to focus on a development strategy which relies on the mechnical transfer and adoption of DC technologies:

a) Developed countries permit only a selective transfer of technology in order to maintain North-South dependency structures. The dependency mechanism is likely to be shifted to a higher level if underdeveloped countries persist and succeed in massively acquiring DC technologies or in producing them on license on their own. DC control will then be exercised in more indirect ways.

b) It is not at all clear what a "Listian" development strategy of self-centered development would entail for the choice of technology. But it is unlikely that the technologies offered by the developed countries today can fit into such a strategy.

c) DC technologies are in many instances incompatible with the realization of selfreliance, cooperation and democratic participation. Development on this basis will require appropriate technologies, and they will be different from those found in developed countries today.

The conclusion is that a strategy of selfcentered development has to be combined with a policy of indigenous technology development, that is, a policy of selective delinking from the developed countries when it concerns technology and technical knowledge.

The other possible combination — technological self-reliance and integration into the international trading system — will not work either. It would burden the underdeveloped countries with the costs and risks of technology development only to see MNC and DC enterprises use their flexibility and financial power to later take over emergent markets for these technologies. The argument, that by "stimulating local innovation and reinforcing other development efforts, simple technologies can lead to self-sustaining development" (Norman, 1978:13), will only hold if the selfcentered development strategy is chosen at the same time.

Such a technology development strategy demands foremost the establishment of indigenous capabilities to create know-how, to embody it in technologies and to apply these technologies in organizational and productive efforts. It is above all selfreliance of this type that counts. A different type of development is difficult to conceive if the super-structure of knowledge, conceptions, and technological orientations is not created through selfreliant effort.

Concretely this means to learn from other underdeveloped countries and their experiences with "alternative" technologies. It is therefore important to construct national and international UDC *information, exchange and cooperation systems and organizations* with respect to technology and technology applications (Senghaas, 1977).[6] This would not only help to weaken the influence of DC technologies. It also would lower the real economic costs of producing alternative technologies. At the same time it would favor the strengthening of UDC ties in general.

It also means that technology has to be evaluated on more than one dimension. Green (1978:711) points out that the Chinese have always striven to progress along several dimensions at the same time. That is, the choice of technology, even of alternative or intermediate technology, cannot be based only on the criteria of optimal capital-intensity and mechanization, but has to include other important values such as the facility with which it supports learning, local repairing and technology adaptation, the development of better technologies, etc. (Bagchi, 1978:228).

Finally, it is essential that all attempts be made to develop social technologies which are supportive of selfreliant, cooperative, and democratic behavior. This means above all the elaboration of information, accounting and decision-making systems at micro and macro levels which would give weight to the *exercise* of selfreliance and democracy in the factory, the community, and the larger political system. This means that accounting systems, including national accounting systems, have to be designed in such a way that, e.g., time spent on learning and strengthening selfreliant capabilities and on participatory activities is measured as a positive contribution to economic and social welfare, rather than being indicated as "costly" or unproductive activities hindering the attainment of maximal material production. In this area too there is a need for the underdeveloped countries to carefully filter the transfer of DC accounting and organizational technologies and to develop through self-reliant efforts indigenous social technologies fully in accordance with their vision of society.

This vision should not consist simply of a reduction of the wealth gap between underdeveloped and developed countries. Striving to develop underdeveloped countries into something resembling contemporary developed countries is a dubious enterprise. The developed countries will continue to develop during the time needed by the underdeveloped ones to approach the position of the developed countries today. There are strong indications in the current deep crisis that developed countries will be forced to undergo substantial restructuring before too long. Advocating a development model based on past DC experiences, even highly successful ones, is very questionable in view of the possibility that this type of structure may be already historically doomed. Even if the underdeveloped countries should manage to start reproducing the type of system found in most developed countries today, they are likely to find that the future world system will be in any case substantially different from the one which allowed the emergence of contemporary developed countries.

UDC achievement of the conditions found in the developed countries today would surely eliminate many of the conditions which permitted past DC development to take place, indeed if many of these conditions remain today. For instance, there would be no underdeveloped markets to exploit and integrate into their expanding systems. Nor could they rely on abundant and cheap natural resources such as oil. Future UDC development will have to take place within a new set of constraints which are emerging together with the social processes producing them.

The question of technology and the transfer of technology is linked fundamentally to the desirability, and even the possibility, of pursuing a development model which belongs to the past and which may only be marginally relevant to the future. This suggests that future development of underdeveloped countries has to be based to a substantial degree on technologies which do not yet exist either in the DCs or the UDCs and which neither can know with any certainty what they will entail.

NOTES

1. Moran (1978) argues that competing MNC, among them non-american ones, have introduced competitive market structures into the larger underdeveloped countries (particularly in Latin America). They have thereby contributed to eroding one important dependency structure. The prototype example is the car industry in Latin American countries where the local Ford or GM monopoly has been replaced with oligopolistic market structures with Fiat, Renault, VW and others occupying important market segments. (Of course this means that most often they use inefficiently small assembly plants.) Similar developments can be observed in industries such as consumer appliances, food processing, fertilizers, etc.
2. This point is also discussed in Chapter 7 above in the context of productivity comparisons between Yugoslavia, the U.S., and underdeveloped countries.
3. Bennaceur and Gèze (in Ernst, 1980) mention that of similar plants operating in an underdeveloped country, the one operated by a foreign MNC is performing better than the one under national management control (built on a turn-key basis).
4. We stress here the production side and factors affecting socio-technical systems of production. Any thorough analysis should include consideration of consumption processes and the distribution and use side of production processes.
5. The case is taken from Vail (1977). We have simplified it to illustrate our approach to the analysis of technology adoption and socio-cultural system comparability.
6. But one should not forget to account for the real differences between underdeveloped or developing countries. Otherwise the transfer and exchange of UDC technologies will lead to failures. The resultant disappointment would return to favor DC technologies.

REFERENCES

Adler-Karlsson, G. 1978 "The Unimportance of Full Employment." *IFDA-Dossier* (Nyon, Switzerland), Nr. 2, November.

Bagchi, A.K. 1978 "On the Political Economy of Technological Choice and Development." *Cambridge Journal of Economics*, 2:215-232.

Braverman, H. 1975 *Labor and Monopoly Capital.* New York, Monthly Review Press.

Burns, T.R., T. Baumgartner and P. DeVillé 1985 *Man, Decisions, Society.* New York, Gordon and Breach.

Burns, T.R., L.R. Karlsson and V. Rus (eds.) 1979 *Work and Power.* London, Sage.

Cherns, A. 1978 "Spontaneity and Participation in Work and Community." Uppsala, 9th World Congress of Sociology.

Corm, G. 1978 "Saper l'ideologie du développement." *Le Monde Diplomatique*, April.

Dean, G.C. 1972 "Science, Technology and Development: China as a Case Study." *China Quarterly*, Nr. 51, pp. 520-524.

Edquist, Ch. and O. Edqvist 1979 *Social Carriers of Technology Development.* Stockholm, SAREC.

Emmanuel, A. 1972 *Unequal Exchange.* New York, Monthly Review Press.

Ernst, D. (ed.) 1980 *The New International Division of Labour, Technology and Underdevelopment.* Frankfurt, Campus.

Green, R.H. 1978 "Transferability, Exoticism and other Forms of Dogmatic Revisionism." *World Development*, 6:709-713.

Grow, R.F. 1975 "The Diffusion of Soviet Industrial Technology and Regionalism in China." Washington, D.C., International Studies Association Meeting.

Haraszti, M. 1976 *Salaire aux pièces.* Paris, Seuil.

Hettne, B. 1978 "Selfreliance versus Modernization: The Dialectics of Indian and Chinese Development Strategies." Gothenburg, University of Gothenburg-Department of Peace and Conflict Research Discussion Paper.

Hymer, S. 1972 "The Multinational Corporation and the Law of Uneven Development." In J.N. Bhagwati (ed.), *Economics and the World Order.* New York, Macmillan.

Jacobsson, St. 1979 "Technical Change, Employment and Distribution in LDCs." *Lund Letter*, Nr. 13 (June).

Kates, J. 1978 "Science, Industry and the World Order. " Amsterdam, 4th international Congress of Cyvbernetics and Systems.

Kindleberger, C.P. 1956 *The Terms of Trade.* Cambridge, MIT Press.

Kuhn, Th.S. 1963 "The Essential Tension: Tradition and Innovation in Science." In C.W. Taylor and F. Barron (eds.), *Scientific Creativity.* New York, Wiley.

Lasch, Ch. 1977 "The Siege of the Family." *The New York Review of Books*, 24 (November 19).

Leddy, J.M. 1977 *GATT plus: A Proposal for Trade Reform.* Washington, D.C., Atlantic Council.

Lippit, V.D. 1978 "Economic Development in Meiji Japan and Contemporary China." *Cambridge Journal of Economics*, 2:55-81.

Lövbräk, A. 1976 "The Chinese Model of Development." *Journal of Peace Research*, 13:207-226.

Marglin, S. 1974 "What do Bosses do?" *Review of Radical Political Economics*, 6 (Summer).

Moran, T. 1978 "MNC and Dependency: A Dialogue for Dependentistas and Non-Dependentistas." *International Organization*, 32:79-100.

Norman, C. 1978 "Mass Production or Production for the Masses?" *Agenda*, 1(July-August):11-16.

OECD 1974 *National Accounts and Development Planning in Low-Income Countries.* Paris, OECD.

Ravignan, F. 1979 "De l'Europe au delà ..." *Le Monde*, April 11.

Rosanvallon, P. 1976 *L'âge de l'autogestion.* Paris, Seuil.

Rostow, W.W. 1960 *The Stages of Economic Growth.* Cambridge, CUP.

Sachs, I. 1977 "Civilization Project and Ecological Prudence." *Alternatives*, 3:1-18.

Senghaas, D. 1977 *Weltwirtschaftsordnung und Entwicklungspolitik.* Frankfurt, Suhrkamp.

Senghhas, D. 1975 "Friedrich List und die Neue Internationale Ökonomische Ordnung." *Leviathan*, Nr. 2, pp. 292-300.

Shawcross, W. 1977 "The Precarious Country." *The New York Review of Books*, 24 (July 14).

Shorter, E. and C. Tilly 1974 *Strikes in France, 1830-1968.* Cambridge: CUP.

Tsurumi, K. 1977 "Some Potential Contribution of Latecomers to Technological and Scientific Revolution. A Comparison between Japan and China." In R. Dahrendorf *et al.*, *Scientific-Technological Revolution: Social Aspects*. London, Sage.

Vail, D.J. 1977 "Technology for Ujamaa Village Development in Tanzania." Toronto, International Studies Association Meeting.

Watanabe, T. 1980 "For a more Proletarian Technical Revolution." *China Newsletter*, Nr. 29 (December), pp. 2-5.

Wheelwright, E.L. and B. McFarlane 1970 *The Chinese Road to Socialism*. New York, Monthly Review Press.

Author Index

Subject Index

356

For Product Safety Concerns and Information please contact our EU
representative GPSR@taylorandfrancis.com Taylor & Francis Verlag GmbH,
Kaufingerstraße 24, 80331 München, Germany

Printed and bound by CPI Group (UK) Ltd, Croydon, CR0 4YY
08/05/2025
01864350-0001